Unbelievable Happiness
and Final Sorrow

Unbelievable Happiness and Final Sorrow

THE HEMINGWAY-PFEIFFER MARRIAGE

Ruth A. Hawkins

The University of Arkansas Press
Fayetteville • 2012

ISBN-10: 1-55728-974-3
ISBN-13: 978-1-55728-974-2

16 15 14 13 12   5 4 3 2 1

Text design by Ellen Beeler

∞ The paper used in this publication meets the minimum requirements of the
American National Standard for Permanence of Paper for Printed Library
Materials Z39.48-1984.

Library of Congress Cataloging-in-Publication Data

Hawkins, Ruth A., 1947-
    Unbelievable happiness and final sorrow : the Hemingway-Pfeiffer marriage /
Ruth A. Hawkins.
        p. cm.
    Includes bibliographical references and index.
    ISBN 978-1-55728-974-2 (casebound : alk. paper)
    1. Hemingway, Ernest, 1899–1961—Marriage. 2. Pfeiffer, Pauline. 3. Authors,
American—20th century—Biography. 4. Authors' spouses—United States—
Biography. I. Title.
PS3515.E37Z6144 2012
813'.52—dc23
[B]
                                                                  2012002458

This book is dedicated to the two men in my life—
my husband, Van, and our son, Curt

CONTENTS

PREFACE

When I began researching Pauline Pfeiffer Hemingway and her family nearly fifteen years ago, I was surprised at what little attention the Pfeiffers had received. Though the Pfeiffers were mentioned by many Hemingway scholars, this family's impact on Ernest Hemingway and his writing career essentially was neglected. Today, that hasn't changed significantly, and much of what is written is inaccurate or does not capture the family's true contributions. Only a few writers, such as Michael Reynolds, have suggested the breadth of the Pfeiffers' influence, and it was Reynolds who convinced me that this book should be written.

I attribute the lack of attention to the Pfeiffers to two things: (1) they were an extremely private family and did not publicly discuss their relationship with Hemingway, and (2) Pauline had the bad luck to die before Ernest, leaving the slanted picture that he painted of her as her lasting legacy. His other three wives had the good health and the good sense to outlast him and contribute their own views of life with Hemingway, thus balancing out the record, if not actually setting things straight.

In spite of the greater attention given to Hemingway's other wives, Pauline lived and worked with him during his most productive period as a writer and bore two of his three children. Thus, she deserves more than to be dismissed as a man-chaser who went after Hemingway and broke up his marriage, got what she deserved when the same thing happened to her, and ultimately wound up in an unmarked grave.

Even Pauline's uncle Gus Pfeiffer, acknowledged as Hemingway's financial backer, is mostly ignored except as the man who wrote occasional big checks that helped Hemingway get through the rough spots. Yet Uncle Gus had a profound influence on Hemingway's career, including gathering research materials, providing sound advice, and enabling him to live the lifestyle necessary for his writing success.

This book maintains that Pauline played a major role in Hemingway's life, as did her entire family. Even after casting her aside as a wife, Hemingway lamented that he missed her editing skills. Along with Pauline's support as helpmate and critic and Uncle Gus's financial support, the unconditional love Hemingway received from his mother-in-law at one time rendered this relationship closer than that with his own mother. Letters written to Mary Pfeiffer show a dramatically different and deferential Ernest Hemingway, one who seemed anxious to remain in her good graces. Though he did not have the same kind of relationship with his father-in-law,

Hemingway admired and respected Paul Pfeiffer's business acumen, even though he maintained some distance.

The influence of Virginia Pfeiffer, Pauline's sister, has not been explored by Hemingway scholars, yet his attempts to figure her out undoubtedly provided much of the material for his fascination with sexual predilections and blurred male-female relationships. What is more, his inability to win Virginia kept him fascinated with her and made life intriguing and entertaining, until she turned on him for the way he treated Pauline.

Rather than Pauline being the shrewd man-hunting female who calculatedly took Hemingway away from his first wife, the record suggests that she was a naive woman, inexperienced with men, who became enamored of Ernest beyond all ability to judge or care about right and wrong. Not only did Pauline have the misfortune to fall in love with him, but she continued to love him until the day she died. It is questionable, however, whether Ernest ever truly loved her, though a strong sexual chemistry existed for a time. More likely, he loved everything she brought to the marriage—her family money, her editorial skills, her strong belief in him, and her devotion to his every need.

Unfortunately, Pauline made a lot of bad choices—including giving up her own career to build his. Though witty and intelligent, she had little ambition of her own and chose to promote the man she loved, rather than attempting anything in her own right. Perhaps her greatest failing, however, was in her role as a mother. When married to Ernest Hemingway, one often had to choose between being a wife and being a mother. Pauline chose being his wife, and in the end she lost both her husband and, to a degree, the respect of her children.

Despite her faults, Pauline and her family deserve recognition for the major impact they had on Ernest Hemingway financially, emotionally, and artistically. Their support, which enabled him to develop the literary style that ultimately brought him the most prestigious prizes in literature, is the focus of this book.

ACKNOWLEDGMENTS

As with any book more than ten years in the making, there are numerous people who contributed to this effort. While it is not possible to list everyone by name, there are some who deserve special recognition, beginning with the couple who started me on this journey, Sherland and Barbara Hamilton of Rector, Arkansas. The Hamiltons continued to encourage me over the years, along with the equally gentle prodding of Rosemary Janes (whose family acquired the Pfeiffer property in 1950) and current and former staff of the Hemingway-Pfeiffer Museum and Educational Center in Piggott, especially Diana Sanders, Deanna Dismukes, Johnna Redman, and Karen Trout.

Others recognized the significance of Piggott and the Pfeiffers long before I started writing this book, and some of their early essays and interviews provided a good starting point. Among them are Anita Allman, Ellagene McNiel Gilman, Ruth Gwin, Marie Hillyer, Linda Lingle, and Linda Rouse. Most important to this project in the beginning, however, was Ken Wells of Piggott, who once played with the Hemingway children. Ken recognized the need for a book and turned over his notes to me, along with introducing me to sources in Piggott and to the Hemingway family. Early assistance from Ken, as well as Piggott attorney John Lingle, will not be forgotten. Additionally, Don Roeder of Piggott helped in many ways and paved the way for in-depth interviews with one of the book's informants, Matilda Pfeiffer, sister-in-law of Pauline Pfeiffer Hemingway.

From the scholarly community, I am grateful to Michael Reynolds, who challenged me to do this book, and to Bernice Kert, for her valuable advice. I am sorry that I did not finish it in time for them to read it. Rose Marie Burwell and Susan Beegel also were sources of encouragement along the way.

This book is largely based on letters and oral history interviews. I appreciate the time and memories contributed by all who shared their stories, and they are acknowledged in the bibliography. Several should be singled out, however, including Matilda Pfeiffer, George Pfeiffer, Laura Archera Huxley, Jay McEvoy, Louise Pfeiffer, Jack Hemingway, Patrick Hemingway, and Gregory Hemingway. All were helpful not only in sharing information but in steering me in the right direction for other sources. Several interviewees cited here and in the bibliography are now deceased, and I am honored to have known them and heard their stories firsthand.

I did not realize how much I enjoyed research until I started spending time in libraries across the country. The staffs of the Ernest Hemingway

Collection at John F. Kennedy Library, Princeton University Library, Stanford University Library, University of Missouri—Columbia Records/ Registration Office, and Monroe County Library in Key West were especially helpful. Jewel Devin at the Cedar Falls (Iowa) Public Library, Nancy Hamilton in Michigan, and the sisters at the Academy of the Visitation in St. Louis went out of their way to assist with finding information and materials.

Visiting Hemingway sites to walk in Ernest's and Pauline's footsteps also was enlightening. Special thanks to Virginia Cassin, at the Ernest Hemingway Birthplace Home in Oak Park, Illinois; Michael Morawski, at the Ernest Hemingway Home and Museum in Key West, Florida; Gladys Rodriguez Ferrero, associated with the Ernest Hemingway Museum (Finca Vigia) in Cuba; Steve Paul, who developed a great tour of Kansas City sites; residents of the former Pfeiffer colony at Aspetuck, Connecticut; and Ernest H. Mainland, who gave me a great introduction to Petoskey, Michigan, and Windemere Cottage. Thanks also to the Gustavus and Louise Pfeiffer Research Foundation, Sarah Pfeiffer McCarthy, Irene Leonardi Tortoreto, Robert Baldwin, Dian Kammeyer, and John Hemingway for their support and assistance.

I am indebted to Patrick Hemingway and the Hemingway family for permission to quote from the unpublished writings of Ernest Hemingway and the unpublished letters of Paul and Mary Pfeiffer and Pauline Pfeiffer Hemingway. Thanks as well to the Ernest Hemingway Foundation, Ernest H. Mainland, Lucy Dos Passos Coggin, John Sanford, Hillary Hemingway, Scott Donaldson, Peter Hays, Tim Page, the Ketch and Yawl Press (2007 revised edition of *Papa in Key West*), Pineapple Press (1996 revised edition of *My Brother, Ernest Hemingway*), and others cited in the footnotes.

My research was made much easier thanks to the assistance of three of my dearest friends and colleagues—Diana Sanders, Paula Miles, and Benita Walker—who painstakingly typed transcripts of letters and oral history interviews and provided other assistance over the years. Diana's efforts also have contributed significantly to making the Hemingway-Pfeiffer Museum and Educational Center a major asset to northeast Arkansas.

I am grateful to the staff at the University of Arkansas Press and to Carol Sickman-Garner, whose attention to matters of style made this a better book. I am learning that no book is ever finished, and any errors or omissions are entirely mine.

Finally, my deep appreciation to my husband, Van, who patiently edited various versions of my manuscript and made judicious cuts and suggestions, and to my son, Curt, who assisted in organizing the letters and may not remember a time when I was not working on this book.

CHAPTER 1

Introduction

When Ernest Hemingway met the Pfeiffer sisters in late March 1925, he found Virginia far more fetching than her older sister, Pauline, who later became his second wife. At the time, Virginia gave him the attention he craved, while Pauline thought him boorish. Pauline was working in Paris for Main Bocher, editor of the *Vogue* magazine French edition. Previously a writer for *Vogue* in New York, she used the opportunity to become part of the Paris social scene. When her sister, Virginia, joined her in France for an extended visit, they each found their niche in Paris.

In those heady days and nights in the enchanted city, cafés and bars served as rendezvous for American expatriates and tourists who came together to share ideas and plan activities. Each establishment catered to a distinct clientele and took on its own personality. Pauline's tastes favored the expensive Right Bank spots, where she dined on Portuguese oysters with friends at Prunier's, or sipped Bloody Marys with colleagues at the elegant Ritz Hotel. When Pauline crossed to the more avant-garde Left Bank, she sought out places in the upscale St. Germain district, such as Café de Flore and Aux Deux Magots, which catered to journalists, Sorbonne professors, and working intellectuals. Her more adventurous sister, Virginia, preferred Café Rotonde on the Left Bank, where tourists flocked to observe revolutionaries, Greenwich Village transplants, and assorted misfits who uniformly aimed for nonconformity. Another likely spot for Virginia, the noisy Café du Dôme, drew struggling artists and expatriates attempting to be seen and make connections.

Paris in those days worked like a magnet, pulling in writers, artists, musicians, and intellectuals. Europeans and Americans learned to dance the Charleston from a new Paris sensation, an African American cabaret queen known as Bricktop for her red hair, but born Ada Beatrice Queen Victoria Louise Smith in Alderson, West Virginia. Along with sipping Pernod and listening to Cole Porter's music, patrons filled cafes, bars, studios, and salons with spirited discussions of intellectual topics. Alive with creative energy at all hours of the day and night, citizens of Paris learned to live with outrageous lifestyles and behaviors. Wealthy Americans reveled in the deliciously hedonistic atmosphere, while indigent artists and unknown writers found inexpensive living and a supportive environment. Hemingway perhaps captured the French capital best when he wrote more than a quarter century later, "If you are lucky enough to have lived in Paris as a young man, then wherever you go for the rest of your life, it stays with you, for Paris is a moveable feast."[1]

Shortly after the Pfeiffers became part of this frenetic city, Pauline became friends with Kitty Cannell, fashion editor for the *New York Times* in Paris. For months Kitty had been telling Pauline she wanted to introduce her to another of her friends, Hadley Richardson Hemingway. Although they had not previously met, Hadley and Pauline had grown up in nearby St. Louis neighborhoods. They also shared a mutual friend in Katy Smith. Katy had attended Mary Institute in St. Louis with Hadley and later become friends with Pauline at the University of Missouri School of Journalism. Katy provided another link as well. While growing up in St. Louis, she had spent summers in Petoskey, Michigan, where she and her younger brother Bill met and became friends with Ernest Hemingway. In October 1920, Katy introduced Ernest to Hadley, eight years his senior, and they fell "cockeyed in love" and married less than a year later.[2] Shortly after their marriage, they moved to Paris, where Ernest pursued his writing ambitions while living on Hadley's trust fund.

Though Pauline and Hadley had much in common, a meeting between the two did not take place earlier because the Hemingways were away when the Pfeiffer sisters arrived in Paris. Ernest and Hadley passed most of winter 1924–25 in Schruns, Austria, skiing and celebrating the pending New York publication of his first book, *In Our Time*. As soon as they returned, Hadley received an invitation for tea at Kitty Cannell's apartment near the Eiffel Tower to meet the Pfeiffers.

The sisters showed up around four in the afternoon looking like Japanese dolls, according to Kitty. Both petite, with "bones as delicate as a small bird's," they had bright, almond-shaped eyes and black bobbed hair stylishly cut across the forehead in thick bangs. Perfect grooming and fashionable outfits enhanced their striking physical features. For protection from the chilly weather, Pauline wore a new chipmunk coat from a top Paris designer. "It was the only one any of us had seen and she looked as cute as a little chipmunk in it," Kitty recalled, noting that Hadley looked rather dowdy by comparison.[3] Even though only four years older than Pauline, Hadley had a seventeen-month-old son by Ernest and had not regained her former figure.

The four women passed a good part of the afternoon swapping stories about St. Louis and Paris, hearing about Pauline's job at *Vogue,* and discussing fashions. Pauline, though nearing thirty at the time, had a schoolgirl crush on her *Vogue* editor. "Everything about him was 'ambrosial'—the superlative of the moment," Kitty remembered, and Pauline could not stop talking about him.[4]

Later in the afternoon, Kitty's sometime lover Harold Loeb came in with Ernest, both still keyed up from a boxing workout. Loeb, also a writer, occupied the apartment adjoining Kitty's. The previous fall he had introduced Ernest to the Paris representative for Boni & Liveright, the New York firm that agreed to publish his book. Both men joined the women's conversation and found the Pfeiffer sisters well versed on many topics. Pauline and Virginia clearly set the tone, liberally dispensing the light banter considered smart in Paris intellectual circles. In Kitty's view the sisters complemented each other. Pauline appeared more interesting and witty, while Virginia seemed more spirited and outgoing. "They were more than twice as cute as if there had only been one of them," Kitty recalled. "The one who was a little older (Pauline) benefited by the looks of the younger, and Virginia shone in the witticisms of the one who was a little brighter."[5]

Ernest related tales of his recent skiing trip to Austria with Hadley. As the more athletic of the sisters, Virginia found his stories interesting and followed him into the kitchen, where she spent much of the evening pumping him for more information—much to Ernest's delight. When the Pfeiffers left the party, Pauline chided her sister for spending so much time alone with Ernest in the kitchen.[6] It seemed particularly inappropriate, according to Pauline, since his wife in the next room was the guest of honor and the one they were supposed to be getting to know. Besides, while Pauline liked Hadley, Ernest did not impress her. Back at Kitty's apartment, Ernest expressed his view of the Pfeiffer sisters. Virginia, who took such an interest in hearing his stories, struck him as a prettier version of her more stylish older sister. Shortly after they left, he joked, "I'd like to take Virginia out in Pauline's coat."[7]

While Pauline and Virginia differed in their opinions of Ernest, both found Hadley a fine person and worth getting to know as a friend. A few days after their initial meeting at Kitty's, Pauline and Virginia followed up on their new friendship with Hadley by calling on her at the Hemingways' apartment over a sawmill on the Left Bank. The apartment fell far short of

Pauline's Right Bank apartment on the rue Picot, just off avenue Foch, in the wealthy American enclave of Paris. Pauline was shocked to find a cold apartment and the Hemingways' baby with a bad case of sniffles. Ernest was reclining on the bed, reading, unshaven, and slovenly, and did not bother to get up. Pauline thought him oafish and insensitive to Hadley, reaffirming her initial first impressions.

Apparently, however, his ruggedness appealed to Virginia. Later that week, when Pauline visited friends for the weekend, Virginia remained in Paris. Leaving a Paris restaurant after dining alone one evening, she encountered Ernest having dinner with Gertrude Stein and Alice B. Toklas. He motioned for her to join them for a glass of wine. As one glass became a full bottle, Ernest's other dinner companions departed, leaving him alone with Virginia. After the wine, he accompanied Virginia back to her quarters, a visit suggestive of more than conversation.[8]

When Pauline returned, she and Virginia continued to visit Hadley, as well as participate in social activities with Ernest and Hadley together. Throughout the remainder of her stay in Paris, Virginia also enjoyed Ernest's company on other occasions not shared with her sister. While some Hemingway biographers dismiss the idea of any personal relationship between Ernest and Virginia, pointing out that Virginia preferred the company of women, her friends claimed that she reveled in good times with great friends, male or female, and Ernest ranked high on the list. Although attracted to him, at that stage of her life Virginia avoided getting serious with any man—or woman—and certainly not a married man. Thus, he was a safe, and yet dangerously exciting, choice.[9]

Ernest found Virginia intriguing and paid close attention to her stories of growing up in a wealthy family. Virginia's father, Paul M. Pfeiffer, possessed extensive land holdings in the Piggott, Arkansas, area. Her uncles Henry and Gustavus Pfeiffer owned William R. Warner Co., Inc., a pharmaceutical manufacturing firm, and Richard Hudnut Perfumer, both international companies headquartered in New York. Ernest's financial circumstances stood in stark contrast to the Pfeiffer sisters. With Hadley's meager trust fund supporting them as he struggled to make it as a writer, Ernest must have found Virginia's interest potentially rewarding in more ways than one.

The early relationship between Ernest and Virginia ended, however, when she returned to Piggott to spend fall and winter with her parents. By the time she came back to Paris the next spring to visit her sister, rumors of Pauline's romantic involvement with Ernest were the talk of the Left Bank literary set. The relationship made no sense to Virginia, particularly given her sister's strong early opposition to Ernest. Even more important, she could not believe that Pauline's professed strict adherence to Roman Catholic teachings had allowed her to enter into such a relationship. Skeptical of Ernest's intentions from the beginning, Virginia questioned whether Ernest loved Pauline or the thought of Pfeiffer family money. Regardless, Virginia determined to keep her sister from knowing that she was not the first Pfeiffer to attract Ernest's attentions.[10] As much as Virginia enjoyed the writer's company and might have wanted to pursue her own relationship with Ernest, she realized Pauline loved him and chose not to interfere.

This complicated start marked the beginning of Ernest's association with the wealthy and intensely private Pfeiffer family. The relationship went beyond Pauline and Virginia to include their uncle Gustavus A. Pfeiffer, Ernest's financial angel; their father and mother, Paul and Mary Pfeiffer, who became surrogate parents; and their brother Karl, who quail-hunted with Ernest. The Pfeiffers readily accepted Ernest into the family when he married Pauline, and they provided enormous support to the couple throughout their marriage. When Ernest betrayed Pauline and divorced her, he cut himself off from Pfeiffer resources that had sustained him for years— a loss perhaps harder to reconcile than the absence of their daughter.

CHAPTER 2

The Pfeiffers

The Pfeiffer wealth that attracted Ernest Hemingway was earned, not inherited, by a large family spread across two continents. Pauline, like most of her Pfeiffer relatives, moved easily across the distances that separated them. Despite geographic barriers, family members remained unusually close—both personally and through business dealings. They also shared a deep appreciation for history, culture, and community service. To understand their closeness and family values requires going back several generations.

Pauline's grandfather Heinrich (Henry) Pfeiffer was the first to arrive in the United States. Born January 14, 1830, Heinrich was among fifteen children of a prominent family from Kempten in Southern Bavaria, now part of Germany. Today a bustling commercial center, Kempten then seemed like a romantic postcard scene that inspired music and poetry. Located in the foothills of the Alps on an eight-thousand-foot plateau, the quaint town was nestled amid snow-capped mountains, rippling mountain streams, dark green pinewood forests, and rolling landscapes with deep long valleys. On one of many pilgrimages to the birthplace of his father, Pauline's uncle Gus described it as a place where "the elements of Nature seem to combine to foster simplicity and depth and breadth of character, and the qualities of goodness and honesty."[1]

Family roots stretched back to Hans Pfeiffer, who migrated in 1607 to Kempten, apparently from nearby Alt Rothenburg, in Austria.[2] The family included many brewers, and Heinrich's father, Johannes, continued this tradition. He owned a popular inn and brewery, the Schwarzer Adler, in the heart of town, on Baeckerstrasse, where he sold beer and raised his children.

Heinrich was a romping, mischievous boy who played hard in the narrow streets among centuries-old buildings and the ruins of the Burghalde, a complex built by the Romans in the third century. Located on a hill seventy-five feet above the streets, the remnants of the Burghalde included a wall partially surrounding a picturesque tower, along with a well dug so deep that you could drop a pebble and count to seven before it hit water.[3]

Heinrich worked as hard as he played, rising early to assist his parents with chores at the inn and catering to guests from around the world. He dreamed of becoming such a traveler and determined early to one day make his way to the United States. By age twenty-one the young man had saved enough money to make the trip. Heinrich departed Kempten in 1851 and went to Pennsylvania, where he established a brewery.

After several years of hard work and success, he returned to Kempten to marry his childhood sweetheart and bring her to the United States, only to find that his sweetheart had married someone else in his absence. Undaunted, Heinrich set about finding a wife and discovered Anna Barbara Kluftinger. Known by her close family as Babette, she also came from a large family—one of the oldest and most respected in Kempten. Her family traced its ancestors in the town to 1394, including a long line of master butchers, as well as politicians and a poet.[4]

Barbara's father, Markus, an innkeeper like Heinrich's father, operated the Keck Inn, located on a hill overlooking Kempten, just three-quarters of a mile from the Schwarzer Adler. He also served as landlord for St. Stephan's Lutheran Church, next door to the inn. Markus married Katharina Magdalena Walch of nearby Kaufbeuren on April 18, 1831, and the couple had thirteen children, including Barbara, born February 6, 1835.

Barbara's early years were spent playing in and around the church grounds, including the Keck Kapelle (chapel), while her father tended to his duties. The Kapelle, filled with frescoes dating to the thirteenth century, was later bought and restored by the Kluftinger family, thus attracting artists from throughout Europe.

When her mother died during the birth of the last child, nine-year-old Barbara, as the oldest living sister, took charge of the younger children. During Barbara's teenage years, she left Kempten to work for a family in Switzerland, as was customary for many young girls in southern Bavaria. When she was nineteen, her father died, and she returned home to resume caring for her younger brothers and sisters.

Shortly thereafter she met Heinrich, the adventurous and successful young man back from the United States, and quickly agreed to marry him on condition that he take her to America. Married April 3, 1856, at St. Stephan's Lutheran Church, they set sail soon thereafter. The newlyweds settled in Lewistown, Pennsylvania, where Heinrich continued his brewery business. After the birth of their first son, Henry, on March 3, 1857, the family traveled to Dubuque, Iowa. They moved on again, partly by covered wagon, to Cedar Falls, Iowa, in Black Hawk County, where Heinrich established another brewery. At that time, Cedar Falls was little more than a settlement in Indian Territory called Sturgis Falls. Indians still roamed the countryside, and small bands sometimes came to the Pfeiffers' door for food.

Heinrich and Barbara named their second son, born in Cedar Falls shortly after their arrival, George Washington Pfeiffer, as an affirmation of their "American Choice."[5] In time, eight additional children resulted from this union, including Emma, Rose, Jacob (Jake), Leonard (Lony), Paul Mark, Ernest, Gustavus Adolphus (Gus), and William (Will). Paul Mark, Pauline's father, born February 15, 1868, was their seventh child.

Their extended family grew larger when Barbara's younger sister Sabina Amelia immigrated to Cedar Falls in 1866 with her husband, Matthew Gering, and three children. After two additional children were born, the Gerings moved to Plattsmouth, Nebraska, but a strong bond between the two families continued through successive generations, including Pauline's later engagement to a cousin from Nebraska.

Heinrich and Barbara stressed to their children such principles as hard work, honesty, and thrift. And above all, they taught the importance of family. Harris Franklin Rall, a friend and minister, recalled Heinrich as a man of few words who often taught profound lessons to his children. One such lesson came when two of the brothers got into a fight with each other, and their father suddenly appeared on the scene. Their worst fears seemed confirmed when he sent one to cut a rod from the nearby willow hedge. He told him to break the staff into two parts, an easy task. Then Heinrich broke the halves into shorter pieces, tied them together, and handed the bundle to his sons, challenging them to break it. That, of course, they could not do. Heinrich's message followed: "You will have plenty to fight against when you go out into the world. Don't fight each other. Stand together and nothing can touch you."[6]

Both Heinrich and Barbara were strong role models for their children, particularly because their personalities complemented each other. Heinrich, a rather quiet man, was considered patient, kind, and easygoing. Though highly principled, he was somewhat reserved in matters of religion. Barbara, on the other hand, was the epitome of the pioneering, evangelistic spirit of aggressiveness, hard work, strong will, and devotion to Christian service. Although small in stature beside her husband and eight boys, she ruled the family with her outspoken beliefs. After arriving in Cedar Falls, she had joined the Evangelical church, an outgrowth of the Methodist movement that ministered to German Americans in their own language. Arriving home from services one day, she declared beer the work of the devil and opened all the spigots of her husband's beer casks, flooding the cellar.[7] Her actions successfully ended Heinrich's career as the town's first and only brewer. In his usual manner of taking things in stride, Heinrich simply shifted gears and invested in a farm outside of town. The entire family worked hard to develop the farm, not an easy task, and managed to eke out a living.

When an 1871 flood ruined their crops, the Pfeiffers "farmed out" several sons to friends and relatives to keep everyone fed and clothed, including sending one son to live with Barbara's younger brother Leonhard in Europe. A bachelor with no children, Leonhard had become quite wealthy in the hemp business, with properties in Kempten, Bavaria, and Bologna, Italy. When Kaiser Wilhelm I appointed him German consul general for northern Italy, he asked Barbara to allow her oldest son, Henry, to live in Bologna with him to learn the hemp business and assist with his diplomatic duties. Barbara refused to send Henry but instead reluctantly sent her second son, George Washington, known as Washington.

The fourteen-year-old country boy, who had never seen a city or an ocean, quickly learned Italian, improved his German, and took on Old World refinement and culture, eventually becoming a partner in his uncle's business. Though he left for Europe before the birth of the two younger Pfeiffer children, Gus and Will, Washington became a hero in their eyes through his letters and books from Germany and Italy.

In May 1881 Heinrich and Barbara celebrated their twenty-fifth wedding anniversary and received a treasured anniversary gift—unification of their entire family—when Washington made his first trip home since departing for Europe ten years earlier. Washington brought some flavor of the Old World into the Pfeiffer home, and the event had a lasting impact on the family. During Washington's visit, he advanced the family's personal fortunes by helping his father stock the farm, which lacked livestock and equipment. Washington contributed horses, cattle, hogs, and several pieces of machinery to turn the farm around.[8] Not only did his contributions keep his father from going into debt, but they gave his family the means to work the farm more efficiently. Over the successful ensuing years, the Pfeiffers plowed farm profits into charities and diverse business opportunities, thus taking their place among the town's most highly respected citizens.

Years later, their legacy in Cedar Falls lived on through the philanthropy of their children. The Pfeiffer family home at Eleventh and Grove became the site for the Western Old People's Home, a retirement residence built with contributions from the Pfeiffer children, and early residents received a gold piece at Christmas from the Pfeiffers for many years. Other Pfeiffer property became the Washington Park Golf Course and Country Club (in memory of Washington Pfeiffer) and Pfeiffer Spring Park. Pfeiffer funds also built the town's Zion Evangelical Lutheran Church, provided organs for five churches in the community, and funded purchase and maintenance of a Victorian mansion for use by the Cedar Falls Women's Club.

As the Pfeiffer children entered adulthood, they carried with them their parents' pioneering and entrepreneurial spirit. The oldest brother, Henry, introduced the family to the pharmaceutical business. After Henry's first job at Miner's Flour Mill, he apprenticed himself for three years to Anton Sartori, owner of the Corner Drug Store in Cedar Falls. Meanwhile, he married Annie Merner in 1882, and they set up housekeeping in an apartment above the drugstore. At the end of his apprenticeship, Henry obtained a certificate qualifying him to fill prescriptions and operate a drugstore. An important opportunity came just one year later, when his employer moved to western Iowa and sold Henry the Cedar Falls business. Soon, Pfeiffer's Corner Drug Store became a popular and lively business in Cedar Falls and environs.

Finding that he needed a bright young clerk for his growing business, Henry asked his brother Paul to help him. Paul's business ability had manifested itself at an early age. When no more than nine years old, he successfully marketed the family's garden and dairy produce. Besides being a good salesman, Paul proved good at collecting debts, even from people notorious for not paying their bills. Family members liked to tell how Paul, though a young boy, collected from a hotelkeeper known by all to be a slow payer. Paul waited until the man engaged in conversation with a hotel guest, then asked him for payment of his vegetable bill. Cornered, the hotelkeeper paid up to avoid embarrassment.

When Paul went to work for his older brother, he applied his keen skills to the drugstore business. During the early years of Paul's clerkship, a Chicago publisher, Belford, Clark & Co., marketed novels and other books with expired copyrights. Discounts ranged from one-third to one-fourth of their original prices. To promote these books, the company organized book sales in towns with populations of three thousand or more. Publishers picked the most popular store in each town, including Pfeiffer's Corner Drug Store in Cedar Falls, for their promotions. These innovative drugstore book sales proved highly successful for the Pfeiffer store and introduced Paul to the fascinating world to be found through literature. He became acquainted with great writers and ideas by reading fiction, history, and philosophy.

After ten years of success in the retail drug business, Henry partnered with a friend in 1891 to organize Allan-Pfeiffer Chemical Company in St.

Louis. His departure from Cedar Falls also led to a change for Paul, who by then felt ready to go out on his own. Paul soon acquired a drugstore in Parkersburg, Iowa—just twenty miles from Cedar Falls, in neighboring Butler County. With an entrepreneurial personality and dislike of day-to-day operations, he turned to his family for administrative help. Like his brother Henry, who had given Paul his start in Cedar Falls, Paul gave his younger brother Gus the opportunity to join him. With a year at the Illinois College of Pharmacy completed, Gus moved to Parkersburg to help his brother. Paul quickly made Gus his partner and gave him stock in the Pfeiffer & Company drug firm. Gus handled daily business operations, which freed Paul to pursue other opportunities, including working as cashier in a local bank in which he had eleven thousand dollars' worth of stock. By then Paul, approaching twenty-five and financially secure, wanted to marry and begin a family.

He found the right girl shortly after moving to Parkersburg in Mary Alice Downey. An Irish girl from a devout Catholic family, Mary was born April 4, 1867, the seventh of nine children. Her parents, both from Ireland, had arrived separately in the United States with their families during a potato famine in the 1840s. Daniel Downey came to the United States in 1847 at age twenty-four; Katherine (Kate) Byrnes came a year later at age fourteen, and her family Americanized their name to Burns. Both families settled in Illinois, where Daniel and Kate married on October 19, 1851, moving to Parkersburg, Iowa, some seven years later.

The life they built together was greatly influenced by the early persecution they had experienced as Catholics in Ireland. Daniel vowed before leaving for America that when he had his own family, he would have two things in his home: a chapel where he and his family could observe their Catholic faith and a library where he and his children would always have access to good books and educational opportunities. He succeeded in having both, including the finest library in Parkersburg. When Daniel died on October 5, 1889, his home library became the basis for the Parkersburg Public Library. The collection also contributed to his daughter Mary's voracious reading appetite, a trait she shared with her new husband.

Paul Pfeiffer and Mary Downey married on October 8, 1894, at St. Patrick's Catholic Church in Parkersburg, with Paul's brother Gus and Mary's sister Cora as attendants. Undoubtedly, Paul's marriage to a Catholic girl was not what his mother would have chosen for him. But the newly married couple was a match not unlike his parents'. Like Barbara, Mary strongly and openly expressed her religious convictions, while Paul had inherited the reticence of his father. Although he did not share Mary's religion, he supported her and helped bring up their children in the Catholic faith. In matters other than religion, however, Paul and Mary seemed the reverse of Paul's parents. Like her father-in-law, Mary accepted things as she found them and did not like change, although she adapted when necessary. Paul shared his mother's pioneering spirit and adventurous nature. Like his mother, he looked at life's misfortunes as challenges to be overcome.

One such opportunity presented itself around the time of his marriage, when a devastating fire swept through the entire downtown area of Parkersburg in the summer of 1893, destroying most of the wooden structures. Paul, as bank cashier and owner of a business, joined a committee to rebuild downtown. Undaunted by their losses, committee members announced that the downtown would be rebuilt with magnificent brick structures, all two stories high and from sixty to eighty feet deep. As part of the rebuilding effort, Paul bought a choice lot in partnership with his brother Gus and built one of the finest drugstores in the region.

On January 5, 1895, with the new drugstore up and running, he deeded most of his share to Gus and the remainder to G. N. Clark, who had helped them operate the earlier store. The store was renamed G. A. Pfeiffer & Company. The severance allowed Paul's restless spirit to move on to other opportunities, such as packaging bank deals and developing real estate. Shortly after Paul changed his professional pursuits, he and Mary had a daughter, Pauline Marie, born July 22, 1895.

By the time of Pauline's birth, her uncle Gus was contemplating marriage. In anticipation of this event, and in view of the needs of Paul's family, Paul and Gus together purchased a large home on Buswell Street, not far from downtown Parkersburg. The house, built in the popular Victorian mother-in-law style, had two separate and identical halves. Paul, Mary, and baby Pauline moved into one side shortly after the purchase on February 17, 1896; Gus moved into the other. Four months later Louise Foote, also of Parkersburg, moved into the home as Gus's bride. Exactly one year after their marriage, Louise and Gus had a son named Max. Sadly, he died less than two months later, and they were never able to have other children.

The death of their son and sharing a home with Paul, Mary, and Pauline brought Gus and Louise especially close to their niece. Throughout their lives, they doted on all their nieces and nephews, but none had the strong, early bond that Gus formed with Pauline. The home they all shared, within walking distance of downtown, actually stood on the western edge of town, near rolling hills, cornfields, and a small creek. For much of his life, Paul repeated his parents' pattern of pushing westward, with one foot anchored in the civilizing influence of town life and the other stepping off into undeveloped territory. In each of his successive homes after Parkersburg—St. Louis and Piggott—he lived as far from the heart of town as he could get, while remaining within the city limits.

The turn of the century brought moves and changes for the Pfeiffers, including Gus's return to Cedar Falls, where he acquired half interest in the family's original Pfeiffer Drug Company. Paul and Mary extended their family on March 8, 1900, with the birth of Pauline's brother Karl Gustavus Pfeiffer, born just a few weeks after Pauline, not quite five, rallied from whooping cough.[9]

Paul also enlarged his land holdings, acquiring a ranch of more than one thousand acres in adjacent Franklin County to the west and purchasing a large farm in Allison, just north of Parkersburg. By the end of the first year of the twentieth century, he was raising cattle, horses, hogs, and corn on a large scale.

Although Paul had managers on each farm, he spent much of his time going back and forth from his home in Parkersburg to oversee and develop his properties, making them models of modern farming practices. His concern went beyond outstanding crops, to having the best buildings and equipment. On May 31, 1900, shortly after his purchase of the Allison property, his farming efforts even drew a social note in the local *Parkersburg Eclipse:* "P. M. Pfeiffer let the contract the first of the week for moving one of the large barns on the old Iowa Central Stock farm southwest of Allison. The structure is now on the west side of the road and it will be divided and moved across the road onto the section farm occupied by Wm. Corsaut and purchased by Mr. Pfeiffer several months ago. The barn is 50x50 feet and cost when built $7,700. It is a finely constructed building and will make two as good barns as can be found in Butler County."[10]

Early in 1901, word came from Henry Pfeiffer in St. Louis that he wanted his brothers Paul and Gus to join him in a new venture. The three spent an afternoon in St. Louis on a bench at Forest Park discussing their ideas. Being entrepreneurs, they weighed whether they should get into the growing automobile business or whether they should capitalize on their drug business success. Ultimately, the trio decided to stick with what they knew and formed Pfeiffer Chemical Company, which they located on the St. Louis waterfront in the shadow of Eads Bridge. Henry served as president, Gus as vice president, and Paul as secretary-treasurer.

Gus and Louise relocated to St. Louis almost immediately, leaving brother Jacob Pfeiffer as president and owner of the Pfeiffer drugstore in Cedar Falls. While Henry and Gus got things organized in St. Louis, Paul remained behind to close out his business interests, commuting between

Iowa and St. Louis for a time. On November 14, 1901, the Parkersburg paper ran one last social note regarding the Pfeiffers: "Paul M. Pfeiffer is no longer a resident of Parkersburg, having left for his new home in St. Louis Saturday night of last week. He is connected with the new Pfeiffer Chemical Co. and will devote his time to the interests of that organization, in which his brothers G. A. and Henry are also interested. Paul has been a resident of Parkersburg for many years, and no man has left this community in a long time whose departure is more regretted than his. He has always been public spirited and a pusher in business matters and he will be followed to his new home by the good will and best wishes of a host of friends. He, together with his estimable family, will be greatly missed."[11]

By the time the notice appeared, Paul, Mary, and their children, Pauline and Karl, resided in St. Louis, their home from the time Pauline started first grade until she graduated from high school. The fourth-largest city in the nation at the turn of the century, St. Louis was experiencing a building frenzy in preparation for hosting the 1904 World's Fair that gave the city an air of excitement. By the time the fair opened, St. Louis boasted more than one hundred hotels, and automobiles had become a common sight on city streets. As downtown office buildings, financial institutions, and manufacturing facilities replaced residential areas, new neighborhoods developed first to the north and south, then to the west, in the early 1900s.

Paul's family settled into a new two-story reddish-brown brick Victorian house at 5129 Morgan Street, on the western limits of the city. Henry and his wife, Anna, lived a few doors down, in a virtually identical house. Gus and Louise lived just one block over, at 5101 Kensington Avenue. Sally Smith Benson immortalized the neighborhood in her memoir *Meet Me in St. Louis*. Sally lived at 5135 Kensington, and Blewett Wagoner, who became "The Boy Next Door" in the musical version of her book, lived at 5137 Kensington. The Hodiamont streetcar, the basis for the musical's "Trolley Song," ran along the alley just behind Kensington Avenue.

When the Pfeiffers moved in, the neighborhood was in the midst of a building boom, with small retail businesses being established to cater to the growing residential population. Individual vendors further serviced the neighborhood, making their rounds with items such as ice, milk, produce, and bakery goods. Its location near Forest Park and close to some of the most fashionable homes in St. Louis made the growing neighborhood a sought-after place to live at the time.

Paul took the streetcar downtown each day but soon tired of his office job. After the second year in business with his brothers, he resigned to pursue land development, maintaining a small office at Pfeiffer Chemical

Company. In 1908 Pfeiffer Chemical Company expanded by acquiring William R. Warner, a major drug manufacturing business, and transferred its base of operations to Warner headquarters in Philadelphia and eventually to New York. Henry and Gus relocated to the East Coast, but Paul chose not to move his family to an even larger city, nor did he have any interest in being more actively involved in the St. Louis operations. Their sister Emma's son Garfield Merner took charge of the St. Louis branch. Merner was not the only member of the next generation of Pfeiffers to become involved in the family businesses. In a curious reversal of his own situation, Washington sent his second son, C. Leonard Pfeiffer, from Italy to the United States at age fourteen to live with and work for his uncle Jacob in Cedar Falls and later his uncles Henry and Gus in New York.

Though Paul remained in St. Louis for a time, continuing problems with asthma and his brothers' relocations gave him few reasons to stay, but a return to Iowa held little appeal. Paul's father had died in 1903, and in January 1908 the Pfeiffers received word of "Grossmutter Barbara's" serious illness at her daughter Emma Merner's home in Los Angeles. Paul and his brothers maintained a bedside vigil until her death on February 22, 1908. True to her nature, Barbara imparted some final wisdom to her children gathered around: "What I gave, I take with me. What I kept, I leave behind."[12]

With many Iowa ties undone, including the death of Mary's mother in Parkersburg in 1909, Paul looked south for opportunities. For years he had heard stories about vast expanses of land in the Mississippi River Delta, where railroads hauled out timber for mills in the north. An adventurous entrepreneur could buy the land for almost nothing, drain the swamps, remove the stumps, and harvest a fortune, Paul surmised. Numerous versions of Paul's search for just the right spot became legend in Piggott. The story told by family holds that during Paul's return to St. Louis by rail from a trip to New Orleans, the train was halted by St. Francis River flooding. Passengers sat stranded for several days south of Piggott. While waiting for the water to recede, Paul roamed the area, observed the land, and asked questions of the locals. He discovered exceptionally fertile land between Crowley's Ridge in Eastern Clay County and the St. Francis River.

Once back in St. Louis, Paul began buying large tracts of land in the Piggott area, with more than one hundred land transactions totaling approximately thirteen thousand acres between 1902 and 1913. When his brothers departed for Philadelphia, Paul began regularly commuting between St. Louis and Piggott, dividing the vast acreage into forty- and eighty-acre farmsteads for lease to tenant farmers. To attract good farmers, he offered reasonable contract terms and made sure each farm had a house, barn, chicken house, smokehouse, outdoor toilet, corncrib, and wooded lot.

Paul gained a reputation as one of the "fairest men ever to set foot in Clay County," but apparently not everyone held such a high opinion of him.[13] One encounter with a disgruntled renter landed him in a hospital in the nearby town of Paragould, in neighboring Greene County. An article in the October 14, 1912, issue of the Paragould paper gave an account of the incident:

> Paul M. Pfeiffer of St. Louis was taken to Paragould last night from St. Francis, Ark. and placed in a sanitarium, suffering from dangerous knife wounds in the back, alleged to have been inflicted by Capt. Geo. M. Jackson, a socialist leader of Clay Co. Pfeiffer had been to Jackson's house and Jackson is said to have demanded some improvements made on the building, which was owned by Pfeiffer. Jackson, when the request was objected to, became angered, it was said, but Pfeiffer being used to dealing with Jackson and knowing his moods, paid no attention to his anger. It is alleged that just as Pfeiffer was leaving Jackson's yard the latter stabbed him with a knife, the weapon entering under the shoulder blade and going through to the lung. Physicians say Pfeiffer is in a dangerous condition, but may recover. Pfeiffer is a capitalist of St. Louis, and owns a great deal of land in Clay Co. He spends much of his time looking after his interests in the Eastern district.[14]

Though the stabbing did not dissuade the "capitalist" from moving to Arkansas, other more powerful persuasions kept him in St. Louis for a time. Mary expressed concern that Piggott lacked a Catholic church and Catholic schools. With Pauline entering her senior year of high school, timing seemed bad for leaving the advantages offered by a city of 713,000 people to move to a town of 1,300. Once Pauline finished school, however, that major hurdle came down.

CHAPTER 3

Pauline

Pauline began first grade in the fall of 1901 at Academy of the Visitation on Cabanne Avenue, adjacent to her residential St. Louis neighborhood. The school had relocated in 1892 from downtown, and the Sisters of the Visitation built an imposing chateau-like structure as their new school and convent. With its turrets and buttresses, students thought it resembled a fairyland castle or a hiding place for ghosts. Indeed, Pauline's Catholic education and concern about church dogma would rise up to haunt her later in life.

The rigorous academic program included a philosophy based on "Gospel virtues of optimism, gentleness, joy, humility, and inner freedom."[1] The school for young ladies accepted both day students and boarders in grades one through twelve. Pauline may have boarded for the first few months of the school year, since Paul and Mary did not move to St. Louis until November. More likely, however, Pauline came to St. Louis early and lived with Uncle Gus and Aunt Louise until her parents arrived.

Living in St. Louis at that time offered Pauline unexpected educational opportunities. The Pfeiffers resided less than a mile from Forest Park, where groundbreaking ceremonies on December 20, 1901, announced the coming St. Louis World's Fair. Planned in honor of the 1803 Louisiana Purchase centennial, the grand scale of exhibitions delayed an official opening until April 30, 1904. The more than two years of preparation provided great entertainment for residents. Watching the Grand Basin and ornate buildings emerge from undeveloped land on the west side of Forest Park amazed onlookers perhaps as much as later contact with people and products from all over the world. The same architect who had built the Sisters of the Visitation's "chateau" a few years earlier constructed the fair's Palace of Liberal Arts.[2] The convent/academy seemed monumental at the time, but it paled by comparison to the grandiose exposition palaces that seemed to appear as if by magic.

For Pauline and her classmates, the seven-month fair became an extended classroom. Nuns took students to exhibits for enrichment and brought speakers and entertainers to the school after appearances at the fair. One such entertainer, an Irish tenor named John McCormack, became one of the supreme vocal artists of the twentieth century, with a successful forty-year professional career. His rendition of "I Hear You Calling Me" reverberated in the halls of the academy for years to come.[3]

When the fair closed at the stroke of midnight on December 1, 1904, it was a merry yet sad occasion, remembered by some residents as "one of the wildest nights ever witnessed in St. Louis." As midnight approached, the fair president raised his arms toward palace-like buildings with all their thousands of glittering lights and pronounced, "Farewell, a long farewell, to all thy splendor," as he threw the switch casting the fairgrounds into total darkness.[4]

Life in the Pfeiffer neighborhood returned to normal after the fair closed, which for nine-year-old Pauline meant games with brother Karl and neighbors in vast backyards and along tree-lined streets or playing paper dolls alone in her room. Two additional playmates had joined Pauline and Karl at home—Virginia Ruth, born March 27, 1902, and Paul Mark, born October 19, 1907. Paul Mark was called Max to distinguish him from his father and to honor the memory of his cousin, Uncle Gus's child, who had died in infancy.

Along with tending children and keeping house, Mary devoted time to Catholic charities, including the Sisters of Mercy Industrial Home and School for Girls, down the street from the Pfeiffer home. On several visits to take clothing in 1911, Mary noticed a nine-year-old named Julia who went door to door with one of the nuns each day to beg for alms. Feeling sorry for the young girl, Mary contacted her unmarried sister, Cora Downing, to arrange for the child to become her ward. Mary thought putting the two together would promise a new life for Julia and prevent Cora from being alone. Years later Julia's daughter, Sheila Tybor, recalled, "My mother remembered sitting on the judge's lap and him saying, 'Would you like to go with this nice lady and live in Montana?" Julia quickly said yes, and Cora went on ahead to homestead 145 acres in Nowhere, Montana. Julia started west alone with her doll, traveling by train, stagecoach, and buckboard to reach her new home.[5]

Though Cora braved the western frontier, her sister Mary preferred the cultural advantages of a big city. The trolley that ran through the Pfeiffers'

St. Louis neighborhood provided easy access to libraries, museums, art galleries, plays, and concerts. Karl recalled that their father took them to see every Shakespeare play performed while they lived in St. Louis. With her flair for the dramatic, Pauline enjoyed participating in the school's religious pageantry and historic celebrations, including the annual May processional to the Shrine of the Sacred Heart and her First Communion and Confirmation ceremonies on May 2, 1907.

Virginia joined her sister at the academy in the fall of 1908. Though both excelled as students, Virginia delighted in seeing just how far she could push school regulations. Less daring than her younger sister, Pauline indulged only in minor forms of rebellion that mostly involved variations on the required school uniform. Explicit rules governed uniforms, but Pauline attempted to find as many ways as possible to assert her individuality, such as placing a bow in her hair or adding forbidden trim to her sleeve cuffs. After she became a fashion writer in Paris, her former classmates noted in an alumnae bulletin, "Had we foreseen her then as the future arbitrator of American fashions, how we would have aped her variations of that old black uniform! The ripped hem of her skirt might have started us all on the uneven hem-line years before Paris cabled it over."[6]

By her senior year, Pauline anxiously awaited graduation. Her French book includes a calendar drawn on the inside cover with each day checked off, along with miscellaneous notes and doodles. The back cover of her French textbook includes a poem written about her ten close-knit classmates:

I wiggled and wiggled and wiggled again
But quiet as death were the rest of the ten.
I looked at each one in the most pleading way
My looks were ignored, no attention they'd pay
Ag read the bible and Peg bit her lips
Amy C. sat with her hands on her hips
Doll wiggled her tongue; Mable fingered her collar
Aimee B. chin on neck her text tried to foller
Amy Dean ate a chocolate immense round & fat!
Oh gee! But I did awfully want some of that!
Lucile chewed her gum; Marguerite did the same
then to vary the scene tried to backhand her name
Baby was hopeless, she's of studious turn
Ok study all nine; I don't Give a durn![7]

Pauline graduated on June 11, 1913, as a student of merit and recipient of the English prize. Less than a month later, she moved with her family to

Piggott, her schooling no longer an obstacle to relocation. Paul quickly eliminated another barrier by promising his wife a chapel in their residence at Piggott to compensate for lack of a Catholic church.

Their new home was a two-story white Colonial Revival farmhouse, built in 1909–10 by the town's master builder, W. D. (Buck) Templeton, as his personal residence. A large house by the town's standards, it had been designed by Templeton to accommodate his large family, which ultimately included twenty-three children. When Paul first offered to buy the house, Templeton refused. He eventually relented after Paul paid him the handsome sum of $5,500 and gave him a deal on twenty acres of Pfeiffer-owned property east of town.

The house was solidly constructed, with spacious rooms downstairs and five bedrooms upstairs. In addition, it had features not available to most homes in town, including wiring in anticipation of electricity coming to Piggott and a well in the corner of the kitchen for convenient access to water. Other features were carryovers from Templeton's commercial buildings, including pressed tin ceilings in every room and glass-paneled doors throughout the house.

An orchard had been planted across the street, and behind the house sat a barn that included a hayloft, large and small animal stalls below, and a sheltered pass-through area for carriages. Having no animals, the Pfeiffers used the barn for storage space until fifteen years later, when their son-in-law sought its privacy to compose one of his greatest works.

Though the house on Cherry Street hill was perched on the outskirts of town, it stood just eight blocks from the town square. Fields and wide-open spaces bordered it on the west, and the town's three-story brick school sat directly across the street. The location met many needs, with Max starting school, Virginia entering fifth grade, and Karl going into seventh grade.

The Pfeiffers moved into their new home on July 4, and Pauline set about helping her mother get the family settled. The music room became a chapel, and a priest came from Paragould, thirty miles away, to consecrate it as a place of worship. Each day began with devotionals in the chapel, and the Paragould priest caught the train to Piggott one Sunday a month to say mass. After mass on those days, the priest stayed for a huge Sunday dinner and an afternoon playing pinochle with Paul until the return train's whistle blew. On other Sundays each month, Mary Pfeiffer and the children took the train to Paragould for mass.

With Pauline's help decorating, Mary filled the house in Piggott with sturdy, top-of-the-line furniture—mostly Mission-style oak, manufactured and signed by Gustav Stickley. This much-sought-after furniture of the day contrasted with Victorian-era gaudiness and suited Mary, not one for frills or ornamentation. Mary kept the colors chosen by the structure's previous owners, but added a thin oak veneer to dress up its pine floors. The addition of a fireplace made the house more like their St. Louis home. Soon after its addition, however, the fireplace nearly proved Mary's undoing.

While dressing young Max in front of the fireplace on a Sunday morning, Mary backed too close to the hearth and caught her long apron on fire. By the time she realized it, the blaze had gained considerable headway. She frantically called for Paul, who ran in and tore away her burning clothes. In the process, he severely burned his hands and arms. Mary suffered major burns along the entire right side of her body. After physicians treated them at home, Paul managed to recover rapidly, but Mary did not fare as well. More than a week after the accident, concerned doctors moved her to the hospital in Paragould.[8] She remained for several weeks while doctors monitored her progress, and months later she finally recovered. Pauline assumed many of her mother's household responsibilities during Mary's recuperation.

How much time Pauline spent in Piggott after her mother's recovery is unknown, but by 1915 she wanted to continue her formal education. Pauline had graduated from high school well grounded in English, Latin, French, and history and hoped to pursue a career utilizing her writing talents. She entered the University of Missouri at Columbia that fall and graduated in just three years from the School of Journalism, the first such school in the nation.

While in Columbia, Pauline concentrated primarily on her classes, including heavy course loads and summer school. She did not participate in many purely social activities, nor did she share in sorority or residence hall living. Instead, she lived in an apartment close to campus, first on Missouri Avenue, just north of Jesse Hall, where many of her basic classes met, then on Rosemary Lane, just east of her journalism classes in Switzler Hall. Pauline's enrollment automatically made her a member of the Women's Self-Government Association, which addressed the concerns of women regarding their lives on campus. As an Arkansan, she also belonged to the Dixie Club, comprised of students from southern states.

Pauline formed some strong friendships in Columbia, including one with Clara Dunn, who remained a friend throughout her life. Clara, a year ahead of Pauline, came from a wealthy family in Monroe City, Missouri, and gained substantial popularity, including election as Yearbook Queen during her senior year. Other students from St. Louis included Sybil Burton and Katy Smith, who both had a lot in common with Pauline. Sybil had lived in the same St. Louis neighborhood, but had gone to public schools. Pauline and Sybil took daily walks together in Columbia and considered themselves somewhat rebellious, although their rebellion centered on such issues as refusing to have their photographs taken for the yearbook.[9] In addition to their St. Louis connections, Pauline and Katy shared stories of summers in Michigan. Pauline's family regularly spent summers at a resort in Frankfort, Michigan. Katy and her brothers summered just one hundred miles north, in Petoskey, where Ernest Hemingway and his family took holidays.

Pauline's transcript from the University of Missouri includes such journalism classes as History and Principles of Journalism, Reporting, Feature Writing, News Writing, Editorial Writing, and Copy Editing. With grades slightly above average, Pauline sacrificed high marks for graduation in three years. She was in the tenth graduating class, but already the relatively new School of Journalism had a national reputation. It integrated academic rigor and practical training under the leadership of Dean Walter Williams and instructors such as Charles B. Ross, a member of the faculty from 1908 to 1918. The year after Pauline's graduation Ross joined the *St. Louis Post Dispatch* as chief Washington correspondent and later served as President Harry S Truman's press secretary. While not an A student in most subjects, Pauline probably exemplified the student Dean Williams sought. The school's goal in a 1918 yearbook statement stressed: "Men and women who possess high ideals, mental alertness, clarity of impression and expression, habits of accuracy, and an immense intellectual curiosity—neither sciolists nor pendants—will be more valuable to themselves in journalism because of this possession. They will, also, be more valuable to the community, the commonwealth, the nation, the world—and that's the why of the School of Journalism."[10]

The Columbia newspaper, the *Daily Missourian,* was owned by the School of Journalism and operated by its students. The newspaper served as a community laboratory for journalism classes and provided a practical balance with academic programs. The Daily Missourian Association, comprised of journalism students, selected a nine-member board of directors each year to govern the corporation. Pauline Pfeiffer served on the board during her senior year.

Three years at the University of Missouri gave Pauline a solid background in journalism, and working on the *Missourian* provided a valuable perspective on world events. Many front-page stories focused on World War I, and Pauline and her classmates wrote headlines such as "Italy's Offensive Still Gains Ground," "Germans Continue Advance into Russia," "Fate of

British Empire Hangs on Efforts of Army," and "Turning Point Near on Western Front." Even local campus stories had war-related hooks, with such headlines as "Well-Dressed Coeds May Be Also Patriotic" and "Fewer Students Enroll for Study of German."

Pauline's family had a personal interest in the war as well. With Germany and Italy in conflict, the Germans dispatched Pauline's great-uncle Leonhard Kluftinger back to Kempten, and his property was confiscated in Bologna. Although American citizens, her uncle Washington and his family became enemy aliens due to their German name and relationship to Privy Councillor Kluftinger. Washington, who had married Adelia Rodenbach on one of his trips back to Cedar Falls, fled with his family and four of their five children to Lugano, Switzerland. Their second son, C. Leonard Pfeiffer, still lived and worked in the United States.

Shortly after the family exiled themselves to Lugano, their oldest son, Robert, married his childhood sweetheart, Matilde Valenti, from a prominent Bologna family. The pair immediately came to the United States, where he served as a minister and later became head of the Religion Department at Harvard University and authored a classic textbook on the Old Testament.

George Washington Pfeiffer died at Lugano in August 1917, in the midst of the war. Two months after his death, a headline in the *Columbia Missourian* read "Defeat of Italian Troops at Caporetto." This defeat meant additional turmoil in the Pfeiffer and Kluftinger families, since the loss at Caporetto brought Italian army headquarters to Bologna. People suspected of disloyalty remained in detention there until the end of the war. Pauline's cousin Robert and his new wife, who had an Italian father and German mother, stood by helplessly in the United States, unable to prevent her mother's deportation after being denounced by a maid in Bologna for keeping the German flag in her living room.

The Battle of Caporetto would be fought again more than ten years later in the pages of Ernest Hemingway's novel *A Farewell to Arms*. The author's selection of the Battle of Caporetto and the Italian retreat as a setting for his book stemmed from his days as a cub reporter at the *Kansas City Star*, just 125 miles away from where Pauline edited copy and wrote headlines in Columbia. As Ernest read war headlines about Caporetto in his paper, he resolved to go to Italy and join the action.

Pauline, however, resolved to graduate from college and get a good job. Her graduation on June 5, 1918, placed her into an elite group, and the school's reputation almost guaranteed employment. The class of 13 women and 16 men brought the school's total number of journalism alumni to 149—29 women and 120 men. They came from forty-one of the forty-eight states and seven countries, with 70 serving in the U.S. Army or Navy and 90 percent actively employed in some "profitable form" of journalism.[11]

A highlight of Pauline's senior year, Journalism Week in May, attracted guest speakers from the national media to campus for lectures and public presentations. It also served as an opportunity for journalism students to become personally acquainted with guests through formal job interviews, social events, and acting as student hosts. Victor Morgan of the *Cleveland Press,* just back from the war front in France, gave the keynote speech at an evening banquet. More than likely, Pauline interviewed with him during his visit or somehow made an impression, since that fall she began work as a copy editor on the night desk of the *Cleveland Press.*

Pauline's stay in Cleveland proved brief, however, since she returned to be with her parents after her youngest brother died during the 1918 influenza epidemic. After pouring rain disrupted an afternoon ballgame with friends in the school yard across the street from the Pfeiffers' residence, eleven-year-old Max went home complaining of a sore throat and died the next day, November 5. Due to fear of contagion, Paul and Mary buried him the following day in St. Mary's Catholic Cemetery in Paragould, leaving no time for Pauline to return from Cleveland, Karl from his first year at Notre Dame, or Virginia from boarding school in St. Louis.

Paul wrote to his son Karl that, although they attempted to be brave about it, "it is a heavy cross to bear for both of us. . . . We wanted to keep him so much, sometimes I think perhaps a little selfishly."[12] Several weeks later, Mary wrote to her surviving son, Karl, "I cannot tell you how much I miss him. Every turn I make, something says Max. . . . The silence of death is merciless. If it was not for the thought that he is better off, the loneliness would be unbearable."[13]

Pauline, more like a second mother to Max than a sister, arrived home shortly after the funeral and remained until after Christmas so the entire family could be together through the holidays. Her boss in Cleveland told her he could not hold her position that long but would find a place for her on the staff when she returned. Instead, after the first of the new year, Pauline went to New York, where she had relatives. By then, the Pfeiffer brothers, Henry and Gus, had relocated there from Philadelphia after acquiring the Richard Hudnut Company, manufacturer of perfumes and cosmetics.

Pauline went to work as a reporter for the *New York Morning Telegraph* and roomed for a time with her college friend Clara Dunn. Coincidentally, Sally Smith Benson, from Pauline's old St. Louis neighborhood, also worked at the *Morning Telegraph.* Others on staff included the later feared and revered Hollywood gossip columnist Louella Parsons, just starting her career. Legendary lawman Bat Masterson, at the end of his career, worked as a sportswriter.

Although Pauline was in her midtwenties when she started at the *Morning Telegraph,* an unmarried woman of her background roaming alone in New York appeared unseemly, so she spent much of her time with relatives. Henry and Gus Pfeiffer already possessed distinctive reputations, even in the Big Apple. Those who knew them from St. Louis spread the word that they had kept their business there open until well into the evening, then gone home to hoe their gardens by the light of lanterns hung around their necks. Even after they became millionaires in New York, they arrived at work every morning at seven o'clock. When they entertained at lavish parties, Gus and Henry walked out at bedtime so they could be at work early, leaving guests to enjoy themselves as late as they liked.[14]

By 1921, thanks to her writing skills, Pauline advanced to *Vanity Fair* and *Vogue* magazines, both Condé Nast publications. Her St. Louis connections probably helped as well, since Nast often asked people to join his firm on the basis of chance dinner party conversations. When Pauline met Nast at a social gathering shortly after arriving in New York, she learned that he hailed from St. Louis, had grown up in a Catholic family, and had graduated from St. Louis University Law School.

Pauline started at *Vanity Fair,* then moved to *Vogue,* a more suitable fit for her fashion sense. Despite Nast's ownership of both magazines, their articles and staffs reflected major differences. *Vogue* posited that "if all women are created equal there is no reason for them to remain so."[15] Edna Woolman Chase, editor of *Vogue,* ruled as an autocrat, requiring employees to appear in hats, white gloves, and black silk stockings. *Vanity Fair,* with operations on the same floor as *Vogue,* presented articles that gave people something to talk about at luncheons and dinner parties. Its editor, Frank Croninshield, ran his operation more like an adult playpen, with writers joking, whistling, throwing paper darts, or mocking fashion articles written at their sister magazine.

The *Vanity Fair* staff considered themselves clever and entertaining, and members formulated what they referred to as the "Elevated Eyebrow School of Journalism," meaning one could write about almost any subject, no matter how outrageous, as long as people could talk about it while wearing evening clothes. The editorial content did not avoid serious topics, but such items had to be sandwiched in among references to debutante dinners and French antiques.[16]

Writer Dorothy Parker, who began at *Vogue* in 1915, contributed to the *Vanity Fair* reputation. Dorothy was famous for writing such cutlines as "Brevity is the soul of lingerie," but her wit went unappreciated at *Vogue*. Two years later she moved to *Vanity Fair* as drama critic and, along with managing editor Robert Benchley and drama and picture editor Robert Sherwood, began lunching at the Algonquin Hotel. This event evolved into a legendary gathering for a ten-year period during the 1920s. The Algonquin Round Table had its heyday during Pauline's years in New York, but long after she left, Pauline continued to lunch at the Algonquin whenever in New York.

In 1922 Pauline made her first trip to Europe, traveling with her friend Clara Dunn. She took the opportunity to spend time with relatives still in Germany and Italy, including her great-uncle Leonhard Kluftinger, whose property in Italy had been returned to him after the war. Pauline also attempted to broaden her writing skills while in Europe, contacting old friends in Cleveland to line up feature stories for the Newspaper Enterprise Association (NEA), owned by the *Cleveland Press* parent company, Scripps-Howard. At that time, this service provided comic strips and feature articles for Scripps-Howard newspapers around the country. It later became a syndicated service for all who wished to subscribe.

On April 13, 1922, NEA editor Frank J. Ryan wrote a "To Whom It May Concern" letter for Pauline, which stated: "This letter will introduce the bearer, Pauline Pfeiffer, who is serving as special correspondent for NEA Service, Inc., while making a tour of Europe. Any courtesies which can be extended to her in the gathering of interviews, information, picture and other material for newspaper publication will be appreciated by the undersigned."[17]

Upon her return to New York in September, Pauline renewed her acquaintance with second cousin Matthew Herold of Plattsmouth, Nebraska, grandson of Sabina Amelia Kluftinger Gering. After completing his law degree at Harvard, Matthew had practiced in New York and become the attorney for Henry Pfeiffer and Gus Pfeiffer's pharmaceutical enterprises. The two saw each other regularly and got along well together. Though not madly in love, they somehow concluded they should get married. At that time, Pauline lacked experience with men, felt comfortable with her career, and loved being around family, so it seemed the right thing to do.

"I remember it well," recalled Matthew's younger sister, Ursula Herold Harris, who attended boarding school and came home to Plattsmouth for Christmas break. Matthew returned from New York as well, along with their brother Henry. When Ursula returned from an outing one afternoon, Henry greeted her with "You should have seen the fur fly today. Matt just announced he was engaged to Pauline." The "fur was flying" not just because they were cousins, but because Pauline was Roman Catholic and Matthew's family members were ardent Episcopalians.[18]

Still, Matthew and Pauline planned to marry the following summer in Bologna, Italy, at Villa Favorita, the imposing home of their mutual great-uncle Leonhard Kluftinger. When Ursula visited Virginia Pfeiffer in New York over spring break, they planned a European trip together for the wedding. In the meantime, an offer came from *Vogue* for Pauline to transfer temporarily to the Paris bureau. She did so, subletting her apartment to her friend Connie Degnan. With the wedding postponed, Ursula recalled that Pauline told Connie to "take good care of Matthew, and don't let him go out with any other girls. The next thing we know, Matt's engaged to Connie, and Pauline's engaged to Ernest, and that's the end of that."[19]

Pauline's articles had attracted the attention of *Vogue*'s Paris bureau, which opened in 1922. The fledgling subsidiary needed a good writer who also could serve as publicist and assistant to the editor. Arriving in Paris in 1924, she went to work for Main Bocher, *Vogue*'s Paris fashion editor, who became managing editor the following year. When he became fashion editor for the new French *Vogue*, Paris fashions established the standard throughout the world. Designers such as Gabrielle Chanel, Jeanne Lanvin, Madeleine Vionnet, and Callot Soeurs gained the same renown in America and Great Britain as they enjoyed in France.

During his tenure, Bocher made French couture collections big news with sharply written forecasts, an eye for accuracy, and a penchant for the latest and most startling details. Bocher invented such phrases as "off-white," "dressmaker suits," and "spectator sports clothes." He demanded a discerning eye from Pauline and other reporters, so she passed the first few months in Paris adjusting to her new job and applying the French she had learned in high school and college. Pauline soon learned that she should have paid more attention to conjugating verbs in French class, rather than writing poems about classmates. She picked up the language quickly, however, by living with a French Catholic family in a wealthy section on the Right Bank. At the time, she did not know any of the writers who lived from one published article to the next on the Left Bank, but that soon would change after she met Ernest Hemingway.

CHAPTER 4

Ernest

Though Ernest Hemingway called Oak Park, Illinois, home, visits to Walloon Lake near Petoskey, Michigan, helped shape his early years. Ernest made his first trip there before he could walk. His parents, Clarence and Grace Hemingway, had discovered this remote retreat the summer before his birth, when they visited a relative's cabin with their seven-month-old daughter, Marcelline. A few canoe trips on the pristine lake convinced them to find a place of their own. They found their spot on the north shore of the lake on a strip of sandy beach with a dock nearby, ideal for swimming, boating, and fishing. Woods around the lake abounded in hiking trails and hunting prospects. Before the Hemingways returned home after their first visit, they purchased four lots, totaling one acre.

Throughout Grace's pregnancy with Ernest, she planned the new summer cottage. Just seven weeks after his birth in Oak Park on July 21, 1899, the family returned to Walloon Lake and finalized plans. This served as Ernest's introduction to a place that provided a deep well from which he drew inspiration for much of his writing. Completed by the following summer, the cottage was christened Windermere by Grace, changed by family usage over the years to Windemere. The name came from a famous lake in England, birthplace of Grace's ancestors.

Ernest Hall, father of Grace Hall Hemingway, came from England with his parents and other siblings in 1855, about the same time that Heinrich Pfeiffer and his bride emigrated from Germany. Like Heinrich and his family, the Halls settled in Iowa and became farmers. Ernest Hall, later called Abba by his grandchildren, from the biblical word for "father," served in the First Iowa Volunteer Cavalry during the Civil War. After returning home, he married Caroline Hancock on November 6, 1865.

Caroline had also moved with her family from England to Iowa, albeit by a more circuitous route. Her mother died when she was ten, and her sea-captain father took Caroline and her younger sister and brother around the world on his cargo ship, the *Elizabeth*. He realized, however, that life at sea poorly suited his children, so he sold the ship. After a brief stay in Australia, they moved to Dwyersville, Iowa, in 1854, at the urging of English friends.

Abba and Caroline Hall settled in Chicago after their marriage, where he established a cutlery business with his sister's husband. The business prospered, as did the family, including Grace, born June 15, 1872, and her brother Leicester, born two years later. Music was the key to harmonious family relationships, and Caroline's prize possession, a melodeon given to her by her father, went everywhere with her. Other members of the family often joined her in performing at public gatherings. Caroline sang soprano, Abba baritone, and Caroline's brother Tyley tenor. When Grace grew old enough, her contralto voice rounded out the family quartet.

Grace's parents immediately recognized and cultivated her musical talents, and she seemed destined for a life in the grand opera. Her parents twice took her to Europe for exposure to fine performances. As Grace grew up, her mother excused her from household chores and learning to cook. "You tend to your practicing," she said. "There is no use any woman getting into the kitchen if she can help it."[1] When Grace was fourteen, her family moved from Chicago to the suburb of Oak Park, Illinois. Anson and Adelaide Hemingway lived across the street with their six children. The oldest of the four boys, Clarence Edmonds Hemingway, one year older than Grace, knew her casually in high school. Not particularly impressed with Clarence, or Ed, as people called him locally, Grace thought him a thin, gawky boy whose clothes did not fit.[2]

Clarence's father, Anson, had come with his parents to Chicago from Connecticut as a child. After service in the Union Army during the Civil War, Anson entered Wheaton College, where he met Adelaide Edmonds and her sister Cordelia. In spite of Adelaide being three years older, Anson married her on August 27, 1867, and they settled in Chicago, where he founded the Chicago Young Men's Christian Association (YMCA) and served as its general secretary for a decade. When it became clear that Anson's salary would not support the education of their children, the Hemingways moved to Oak Park, and he established a real estate business.

Science rather than music bound the Hemingway family together. Adelaide had majored in botany and astronomy in college and enjoyed introducing her children to the wonders of nature. At an early age Clarence collected all kinds of specimens and could name the stars and identify plants and animals. This introduction to science led him to medicine, first studying premed at Oberlin College, then receiving a medical degree from Rush Medical College in Chicago.

He returned to Oak Park as assistant to an established doctor, and Caroline Hall became one of his first patients. While assisting in her cancer treatment, Clarence became particularly close to her daughter Grace, and the two talked for hours. By now, the young doctor had a beard to disguise his youthful appearance, and a summer trip in 1895 to intern at the University of Edinburgh had made him more worldly than the boy Grace remembered from high school. The two fell in love, but Grace wanted to pursue a career in music. A few weeks after her mother's death, on September 5, 1895, Grace went to New York to study at the Art Students League and made her concert debut at Madison Square Garden the following spring. Though the Metropolitan Opera offered Grace a contract, Clarence wanted her to come home, and her father invited her to make a summer trip with him to Europe. Urging from the two men in her life brought her home, along with her concerns about sensitivity to stage lighting from a childhood illness.

After her return from the Europe trip, Grace married Clarence on October 1, 1896, and they moved in with her widowed father. The bride believed it would give them much more room than they could otherwise afford, with Clarence just beginning his medical practice. This arrangement also suited Clarence, who, busy with patients or other activities, seemed to like the idea of not being head of the household. Grace's uncle Tyley Hancock, a salesman who traveled throughout the Midwest, also stayed in the Hall-Hemingway home whenever business brought him to the Chicago area. Tyley, a great storyteller, delighted in telling tales of sea voyages made with his father and sisters when he was still a boy.

The living arrangements came to an end when Abba died shortly before Ernest's sixth birthday. Soon afterward, Grace sold her father's house and moved the family to a nearby rental house, awaiting completion of a larger residence to accommodate the growing family. By then Marcelline and Ernest had two new sisters, Ursula, born in 1902, and Madeline (Sunny), born in 1904. Later two additional children joined the family, Carol in 1911 and Leicester in 1915.

The family moved to its new home on Kenilworth Avenue in fall 1906. Designed by Grace, it had a huge, acoustically balanced music room, complete with balcony, dais for student recitals, and Steinway piano. At the opposite end of the house, a doctor's office and waiting room for patients provided space for Clarence's medical practice. The house also had space for two servants and a guest room to accommodate Uncle Tyley.

Despite long hours with his medical practice, Clarence did most of the household's marketing, cooking, baking, canning, and meal preparation. Family members loved to tell the story of his interrupting a house call to phone home and tell them to take a pie out of the oven. He passed on to his children the love of science and nature he had inherited from his mother. Clarence taught them how to make a fire, cook in the open, make bullets, prepare animals for mounting, identify plants and animals, find their way in the woods, and handle guns properly—knowledge that Ernest would draw from in his later writing.

Especially important for Ernest's store of experiences, Clarence taught his children how to hunt and fish. He believed, however, that killing for sport was wrong and that one should kill only what one could eat. On one occasion at their summer retreat in Michigan, a neighbor brought his dog with a mouthful of porcupine quills to Clarence. The dog, clearly in pain, whimpered as the doctor removed them one by one. Ernest and a friend found the porcupine that had inflicted the damage and killed it, believing their action justified. When Clarence found out, he made them cook and eat the porcupine. No amount of cooking could make it taste like anything but shoe leather.[3] Ernest later passed on all these lessons from his father to his fictional character Nick Adams, who never caught more trout than he needed for his meals and who was always careful not to touch those he let go with a dry hand, lest he upset the delicate mucus that covered the fish.[4]

Clarence, the disciplinarian in the family, remained unbending in his rules and expectations for his children. He deplored idleness, drinking, dancing, smoking, playing cards, and recreation on Sundays. Illness served as the only excuse for missing church and Sunday school. Grace, on the other hand, took a permissive approach with her children, believing they should be given latitude to develop creativity. She enjoyed lavishing gifts on them, particularly on birthdays and at Christmas, as well as planning parties and picnics. While Clarence taught the children about the outdoors, Grace gave them music lessons, took them to concerts and operas, and exposed them to painting and drawing. In return, Grace expected her children to behave and to appreciate the sacrifices she made for them. She also expected to have her way on most decisions in the household.

Clarence and Grace had differing opinions about money as well. She justified spending lavishly on clothes, their home, and their children because of income from the singing, piano, and voice lessons she gave in their home. Many of Clarence's patients could not pay for services, and Grace's earnings comprised a major part of the family income. With music students keeping her busy, Grace had neither time nor patience for household chores, so servants performed these tasks. When Marcelline once asked why she did not act like other mothers, Grace replied, "Well, you see, dear, I do these things because I can, but I pay out of what I earn in my professional life for the cook and the laundress and the nursemaid who do the work that other girls' mothers have to do."[5]

Grace's youngest son, Leicester, recalled, "Whenever there was a serious emotional crisis she rushed to her room, drew the shades, and declared she had a sick headache. Having her wishes crossed always produced a crisis, and there were hundreds of them while we children were growing up."[6] Later, taking separate vacations averted some of the problems. In 1909 Grace began taking each of her children individually for a vacation to Nantucket, beginning with Marcelline. Grace believed that she needed time alone with each of her six children.

Ernest made the trip with her in 1910 and saw an ocean for the first time. On the way home they visited historic sites in Boston, Cambridge, Lexington, and Concord, and Grace delighted in showing him places she had visited as a child with her parents. The experience, along with his remembrance of Uncle Tyley's stories, prompted one of Ernest's earliest writing efforts, "My First Sea Vouge," in April 1911. His essay told of his uncle Tyley sailing the world, except that Ernest made Martha's Vineyard the starting point for the voyage and changed his uncle's siblings from two sisters to one brother—perhaps wishing for a brother who did not arrive until four years later. Grace dreamed of having twins, and when Ernest arrived a year after Marcelline, she indulged her fantasy by dressing Ernest and Marcelline alike—sometimes in dresses, sometimes in overalls—and having both with their hair cut in bangs across the forehead. Grace even had Marcelline repeat kindergarten so that she and Ernest could enter first grade together.

Ernest's childhood revolved around family activities that sparked his interest in new adventures. His parents took him to Pawnee Bill's Wild West Show, the Ringling Brother's Circus, and other attractions that came to the area, and he belonged to the Agassiz Club, a nature study group led by his father. Ernest developed his father's appreciation of the outdoors, but his mother's attempts to teach him voice and cello never succeeded. Uncle Tyley whetted Ernest's desire to experience the world beyond Oak Park, and visits from his uncle Will Hemingway, a missionary doctor in China who knew the Dalai Lama, exposed Ernest to a life difficult to imagine.

Ernest's creativity, fueled by family experiences, put drama in the most mundane events. His highly exaggerated stories might have been punished as lies in other households, but they became humorous in his own. At an early age, when he told a particularly tall tale, Grandfather Hall told Grace,

"If he uses his imagination for good purposes, he'll be famous, but if he starts the wrong way, with all his energy, he'll end in jail, and it's up to you which way he goes."[7]

Ernest received much of his temperament from his mother. Like Grace, he held grudges. Grace had a tendency to store up injustices done to her, so that on occasion even the smallest thing triggered a litany of perceived wrongs. Clarence, on the other hand, reacted immediately and moved on. Though a loving father, Clarence had his dark side, and his moods toward his children sometimes changed instantly. Occasionally these traits showed up in Ernest, who remembered a time when he got so angry with his father that he took a gun and drew a bead on him from a hiding spot in the wood-shed while his father worked among his tomato plants.[8] Ernest's black moods became more pronounced as an adult, leading periodically to verbal attacks on friends, wives, children, or others who crossed him.

While sometimes frustrated by his father's moods, Ernest greatly admired his father's physical courage and medical skills. On more than one occasion, he benefited firsthand from his father's abilities. One morning at Walloon Lake, Ernest fell while running with a stick in his hand, and it went through the back of his throat, gouging his tonsils. Fortunately, his father managed to stop the bleeding, but the injury took a while to heal. Clarence taught him to concentrate on whistling whenever the pain became unbear-able, a technique that became Ernest's typical reaction to pain. On another occasion, while boating on the lake, Ernest caught a fishhook in his back and implored his sister Sunny to cut it out. Wisely, she refused, and his father got it out with minimal pain when they returned.[9]

One time the doctor had to operate on himself. Fishing well away from the nearest town, Clarence developed blood poisoning in his arm. When his arm hardened and throbbed, he knew it had reached a dangerous stage, and he must do something. Clarence made the men with him hold him down, while he plunged the knife into his arm to drain the poison, screaming with pain as he did so.[10] Early on, Ernest gathered through such examples that personal courage made the man. Before the age of three, he claimed to be "fraid a nothing," a statement he attempted to prove throughout his life and a characteristic sought by the heroic Nick Adams in many of Hemingway's later short stories.[11]

Ernest achieved an average academic record in high school, and his defi-cient eyesight and small stature until age fifteen limited athletic possibilities. He took up boxing to compensate, and when his growth spurt came, he sometimes bullied others. Ernest believed that a man must win at everything he tried. So fishing, hunting, tennis, and boxing became not just sports—

they tested his manhood. He worked just as hard throughout high school to develop his writing skills and completed articles and columns for the school literary magazine and school newspaper.

His mother hoped that upon high school graduation in 1917 Ernest and Marcelline would attend Oberlin College, but only Marcelline went to Oberlin. With growing U.S. involvement in World War I, Ernest preferred military service, but defective eyesight prevented his enlistment. Instead, his uncle Tyler Hemingway, in Kansas City, used his influence to get Ernest a job at the *Kansas City Star*, one of the nation's outstanding newspapers.

Ernest arrived in Kansas City in October 1917 and became a cub reporter covering the police beat. Although he joined the Missouri Home Guard and went on maneuvers each weekend, he felt dissatisfied. After a few months at the paper, Ernest learned through a fellow reporter that the Red Cross needed ambulance drivers, no eye exams necessary. Ernest quit the *Kansas City Star* in spring 1918 and left for Europe, stopping first in New York for training, then went on to France before being assigned to the Italian sector. Anxious to see action, he volunteered to assist with the rolling canteen, a bicycle brigade that delivered supplies to men at the front. On the evening of July 8, 1918, as he delivered chocolates, cigarettes, and mail to the front lines, a trench mortar exploded, killing one of the men next to him. Ernest fell wounded, with more than two hundred pieces of shrapnel and an Austrian machine-gun bullet in his leg, but he apparently managed to carry a wounded soldier to safety before collapsing from the pain. Ernest earned the Italian Medal of Valor for his act.

While hospitalized in Milan, Ernest fell in love with his nurse, Agnes von Kurowsky, who became part of the composite heroine in his later novel *A Farewell to Arms*. Despite their eight-year age difference, Ernest decided he wanted to marry the older nurse. After returning to Oak Park in January 1919 to recuperate, he wrote to her regularly, and she responded. In March, however, Agnes wrote to end the relationship as gently as she could, telling him she loved an Italian military officer. The news crushed Ernest. His sister Marcelline recalled that he became sick and grieved for days after receiving her letter.[12] With Agnes's rejection, some of his confidence and self-image crumbled. For a while, the now-worldly man just back from Italy, tested in war and wounded in battle, enjoyed the status of a hero in his hometown. For four months after his return, Ernest continued wearing his uniform to maintain his admired persona, but eventually this adulation grew tiresome, even with his family.

Ernest's father had changed in the young man's absence as well. Ernest found him more rigid, more withdrawn, and much less interested in hunting and fishing. Clarence seemed stressed by financial worries, particularly when Grace proceeded, over his objections and using her own money, to build a separate cottage retreat for herself at the lake. Clarence frequented the lake house less, believing financial pressures required him to devote more time to his medical practice, and he became jealous and controlling about his wife's friendship with Ruth Arnold, her former music student, live-in family companion, and nursemaid to the children.

Clarence worried as well about his son finding a job and pulling his weight in the family. Ernest drifted among Oak Park, Walloon Lake, and part-time jobs in Toronto and elsewhere for nearly a year and a half before his mother lost patience with him. The breaking point came during the summer of 1920 at Windemere Cottage. Clarence had stayed home to tend patients, and Ernest's mother expected her son to do many of the chores normally taken care of by his father. Instead of helping, Ernest created more work for his mother by dropping in with his buddies for meals, then heading back across the lake.

Misunderstandings and arguments between mother and son resulted in Grace presenting Ernest with a letter after his twenty-first-birthday celebration, letting him know he was no longer welcome at Windemere. In the letter she compared a mother's love to a bank account in which each child starts out with a healthy account balance and continues to make withdrawals throughout childhood. As the child gets older, she explained, he is expected to make some deposits of his own through various acts of love and kindness. In Ernest's case, however, his account was overdrawn. She told him not to come back "until your tongue has learned not to insult and shame your mother" and added, "When you have changed your ideas and aims in life, you will find your mother waiting to welcome you, whether it be in this world or the next—loving you and longing for your love."[13]

Ernest left Windemere and joined an older crowd at the lake, including Bill and Katy Smith. He developed romantic feelings toward Katy, the same age as Agnes. That fall Ernest rode with the Smiths to Chicago, where he moved in with their older brother, Y. K. (Kenley) Smith, and his wife. In Chicago he worked on his writing style while holding down various odd jobs, including writing articles for the *Toronto Star,* serving as a sparring partner, and eventually doing a magazine column. Through Kenley he met Sherwood Anderson, a writer at the peak of his career. Anderson took a paternal interest in Ernest and influenced his writing, not so much in style as through his understanding of what it took to be a writer. Ernest learned from Anderson the business aspects of writing, broadened his reading interests, and came to appreciate standards of literary excellence that reached beyond fiction writing for the *Saturday Evening Post.*

Ernest met someone else who changed his life as well. Katy's friend from St. Louis, Hadley Richardson, had recently lost her mother, and Katy suggested she come to Chicago for an extended vacation to rest from the ordeal of her mother's illness and death. Hadley stayed with Katy's brother and his wife, along with assorted bachelors who periodically lived there as well. Hadley first felt taken aback by the crew of brash young men, including the especially attentive Ernest. Though twenty-nine, she had far less social experience than the twenty-one-year-old, who was at her side almost constantly during the three-week visit. Later Ernest claimed he knew he would marry Hadley the minute he met her. Whether this is true or not, they visited back and forth between St. Louis and Chicago and by the following spring planned to marry. The wedding took place on September 3, 1921, at Horton Bay, near the Hemingways' summer retreat, and Grace offered Windemere Cottage for their honeymoon.

Although Ernest lacked a full-time job when they married, Hadley had a small trust fund that yielded about three thousand dollars per year. Ernest's goal was to return to Italy, and Hadley assured him that if they lived frugally, they could live on income from her trust and his freelance fees from the *Toronto Star.* Sherwood Anderson convinced them, however, that if Ernest wanted to be a serious writer, he should go to Paris, where expatriate writers could teach Ernest about the literary world.

When Ernest and Hadley departed for Paris in December 1921, Anderson sent along several crucial letters of introduction. One, to Lewis Galantière, a Chicago writer associated with the International Chamber of Commerce in Paris, suggested that Hemingway, "a friend of mine and a very delightful man," would be worth getting to know and would probably be settling in the Latin Quarter since he and his wife would not have much money.[14] The second letter, to Gertrude Stein, referred to Hemingway as "an American writer instinctively in touch with everything worth-while going on here."[15]

Hemingway took a while to summon the courage to follow up on Anderson's letters of introduction, but he soon penetrated the literary circle. Gertrude Stein and poet Ezra Pound became mentors. Ernest sought to take the best from each person he met, as well as to use their connections to get work looked at and published. Margaret Anderson, who with Jane Heap published the *Little Review* in the early 1920s, accepted some of his early essays after rejecting his first submissions. Ernest struck Margaret as "simple," and she recalled that he fancied her as soon as they met, in spite of being newly married. In fact, she claimed that he "had become so 'gooey' that she had been forced to avoid him."[16] Ernest wrote to *New Yorker* journalist Janet Flanner some ten years later that he never met a "nicer or more flutter-brained legendary woman, nor a prettier one . . . than Margaret."[17] His flirtations with other women became a pattern that was repeated throughout his marriage to Hadley and successive wives.

When Hadley became pregnant, she and Ernest determined to have the baby in Toronto, where Ernest could write for the *Toronto Star* until they returned to Paris. So they headed to Canada in the fall, and John Hadley Nicanor Hemingway was born on October 10, 1923. Named partially for a bullfighter they met in Spain and in recognition of their new interest in the sport, he was called Bumby by both his parents because he felt so round and solid when they held him.[18] When only three months old, Bumby accompanied his parents back to Paris, where they found an inexpensive apartment above a sawmill.

By the time they returned, Ernest had started reaping the benefits of his contacts in Paris and the many expatriate magazines and presses that published each other's work and launched literary careers. Two limited-edition Hemingway books were privately published, both through Ezra Pound connections. Robert McAlmon, a poet friend of Pound, published *Three Stories and Ten Poems* through his Contact Publishing venture. Bill Bird released *in our time,* a series of sixteen sketches written by Ernest and edited by Pound, through his Three Mountains Press. New influences came into Ernest's life as well. He crossed paths in Italy during World War I with the widely traveled American novelist John Dos Passos, but they did not get to know each other until 1924, during one of Dos Passos's quick trips through Paris, after publication of *in our time.* Dos Passos predicted Hemingway would become "the first great American stylist."[19] Donald Ogden Stewart, a Yale graduate and writer of humorous fiction, became another member of the growing entourage, encouraging Hemingway's literary interests, as well as an interest in bullfighting.

Hemingway treated each early contact in the Paris literary circle as an additional chapter in his development as a writer. When Ford Madox Ford arrived in Paris in 1924 to start a new literary magazine, *transatlantic review,* Ernest assisted by editing articles for the magazine. Working at the *transatlantic review* office, Ernest encountered Harold Loeb, editor of *Broom,* who intervened in getting Ernest's first book published in the United States. In the fall of 1924, Loeb took Hemingway to see an old friend, Leon Fleischman, who had moved to Paris and become the European representative for the New York publishing house Boni & Liveright. At the end of the evening, Hemingway left his short stories from the limited edition of *in our time* for submission to Horace Liveright. In the meantime, novelist F. Scott Fitzgerald wrote to his own editor about Ernest. Though he had not met Hemingway, he had read some of his articles and stories and now wrote to Scribner's star editor, Maxwell Perkins: "This is to tell you about a young man named Ernest Hemmingway, who lives in Paris (an American) writes for the transatlantic Review & has a brilliant future. Ezra Pount published a collection of his short pieces in Paris, at some place like the Egotist Press. I havn't it hear now but its remarkable & I'd look him up right away. He's the real thing."[20]

Perkins tried to make contact with Ernest, but did not reach him until after his book contract with Boni & Liveright, an arrangement that almost did not happen. When Loeb was in New York after the first of the year to check on details for his own book, *Doodab,* about to be published by Liveright, he inquired about Hemingway's manuscript and found that the publisher planned to mail it back to him.

"Hold it. Give it another reading," Loeb pleaded. "I know what I'm talking about."[21]

In the meantime, Sherwood Anderson also contacted Liveright directly on Ernest's behalf to convince them of the importance of Ernest's book. With Anderson at the peak of his reputation, the publishing firm did not wish to upset its star author and therefore accepted the book. Ernest and Hadley were still celebrating the good news when they met Pauline and Virginia Pfeiffer at Kitty Cannell's apartment.

A January 1925 letter to Ernest Walsh, who wanted a profile for his new literary magazine *This Quarter,* essentially summed up Ernest's view of his life to that point:

> As near as I can figure out am 27 years old. [He was actually not quite 26.] 6 feet tall, weight 182 lbs. Born in Oak Park, Illinois, served in war on Italian front, Wounded, profession newspaper correspondent, married Hadley Richardson Sept. 3, 1921, one son, John Hadley Nicanor, B. Oct. 10, 1923, Author of Three Stories and Ten Poems, Contact Publishing Co., Paris and In Our Time, Three Mountains Press, Paris. Edited Transatlantic Review for Ford Madox Ford during latters absense in America. Edward J. O'Brien dedicated Best Short Stories of 1924 to. Amusements Boxing, Trout fishing, ski-ing and bull fighting. Prefers to do the first three and watch the latter. State of health, good. Very fond of eating and

drinking. Lives in France for that reason among others. Believes Gertrude Stein to be a great writer. Tried to keep Transatlantic Review alive in order to Publish her "Making of Americans." Failed. Friend of Ezra Pound. Believes Pound greatest living poet. This is not friendship. Would like to make bet on subject. Believes other great living poets would admit it. Few great living poets living. Fond of horse racing.[22]

CHAPTER 5

Three's a Crowd (1925–1926)

After Kitty Cannell's party in March 1925, Pauline had little time for socializing. April 1925 marked the grand opening of the International Exposition of Decorative and Applied Arts, which provided much material for the news media and magazines such as *Vogue*. The exposition featured exhibits from twenty-one nations and ranged from the latest automobile designs to tiny bottles of French perfume. Of special interest to *Vogue*, the opening exhibit of thirty manikins displayed creations from ten leading Paris dressmakers and milliners—Worth, Callot, Paquin, Vionnet, Jenny, Lanvin, Redfern, Driscoll, Beer, and Cheruit. By the time the exposition closed six months later, it had attracted 8.5 million visitors and left the Eiffel Tower as a permanent Paris landmark.[1]

Although the exhibition and other duties at *Vogue* occupied much of Pauline's time, she and Virginia managed to cultivate their growing friendship with Hadley. Pauline enjoyed listening to Hadley play the piano and admired her maternal instincts, as well as the sacrifices she made to support Ernest. The Pfeiffer sisters also took up the Hemingway social agenda, which varied from bike riding and boxing matches to art openings and patronizing various Paris cafes and restaurants.

That fall a new sensation burst onto the Paris social scene in the form of an exotic entertainer named Josephine Baker. After Baker performed her Danse Savage, clad only in a girdle of feathers, she went from being a member of the Harlem touring cast of La Revue Nègre to being the reigning queen of the Paris nightclub scene for more than fifty years. Ernest thought her "the most sensational woman anybody ever saw. Or ever will." And after dancing with her one night at the Montparnasse café Le Jockey, he later told a friend, "She never took off her fur coat. Wasn't until the joint closed she told me she had nothing on underneath."[2] Though perhaps not as exciting as dancing with Josephine Baker, the six-day bicycle races also became one of Hemingway's new passions. His friend John Dos Passos, now back in Paris, often attended with Ernest and Hadley, the Pfeiffer sisters, and other Hemingway friends. Dos Passos recalled that they would stop along narrow market streets for wine, cheese, crunchy rolls, a pot of pate, and "perhaps a cold chicken," then sit up in the gallery to eat, drink, and enjoy the races.[3]

Along with new places came new faces. Though F. Scott Fitzgerald supported Hemingway's work, the two writers did not meet until the spring of 1925. At the time, they each had something the other needed. Fitzgerald had just published *The Great Gatsby*, and Hemingway was beginning his literary climb. Hemingway envied Fitzgerald's money and commercial success; Fitzgerald admired Hemingway's intellectualism and his circle of friends. Scott and his wife, Zelda, happily joined the circle.

Other new friends included Gerald and Sara Murphy, wealthy Americans who became den parents to the growing pack. The Murphys arrived in Paris with their three small children in 1921 and took up residence in an elegant apartment on the Right Bank. They avoided other well-connected Americans in Paris, however, preferring the more energizing company of artists and intellectuals on the Left Bank. Heir to the Mark Cross fortune, Murphy painted, but his greatest talent was encouraging and stimulating the careers of others. The Murphys believed Hemingway probably had more potential than anyone else around them. Through the Murphys, Hemingway met Archibald MacLeish. A Yale graduate with a Harvard law degree, MacLeish had left a prestigious practice in Boston to pursue his dream of becoming a poet. He moved to Paris in 1923 with his wife, Ada, a concert pianist, and their two children.

Hemingway's old childhood friend Bill Smith also arrived in Paris to join the coterie. Pauline and Virginia Pfeiffer enjoyed being on the periphery of this group, particularly when the circle widened to include Right Bank people, with whom they had much more in common. In this company, Pauline's education, her sense of style, her money, and her independence gave her freedom to revel in the role of a thoroughly modern woman. For the 1920s female, that also meant mastering light banter and flirtations, hallmarks of a flapper personality. While Pauline had little real experience with men, and in fact was quite naive on the subject for a woman her age, she knew how to flirt with both men and women and how to play the coquette female. For example, after most of the Hemingway entourage departed for bullfights in Spain that summer, leaving Pauline and Virginia in Paris, Pauline wrote to her friend Katy Smith: "I have just bid Bill godspeed to the bulls. Really, my dear, you have two super brothers. I would marry either of them. I have a little money of my own, have a calm, even temper. Don't you think you could arrange something for me? However, the object of this letter is not to marry myself off . . . but to plead with you with all my charm, which you know is now considerable, to come on over here this autumn."[4]

Later that summer Pauline toyed with Harold Loeb, no longer involved with Kitty Cannell, writing to him about personal items she may have left in his coat pocket the last time they partied together. She wondered if he could find her lipstick, handkerchief, and gloves and send them to her as soon as possible.[5] She used this ploy often to remain in people's thoughts, though she had no real romantic interest in them, and she did not overlook Ernest in the game. Bill Smith recalled that she approached Ernest with the line, "I was talking to someone about you just the other day."

"Oh, and what did he say?" Ernest bantered back.[6] Ernest did not merit special flirtations at first because, in addition to being Hadley's husband, he apparently did not register high on Pauline's list of desirable men. Nor did her initial opinion of him change much over the summer. So if Ernest paid more attention to Virginia than Pauline, no one noticed or cared, particularly since another new woman created a more public diversion.

Duff Twysden, a twice-divorced English woman, claimed her second husband beat her when drunk, and she escaped his abuse by falling in love with her cousin Pat Guthrie. She and Pat then ran off to Paris and became faces in the Left Bank crowd. Although Duff lived with Guthrie, she had a string of admirers and various relationships with other men. Those smitten by her included Ernest and Harold Loeb. While not particularly attracted to Ernest, Duff enjoyed his overtures, as well as the drama of open flirtation. She mesmerized Ernest, and he saw it as confirmation of his manhood that he could capture the attentions of a woman being sought after by so many others. Later she shifted some of that attention to Loeb, making an awkward summer for the bullfight crowd in Pamplona—including Ernest, Hadley, Loeb, Duff, and her fiancé Guthrie. The vacation ended with no one on speaking terms, and it gave Ernest the basis for his first novel, *The Sun Also Rises*.

When Ernest returned to Paris that fall, his mood darkened. Adding to Duff's earlier rebuff, several short story rejection slips awaited him from publications including *Little Review* and *Dial*. Additionally, in mid-October Virginia Pfeiffer left for New York to see her friend Clara Dunn, her sister's former roommate, with whom Virginia maintained a close relationship, before returning to Piggott. Her departure effectively ended any clandestine relationship with Ernest, whose interest to that point may have been her balance sheet as much as her personality. Now he was perhaps even more intrigued by a woman who would choose to be with another woman instead of with him. It was a blow to his ego, but a source of continuing fascination that made Virginia all the more interesting. Six years later Ernest wrote a short story, "The Sea Change," about a man and a woman saying their goodbyes in a bar after a wonderful summer together. The woman is leaving Paris to spend time with her lesbian lover. She insists, however, that she loves him, in her own way, and promises to return if he wants her back. But the man believes her choice is a perversion and tells her he does not want her back.[7]

When published in 1933 as part of *Winner Take Nothing*, Ernest called it a completely made-up story. At other times, he gave different explanations of its source. In "The Art of the Short Story," he wrote, "I had seen the couple in the Bar Basque in St. Jean de Luz and I knew the story too too well."[8] Much later he told literary critic Edmund Wilson that the story had grown out of a three-hour conversation with Gertrude Stein about lesbianism, "and I was so sold on her theory that I went out that night and fucked a lesbian with magnificent results; ie we slept well afterwards."[9]

After Virginia left for New York and Piggott, leaving her sister in Paris, Pauline spent more time with Hadley, often going by the Hemingways' apartment in the evenings after work. Ernest shared his writing with her, and her opinion of him began to change as she recognized his talent. He also started looking at her differently. In addition to having the same financial credentials as her sister, Pauline brought the added advantage of being a practiced editor and critic.

Boni & Liveright's publication of Ernest's book *In Our Time* on October 5, 1925, brought him irritation rather than excitement. He found himself sharing the spotlight with the simultaneous publication of a sentimental novel, *Dark Laughter*, written by his mentor Sherwood Anderson. Already aggravated that he had missed an opportunity to sign with Scribner's, and that Liveright had required him to cut one story and significantly alter another, now reviews of his book compared him to Anderson and noted Gertrude Stein's influence. Resenting the notion that others had contributed to his success, Hemingway decided to write a parody of *Dark Laughter* and sever his association with Anderson, despite the fact that Anderson had opened the doors to Paris for him.

Early friends who understood the depth of Hemingway's debt to Anderson were appalled by the satire, eventually published as *Torrents of Spring*. Pauline, however, thought the draft he zipped off in just ten days was one of the funniest things she had ever read. She encouraged him to get it published, and Fitzgerald agreed. More than likely, both saw it for what it probably was—a way to free Ernest from his publishing contract. While Boni & Liveright had rights to his next two books, the firm would look askance at publishing such an obvious parody of its star writer. Thus, a rejection might leave Ernest free to sign with another publisher. With Hemingway probably orchestrating such a scenario, Fitzgerald wrote a letter to Liveright regarding *Torrents,* suggesting "it might interest you to know that to one rather snooty reader, at least, it seems about the best comic book ever written by an American."[10] He added that in a sense he hoped they didn't like it because he would love to see it go to his own publisher. Perhaps Pauline and Fitzgerald would not have thought it quite as funny if they had known or understood the extent of Anderson's support for Hemingway. But Hadley had been there almost from the day that Y. K Smith introduced the two men, and she recognized Ernest's parody as a cruel way to repay Anderson's friendship. For Hemingway's part, however, aside from a way to possibly sever his contract, he needed to serve public notice that he was his own person as a writer.

The entire ordeal put a strain on Hadley's friendship with Pauline, since Hadley believed Ernest would never have tried to publish it without Pauline's encouragement.[11] Nevertheless, it was hard not to like Pauline, who flattered Hadley and showed great interest in her musical talents. Both Hadley and Ernest saw her as a great conversationalist and appreciated her company. By November Ernest wrote Harold Loeb, "We've been seeing a lot of Pauline Pfeiffer."[12] The next month he told Bill Smith about Pauline's merits as a good companion and literary critic. "Pauline and I killed on a Sunday two bottles of Beaune, a bottle of Chambertin, and a bottle of Pommard," he wrote, "and with the aid of Dos Passos a q[uart] of Haig in the square bottle, and a quart of hot Kirsch."[13] Paradoxically, although Pauline enjoyed partying with Hemingway and his crowd, she lived with a devout French Catholic family, attended mass, abstained from meat on Fridays, and observed all holy days of obligation. She considered herself fortunate to be living with such a fine family, but had her doubts about some French Catholics. "They are a genre unto themselves," she told the nuns back at her former school in St. Louis. "I fear their consciences were not prudently formed when they were children, for they follow their own inclinations in all things. They eat meat on Friday, arrive at Mass at any time, if at all, and when traveling they take a church holiday. But they pour into the churches on all fete days and all business is suspended. Virginia, who sometimes rebels against the rigours of her early training, says she intends to bring up all her children French Catholics."[14]

She could not have known at the time that it would not be long before she would be following her own inclinations when it came to Ernest Hemingway. With Virginia home in Piggott, Pauline faced the Christmas holidays alone and quickly accepted when Hadley suggested she accompany the Hemingways on their ski trip to Schruns. Though not particularly excited about skiing, Pauline thought it a good way to escape the rain and miserable weather in Paris. Shortly before the trip, Kitty Cannell, walking down a Paris sidewalk, encountered Pauline in a gorgeous designer suit, lugging a pair of skis and struggling against the wind. Pauline told her about the upcoming holiday at Schruns with Hadley and Ernest, and Kitty recalled being quite surprised, not realizing they had become that friendly.[15]

Ernest, Hadley, and Bumby left for Schruns on December 12, and Pauline joined them on Christmas Eve. At first Hadley welcomed Pauline's companionship, since Ernest wrote much of the time. Being around Ernest while he wrote gave Pauline another perspective on him, and his strict discipline impressed her. Their first days together followed a predictable routine. Ernest spent the mornings writing, and he took a break in the afternoons for skiing. The evenings passed in long conversations or in playing three-handed bridge.

Though Ernest tried teaching Pauline to ski, she preferred reading inside by the fire. Thus, the relationship between the three settled into a pattern. Hadley and Pauline shared morning activities, often doing things with Bumby, while ski afternoons became Ernest and Hadley's time together. Evenings belonged primarily to Pauline and Ernest, and they devoted hours to discussing his writing. Thus, Pauline gradually shifted her attention from Hadley to Ernest, sitting patiently while he read portions of his short stories to her, along with drafts of his first novel. Pauline lifted Ernest's spirits and confidence, and the author came to value her opinion as he worked on rewrites for *The Sun Also Rises*.

Hadley observed the relationship blossoming but underestimated its nature. Ernest, for example, included Pauline in the pet names they enjoyed bestowing on each other, with Ernest becoming Drum, Hadley, Dulla, and Pauline Doubladulla. Since other women often accompanied the Hemingways on holidays, such playfulness did not upset Hadley. On one occasion early in the Hemingways' marriage, two female friends had joined them for two weeks of skiing and called themselves "the harem," with Ernest becoming "the Moslem."[16]

In this situation, however, Pauline felt something happening that she did not anticipate at the outset of the trip and could not seem to help. She fell in love with Ernest, and her lack of experience with men gave her few defenses for fighting her growing feelings. While some Hemingway biographers say she came to Paris looking for a man and pursued Hemingway on this trip, chances are that the opposite happened. Ernest more likely pursued her, since she came from great financial wealth and Hadley's resources were dwindling. Pauline's keen editorial eye may have sealed the attraction for Ernest. Even if Pauline came to Paris in search of a man, biographer Michael Reynolds points out that Ernest was her least likely choice.[17] Pauline, single, wealthy, college educated, and devoutly Catholic, hardly seemed a fit for Ernest, married with a child, with no formal education beyond high school, struggling as a writer, and apparently possessed of few moral scruples.

Later, however, as Ernest recalled those days in a version of A *Moveable Feast,* published after his death, he laid all the blame for the breakup of his marriage on Pauline. Accusing her of using the old trick of "becoming the temporary best friend of another young woman who is married," he managed to absolve himself of any active role in the scenario that began to play itself out:

> When the husband is a writer and doing difficult work so that he is occupied much of the time and is not a good companion or partner to his wife for a big part of the day, the arrangement has advantages until you know how it works out. The husband has two attractive girls around when he has finished work. One is new and strange and if he has bad luck he gets to love them both.
>
> Then, instead of the two of them and their child, there are three of them. First it is stimulating and fun and it goes on that way for a while. All things truly wicked start from an innocence. So you live day by day and enjoy what you have and do not worry.[18]

In a later edition of A *Moveable Feast,* which restores some of the original material edited out of the first version, Hemingway accepts some of the blame, but only in the sense of being too blinded by his new love for Pauline to be repelled by her actions.

Perhaps not coincidentally, Ernest's affections for Pauline developed around the time Uncle Gus increased her trust fund to $60,000, with a $250-per-month yield. The gift came, Gus explained to Pauline, out of "love and affection" and a "desire to share the prosperity which has come to us." His motive was to enable her "to better and more successfully evolve your personality and attain your hopes and ideals."[19]

An affair with a married man surely did not fall within the hopes and ideals Gus had in mind. Pauline arrived back in Paris on January 14, 1926, two days after her scheduled return to *Vogue,* and had trouble concentrating on work. Her mind was in Austria, where Ernest and Hadley planned to remain until spring, and she experienced strong feelings of both desire and guilt. Pauline immediately recognized that she lacked the will to end the situation. She genuinely liked Hadley, but she could not turn away from Ernest.

Pauline wrote to both of them the minute she got back, attempting to convince Hadley and herself that her feelings extended to both Hemingways. The letters also let Ernest know that she thought about him constantly. When not writing, she ran errands for them, returning their books to the library, sending pecans, or finding things to do for them in Paris. She reassured Hadley of her friendship with the entire family by sending money to buy presents for Bumby and referring to him often in her letters through such observations as the carpet being installed in her bedroom looking "about the color of Bumbi's beret."[20] Pauline even indicated that she might include Bumby in her new trust fund.

Not long after Pauline's return to Paris, Ernest made plans for a trip to New York to end his contract with Boni & Liveright and line up a new publisher. The anticipated rejection of *Torrents of Spring* had arrived during the holidays, with Liveright indicating that protecting Anderson would not have stood in the way if they thought it a book worth publishing. While it possessed some bright spots, like Hadley they viewed it overall as in "rotten taste and horribly cruel."[21]

Though the Liveright rejection came as no surprise, Pauline seethed over it when she arrived back in Paris. She wrote Hadley and Ernest, "I think there must be something rotten about a firm that hasn't anyone in it that thinks Torrents of Spring is funny." She then boldly suggested: "I would like to take this up with Liveright. For Liveright's own good. Perhaps if Mr. and Mrs. Hemingway should go to America, or just Mr. Hemingway should go to America, I might go with them or just him and tell them a few things. I have learned to be a very forceful speaker writing for Vogue, and I would be glad to be as forceful as possible. Damn it to hell, gentlemen, I could begin and then go on from there."[22]

Pauline knew that Ernest did not want the contract with Liveright, but it provided a way to let him know of her interest in the trip. Short of that, she suggested that he at least stop by Paris on the way and drop off a draft of *The Sun Also Rises* for her to read during his absence. Better yet, she suggested, perhaps Hadley would come along and spend time with her in Paris while Ernest stayed in New York.

Ernest embarked for New York via Paris in late January, leaving Hadley and Bumby at Schruns. Pauline, well aware when she invited Hadley that she probably would not leave Bumby behind with a nurse, delighted in the chance to see Ernest alone in Paris. "I feel he should be warned that I'm going to cling to him like a millstone and old moss and winter ivy," she wrote Hadley before his arrival.[23] At that time of year, Pauline was kept busy with designer shows, but she managed time away with Ernest while he stayed in Paris. Toward the end of his visit she wrote Hadley, "I've seen your husband E. Hemingway several times—sandwiched in like good red meat between thick slices of soggy bread. I think he looks swell, and he has been splendid to me."[24]

After Ernest departed for New York, Pauline continued to write Hadley, perhaps to assuage her guilt. "I have exactly ten minutes intervening between me and lunch, and I hasten to devote them to you—tho I have no letter to answer," she told Hadley. "I trust there is a faint mauve reproach in that last, for here I am going to three collections a day, working like a mad thing, and there are you walking in the sunshine, playing the piano, skiing down precipices."[25]

Things went well for Ernest in New York. After meeting and parting amicably with Liveright, he met with Maxwell Perkins at Scribner's, who accepted *Torrents* and *The Sun Also Rises* for publication. Fitzgerald had alerted Perkins earlier that they could probably get Hemingway's first novel if they agreed to take the parody as well. While in New York, Ernest also made the rounds of his journalist friends, including Dorothy Parker and Robert Benchley. By then, Parker and Benchley had tired of the New York scene and found the Algonquin Round Table too crowded, so they decided to check out Paris. Departing New York on the boat with Ernest, they heard repeatedly of his anxiousness to see Hadley and Bumby at Schruns. Once they arrived in Paris, however, Ernest seemed in no hurry to go on to Austria. In fact, he stayed in Paris for several days, showing them the sights and taking them to dinner.[26] Neither Parker nor Benchley realized at the time that they were providing an excuse for Ernest to see Pauline when she could get away from work.

After Ernest returned to Schruns, Pauline continued her letters to both Hadley and Ernest in an effort to keep up the pretense that nothing had changed. Whenever she did not hear back from Hadley immediately, Pauline became concerned that Hadley had found out about the relationship. "Hadley, sweet," Pauline wrote on March 16, "I detect a falling off of the letters from your quarter. Isn't there something can be done about this? And done with a fair amount of dispatch?"[27] Pauline also attempted to make Ernest jealous, while assuring Hadley that her interests focused on men other than Ernest. One message to Ernest read, "This isn't a letter, but just written to tell you that I think your friend Robert C. Benchley is awful swell and I am very VERY fond of him."[28]

Pauline also tried to hide her feelings for Ernest by relating incidents with other men, including her boss. One morning Pauline was working with Main Bocher at his home on an article request sent from New York. When no ideas came forth for the direction of the feature, they decided to prime the creative pump with a little wine. One bottle led to another, until eventually Pauline became tipsy. She took great delight in reporting to Ernest and Hadley that Bocher's nose appeared to move around on his face. "I didn't like to say push your nose back into the middle of your face, Mr. Bocher, because in a way I am not Mr. Bocher's equal," Pauline wrote. "But I got so worried about the nose, which finally got on the point of falling off the side of the face, that I thought the only thing I could do gracefully, and without loss of time, was to leave, so I did."[29]

Pauline even suggested that she might have a romantic interest in John Dos Passos. After Dos Passos shared a brief skiing holiday with Ernest and Hadley in early March, Pauline wrote to inquire how the visit went. An aside to Hadley read, "Hadley, this is of course private, but was there any where about him. . . . anything resembling a jewel casket? Everything between the hot Spanish suitor and me has now been placed on the high love plane."[30] The idea of Dos Passos presenting her with a ring was a ploy on Pauline's part. Despite her efforts to divert attention, friends such as Joan Boyle noticed that Pauline did not take her usual interest in the Paris fashion collections. Joan worked at the *Vogue* office in New York and came to Paris to assist during designer openings. Once the shows ended, Pauline and Joan visited Joan's sister Kay, who lived at Grasse in southern France with Hemingway's friend Ernest Walsh. A week prior to their visit, a letter a day arrived from Hemingway for Pauline. Joan attempted to explain to her sister the close relationship between Pauline and Hadley, and that Ernest had asked Pauline to pick up a brand of perfume bottled in Grasse, and lingerie found only in Cannes, for him to give as a surprise to Hadley.

"Pauline talked to us brightly and efficiently about Hemingway, speaking with authority, and even a trace of condescension, of the difficulty he had getting words down on paper," Kay recalled. Pauline also told them she was converting Ernest to Catholicism, noting, "The outlet of confession would be very good for him."[31]

The first evening of the visit, Walsh read excerpts aloud from an editorial he had written for *This Quarter,* in which he praised Robert McAlmon. Pauline seemed anxious for him to finish and said she didn't want to hear about McAlmon because he had spread vicious lies about Hemingway, including the charge of Hemingway being a closet homosexual. Walsh slammed his hand down on the kitchen table and shouted, "Christ! McAlmon was the first to publish Hemingway!"[32] Pauline responded that Ernest owed him nothing, noting that if a debt existed, Ernest had paid it back with other favors to McAlmon. Walsh claimed that Ernest stopped writing him after that incident, though not before providing his own explanation about the letters to Pauline. "We saw Pauline Pfeiffer the other day," Ernest wrote to Walsh. "She'd visited with you and said you were well. I wrote her at your address to pay her some money I borrowed going through Paris. She bought me some night gowns for Hadley."[33] By the end of that year, when Walsh died of tuberculosis, it was common knowledge that the relationship between Hemingway and Pauline was not about buying nightgowns for Hadley.

The Hemingways returned to Paris from Schruns at the beginning of April, and on April 24 Ernest sent the manuscript of *The Sun Also Rises* to Perkins. With his book finished, the Hemingways undertook a busy social schedule. Ernest reserved a box at the bicycle races and escorted Hadley to parties and events, including drinking and dining with friends at all their favorite places. Throughout that spring, he secretly saw Pauline as well. Later he reflected his dilemma through an unpublished story in which Phillip Haines, a married writer, sleeps with another woman, Dorothy, who is the best friend of his wife, Caroline: "He liked the excitement of the mistress, the luxury, the devotion and it made him treat Caroline better. They had enjoyed a very exciting time and their idea had been that it was all right as long as Caroline did not know."[34]

While Ernest seemed content with the relationship, Pauline's guilt continued to grow, yet she could not bring herself to give him up. One of Ernest's unpublished manuscript fragments reflected her conflicted emotions: "Dorothy had thought it was a great sin, however, and it was only justified to her by how much they loved each other. Even then it was not justified. It was too great a sin."[35]

When Virginia returned from Piggott in the spring, everyone seemed to know of the affair except Hadley, who may have chosen to ignore her suspicions. In spite of the romantic relationship, Pauline attempted to maintain her supposed friendship with Hadley. Toward the end of April Virginia and Pauline invited Hadley on a trip with them through the Loire Valley to visit castles and gardens. They traveled in Virginia's rental car, stayed in the best hotels, and ate at elegant restaurants, all at Pauline's expense. During the trip, however, Pauline's mood changed dramatically, reaching a point where she either talked excessively or turned silent and sullen, snapping when Hadley asked her anything.

Finally Hadley realized that a serious problem existed and baited Virginia one afternoon: "Don't you think Ernest and Pauline get along awfully well together?" Virginia hesitated and said, "I think they're very fond of each other." Hadley recalled, "It was the way she said it. It was like an announcement. I seized the situation. Suddenly it was immediately clear to me."[36] When Hadley returned to Paris she confronted Ernest. Instead of being remorseful, he became angry with his wife, blaming her for the mess. If she hadn't brought the affair out in the open, he argued, it would not be a problem. For his part, Ernest saw nothing wrong with the status quo.

A short time afterward, Hadley ran into Kitty Cannell, who asked about the ski trip at Schruns with Pauline. "Well, you know what's happening," Hadley replied coldly. "She's taking my husband."[37] For a time Hadley attempted to go along with Ernest's insistence that they proceed as if nothing had happened. It proved virtually impossible, however, especially since they had made so many plans involving Pauline, including inviting her to join the group going to Spain for summer bullfights. To complicate matters even more, at the end of the Schruns trip Pauline had invited them to spend the following winter in Piggott, where she would get them a house. All that now would have to be undone or endured.

Under the circumstances, Hadley looked forward to a Madrid trip with Ernest in May. Bumby's planned stay with the Murphys at their Cap d'Antibes villa on the southern coast of France would give Hadley a rest and Ernest quiet time to write. It also meant they would have time to themselves for sorting things out. Before they departed, however, Bumby came down with a bad cough, and Hadley could not send him to the Murphys. Ernest went on to Madrid alone on May 12, apparently without a thought as to whether he should stay and help Hadley care for their son.

Pauline had departed Paris a week earlier to spend time with her relatives in Italy. During Ernest's stay alone in Madrid, he clearly conveyed that Pauline would remain a part of his life, even if he continued his marriage to Hadley. A letter to his father indicated that he planned to live with Hadley in Piggott that winter. "In Piggott I figure that I will be far enough away from people so they won't come and bother and I can work," he told him. "I will be working on another novel and some gents when they are working on a novel may be social assets but I am just about as pleasant to have around as a bear with sore toenails. Pauline Pfeiffer who was down in

Austria with us and is going to Spain this summer lives in Piggott when she's in the states and is getting us a house there."[38]

While Hemingway was in Madrid, Scribners released *Torrents of Spring*. He wrote to Sherwood Anderson in advance of its publication, assuring him that the parody, written in good fun, should not upset him. He told Anderson: "You see I feel that if among ourselves we have to pull our punches, if when a man like yourself who can write very great things writes something that seems to me, (who have never written anything great but am anyway a fellow craftsman) rotten, I ought to tell you so."[39]

As it turned out, Anderson was less offended by the book than by Hemingway's attempt to explain himself. "Damn it, man, you are so final—so patronizing," he responded. "You always do speak to me like a master to a pupil. It must be Paris—the literary life. You didn't seem like that when I knew you. . . . Come out of it, man. I pack a little wallop myself."[40]

Shortly after Hemingway left for Madrid, Sara Murphy wrote to Hadley that she and Bumby should come on to Cap d'Antibes in spite of his illness. Bumby would be helped by the sunshine, and Ernest could join them when he finished his writing and Bumby overcame the flu. Hadley accepted the offer, but after their arrival discovered that Bumby had whooping cough and needed to be quarantined. Hadley and Bumby moved into a spare cottage leased by the Fitzgeralds, who moved to a larger villa with a private beach. Although the Murphys treated mother and son well, Hadley never felt particularly comfortable around Gerald and Sara, with all their money, their fashionable clothes and impeccable taste. Her own clothes were old and misshapen, and she had never quite regained her pre-pregnancy figure. Competing was an impossibility, since her small trust fund was being stretched to support a family of three. Being apart from the other guests, including the Fitzgeralds and the MacLeishes, only heightened Hadley's sense of not belonging.

Pauline wrote Hadley after the quarantine that she would come and help take care of Bumby to give Hadley some relief. She had had whooping cough as a child and thus should not be affected by the exposure. Undoubtedly Pauline was the last person Hadley wanted to see, but Pauline found an ally in Ernest, whose letters to Hadley from Spain pressured her to accept his lover's offer. Hadley feared that if Pauline did not come to Cap d'Antibes, she might join Ernest in Madrid, and Ernest would forego the visit to the south of France. Thus, Hadley extended an invitation, and Pauline arrived about the same time as Ernest and moved into the rented villa with them. When the Fitzgeralds' lease on the villa expired, Pauline rented two rooms at the Hotel de la Pinede in Juan les Pins, a nearby town, and asked the Hemingways to be her guests. Bumby and his nurse, Marie Rohrbach, occupied a small house nearby.[41]

Hadley recalled that the summer consisted of three bathing suits on the line, three breakfast trays, and three of everything. Pauline, an early riser, came to the Hemingways' bedroom each morning, wearing a robe over tomboy pajamas, and crawled into bed with them. The three shared breakfast in bed, along with a lot of playfulness that took on sexual overtones definitely not appreciated by Hadley.[42]

After breakfast they usually went swimming at a private cove. Pauline tried to teach Hadley how to dive, but a childhood back injury made it too difficult. Sometimes Hadley and Pauline swam by themselves while Ernest wrote. On one occasion Pauline suggested that they sunbathe in the nude to get an all-over tan. Pauline's slim body turned a golden brown, but Hadley's fair skin freckled, then burned and peeled. Hadley enjoyed bicycling, and after drinks and lunch, the three rented bicycles and rode all over the area. "I came back from that awful summer absolutely in bloom with the best color I ever had," Hadley recalled.[43]

In July most of the group moved on to Pamplona for the bullfights after sending Bumby to Brittany with his nurse. Although everyone treated her well, Hadley felt like an outsider. She suspected that some of them, including Sara, sympathized with Ernest and Pauline. Part of her insecurity came from her lack of fashionable clothes and sense of style, making it impossible to compete with Pauline and others who wore linen trousers during the day and flowing dresses at night.[44]

When the bullfights ended, Pauline returned to her job in Paris, while Hadley and Ernest went to Madrid. Pauline continued to write letters to both of them, but meanings between the lines became clear to Hadley. In one letter Pauline wrote, "I'm going to get a bicycle and ride in the bois. I am going to get a saddle too. I am going to get everything I want. Please write to me. This means YOU Hadley."[45]

Constant arguments between Ernest and Hadley in Spain signaled a marriage irretrievably broken, and they took up separate residences upon their return to Paris. Gerald Murphy offered Hemingway use of his vacant studio. The Murphys thought the world of Ernest, but they never felt that he and Hadley were a good match. They also preferred Pauline's company to Hadley's, despite deploring the breakup of a marriage.[46] Sympathetic to Ernest's situation, they put four hundred dollars in his bank account in September, before departing for the United States, saying, "We found we couldn't leave Paris without acting on the hunch that when life gets bumpy, you get through to the truth sooner if you are not hand-tied by the lack of a little money."[47] Gerald gently suggested that, while Ernest and Hadley obviously cared for each other, it seemed to him that they wanted different things in life. "You and Hadley should go away from each other. . . . What situations need is space and distance as well as time. But above all things you should act."[48]

Hadley at first hoped that Ernest and Pauline's closeness eventually would push them apart. Once Ernest tired of the overheated relationship, Hadley believed, the fire would burn itself out. It had happened before with other women, and they came through with their marriage intact. Now Hadley decided perhaps the reverse might work. If Ernest and Pauline did not see each other for a while, maybe the ardor would cool. Therefore, she suggested a solution to Ernest. If Pauline and Ernest did not see each other or communicate for one hundred days and still felt the same way at the end of the period, she would give him a divorce. Pauline and Ernest agreed to the conditions.

In early September Ernest wrote to Fitzgerald, "Our life is all gone to hell which seems to be the one thing you can count on a good life to do. Needless to say Hadley has been grand and everything has been completely my fault in every way. That's the truth, not a polite gesture."[49] On the same day, he wrote Anderson, "Piggott is shot to hell now along with a lot of other things."[50] Pauline headed to Piggott alone but planned to return in one hundred days.

CHAPTER 6

The One Hundred Days (1926)

Ernest and Pauline considered the one-hundred-day separation a great challenge and, like any other test of perseverance, one that would make them stronger for having survived it. Ernest took Pauline to Boulogne on September 23 for her transatlantic crossing, and they spent their last evening together with a meal of sole and partridge at Hôtel Meurice. Over dinner and brandy they worked out a code for various contingencies in the event they needed to communicate through public cables. A message of "Hurry" from Ernest or "Coming" from Pauline meant they would reunite immediately. "Started" meant that Hadley had begun divorce proceedings. Other terms such as "Bears," "Jesuits," and "Cubists" each had coded meanings, which remain unknown.[1]

At the end of Pauline's first day aboard the *Pennland*, she wrote about comfortable, warm, solid feelings and her plans to make it through the three months by writing long letters to Ernest. Some things might sound "stupid," she warned, "but by writing you everything I can keep you very close to me and very much in my life until I see you again in the same town in the same hotel in the same clothes and then never leave you again all our lives."[2] After four days at sea, however, the separation no longer seemed like such an adventure, and she wanted to take the next boat back. She became far less circumspect about their relationship and wrote to Ernest, "Darling, if you think it's a good thing to do, I don't care if you say to Hadley that we were living together in Paris. I don't care at all. I mean this. You tell anybody anything you want."[3]

By the time the *Pennland* docked in New York on the morning of October 4, Pauline was having serious second thoughts about the whole idea of being apart for three months. Uncle Gus met her at the ship, along with her favorite cousin, Garfield Merner, to make sure the trip had gone well and to exchange family news before facing Monday morning at the office. Her uncle had arranged for her to stay at his favorite hotel, the Waldorf-Astoria, but she arrived to find the room unready. When the St. Louis Cardinals won the second game of the World Series the night before, after an opening victory by the New York Yankees, Cardinal fans partied into the night and took their time getting up and out of the hotel. While waiting, Pauline wandered around the city, eating lunch by herself, desperately missing Ernest, and trying to occupy time with such mundane purchases as hairpins.[4] When she arrived back at the hotel to check on her room, Pauline's spirits picked up after finding that a letter from Ernest awaited her. Written before he left Boulogne, the letter strengthened her resolve, and Pauline felt reassured by how "solid and calm" he sounded.[5] Even though dated a week earlier, his words convinced her to remain equally strong.

Pauline stayed several days in New York to visit with Uncle Gus, Aunt Louise, and other relatives, including cousin Matthew and his wife, Connie. After Pauline and Matthew broke off their engagement, he married her friend Connie on January 7, 1925. "I think from appearances that he's awfully glad he didn't marry me," Pauline wrote Ernest. "And certainly I feel the same."[6] Pauline also enjoyed time with friends she shared with Ernest, since it made her feel closer to him. The Murphys had returned to New York several days ahead of Pauline, and John Dos Passos arrived as well. The Murphys told Dos Passos about the split between Hadley and Ernest, and Dos Passos questioned Pauline about it one evening. They treated her really "swell," she reported to Ernest, adding that the Murphys were "adorable" and "Dos was exactly like Dos—so much like Dos you wouldn't believe it." [7] The four friends passed evenings drinking at Gerald Murphy's family home and making the rounds of the jazz clubs on Lenox Avenue. The Harlem Renaissance was in full swing, and performances rivaled anything Pauline had seen in Paris.

Pauline made time for lunch at the Algonquin with her *Vogue* friend Joan Boyle, which included a chance meeting with Robert Benchley. Like Dos Passos, Benchley questioned her extensively about Ernest, which led Pauline to suspect that he, too, knew about their relationship. Regardless, she enjoyed the conversation and decided to count him among their joint friends.[8] Pauline used some of her time in New York for business, including dropping by Scribner's to learn the publication date of *The Sun Also Rises*. More important, she wanted a chance to hear firsthand all the good things said about Ernest. She delivered materials to *Vogue* from the Paris office, and editors there asked her to consider working in the New York office for six weeks, beginning the day after Christmas. Pauline did not tell them she hoped to be back in Paris making wedding plans by then, but instead kept the offer in mind as a contingency plan.

A week after her arrival in New York, Pauline departed by train, arriving in Piggott two days later. Her mother, Mary, met her at the train station, where Pauline had the awful task of breaking the news that she loved a married man. Fortunately she avoided her father, who was in Memphis, involved with the cotton market, so she did not have to face him that day. As Pauline suspected, the news devastated her mother, who asked about Hadley and the child involved. She could not have taken Hadley's situation more to heart, Pauline lamented, than if Hadley had been her daughter.[9]

Mary also realized the great guilt that Pauline was carrying and suggested they not talk about it for a while and certainly not break the news yet to her father. In her own way, Mary believed Hadley might be right about the one hundred days, and perhaps emotions would diminish with the separation. If such became the case, then her daughter's broken heart would be dealt with, but Paul Pfeiffer would never know his daughter had almost broken up a marriage.

In Piggott, Pauline attempted to pass the time in a daily routine designed to help her get in great shape for Ernest. Her basic schedule included rising at 7 A.M. for breakfast, milk at 10:30 A.M., Spanish lessons until lunch at 12:30 P.M., a letter to Ernest while her mother napped, a two-hour walk, milk at 4 P.M., dinner at 6:30 P.M., milk before bed at 10 P.M., and lots of reading in both French and Spanish.[10]

To vary her exercise, Pauline talked a. boy into renting his bike to her in the afternoons while he attended school across the street. Sometimes her mother accompanied her on walks; other times she waited for the evenings to go downtown and back with her parents for a movie or a traveling show. One night walking home with her parents, Pauline missed Ernest so much that she left her parents when they arrived at the edge of the yard and crossed the street to the school to continue walking away her anxieties. She later wrote to Ernest, "I walked along through the school house yard and it was so lovely, and so lonely. The school house is on a hill with a lot of bare ground, with trees around the edge. And the moon was full and faintly yellow—the way that moonlight is just a little yellow in October, and it was clear and crisp."[11] The moonlit country night made her think perhaps she would miss Ernest less in a bustling city. Then she remembered that while in the city she had thought being in the country would make things easier.

To make the time apart go faster, Pauline immersed herself in small-town activities, with drilling for oil being the biggest event of her visit. A well started in September on the north side of Piggott had plunged thirteen hundred feet through almost solid rock by the time she arrived. Her father, who thought it a pipe dream, discounted hitting oil before eighteen hundred feet, if at all. Despite her father's skepticism, Pauline eventually bought three units in the well at ten dollars apiece—one for herself, one for Ernest, and one for Virginia. "The well is really very exciting," she told Ernest, "as practically all the men who are involved have given up their regular employment and hover about expecting deliverance hourly."[12] Piggott residents would be beside themselves if the well came in, she told him, since no one in town seemed to have more than ten dollars to his name. Even the circus canceled its Piggott appearance due to the poor cotton crop and price slump. In the end, the well provided entertainment, but no money. For Pauline, however, the diversion seemed well worth her thirty-dollar investment.

Fortunately for Pauline, her mother and father read widely and loved discussing what they read, which helped pass many evenings. During that winter in Piggott, Pauline polished off an eclectic reading list, including such books as *Lys Rouge, The Story of Philosophy, Lollie Willows, La Mujer Fantastica, Orphan Angel,* and *Las Corridas de Toros en la Actualidad.*[13] Her most exciting reading, however, consisted of reviewing and critiquing Ernest's work. His correspondence generally included drafts of short stories and other work in progress, and he anxiously awaited her editorial comments. Pauline's work editing for the man she loved became not a job, but a passion. When his third book, *The Sun Also Rises,* came out on October 22, first reviews lacked enthusiasm. She wrote to encourage him, saying, "Remember, no matter what the critics say, we know about that book. . . . We know things that are the matter with it, and we know there is some swell writing in it."[14] On another occasion she wrote, "I'll probably turn into a Svengali when I'm married to you, for I'm so darn crazy for you to write swell. The critics are so funny. They know things and they don't know things."[15]

Pauline's sharp editorial eye and encouraging comments were exactly what Ernest needed at this early stage of his career. In her letters, Pauline was a tactful critic when he missed the mark, while lavishing praise when he wrote well. Referring to a poem about their friend Dorothy Parker, she told him, "I didn't like the Dotty poem much Ernest—about twelve tents [tenths] out of water maybe," meaning he had gone too far in attempting to make his point.[16] Later she pronounced it shrill, "like ordering a lot of clothes for an elephant and putting them on a mouse."[17] On the other hand, after reading the draft of his short story "In Another Country," she wrote, "It's swell, and straight, and beautifully finished. Also just enough out of water. I can't find any fault with it at all."[18]

Ernest's poem being too much "out of water," while the short story was "just enough out of water," was a reference to the iceberg theory associated with Hemingway's writing style, which held that a good writer should show only the tip of the iceberg, leaving the rest beneath the surface for readers to discover. "Anything you know you can eliminate and it only strengthens your iceberg," Hemingway commented years later in "The Art of Fiction XXI."[19] The actual term probably should be credited to Hadley, who once told Ernest he had "a magnificent grip on the form back of the material no matter how strange it is, like the icebergs."[20] Regardless, it was a writing style that Pauline appreciated, and she worked closely with Ernest to perfect it.

While Pauline edited manuscripts in Piggott, Ernest spent his time in Paris alienating old friends whom he no longer needed. At a party one evening he insisted on reading the Dorothy Parker poem that Pauline did not like. Some of Dorothy's friends, including Don and Beatrice Stewart, thought the poem highly insulting, and it marked the beginning of the end of Ernest's relationship with the Stewarts. Additionally, with publication of *The Sun Also Rises,* many characters easily identified as Ernest's friends grew enraged at their portrayals and had nothing more to do with Hemingway. Harold Loeb, in particular, had good reason to be incensed at Hemingway's characterization of him as Robert Cohn, an insufferable, lovesick bore. Though Loeb did not look or act like the fictive Cohn, Hemingway had used Loeb's easily recognizable background in constructing the character. Both descended from wealthy Jewish families (Loeb's pedigree included the Guggenheims as well as the Loebs), graduated from Princeton, edited an expatriate magazine in Paris, broke with a mistress, and had a brief fling with a permissive Englishwoman. Thus, readers who became acquainted with Robert Cohn through the book figured they also knew Harold Loeb— not a flattering assumption.

In *The Sun Also Rises,* Cohn is one of many men who sleep with Lady Brett Ashley (based on Lady Duff Twysden), with her favors also extended to her fiancé, Mike Campbell (based on Pat Guthrie), and writer Jake Barnes (based on Hemingway). Unlike Brett's other partners, Cohn has the misfortune to fall in love with her and attempts to be protective of her, prompting her fiancé to jab, "She's slept with lots of better people than you."[21] In a public confrontation, with all the summer people gathered around the table in Pamplona, Campbell pushes Cohn further with, "Why do you follow Brett around like a poor bloody steer? Don't you know you're not wanted? I know when I'm not wanted."[22] After helping Ernest get his first book published, serving as his tennis and boxing partner, introducing him to Pauline, and being an all-around friend, Loeb could not believe the slap in the face that Ernest had delivered. When the two men encountered each other at Brasserie Lipp café shortly after the novel's publication, neither acknowledged the other, and they never met or spoke again.[23]

Hemingway occupied much of his time during the separation from Pauline working on stories for his next book, *Men Without Women,* though he certainly was not without women personally and at the time had at least one too many. He whiled away much of his leisure time with Virginia, who remained in Paris when her sister went home for the one-hundred-day separation. Ernest at first planned to dedicate *Men Without Women* to Virginia in appreciation for her companionship and her help in getting through the three months without Pauline. Later, he had second thoughts about the appropriateness of dedicating a book almost totally devoid of females to Virginia and dedicated it instead to a male friend, American poet Evan Shipman. Ernest may have sought other ways to express his appreciation to Virginia. Whatever the early relationship between Virginia and Ernest, it forever changed after his affair with Pauline. Some of Virginia's friends claimed she never married because Ernest remained the only man she loved. Others claimed she never married because she could not find a man as wonderful as her father or one who wanted her and not her money.

One friend from Piggott, Ayleene Spence, believed a combination of all of the above. She suspected early on that Virginia loved Ernest from the way she talked about him when at home in Arkansas. "She was intrigued with him when she met him in Paris," Spence recalled. "And I can see from what she told me about him that a woman would be attracted to him."[24] Later, after Hemingway's marriage to Pauline, Spence remembered Virginia laughing about people in Paris being confused as to which Pfeiffer Ernest planned to marry. While Virginia cared for Ernest, and may have loved him, Spence believed she would have been reluctant to marry him, even if he had never taken up with Pauline. Virginia never overcame the suspicion that Ernest valued Pfeiffer money more than either of the sisters. Besides, Ernest lacked the qualities of Paul Pfeiffer, the father Virginia adored. Paul's confidence and self-assurance allowed him to revel in the accomplishments of others. Ernest believed that anyone else's success diminished his own.

Virginia and Ernest apparently spelled out the terms of their relationship during Pauline's forced absence from Paris and arrived at a situation that seemed to work for both of them. With Ernest as her brother-in-law, Virginia could be around him as much as she wished without raising eyebrows, especially since most people assumed her sexual interest leaned toward females. Ernest, on the other hand, would have the best of both sisters: a wife who loved him and dropped her own career to assist with his and a sister-in-law who possessed a wonderful sense of adventure and kept things fresh and exciting. During their three months together in Paris, Ernest and Virginia dined together, ran errands, took trips, and attended various events. When Ernest made a trip to Spain with Archibald MacLeish, he gave his tickets for a boxing match to Virginia and a friend, and she sent a lengthy letter to him in Spain telling all about it. Without him around, though, Paris wasn't the same. "Time isn't going so fast in spite of this being a full week," Virginia told him.[25]

In addition to her notes and letters to Ernest, Virginia transferred her sister's letters and consoled Ernest when he did not hear from Pauline. For the most part, Pauline and Ernest wrote daily. Occasionally Pauline stuffed a number of letters into one envelope so the small-town postmaster would not be suspicious about her sending letters daily to a man in Paris. Other times she sent letters to Virginia to be passed along to Ernest. The longer Pauline stayed in Piggott, the more her Catholic conscience worked on her. "Pauline was in a fix about getting married to Ernest," her sister-in-law Matilda Pfeiffer recalled. "Because after all, she was Catholic, and he was married to this other woman. And Ernest wasn't Catholic. . . . But Pauline —she was just so crazy about him—and he wanted to marry her."[26]

As the separation went on and the guilt continued to grow, Pauline became deeply depressed, and Ernest seemed helpless to do anything about her mood, particularly being an ocean away. In one letter that crossed mid-ocean with some of hers, he responded to her dark mood by writing a long, rambling letter. "All I can think," he told her, "is that you—that are all I have and that I love more than all that is and have given up everything for and betrayed everything for and killed off everything for—are being destroyed and your nerves and your spirit broken all the time day and night and that I can't do anything about it because you won't let me."[27]

Before she received this letter, however, Pauline had hit bottom and started her climb back up. Her concern at last centered on unfairness to Hadley. After a four-day fit of depression in which she sent no letters or cables to Ernest, she somehow emerged with a clear head and summoned strength to write a lengthy letter to Ernest in which she admitted, "We were so cock-eyed crazy about each other, and so very scared we might lose each other—at least I was—that Hadley got locked out."[28]

Pauline accepted more guilt for not considering Hadley's feelings than Ernest, but she now realized Hadley's wisdom in suggesting the one-hundred-day separation. It needed to be a time for everyone to really think things through and not just stick it out. During the times that Hadley did not hate her, Pauline surmised, "she must know that I was just blind dumb."

As Pauline reflected on the situation, Ernest heard similar concerns from Hadley in Paris. When Hadley discovered that Pauline and Ernest were writing daily, she informed Ernest that this did not seem to her to be a one-hundred-day separation. A true one hundred days apart meant no communication whatsoever. Ernest made the mistake of conveying this to Pauline before knowing her current frame of mind. Pauline surprised him by agreeing with Hadley and favored beginning the three months again. Ernest then feared the loss of both Hadley and Pauline. On November 2, in what she assumed would be her last letter for another three months, Pauline told Ernest that "if at the end of three months Hadley says three months more, we will go three months more. Because we can. . . . As for me, I get surer and surer that I am in love with you all the time."[29] Pauline assured him not to worry, and even her mother, realizing how much she loved him, came around to the idea that Pauline would marry Ernest. Her mother's conversations shifted from saying, "If you marry Ernest," to "When you marry Ernest," and Pauline took that as great progress.

Amid all the reassurances, Pauline explained to Ernest how she planned to get through the next three months, since he would not hear from her after that letter went in the mail. She would probably take the job at New York *Vogue* for six weeks, starting the day after Christmas. Also, she would encourage Virginia to come home to help pass the time, particularly since their parents wanted Virginia to return to the States and form a plan for her life. Pauline also decided to contact the Murphys and Dos Passos and occasionally pass news along to Ernest through them. The letter closed with "Ernest is perfect and what I shall pray every night to St. Joseph is 'Dear Saint Joseph, send me a good, kind, attractive Catholic husband, and I think Ernest is perfect.' And God keep you, dear, dear Ernest, and bless you and help you."[30]

On the same day that she sent the letter to Ernest, Pauline sent a letter to Hadley as well, apologizing for any misunderstanding. She assured Hadley that she did not want her to proceed with the promised divorce until absolutely certain and with no regrets. "You don't think of me as a very trustworthy person, I suppose," she told Hadley, "but you know what I always said about you—that you not only couldn't do a low thing, you didn't even think one, and I still feel the same way, so perhaps it would be best if we both just trusted you."[31]

Pauline's response to the new timeline struck Ernest as a little too matter-of-fact, and she did not seem sufficiently distraught. Pauline no longer missed him the way he missed her, and he feared that perhaps her conscience would prevail after all. In a long, self-pitying letter, he attempted to rid himself of his demons and nightmares. Things had changed from the beginning of the separation, he told her. At first just plain lonesome, he had pulled through because he believed it to be just a matter of time before she returned. Now not only was he lonesome, but he feared she might not come back.

"Last fall I said perfectly calmly and not bluffingly and during one of the good times," he wrote, "that if this wasn't cleared up by Christmas I would kill myself—because that would mean it wasn't going to clear up." By killing himself, he reasoned at the time, he would remove the sin from Pauline's life and spare Hadley the trouble of a divorce. Earlier Pauline made him promise not to entertain such thoughts, but now everything seemed to be out of control, "and you have broken your promises and I should think that would let me out," Ernest reasoned.[32]

The next time Hadley saw Ernest, he appeared so emotionally roiled that she felt sorry for him and decided to let him off the hook. Besides, after reflection, Hadley realized that she should not be the one forced to make a decision about when to proceed with the divorce. On November 16, 1926, she wrote to Ernest canceling the conditions she had placed on the divorce. She also suggested that from that point forward, their communications regarding divorce should be in writing to avoid any misunderstandings.[33] Immediately after Ernest received the letter, he asked Virginia to send a cable to Pauline saying that Hadley had ended the three months' separation and would start divorce proceedings as soon as possible. An elated Pauline quickly wrote to Ernest that she was "cockeyed happy."[34] Though she had no idea why Hadley had changed her mind, Pauline hoped Hadley had met someone and fallen madly in love.

Whatever the reasons, Pauline proposed to delay her return to Europe until after Christmas since she previously had made plans to go to New York with her family for a holiday celebration with brother Karl and his wife Matilda. She also matter-of-factly told Ernest about negotiations with *Vogue* and that she might take the *Vogue* job for six weeks after Christmas, provided they agreed to the salary she wanted. The extra money would help them, she thought, and divorce proceedings might go better without her there. Pauline asked Ernest's opinion, making it clear she would do what he thought best. Ernest wrote back to say that he did not know what to advise her, particularly since it sounded like she wanted to take the *Vogue* job and did not seem to be in such a great hurry to get back, even though he anxiously awaited her return. As for the money, living in New York for six weeks would probably eat up most of what *Vogue* paid her. [35] When *Vogue* offered only seventy-five dollars per week, instead of agreeing to her demand for one hundred dollars, it was much easier for Pauline to give in to Ernest's not-so-subtle insistence that his interests be served.

In addition to these considerations, Pauline worried about Virginia, drifting around Paris without any goals for her life. She warned Virginia that their parents might withdraw financial support "in a faint sad hope that it may do some good. They are really worried about you. Of course, I always worked and certainly I have turned out no comfort to them, but that is what they think, anyway."[36] Pauline suggested that if Virginia came home for Christmas, they probably could return to Europe together after the holidays, provided Virginia presented their parents with a plan for how she would occupy her time in Paris.

Virginia continued to vacillate. She wrote one letter indicating that she might come home for Christmas but wanted to consult with Ernest about his plans first. In another, Virginia claimed that she would stay in Europe over the holidays and probably attend the Sorbonne in the spring. "Mother is pleased about Jinny and the Sorbonne," Pauline wrote Ernest. "I think she would really be delighted if Jinny would be firm enough to say she didn't think she would come home Christmas because of other plans, ANY plans from Jinny would do the family no end of good."[37]

Ultimately Virginia decided to go with Ernest and the MacLeishes to Gstaad for a Christmas skiing trip. By then Ernest clearly exhibited depression about Pauline's decision to delay her return until after Christmas, and Virginia chose to be there to help him through the holidays. Pauline did not recognize the depths of Ernest's depression until she received his December 3 letter, in which he wrote, "You see Pfife I think that when two people love each other terribly much and need each other in every way and then go away from each other it works almost as bad as an abortion. . . . The deliberate keeping apart when all you have is each other does something bad to you and lately it has shot me all to hell inside."[38]

Ernest's abortion analogy, along with Pauline's and Ernest's actions during that period, promotes speculation. Pauline's letters to Ernest after returning to the States made constant reference to regaining strength, getting healthy, and following a regimen of three glasses of milk (a blood coagulant) each day. Further, in another of Ernest's letters to Piggott he wrote, "Maybe you'll come back and maybe there will be something left of you and maybe we'll have a little guts and not try self sacrifices in the middle of surgical operations."[39] Any "surgical operations" in the form of an abortion likely would have been the previous May, with Ernest in Madrid alone and Pauline ostensibly visiting relatives in Italy. Learning mid-trip that she might be pregnant would account for Pauline's sudden and drastic mood swing, noted by Hadley and Virginia in April during their drive through the Loire Valley.

Meeting Ernest in Spain in May for such an abortion would possibly explain the author's note to his father at that time, in which he mentioned that he had just returned from mass.[40] Attending mass seemed a curious event for Ernest, who was not particularly religious and had been raised Protestant. Perhaps he attended with Pauline—a Catholic woman who felt in need of absolution. An abortion during the spring also would account for Ernest's brutish insistence to Hadley that Pauline join them that summer at Juans les Pins. Ernest's concern for Pauline's health after the surgery apparently trumped any sensitivity to Hadley's feelings. While the summer on the coast was miserable for Hadley, she also recalled that Pauline looked "unhappy and forlorn."[41]

After Ernest and Pauline married, Ernest wrote a short story on their honeymoon titled "Hills Like White Elephants," promoting further speculation. The story deals with a man and a woman at a train station in Spain discussing whether or not to proceed with an abortion, although the word *abortion* never appears in the story. The man pushes the woman to have the abortion. Ernest insisted this story was "totally made up," yet he also called it a "hard" story, meaning one with considerable depth beneath the surface.[42] His notation across the bottom of the last page, "For Pauline –well, well, well," seems an odd choice of literary gifts to give his new bride unless there was something more to the story.[43]

Years later, when his marriage to Pauline fell apart, Ernest wrote another telling passage in *To Have and Have Not*. After a fight between a married couple, Richard and Helen Gordon, Helen throws at Richard: "Love is just another dirty lie. Love is ergoapiol pills to make me come around because you were afraid to have a baby. Love is quinine and quinine and quinine until I'm deaf with it. Love is that dirty aborting horror that you took me to. Love is my insides all messed up. It's half catheters and half whirling douches. I know about love. Love always hangs up behind the bathroom door. It smells like Lysol. To hell with love. Love is you making me happy and then going off to sleep with your mouth open while I lie awake all night afraid to say my prayers even because I know I have no right to any more."[44]

Whatever happened before Pauline left for Piggott, Ernest remained convinced that she changed during the one-hundred-day separation. Ernest told her that he longed for a letter with the intimacy of earlier letters. Instead, her letters seemed to be news bulletins written in haste to catch the mail. "All the letters before your bad time sounded as though you loved me more than anything in the world and when one came I used to be just cock-eyed happy," he lamented. "Then since, there was just the grand last letter but it seemed as though there wasn't any joy any more—just loyalty—and I was afraid maybe you had really given me up "[45]

Pauline received this letter prior to the trip to her brother's house in New Jersey and immediately wrote to assure him that all was well and soon she would be back in Paris. If he wanted anything from the States, Ernest should send her a cable in New Jersey and sign it "Jinny." Most of her family remained unaware of their relationship, and "I'm rotten at hiding things," she told him. "But pretty soon there won't be anything to hide. And I love you, and I love your last three letters—you are so lovely—and I am loving you HARD as you advised, and did even before you mentioned it. Have a beautiful time in Gstaad with the MacLeishes."[46]

On Christmas Eve, Ernest joined Virginia and the MacLeishes at Gstaad. After Hadley's agreement to divorce, he let his friends know, and their responses did little to cheer him up. F. Scott Fitzgerald, en route to New York, wrote that Ernest's news depressed him. Even though he expected it, he regretted not hearing firsthand from Ernest about what had gone wrong. "Anyhow I'm sorry for you and for Hadley and for Bumby," he wrote, "and I hope some way you'll all be content and things will not seem so hard and bad."[47]

Meanwhile, Pauline wrote her last letter during the separation to Ernest from her brother's house. Though Christmas Day fell on a Saturday, the holiday stretched through Monday for her since Ernest's gift arrived in New York too late to be delivered across the river to Orange, New Jersey. "But anyway, every thing is swell," she assured him. "And so am I. But I'm just cockeyed lonesome to see you. . . . I am too long away from Ernest. I have a need of Ernest near."[48] Before year's end she headed back to him.

CHAPTER 7

Wedding Plans (1927)

Pauline left for Europe on December 30, 1926, aboard the *Cleveland* and 10 days later stepped onto French soil. Ernest met her at Cherbourg 106 days after putting her on the ship from Boulogne for the one-hundred-day separation. When the lovers spotted each other, both liked what they saw. Ernest had lost weight and looked trim, with a stylish mustache; Pauline had put on a little weight and looked less gaunt than when she departed. They immediately returned to Gstaad for a continuation of the holiday ski trip with Virginia and the MacLeishes, and Ernest reveled in the devoted coterie. In many ways, having Virginia and Pauline both present reminded him of the previous year in Schruns with Pauline and Hadley. This combination, however, seemed less threatening. Even their friends considered the Pfeiffers a pair, with friends such as Gerald Murphy referring to them as "the Sister Act."[1]

Skiing filled the next few weeks, and pictures of Ernest taken at that time show no trace of the depression suffered before Pauline's return. He appears happy, smiling, and full of self-confidence. Even his wardrobe looks improved. No longer the rumpled oaf Pauline perceived him to be early in her friendship with Hadley, the Ernest in these photos appears debonair in tailored slacks and a white ski sweater matching Pauline's.

While Ernest and Pauline skied, Hadley received her judgment of divorce from him. The decree gave her custody of Bumby, with Ernest having full visitation rights. Ernest, however, could not marry yet. A French divorce involved a number of steps before becoming final and even more red tape before freeing him to marry. The schedule involved signing final papers on March 10, with the final decree to be issued on April 14. After the decree, Ernest had to file papers with the mayor in his district, a process expected to take until late April.

Ernest returned to Paris briefly in mid-February to take care of business matters, see Bumby, and have their picture made together. By then the MacLeishes were on a tour of Eastern Europe with the Murphys, and the Pfeiffer sisters had the ski slopes to themselves, which quickly grew tiresome. They urged Ernest to bring Bumby back to Gstaad on his return from Paris, suggesting they make "an entire album of pictures of him."[2] Since they planned a return to Paris on March 10, it gave Bumby a ten-day holiday and provided a break for Hadley. While Ernest logged most of his time skiing or writing, Pauline and Virginia alternated supervising Bumby's naps and meals. Both women expressed great affection for him, and Bumby grew close to his future stepmother. At a precocious age, Bumby asked lots of questions that his father often begged off on, suggesting that he ask Pauline instead, since she knew about everything. The frequent phrase "Pauline knows" soon became "Paulinos" for young Bumby and remained his nickname for his stepmother.[3]

Ernest and the Pfeiffer sisters, with Bumby in tow, arrived back in Paris in time for Ernest to sign final divorce papers. Long before the return, however, Ernest became restless. The days with Pauline and Virginia and nights with Pauline offered their charms, but going that long without male companionship bothered Ernest. An invitation to travel to Italy with Guy Hickok, his longtime friend and Paris correspondent for the *Brooklyn Daily Eagle,* struck him as a solution. While Pauline hated being apart again after such a long separation, she nonetheless recognized his need for "the promotion of masculine society" and suggested that she hoped the trip would last him a long time, "for I'm very sure your wife is going to be opposed to them."[4] Much had to be done, however, for Pauline to become his wife. With Ernest off on his trip, Pauline could work through all the details without enduring Ernest's impatience with everything involved in such a complicated Catholic wedding.

The night before he left, Ernest and Pauline had dinner with the Hickoks, and she took care of one important detail by signing her new will, leaving ten thousand dollars to Bumby and everything else to Ernest. Guy and Mary Hickok witnessed the document. Ernest and Guy set out the next morning on what started as a three-week tour of Italy, including a visit to Ezra Pound. In reality, they returned in ten days, still plenty of time for Pauline to put matters in order. To determine requirements for the marriage, Pauline paid a visit to her friend, Father Gabriel MacDarby, rector of St. Joseph's, the only English language Catholic church in Paris. Being married in a French church meant living in the parish for at least three months. Thus, it seemed logical for the marriage to take place in St. Honoré d'Eylau at Place Victor Hugo, two blocks from Pauline's rue Picot apartment. A civil ceremony at the mayor's office had to proceed prior to the church ceremony.[5]

One big obstacle, annulment of Ernest's first marriage, required his marriage certificate, evidence that it had taken place outside the church, and the name and address of the person he had married. Then Ernest, like Pauline, had to provide a certificate of baptism in the Catholic church. Ernest claimed to friends that his baptism had taken place while he was hospitalized in Italy during World War I and once insisted to Ernest Walsh, "If I am anything I am a Catholic. Had extreme unction administered to me as such in July 1918 and recovered. So guess I'm a super-Catholic."[6] Pauline wrote Ernest, suggesting that while traveling in Italy he ask for registration of his baptism at the hospital where he convalesced or other paperwork provided in wartime circumstances. Perhaps he might even find the priest who had baptized him. Locating these papers would make things go much faster, and if he rounded up the necessary documents they could begin the process immediately.

Another major detail involved finding a place to live. As soon as Guy and Ernest departed, Virginia and Pauline began apartment hunting, which proved frustrating. After discarding all printed listings and agents' leads, they eventually found an unfurnished apartment recommended by Archie and Ada MacLeish at 6 rue Feron in the sixth arrondissement. It seemed to Pauline to be just about the right size—a big bedroom and salon, large dining room, sun room, kitchen, two bathrooms, small office for Ernest, and another small room for a maid, guest, infant, or storage. Located in a quiet, respectable area between St. Sulpice Catholic Church and the Luxembourg Gardens, the apartment caught the sun on one side all morning and on the other all afternoon. Its location made it suitable to Pauline, while being on the Left Bank suited Ernest. A problem loomed, however, with rent of nine hundred francs a month and the equivalent of a three-thousand-dollar up-front deposit.[7] Pauline believed that Uncle Gus, expected in Paris on business the last day of March, would cover the deposit. Thus, Ernest's investment in Pauline's financial resources began to pay dividends even before the marriage.

These many items kept Pauline busy, and cleaning up the Murphys' apartment where Ernest lived alone as a bachelor added to her chores. Pauline sorted and piled stacks of papers and manuscripts, clothes for laundering, sweaters to be dyed, and other things to be mended. Additionally, she gathered letters and other mail to be opened, sorted, and sent to Ernest or stacked for his return, feeling confident that the writer's life would be more organized with her in charge. While Pauline enjoyed helping her husband-to-be, cleaning did not suit her, and she realized a maid would be necessary after they married.

One afternoon Pauline ran into Bumby and his nursemaid, Marie Rohrbach, in the park. Marie served as cook and housekeeper for Ernest and Hadley, and Marie made it known to Pauline that she would like to work for her. Pauline all but committed, without giving it much thought. That evening she received a note from Hadley, stating that she did not appreciate the idea of Pauline and Ernest starting their life together by appropriating part of Ernest's life with Hadley. Pauline respected Hadley's feelings and rescinded the offer to Marie. "I was so pleased about getting a good cook that I didn't consider the ramifications," she wrote to Ernest. "You can't build an old house with new bricks or the other way round or can you? Anyway Paris is full of good cooks."[8]

When not planning her new life with Ernest, Pauline joined Virginia for the theater, dinner, and bike rides. Yet within a week of Ernest's departure, Paris lost some of its luster for Pauline. She tired of Virginia and longed for Ernest's return. By March 23, she assured him, "if you will just come back to me you can have your own way all the time. I shall cross you in nothing."[9] It was a pathetic foreshadowing of their future time together.

Nor did Ernest's trip to Italy prove as much fun as expected. Italy had changed radically under fascism, and it disappointed him to see the country under such repression. Huge portraits of Mussolini glared at them from the sides of buildings, and the once gracious, friendly people seemed consumed by suspicion.[10] Ernest found and visited the priest who had baptized him during World War I, but did not come up with a baptism certificate. Priests in World War I Italy did not as a rule hand out baptismal certificates as they moved through hospital wards to anoint the wounded.

After visiting the priest, Ernest broke down in tears.[11] Perhaps his encounter had triggered a stream of thoughts about the life behind him— almost dying at the battlefront, falling in love and being rejected for the first time, having his first marriage fall apart, disappointing his parents, and a host of other regrets. His personal agonies made him unpleasant to be around. At one point during the trip Ernest and Guy argued and did not speak for several days, a difficult situation for two people sharing a room. To make matters worse, Guy found little material of interest for his article, so they decided to cut their trip short. They were less than half a day from Paris when Guy's car broke down. After helping get it towed to a nearby town for repairs, Ernest left Guy to tend to it and caught the first train back to Paris and the adoring female company of Pauline and Virginia.

Ernest had had enough male companionship to last for a while and shortly after his return wrote to F. Scott Fitzgerald, "Pauline is fine and back from America. I've been in love with her for so damned long that it certainly is fine to see a little something of her."[12] He failed to note that he had instigated their most recent time apart. Ernest and Pauline continued their separate residences until the wedding. Not only did it suit Pauline's sense of correctness, but Uncle Gus came to town, and the couple honored his concept of propriety. Gus arrived on March 31 and stayed in Paris during most of April to open a Richard Hudnut branch and take care of other company matters. His first order of business, however, became checking out the apartment Pauline had her heart set on and deciding if he would foot the bill. After seeing the spacious residence and noting how it pleased his niece, Gus agreed. Early in his career, Gus gave lots of thought to happiness in his personal and professional life. As regards his family, he clearly articulated his goals: "Give such financial aid as may be necessary to enable each to live in accordance with his station in life, without lessening individual effort and development."[13]

While Gus always took pleasure in assisting Pauline, he was immediately drawn in by Ernest's charm, and providing the apartment showed support for him as well. Perhaps more important than Gus's financial support at that time, his blessing paved the way for acceptance of the marriage from Pauline's parents. Ernest lacked a comparable advocate on his side of the family. In fact, none of his family knew of his divorce, much less the impending marriage. For months Clarence and Grace Hemingway attempted to learn the truth, after hearing rumors that found their way back to Oak Park. Early in December his mother wrote of rumors of his separation from Hadley. "I trust they are not true," she said, "but you have not mentioned her in any recent letter and I can't but worry a little concerning your happiness."[14]

A week later Ernest heard from his father: "The gossip is about a serious domestic trouble, please write me the truth so I can deny the awful rumors that you and Hadley have had a break. I cannot believe a word of such gossip until I hear from you direct."[15]

Not hearing back from Ernest, his father again wrote toward the end of January: "I firmly believe in you and Hadley as having a home with Ideals and want you to write and tell me why the rumors were spread about. . . . God bless you both and your boy and if any mistakes have been made ask God to guide you aright."[16]

Ernest dreaded telling his parents anything about his life, particularly after his mother's lack of support upon publication of *The Sun Also Rises*.

Her December letter went on at length about what a disappointment he had proven to be and how she could not believe he had wasted his talent writing one of the "filthiest" books of the year. While the book shocked his father also, he more tactfully wished Ernest's future books would have different subject matter.[17]

By early February, Ernest had to write his parents. Hadley planned an extended trip to the United States when the divorce became final and wanted to take Bumby to Oak Park to show him off to his grandparents. Ernest wrote to alert them that Hadley and Bumby would see them in the spring and confirmed that he and Hadley had separated in September. He still made no mention, however, of a divorce or plans to marry Pauline. Ernest closed by letting them know they probably had much cause to feel disgraced if they believed everything they heard. "On the other hand with a little shot of loyalty as anaesthetic you may be able to get through all my obvious disreputability and find, in the end, that I have not disgraced you at all."[18] Ernest failed to recognize the nuances between feeling disgraced by their son and being disloyal to him. The fact that his actions violated their ethical standards was just cause for disgrace but did not translate into disloyalty.

When his marriage plans firmed up, Ernest brought his sister Madelaine (Sunny) in on the secret. Cautioning her not to say a word to any of the family, he wrote, "I know it's hard on the family not to have dope on my private affairs—but they have never merited my confidence nor backed me—and fond of them as I am I can't carry the extra weight of home criticism. I'll tell them in good time."[19] There was undoubtedly a bit of cowardice as well in his delays, but to admit it would have been a violation of his self-image. Ernest brushed past the unpleasantness and went on to outline a possible itinerary for a proposed European visit by his sister. Ernest suggested that if Sunny arrived in May or June he could meet her, show her around as his schedule permitted, and introduce her to his friends. She could then travel around Europe with Pauline's sister, Virginia. "She has a tin can Citroen," he told her. "She is 25 and as crazy as you are. But she talks French and drives a car swell."[20]

When Sunny wrote back to Ernest, suggesting she did not want to intrude under the circumstances, Ernest and Pauline immediately cabled her and sent a lengthy letter to let her know they welcomed her and she would do them a great favor by accompanying Ernest to Pamplona in July. "Pauline can't go this year," he explained, "because I was there with Hadley last year and we don't want to go together until next year and you will be a god send to me."[21] By the time they sent the cable, May wedding plans led Ernest to suggest that Sunny come in mid-June because they would be back from their honeymoon and could spend time with her at their Paris apartment. Ernest and Sunny could depart for Pamplona in early July, while Pauline traveled around Europe with her friend Clara Dunn. "Pauline is crazy about your coming and helped me figure out the wire so don't think you are horning in on anything," he assured his sister.[22] For Pauline, it was not so much being "crazy" about her coming, but taking comfort in the notion that Ernest having his sister around in Pamplona would leave less room for temptation.

The offer tempted Sunny, bored by her work at a dentist's office, particularly since Ernest suggested paying all her expenses in Paris and Pamplona and Pauline seemed supportive of the trip as well. "But then a series of small but upsetting things kept happening, one after the other," she wrote in her book about her brother. "And the following month I finally had to decide, with the greatest reluctance, that I simply couldn't make the trip."[23] One of the "upsetting things" became lack of parental support. Clarence and Grace decided after reading *The Sun Also Rises* that being anywhere near Spain and the bullfights would ruin their daughter. "They can't believe that I would become anything but a prostitute if I ever visited such a place," Sunny told Ernest.[24]

As the wedding approached, Pauline involved Ernest in last-minute details. He made lists and methodically checked things off. The list for the civil ceremony included rounding up birth certificates, signing legal papers, and providing sworn statements before the consulate. The religious-ceremony list included reminders to go to confession, buy a ring, line up attendants, and sign numerous papers. Having sworn to baptism in Italy during the war and a first marriage outside the church, he received dispensation from the Archbishop of Paris on April 25. After that came publication of the banns, which began May 1 and continued through the following Sunday in parish churches of St. Honoré (Pauline's parish) and St. Pierre-de-Montrouge (Ernest's parish). According to his list, Ernest expected to have all day Monday and Tuesday for last-minute details prior to a civil ceremony on Wednesday morning and a religious ceremony on Thursday morning. That provided ample time to pick up rings, decide on a honeymoon location, get tickets, fill out church papers, go to confession, and take care of various financial and literary matters. For some unknown reason, however, both services were moved to Tuesday morning, with the religious ceremony immediately following the civil.

From early May through the wedding, cards and letters arrived from Pauline's relatives. Those greetings garnered great appreciation since most included financial contributions. Thousand-dollar checks arrived from

Pauline's parents, Uncle Henry, and Uncle Gus, and other financial gifts came from assorted aunts, uncles, and cousins. The total could have supported Pauline and Ernest for another year in Europe without other income. Uncle Gus, back in the States by then, wrote, "Although separated by the Atlantic, Aunt Louise and I hope through this note to be among the first to congratulate you and wish you well."[25]

From Villa Favorita, her uncle Leonhard Kluftinger's home in Bologna, Italy, where she had planned to marry her cousin Matthew three years earlier, Pauline received love and greetings from her uncle and many other visiting relatives.[26] Wedding preparations were progressing at Villa Favorita as well, where cousin Anna Pfeiffer (daughter of George Washington Pfeiffer) planned to marry Ettore Leonardi the following month.

A letter to Pauline and Ernest from Uncle Henry in New York read, "Dear Niece and Nephew . . . Marriage is a natural step that should lead to great mutual happiness, and your Aunt Annie and I congratulate you upon having taken this step, and wish you a long and happy married life together."[27] Annie enclosed her own letter saying, "Uncle Gus told us much about Ernest's life and work and he spoke very highly of him in every way. You see I am taking Ernest right into the family and not calling him Mr. Hemingway."[28]

"I know this must be an excellent man you have promised to step through life with," Pauline's aunt Kate wrote from Cedar Falls, Iowa. "We are pleased to know the gentleman is an American, a Catholic and a writer. A fine combination."[29] Aunt Emma's letter from San Mateo, California, wished them "much joy and a long life happily together."[30] Aunt Harriett in Cedar Falls noted, "Your Uncle Gus thinks you have a fine man for a husband." Writing just three days after Charles Lindbergh's historic May 21 transatlantic flight, Aunt Harriett facetiously added, "Fly over sometime with your husband and spend the day with us now that it's such an easy matter getting over the sea."[31]

In addition to a check, Pauline's father's note included a sprig of bridal wreath cut from their front yard in Piggott, the first to open that season. The evening before the wedding, a telegram arrived from Piggott with the message, "BLESSING CONGRATULATIONS BEST WISHES = FATHER MOTHER."[32] Ernest now had been accepted by a huge family spread over two continents, and one with great wealth and generosity.

On the morning of May 10, Ernest and Pauline stopped long enough to have their Ville de Paris identification cards renewed before being married at the mayor's office in a civil ceremony. Ernest wore a three-piece tweed suit; Pauline appeared in an off-white chemise, pearls, and the short-cropped boyish-looking hairdo de rigueur in Paris. Next, they moved on to Place Victor Hugo for a Catholic ceremony in the side chapel of St. Honoré, with Virginia Pfeiffer and Ernest's banker, Mike Ward, as attendants.

A luncheon prepared by Ada MacLeish at the MacLeishes' home followed, although Ada and Archie could not bring themselves to go to the ceremony. They found it highly distasteful for Ernest to claim being Catholic, rendering his marriage to Hadley invalid because it had taken place outside the church. If that made Bumby a bastard in the eyes of the church, they wanted no part of such hypocrisy.[33] Nevertheless, they attempted to be as supportive as possible. Archie and Ada liked Pauline, a younger, richer, and more stylish mate for Ernest, but they never felt close to her. "She always seemed like somebody you were about to meet," Archie recalled.[34] Ada admitted fondness for both Hadley and Pauline, even given their "very different personalities. I wouldn't say anybody would have been good for Ernest. It would have been better if he had just occasional ladies and didn't marry them."[35]

While Pauline and Ernest completed civil and religious ceremonies, Mary Pfeiffer sat alone at her typewriter in Piggott, trying to visualize being present at the ceremony. Though unable to physically travel to Paris, she made an arduous emotional journey to arrive at acceptance of her daughter's wedding. As Pauline and Ernest exchanged vows in Paris, Mary typed a letter indicating that she had made the journey successfully:

> My dear Children:
> God bless you and keep you always in his care.
> I hope your wedding garments this morning are bright and shining as the sun, befitting those who have come through great tribulations.
> For many months I have been asking our Heavenly Father to make the crooked ways straight and your life's pathway one of peace and happiness, and this morning I feel a quiet assurance that my prayers have not been in vain.
> It is rather a strange sensation to think that today we have a daughter being married away across the sea where we may not look upon her face or clasp her hand, but there is a recompense in the thought that we are gaining a son, grown to full manhood, without our ever having had to give a thought to the many things that go to the accomplishment of that great work.
> My dear Ernest if you are all that those who know you best believe you to be, we are glad to give you our heart's treasure into your keeping.

Your father joins me in sending all blessings and good wishes as also in enclosed financial contribution to your happiness and well being.

Commending you to the care of One who always knows what is best for His children I am, not without some tears, but which I promise will be all wiped away before you see me.

Your loving Mother.[36]

CHAPTER 8

The Newlyweds (1927–1928)

After their wedding, Pauline and Ernest headed south by train with their bicycles on board. Their destination was Le Grau-du-Roi, a small fishing port in the south of France at the mouth of the Rhone River Delta. The flat land in the heart of the marshy Camargue region along the Mediterranean, full of ponds, salt marshes, and stretches of swimming beach, became a perfect getaway haven. Nearly deserted, Le Grau-du-Roi offered solitude. When they wanted company, they rode their bicycles a few miles north to the ancient thirteenth-century town of Aigues-Mortes, a walled crusader city with ramparts still intact. Walking the ramparts and fortifications provided glorious views of the Mediterranean. During their visit, the annual pilgrimage and Gypsy Festival took place some twenty-five miles away, at Saintes Maries de la Mer. Pauline and Ernest stained their faces with berries and got lost among the gypsies.

For three weeks they took in the sea and sun, including some fishing, a lot of swimming, and writing. Before departing, Ernest finished his short story "Hills Like White Elephants" and presented it as a wedding gift to Pauline. While it dealt with abortion, not a likely wedding subject, he considered it one of his "harder" stories, meaning more complex, with much of it submerged below the surface. It suited Pauline, who encouraged him to perfect his "iceberg" style of writing.

It also may have been a great gift to Pauline, transferring the guilt she felt over a possible earlier abortion. If so, most likely it was Pauline who had insisted on an abortion. Though it was a great sin for a Catholic such as Pauline, it was not so public a sin as having a baby out of wedlock, thus announcing her transgression to the entire world. Nevertheless, it must have caused tremendous guilt for Pauline—a guilt Ernest attempted to assuage by giving the insistence on the abortion to the man in the story, rather than to the girl. Hemingway's rapid-fire back-and-forth dialogue, with minimal attribution, makes it easy to get lost in who is saying what or to switch the male and female viewpoints by changing just a few pronouns and transposing the "man" and "girl" references. It must have been a fine wedding present, indeed.

Ernest and Pauline's honeymoon days also found their way into his posthumously published manuscript *Garden of Eden*. In the novel, David Bourne and his wife, Catherine, vacation at Le Grau-du-Roi and ride bicycles frequently into Aigues-Mortes. Catherine cuts her hair short, and they experiment with gender roles and being "the same guy." This is a theme Hemingway explored over and over in his novels and short stories. And it was a phrase Pauline used often in deference to Ernest's continuing fascination with gender roles and merging sexual identities. Ernest would never be able to get away from her for a minute, Pauline suggested early in their relationship, "because we are the same guy."[1] Perhaps she would not have been so quick to play his game had she realized he had played it before with Hadley. "You're a very dear much to be loved guy and I'm the guy to love you," Ernest once wrote Hadley, who reciprocated with "Anything goes doesn't it between [us] honest men."[2]

Upon return to Paris, Hemingway and his new games partner set up housekeeping at the apartment Uncle Gus's money had provided on rue Ferou, quite a step up for Ernest from the sawmill flat he once shared with Hadley. Typical of Ernest's inclination toward accidents, he had cut his foot before departing the Camargue, and it became infected, sending him to bed for ten days with swelling and fever. Since Virginia had completed much of the unpacking and organizing the apartment while they honeymooned, the two sisters shared time doting over the invalid. While recuperating, Ernest attempted to establish a comfortable pattern of correspondence with his new in-laws. His first newsy letter let them know about the wonderful honeymoon trip, progress on the book he hoped to complete by fall, and Pauline's skills in organizing the apartment. Sensitive to his own parents' reaction to his writing, he told Paul and Mary that if they did not mind the stuff he wrote—or could avoid reading it if they didn't like it—he thought he could be a pretty good son-in-law over the next ten to fifteen years.

"The only practical use I might be is to tell you something about your daughters from time to time," he offered. Thus, his first report provided details on both Pauline and Virginia, including information he knew his Catholic mother-in-law would be pleased to hear:

> Pauline is in grand condition and weighs 114 eats all we can pay for at any time, sleeps well, goes to church on Sunday, has a

fine Livret de Famille Chretien, probably misspelled, given her by the fist vicar which she is to present and have stamped every time any of her children are baptized, rode 68 kilometers on the bicycle without getting tired, is now in the other room copying a story after having gotten breakfast and cleaned things up and seems very happy. . . .

Jinny is picking up after the strain of marrying off sister in a foreign country, weighs 110, also goes to mass on Sunday, also keeps ember days, in fact having reminded us of it when there were pork chops for lunch and it hadn't been announced at church spends a lot of time chaperoning Mrs. Dunn who believes that if she will only speak English loud and clear enough any french person will understand if they really want to, and also seems happy. She worked tremendously hard over Pauline's wedding and fixing up the place.[3]

Clara Dunn, Pauline's friend from college, was visiting Europe during the summer with her mother, and Virginia drove them around to see the sights. Ernest welcomed Clara cautiously, concerned about her too-close relationship with Virginia and not quite sure what to think about her after Pauline told him earlier that Clara deplored the idea of Pauline marrying because "she counted on me in her old age."[4] While Pauline assured him that she meant the remark to be funny and that Clara actually supported the marriage, Ernest remained unsure. Pauline, Virginia, and Ernest all shared disdain for Clara's mother, who acted as though she had the "blood of English Kings in her veins."[5] Fortunately for all, she rarely visited the apartment because, as Ernest told his in-laws, three flights of stairs discouraged her, and they lacked a staff of trained servants to suit Mrs. Dunn.

Pauline and Ernest had lived in the new apartment barely three weeks before setting off for Spain. They took in the bullfights together at Pamplona, since Sunny Hemingway backed out on the opportunity. From there they made a pilgrimage, following the bulls and exploring Catholic shrines throughout the country. Their travels took them from Pamplona to San Sebastian, Valencia, Madrid, LaCoruna, Santiago de Compostela, Palencia, and then on to Hendaye Plage at the French border before returning in September to Paris.

While at Hendaye, Ernest received the first of many letters Mary Pfeiffer wrote to her son-in-law. She occasionally wrote to Pauline and Ernest jointly, but usually each received a separate letter. Mary's first letter exhibited self-consciousness about writing to someone rapidly becoming a well-known writer.

"For some time I have been wanting to answer your pleasing and most interesting letter," she told him. "But every time when I would think I was ready, a perverse little whispering imp would say, 'you cannot do that, he is a writer man and you never did anything like that before,' but this morning I reread your good letter and it seemed so easy and natural—as if you had always been writing to me that it gave me courage." [6]

Once she began, the writing was not difficult, and Mary's letter became lengthy and newsy. By the end of the first few paragraphs, Ernest became her son. She felt no hesitancy expressing all on her mind, including the desire for him to bring Pauline home. Not only did her parents want to meet him, but they wanted to be able to see their daughter in a much happier state than when she last visited them.

"Now that it is all in the past I do not mind telling you that her last visit was anything but a pleasure to me," Mary admitted to Ernest. "In fact it was the nearest thing to a nightmare that I have ever experienced in my waking moments, and I would like the remembrance to be erased from my mind in as much as it is possible and feel that it can be done by another visit better than any other way." [7]

She told Ernest he would like Northeast Arkansas, with its heavy vegetation, millions of songbirds, and brooks loaded with fish: "The main industries of a large part of our population are hunting and fishing and there is a complete absence of the elsewhere prevailing spirit of competition. For a long time, this 'content to live where life began' spirit irked me but it has passed and now after periodic excursions into the outer world, I find it restful to return." [8]

Mary's first letter to Ernest even interjected a little humor about the coming European trip for Pauline's uncle Henry and aunt Annie Pfeiffer. She thought Ernest would like Henry, even though Pauline and Virginia tended to focus on his eccentricities and ignored his many sterling qualities. "His great problem is how to dispose of his millions, now that he has them," she said. "Perhaps out of your varied experience you will be able to help him. He is really conscientious in the matter and wants to be sure that he is doing good instead of evil, and it really is not so easy. I do not know from experience but from hearing him talk about it." [9]

Later Ernest told his mother-in-law that they enjoyed their visit from Uncle Henry and Aunt Annie. He appreciated her compliment about his ability to assist Henry in disposing of millions, but his experience "has never included the disposal of anything over 150 dollars a week and that not for long." [10] Actually, Henry did quite well spending his millions without Ernest's help. Rather than giving large gifts, he spread his charitable contributions among many sources. Prior to his death in 1939, his philanthropy filled pages in his gift log. In addition to funding projects at numerous colleges, hospitals, and churches throughout the country and the world, Henry and Annie funded several buildings for a small college in North Carolina renamed Pfeiffer Junior College and later Pfeiffer University.

The rich uncle Ernest helped relieve of his money turned out to be Uncle Gus, who not only advised Ernest on finances but proffered opinions on his writing career. Shortly after the Hemingways returned to Paris, a representative of Boni & Liveright offered Ernest a contract and a three-thousand-dollar advance to return to the publishing house for his next book. Although proceeds from *The Sun Also Rises* went to Hadley, its financial success reassured Ernest that his next book with Scribner's might do equally well. Besides, with Pauline's trust fund, money received from her relatives as wedding gifts, and the likelihood of continuing financial assistance from Gus, Ernest felt flush. He thought enough of Gus's wisdom, however, to seek his advice about what to do.

Gus told Ernest he avoided setting standards for others because ninety times out of ninety they didn't work. That being said, however, he agreed that Ernest should return the check and contract. Pleased with Ernest's self-confidence, Gus told him, "At my age money does not count for much. Doing something worth while—doing well what we undertake—making progress in our life's work are infinitely more important."[11] At that point in his life, Ernest finally had both—money and literary success. Sales of *The Sun Also Rises* had hit twenty-three thousand by the publication date of his new book of short stories, *Men Without Women,* in mid-October. Three months after release, sales of *Men Without Women* had risen to fifteen thousand.

With Ernest's latest book complete, Gus lobbied him for a return to America, which still exuded "the pioneering qualities of courage, initiative and aggressiveness." Gus believed that all civilizations decayed and that Europe existed in an advanced state of decay, while America stood in the vigor of its youth. The energy and restlessness provided ample material for any writer. "You get something in Europe of course," he conceded. "In fact you get a lot—but you miss something & perhaps a lot more by not being here. At any rate there is something to be said in getting the best of both.[12]

By this time, however, Ernest thought of Europe as home, and Oak Park loomed a lifetime away. In September Ernest communicated to his parents about the divorce and remarriage earlier that year. By then, Hadley and Bumby had visited Oak Park and validated many of the rumors that had floated back to them. While she confirmed the divorce, Hadley said nothing about his marriage to Pauline, rightly leaving that detail to Ernest. During Hadley's visit, she enjoyed some private time with Sunny, who recalled Hadley telling her that "if she'd been smart, she would have encouraged Ernest, at the very first sign of his infatuation, to take Pauline off somewhere and burn out the sex appeal they had for each other."[13]

Hadley's visit to Oak Park, which occurred just weeks after Ernest's marriage to Pauline, resulted in a scathing letter to Ernest from his father in which he damned the "love pirates" to hell. "Our family has never had such an incident before and trust you may still make your get-away from that individual who split your home," Dr. Hemingway anguished. "Oh Ernest how could you leave Hadley and Bumby? Put on the Armor of God and shun Evil companions."[14]

In Ernest's response, a rambling letter in which he attempted to smooth things over, he expressed some of the deep-seated hurts inflicted by his parents' lack of support. His letter contained truths, half-truths, and outright lies in his effort to explain his feelings. He apologized for causing them so much shame and disgrace, but felt it inappropriate to discuss his troubles with them. He assured them he loved Hadley and would always take care of her and Bumby. Ernest said that even after the divorce, he would have gone back to Hadley if she had asked. He took responsibility for the breakup and added, "For over a year I had been in love with two people and had been absolutely faithful to Hadley. When Hadley decided that we had better get a divorce the girl with whom I was in love was in America. I had not heard from her for almost two months. In her last letter she had said that we must not think of each other but of Hadley." His father and mother would be much happier, Ernest proposed, if they had some confidence and pride in him as a writer and as a person instead of accusing him of pandering to the lowest tastes in his writing and committing adultery in his marriage. It's easy to wish people in hell when you don't know them, he told his parents, but Pauline was not a "love pirate" who had broken up his home: "I will never stop loving Hadley nor Bumby nor will I cease to look after them. I will never stop loving Pauline Pfeiffer to whom I am married. I have now responsibility toward three people instead of one."[15]

Unlike his family, who felt that his talents should be applied to something other than foul language and taboo subjects, the Pfeiffers read voraciously, with tolerance about what they read. When Uncle Gus read the announcement of *Men Without Women* in the September 25, 1927, *New York Times Book Review*, he placed an advance order to have copies delivered to Pauline's entire family. Ernest, nervous about how his new in-laws would react since he had never met most of them, cabled Gus with the message, "Would appreciate not sending family books until you've read yourself as some stories possibly displeasing."[16] Gus complied and canceled the advance orders but told Ernest he thought his fears groundless since practically everyone in the family was "acquainted with modern writings and literature."[17] After Gus read the book, he thought all the stories good and described "Fifty Grand" and "The Undefeated" as splendid. He quickly reinstated the order for the entire family, telling Ernest: "After reading the stories I failed to discover anything that would shock any of the relatives. Therefore to increase the sale and because I know all were interested, I sent copies as per my previous letter. Confidentially its not easy to shock anyone these days. Everyone from youths (I might almost say infants) up are sophisticated even here in 'Keep in Step' U.S.A."[18]

Even Ernest's devout Catholic mother-in-law praised him, though her tastes ran in a different direction. "I like the way you write but don't always care for your subjects," she tactfully wrote. "Bull and prize fights for instance. I always avoid the latter in the movies whenever I can but am always running into them." She was reading Ludwig's *Life of Napoleon,* she told him, and found it more to her taste. "He makes Josophine very different from what I had always supposed her to be—not so good—and that of course is always interesting."[19] Ernest told Mary Pfeiffer later that perhaps in the future he would select subject matter that appealed to her: "I understand perfectly your not liking fights nor liking much to read about them. The only reason I write about them is because I know about them and have to write about the things I know. As I get older perhaps I'll know about more things and among some of the stories there will be subjects you will like better."[20]

Ernest tried his best during fall 1927 to settle back into a writing routine and started a new novel while at Hendaye. Though he hoped to have it completed by winter's end, he was no further along at the end of January than he had been at Thanksgiving. Uncle Gus tried to provide encouragement by telling him not to worry about releasing it until he was perfectly satisfied:

> Every story & novel it seems to me must breathe the spirit of its author. Otherwise I do not see how it can be either worth while or live. So have the courage to keep at your novel until you can hand it over with the remark to yourself "It's now as I feel it should be."
>
> Henry Ford did it with his new car. His organization, his agents, the public, even his competitors, were impatient. Yet he

delayed & delayed but when the car was finally offered he said "It's the best car we know how to build."

You should also be able to say "It's the best novel I know how to write." Anything less than that fails.[21]

Interspersed with his attempts to write, Ernest and Pauline made the rounds of friends that Ernest had not yet driven off and made some new acquaintances as well. One of their new friends, Harvard graduate Waldo Peirce from Bangor, Maine, loved *The Sun Also Rises* and had sought out Hemingway. At forty-two, the painter spoke three languages and recited bawdy limericks and poems in all of them, thus endearing himself to Ernest. He further charmed the writer by creating a series of cartoon drawings for Bumby's amusement. Bumby and his mother returned to France in mid-October, and Ernest met the ship at Cherbourg. Bumby remained with Ernest and Pauline while Hadley went apartment hunting in Paris. By November she had found a flat on the sixth floor of a modern building, and Ernest helped her get settled in and presented her a copy of *Men Without Women* as a housewarming gift.

Bumby enjoyed spending time with his father and new stepmother. Later in life he recalled that, being young when his father remarried, he assumed two mothers to be the norm and viewed children with only one set of parents as underprivileged. "I think he wanted to be married to both Pauline and my mother," he surmised, "but unfortunately society didn't believe in these things." One of the earliest stories Bumby remembered about Pauline involved her possible clairvoyance. During their first year together, Pauline and his father occupied a table close to the sidewalk at Café de la Paix, near the opera house, when one of Ernest's friends stopped by. After being introduced, Pauline immediately reacted: "You're not alive. You're dead!" Everyone laughed, but later that day the man allegedly died in an auto accident.[22] Bumby believed Pauline's gift probably came from the mystical side of her mother's Irish ancestry.

Virginia Pfeiffer apparently explored this aspect of her heritage as well. During winter 1927–28 she went to a medium who told her she had a very old soul that would not be used again. Virginia's soul, the medium said, actually appeared too worn out to get her through this life. As a result, rather than being naturally kind, Virginia put on a front for people she liked. Virginia laughingly agreed that the description probably hit the mark.[23]

In mid-December the Hemingways, with Virginia and Bumby, traveled once more to Hotel Rossli at Gstaad to join the MacLeishes. Ernest left with a sore throat, which became only one of his worries when they stopped overnight at Montreux. When he got up in the middle of the night to take Bumby to the bathroom, Bumby accidentally stuck his finger in Ernest's eye and cut it with his nail. Ernest's eye began to weep and hemorrhage. To make things worse, he suffered from hemorrhoids, the grippe, and a toothache. Upon arrival in Gstaad, Ernest took to bed for a week. Pauline helped pass the time by reading aloud to Ernest at bedside and tending to Bumby. Pauline's devotion to Bumby went a long way toward easing any harsh feelings Hadley had once felt toward her, and the two women settled into an amicable relationship. "Pauline has sent splendid letters about everything a mother and ex-wife wants to know," Hadley told Ernest. "I am most grateful."[24]

At the end of January, Pauline and Virginia returned to Paris with Bumby, leaving Ernest to ski with Archibald MacLeish. "Bumbi was a lamb on the train," Pauline wrote to Ernest. "We kept waiting all day for the cross hour, but it never came. Hadley wasn't at the station so Jinny took Bumbi around the next morning. She was crazy about Hadley's apartment."[25] Things were not great at the Hemingway apartment when Pauline and Virginia returned. Burst radiator pipes had left the apartment without heat. When Ernest returned, he caught a cold in the unheated apartment and again went to bed. Pauline was getting an early dose of nursing Ernest through many illnesses and accidents.

Ernest claimed to have become Catholic in 1918 while hospitalized in Italy during World War I, and throughout 1927 he immersed himself in the church. In preparation for his marriage Ernest had attended numerous masses, met with lots of priests, given sworn baptism statements, signed annulment papers, attended confession, and participated in marriage rites. Yet nothing made a believer of him quite like the church's miraculous cure of his sexual problems experienced shortly after marriage.

Years later Ernest explained to his friend A. E. Hotchner that he enjoyed a wonderful sexual relationship with Pauline during their entire affair, but once married he had impotence problems. Ernest supposedly made the rounds from doctors to a mystic who attached electrodes to his head and feet and had him drink calves' liver blood every day. While Pauline was patient and understanding, Ernest became discouraged, so she suggested he go to the church just a few blocks away and pray: "I went there and said a short prayer. Then I went back to our room. Pauline was in bed, waiting. I undressed and got in bed and we made love like we invented it. We never had any trouble again. That's when I became a Catholic."[26]

By late fall Pauline was pregnant. In order to have their child in the United States, they planned to leave Europe in March. John Dos Passos convinced them to travel via Cuba and Key West, rather than New York. Having visited Key West in 1924, he wrote Ernest, "It's a vacation paradise, like no other place in Florida. You ought to try it."[27] Uncle Gus offered to have a new car waiting for them in Key West as a belated wedding gift. The Ford Company had begun production of its Model A on December 2, 1927, and received an unprecedented fifty thousand orders. Gus wanted Ernest to be among the first to drive the sporty new vehicle. "Aunt Louise & I are delighted the new Ford is so apropos," he told Ernest. "It's ordered for Miami in March. Rumor states Ford production below expectation so delivery may be a little late. I have confidence Ford will solve his production problems."[28] He suspected that rumors of delay were simply propaganda from "friendly" competition.

In preparation for their departure, Ernest looked through all his trunks for the two manuscripts Gus liked so well—"The Undefeated" and "Fifty Grand." He could find only the first typed draft of "The Undefeated" and an unpublished portion of "Fifty Grand." Ernest sent these and his manuscript of "The Killers" as a gift to Gus for his generosity, with the promise that if he found the other manuscripts upon their return to Paris, he would send them along as well. "You have been very good to us," Ernest wrote, "and I hope that sometime I might justify your confidence."[29]

On the same day he sent the material to Gus, Ernest returned a check for five hundred dollars to Burton Emmett, a Hemingway enthusiast who sought to purchase the manuscript of either "Fifty Grand" or "The Undefeated." Since manuscripts are byproducts for writers, Ernest told him, it would not be good to sell them. He felt it best to give manuscripts to friends, those to whom he could not afford to give other gifts. If they wanted to sell them, so be it. He felt certain, however, that the new owner, Gustavus A. Pfeiffer, would not be interested in selling.[30]

During the two weeks prior to departure, the Hemingways filled their schedule with farewells. They lunched with Gertrude Stein and Alice B. Toklas on February 29, at Pauline's invitation. On March 4, 1928, they dined at the MacLeishes'. When they returned home, Hemingway made a trip to the bathroom in the middle of the night and accidentally pulled the cord to an ancient skylight, instead of the flushbox chain. The decrepit skylight came crashing down on him, slicing a deep gash in his forehead just above his right eye, an injury that would prove fortuitous for American fiction.

Pauline tried to stop the bleeding and called MacLeish to help her get him to the hospital, where he got nine stitches. In his light-headedness and near-delirium from the wound, a flood of memories came back from his injuries during World War I, and he determined that he must write a novel about his war experience. Since the novel he had started in Spain was going nowhere, Pauline told him that they would have to "bleed him" more often if that was what it took to get his creative juices flowing.

While Virginia remained in Europe, the Hemingways boarded the Royal Mail Steam Packet *Orita* on March 17 for the eighteen-day voyage to Havana and the next stage of their new life together. The boat, small and cramped, with almost monastic quarters, made for a rough passage. Pauline wrote Ernest on ship stationery, "Cher Ami, No one would think from the magnificence of this paper that I was writing this note in squallar. . . . but here I am four days out on an English boat and not yet even the offer of a bath."[31] Ernest wrote back: "Miss Pfeiffer or may I call you 'Mrs. Hemingway'?: We are five or ten days out on our trip or tripe to Cuba which promises to extend indefinitely into the future. I have often wondered what I should do with the rest of my life and now I know—I shall try and reach Cuba."[32]

Heinrich and Barbara Pfeiffer family, 1881 reunion in Cedar Falls, Iowa. Paul Pfeiffer front right, Gus Pfeiffer front left. *(Hemingway-Pfeiffer Museum and Educational Center)*

Mary Downey Pfeiffer wedding photo, October 8, 1894. *(Hemingway-Pfeiffer Museum and Educational Center)*

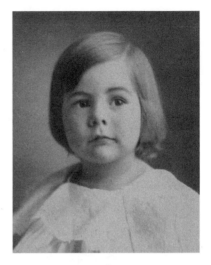

A young Pauline Marie Pfeiffer.
*(Patrick Hemingway Papers,
Department of Rare Books and
Special Collections, Princeton
University Library)*

A young Ernest Miller Hemingway.
(Ernest H. Mainland)

Pauline Pfeiffer (first row, second from right). First Communion at Visitation
Academy, St. Louis, 1903. *(Hemingway-Pfeiffer Museum and Educational
Center)*

Pauline in school uniform in front of her St. Louis home, ca. 1908. *(Patrick Hemingway Papers, Department of Rare Books and Special Collections, Princeton University Library)*

Pauline Pfeiffer, college graduation, 1918. *(Hemingway-Pfeiffer Museum and Educational Center)*

Paul and Mary Pfeiffer in front of the Piggott barn, 1930s. *(Matilda Pfeiffer Foundation)*

Pfeiffer home in Piggott, 1930s. *(Hemingway-Pfeiffer Museum and Educational Center)*

Paul and Mary Pfeiffer, with children Pauline, Karl, and Virginia, in Piggott. *(Hemingway-Pfeiffer Museum and Educational Center)*

Virginia Pfeiffer (right) and Piggott childhood friend Aylene Spence. *(Hemingway-Pfeiffer Museum and Educational Center)*

Matilda (Mrs. Karl) Pfeiffer, Pauline's sister-in-law. *(Matilda Pfeiffer Foundation)*

Gustavus Adolphus Pfeiffer. *(Hemingway-Pfeiffer Museum and Educational Center)*

Sherwood Anderson, Hemingway's early mentor, ca. 1921. *(Newberry Library)*

Ezra Pound inside Shakespeare and Company bookstore in Paris. *(Sylvia Beach Papers, Department of Rare Books and Special Collections, Princeton University Library)*

Gertrude Stein and Alice B. Toklas, 1925. *(Yale Collection of American Literature, Beinecke Rare Book and Manuscript Library)*

F. Scott and Zelda Fitzgerald and Scottie in Paris, Christmas 1925. *(F. Scott Fitzgerald Papers, Department of Rare Books and Special Collections, Princeton University Library)*

Pauline Pfeiffer modeling Paris fashions for *Vogue*, 1925. *(Patrick Hemingway Papers, Department of Rare Books and Special Collections, Princeton University Library)*

Virginia Ruth Pfeiffer in Paris, ca. 1925. *(Hemingway-Pfeiffer Museum and Educational Center)*

Hadley, Ernest, and Bumby in Schruns, Austria, 1926. *(Ernest Hemingway Photograph Collection, John F. Kennedy Presidential Library and Museum)*

Hadley Hemingway and Pauline Pfeiffer, Schruns, winter 1925–26. *(Patrick Hemingway Papers, Department of Rare Books and Special Collections, Princeton University Library)*

Pamplona, summer 1926. From left: Gerald and Sara Murphy, Pauline Pfeiffer, Ernest and Hadley Hemingway. *(Ernest Hemingway Photograph Collection, John F. Kennedy Presidential Library and Museum)*

Virginia Pfeiffer and Ernest Hemingway at Gstaad, winter 1926–27. *(Ernest Hemingway Photograph Collection, John F. Kennedy Presidential Library and Museum)*

Gerald Murphy, Ernest Hemingway, and John Dos Passos at Schruns, winter 1926–27. *(Ernest Hemingway Photograph Collection, John F. Kennedy Presidential Library and Museum)*

CHAPTER 9

Homeward Bound (1928)

After docking in Havana, Pauline and Ernest boarded the *Peninsula &
Occidental* steamship for the ninety-mile trip to Key West. Once they
cleared customs in Key West, Pauline remained with their luggage while
Ernest checked on the yellow Model A Ford Roadster supposedly waiting
for them. As Uncle Gus feared, the car had not arrived. The local Ford
dealership, Trevor and Morris Co., apologized for the delay and put the
Hemingways up in an agency-owned apartment on Simonton Street.

Ernest immediately started on his new novel while waiting on the car.
His fictional hero became Frederic Henry, an American ambulance driver
in Italy during World War I. Frederic falls in love with a British nurse,
Catherine Barkley, during his hospitalization for a leg wound suffered at the
Italian front. Though many details came directly from Ernest's experience,
the story takes place in 1915, much earlier than his Red Cross service in
Italy and prior to the Italian defeat at Caporetto that intrigued Ernest when
he was a cub reporter at the *Kansas City Star*. He quickly got into the story
and, though sweltering in Key West, described snow in the mountains of
Italy. After establishing primary characters, Ernest settled into a routine,
writing during cooler mornings and knocking off to explore the island or
fish in the afternoon.

Once called Cayo Hueso, Spanish for Bone Key, the island had a laid-
back, relaxed atmosphere with the feel of a British Colonial town. Key
West natives, called Conchs, typically eked out a living through fishing or
smuggling liquor out of Cuba. Wooden unpainted buildings set amid brilliant tropical foliage combined with the heat and humidity to give an air of
decay and life in slow motion.

While fishing off the P & O docks two weeks after arriving, an astounded
Ernest ran into his mother, his father, and his father's brother Will. Ernest
had no knowledge of his family's trip to Florida to check on land investments,

since their letter to him telling of their plans had gone to Europe. Nor had Ernest alerted his family of his final plans for returning to the United States via Key West. Since his parents had just one day in Key West, Ernest quickly picked up Pauline and took everyone to a late lunch, then gave his family a cursory tour of the island. Pauline hit it off well with Ernest's parents, despite the awkwardness and their reservations about his remarriage. Grace talked incessantly about her newest passion, painting, and asked Ernest's help in placing some of her work in a Paris show. Ernest tried to discourage her from becoming involved with the highly competitive Paris art world, but Grace held on. If she could get her work into any show at all, she could claim recognition of her work in Paris. Ernest lamely agreed to help.

Shortly after his parents' visit, Ernest and Pauline met Charles and Lorine Thompson, who immersed them in the Key West lifestyle. Charles and his family owned many businesses on the island, so he made a knowledgeable companion. The first time Ernest went deep-sea fishing with Charles, he was hooked. Lorine, a well-read Key West native who taught school, impressed Pauline as much as Charles impressed Ernest. Through Charles, Ernest became so enamored of Key West that he delayed their departure even after the car arrived. Ernest met many of the locals, including Bra Saunders, a professional fishing guide, and Joe (Josie) Russell, owner of a bar called Sloppy Joe's. They all swapped stories, and Ernest could not wait to put the colorful characters together with his literary crowd.

Dos Passos arrived first, pleased that Ernest shared his enthusiasm for Key West and happy to have an excuse to return. Several days prior to Dos Passos's departure for New York, Bill Smith arrived with his sister Katy. Waldo Peirce came shortly after Dos Passos's departure, along with painter Henry "Mike" Strater, Ernest's friend and boxing partner since the day in 1922 they had met at Ezra Pound's studio in Paris. The Smiths, Peirce, and Strater stayed for nearly a month.

Although Pauline enjoyed renewing her old friendship with Katy Smith and developing a relationship with Lorine Thompson, by late April she grew concerned about getting to Piggott. Pauline was approaching her seventh month of pregnancy, the steamy hot weather kept her uncomfortable, and she had not yet seen an obstetrician. Ernest seemed oblivious to the risks, and Pauline's gentle prodding went unheeded since Ernest's writing was going well and he was enjoying time with his friends. Rather than push him, she contacted her father for advice. If Paul Pfeiffer had any major faults, it was being an overly doting father, but this time he had cause for worry. Despite planting season in Arkansas, he rearranged his schedule, boarded a train, and was in Key West within five days of hearing from

Pauline, ostensibly because other business had come up in Florida that gave him the opportunity to travel on to Key West. He had the entire time on the train to build an image of his new son-in-law as egotistical and selfish, and the image was reinforced when he saw his daughter's condition. Paul became worried about other aspects of his character as well when he saw the way Ernest flirted with a waitress at dinner one evening. Shortly after Paul's arrival, he insisted that Pauline take the train to Piggott. The trip cross-country by car in her eighth month would be much too strenuous, he contended. Paul proposed to stay on in Key West until Ernest's guests departed, then return with him by car to Piggott to provide driving assistance to their home.[1]

Pauline's train departed on the evening of May 20, and she arrived two days later in Piggott. During her first evening on the train, she penned a letter to Ernest. "My train arrives in Jonesboro the same minute the Piggott train leaves," she told him. "I'm going to get the conductor to telegraph to hold the train—pleading the belly if necessary. Little Pilar *loves* traveling and kicks constantly. I've taken to kicking back."[2] Pauline and Ernest had decided early in the pregnancy that if their baby were a girl, they would call her Pilar, one of Ernest's pet names for Pauline. Prior to the arrival of Paul and Ernest, the family in Piggott began baby preparations. Lillie Jordan, their live-in housekeeper at the time, remembered that Mary and Pauline made baby clothes for the expected child while waiting for the men to arrive.

It is unknown what Paul and Ernest talked about during their time together in Key West, but Paul saw that Pauline loved Ernest, and apparently he decided to tolerate the man who was not only married to his daughter but about to become the father of his grandchild. Fortunately, Paul loved fishing and accompanied Ernest and his friends on one of their fishing outings, but other than that and their nicknames, they had little in common. Paul was known as "Papa Pfeiffer" or "Father Pfeiffer," and Ernest coincidentally later became known as "Papa," a name apparently bestowed upon him as early as 1926 by Gerald Murphy after hearing it used by Ernest's son. Ernest liked the ring of it and the idea of his friends looking to him as a protective figure. Some of his friends, however, thought it referred more to Ernest's need to always be in charge. That could hardly be applied to Paul Pfeiffer, a quiet, easygoing, unassuming man who would never show up as a bigger-than-life hero in any Hemingway novel. He was nonetheless a hero in Piggott, where he was regarded as an honest man who treated everyone with dignity and respect and who was quick to share any good fortune with his family and his community. Later, friends and family offered varying views of the relationship between Paul and his son-in-law. Pauline's brother, Karl, felt that Paul intimidated Ernest, who attempted to prove himself and measure up to Paul's standards. Karl's wife, Matilda, said Hemingway "was jealous of Papa because Papa was smarter than he was."[3] And Ayleene Spence, a friend close to all the Pfeiffers, believed Hemingway envied his father-in-law because "Mr. Pfeiffer had a good common knowledge of everything," and Hemingway "couldn't talk his language."[4]

Whatever their feelings about each other, they managed to forge an uneasy alliance that marked their relationship over the years. The pair drove off in the new car five days after Pauline's departure by train and made the fourteen-hundred-mile trip from Key West to Piggott in six days. It was a grueling trip, traveling along many gravel roads and spending hot nights in tourist cabins—and things didn't get any better after they pulled into Piggott. When Papa Pfeiffer and Ernest arrived on the last day of May, the town was sweltering in the midst of an unprecedented heat wave, without Key West's cooling gulf or ocean breezes. Ernest immediately wrote Maxwell Perkins that he had come to a "christ offal place."[5] In a letter to his mother the day after his arrival he wrote, "How is Art? Literature is very hot and sweaty today."[6] Ernest did not take kindly to Piggott, and Piggott did not take kindly to him. Most people were perplexed by anyone wearing sandals, shorts, and long hair. Some claimed that Hemingway narrowly avoided being arrested for indecent exposure for appearing on the town square dressed in shorts. Further, he came rolling into town in a fancy car, when most people could not afford a car, much less a brand-new Model A. He had married Paul Pfeiffer's daughter, however, so they tolerated him.

Laud Payne, editor of the local paper, referred to him as a "queer duck" who "would put on a dirty t-shirt, dirty shorts, and tennis shoes. Then he would jog right down the middle of the streets. He looked like a big bear."[7] Residents referred to him as the "big stranger from Paris" and warned their children not to go too near to him, lest they be influenced by any of his corrupting French ways.[8] Children had a totally different opinion, however. He visited with them on the square and gave them money for candy. To pass the time many afternoons, Ernest paid neighborhood children a nickel for every time they shinnied up the drainpipe at the school across the street.[9]

Ernest became anxious to move on from Piggott, but he remained unsettled about going to Kansas City for the birth and wrote his father about coming north. He asked about a good hospital in the Petoskey area, as well as availability of a cottage at Walloon Lake and whether they could get a cook and a nurse. He thought perhaps it might be best for Pauline and the baby to avoid the heat and for him to be out of Piggott after the birth. His father wrote back discouraging the Petoskey plan. Pauline would be far better off in Kansas City, or he would provide obstetrical services in Oak Park. Ernest had no interest in his father being part of the delivery and decided to stick with Kansas City.

The expectant father shelved his restlessness in Piggott and returned to his book, which ultimately became *A Farewell to Arms*. About two hundred pages of his novel, with about two hundred words per page, had been completed before Ernest left Key West. The narrative stood with Frederic wounded and transferred from a field hospital to a new Red Cross hospital in Milan. Ernest left him there while he headed to Piggott, but he hoped to be significantly further along by the time he took Pauline to Kansas City for the delivery.

With a full house in Piggott, the author found it hard to concentrate. Thus, he set up a table in the Pfeiffers' barn, directly behind the house, a relatively small thirty-two-by-forty-foot rectangular structure. Built at the same time as the house, the barn consisted of a high stall for large animals, a low stall for small animals, a passageway in between for carriages, and closed haylofts above. The Pfeiffers used the barn strictly for storage, and Ernest ensconced himself in the lower loft. Occasionally, when it was too hot in the barn, he worked on the large front porch of the Pfeiffers' house, where he caught an occasional breeze.

When writing well, Ernest retreated to the barn at 8 A.M., immediately after breakfast, and did not break until late afternoon. Family members brought sandwiches out for lunch, and Mrs. Pfeiffer sent the housekeeper to the barn at midafternoon with lemonade or ginger ale. "He was always ready to talk when I went in there," Lillie Jordan remembered. "He would quit his writing . . . and look at me and talk and ask me questions. Wednesday was my cookie baking day, so on those days Ernest would want a plate of those cookies—but they had to be warm, right out of the oven."[10]

The family ate a lot of chicken, and a neighbor brought live chickens to the Pfeiffers for Lillie to kill and prepare. She could not stomach the killing part, however, and gladly turned it over to Ernest. "I would go out there sometimes, and he would say, 'You don't have anything for me to drink this time? You must need me to kill a chicken.'" He told Lillie to let him know when the water was boiling, and he'd wring their necks: "He teased me about being such a coward to kill them chickens!"[11] Though Lillie recalled Ernest acting like he enjoyed himself there, he anxiously checked his mail each day for news from beyond Piggott. When Don Richardson, the Pfeiffer farm manager, brought mail from town, Ernest met him and quickly looked through it for anything for him. When Lillie's boyfriend wrote, Ernest taunted her by saying, "I'll give you $5 to let me read your letter." Lillie told him to keep his five dollars: "I'd say, 'Do you see your name on there?'"[12]

On some days Ernest wrote very little at all. He took off to do chores in the yard, shoot clay pigeons, or go off on a tour of the crops with Richardson. Occasionally he spent the entire day quail hunting with Virginia, back from Europe. In her last month of pregnancy, Pauline stayed behind and sewed with her mother. Lillie wondered why, since Hemingway fancied himself a great hunter, he and Virginia never came home with a single quail: "I never did cook any quails. I thought about that a lot. Why he didn't bring any quails in, I don't know. . . . But he and Virginia would talk about what they had done, which had shot first, and who got the most shots. They talked like they just enjoyed their time together. Mrs. Pfeiffer was always glad to sit and listen to them."[13]

By the time Ernest and Pauline departed Piggott, he had completed more than one hundred additional pages of his novel. His fictional hero's relationship with Catherine developed while Ernest wrote in Piggott, and Catherine became an amalgam of Agnes von Kurowsky, Pauline, and Hadley. Shortly before Ernest left Piggott for the birth of his child, his fictional heroine told Frederic, "I'm going to have a baby, darling. It's almost three months along."[14] Ernest told Waldo Peirce he had "worked like a bastard in Piggott" and hoped to have the book finished within the month. He wanted the novel done so that after the birth he could go west, perhaps to Idaho, to hunt and fish. "Piggott is a great place to shoot," he said, "but the law is on," meaning strict enforcement of the hunting season.[15]

Two weeks before her delivery, Pauline and Ernest arrived in Kansas City by car during the Republican National Convention, which resulted in Herbert Hoover's nomination. They settled in with Malcolm and Ruth White Lowry at their home on Indian Lane, a fashionable area of Kansas City. The Lowrys were related to Ernest by marriage through his uncle Tyler, who got Hemingway his first job with the *Kansas City Star*. Ernest's relatives introduced Pauline to Dr. Don Carlos Guffey, who eventually delivered both her children.

Paul and Mary Pfeiffer waited anxiously in Piggott, with good reason to worry about the delivery of a healthy child. Just a few days before Ernest and Pauline left for Kansas City, the Pfeiffers' son, Karl, and his wife, Matilda, had a son in New Jersey, born on June 9 with spina bifida. They named him Paul Mark after his grandfather Pfeiffer. Paul and Mary worried about the additional burden his affliction placed on their son and daughter-in-law, who had lost their oldest child, four-year-old Margaret, to the same illness just eight months earlier. With a healthy and active daughter, three-year-old Barbara, a new baby with special needs, and grief over the death of their first child, Karl and Matilda faced difficult times ahead without Paul and Mary close by to help them.

Pauline went into labor the morning of June 27, and Ernest took her to Research Hospital. After Pauline endured labor all day, Dr. Guffey asked Ernest when he returned from supper for permission to do a Caesarian section. Their nine-pound son Patrick arrived at 7:30 P.M. to an exhausted Pauline. That same evening in Houston, Al Smith received the Democratic nomination for president.

Until Pauline could travel and return to Piggott, Ernest kept his in-laws informed of her progress. Once again, telegrams, letters, best wishes, and checks poured in from the relatives. A letter addressed to "Dear Ernest" came from his mother-in-law, while a letter addressed to "My dear Pauline & All" came from his father-in-law. Mary expressed her sincere appreciation to Ernest for keeping her informed of every detail of Pauline's delivery and recovery. She told him that as soon as Pauline gained strength he must bring her and the baby to Piggott so he could "hie away to the woods and the streams or wherever the call of the wild beckons—and rest up and get back to normalcy."[16] Paul's letter expressed relief, warning his daughter not to get up and around too soon, and he enclosed a birthday check for Patrick and an interest check of $138.48 due Pauline from family investments.

In response to his mother-in-law's concerns about what effect the Caesarian would have on Pauline, Ernest wrote: "The doctor said the wound will take ten days to heal normally. Then she should stay in the hospital another week or ten days and then she can come to Piggott but must stay upstairs and not do any walking up or down stairs or lifting. The doctor said she shouldn't have another baby for three years if she did not want to become a cripple or a corpse."[17]

Uncle Gus and Aunt Louise sent three checks: one for Ernest to pay some of the medical bills, one to Pauline for pin money, and one for one hundred dollars to start Patrick's bank account and put him on the road to "thrift and wealth."[18] Gus told them Patrick's birth in a town where Herbert Hoover had received the Republican nomination, on the date when Al Smith became the Democratic candidate, should bode well for Patrick's prospects for a future presidency. Several weeks later Gus sent a more detailed letter, saying: "Aunt Louise and I are pleased that Pauline triumphed over the trying and serious time. Such suffering as she passed through and the sympathetic agonies I know you suffered will endear Patrick to you both, for you paid a dear price and I know with Patrick was born a new love, a love which makes a new world for you both."[19]

Ernest reported the difficulties of Patrick's birth in graphic detail to his friend Waldo Pierce, whom he addressed as "Capitalista Enorme." And though his reference to the disruption of his novel was no doubt in jest, it subtly conveyed some sense of his underlying priorities throughout the ordeal: "Eighteen hours of labor with the thermometer at 97 then no results at all—Patrick built like a brick shit house across the shoulders—finally the old cesaerian. Nothing for a guy to watch when his affections are involved. Nor in any sense the ideal way to kill time while working on a novel."[20]

Nevertheless, Ernest was back to being the dutiful father when he wrote his parents on July 4 describing a big, strong, and healthy boy: "He is too big in fact as he nearly killed his mother. They had to do a cesaerian finally and I have been very worried about Pauline since but today her temperature is down to 99 8/10 and the gas distention is subsiding. She has suffered terribly."[21] Once more, he took the opportunity to dig his parents regarding their inquiry as to when he might be able to come and see them. "I saw my time clear to run up to Oak Park to pay a visit a while back before the baby was born but when I wrote you advised against it," he chided them. "We can do no jumping around with a baby that age in the summer time and wherever we go must stay for a while. I wrote Dad from Piggott asking about getting a cottage at Walloon but was discouraged."[22] In the follow-up letter he added, "Am taking Pauline and Patrick to Piggott then going out somewhere where I know no one and try and finish the book. I'd love to come to Windemere but can't work and see anyone and would be as pleasant for you to have around as a bear with carbuncles until this book is finished."[23]

On July 18, Ernest drove his new family back to Piggott. While in Kansas City, his hero Frederic Henry returned to the front lines and became part of the Italian retreat at Caporetto, and Catherine left hospital duty in Milan due to the advanced stage of her pregnancy. By the time Ernest and Pauline headed back to Piggott, he had completed 478 pages of the novel and was about two-thirds finished.

"I am no nearer finished on my fucking book than ever," he wrote Waldo Peirce from Piggott. "The bloody heat ruins my head. Also the cries of Patrick." He complained that it was ninety-four degrees when they left Kansas City, ninety-three degrees in Piggott, and never below ninety degrees. "Pauline is well now and getting strong," he added. "Patrick is like a bull, bellows like a bull too. Why you ever wanted to be a father I don't appreciate."[24] Ernest also told Peirce that he would leave in two days for Wyoming. He wasn't sure where in Wyoming, but someplace with a good stream where he could fish half the day and work the other half. And someplace without "*muchachos*" yelling all the time. Some of Ernest's complaining was bluster for his friends. Lillie, the housekeeper, recalled that when he arrived back in Piggott with the new baby, the proud father could not stop talking about him. "Ernest thought he was great," she said. "He was going to teach him how to quail hunt."[25]

First, however, he needed to finish his book without disruptions. Ernest and Pauline celebrated their birthdays on July 21 and 22, and three days later he headed for Wyoming. His wife and son stayed behind in Piggott, along with the first 486 pages of his novel. After once having his manuscripts stolen while married to Hadley, he took no chances on carrying around the unfinished novel until he settled somewhere.[26] Leaving it behind also gave Pauline a chance to read through it more carefully, now that she was feeling better.

Ernest hooked up with Bill Horne in Kansas City to accompany him on the trip west, with the understanding that Pauline would join him upon completion of the book if she felt well enough to travel, leaving the baby with her sister. As Ernest prepared to leave, Pauline wrote to her mother-in-law, apologizing that they could not make it to Michigan or Illinois. "A few months' old baby is nothing, or rather something, to travel with. For the moment I have just dumped Patrick on my family, saying 'Take him.' And am courting the elusive strength."[27]

Pauline's family determined to make sure she followed doctor's orders. In her handwritten letter to Ernest shortly after his departure, Pauline complained that she wanted to use the typewriter, but it was upstairs, along with everything else she seemed to need. "Mother is a dragon about the steps," she complained. "I haven't been allowed upstairs since you left. I'm not allowed to do anything. But I'm getting very strong, and soon there will be a big fight, and then I can do all the things I want."[28]

Pauline missed Ernest tremendously and anxiously sought to join him in Wyoming. "With you away it seems as though I was just a mother, which is certainly not very gripping," she wrote. "But in three weeks I'll begin to get ready to go to Wyoming, where I shall be just a wife."[29] Pauline's statement gives a strong hint that she entered into motherhood primarily because she thought it was what Ernest wanted, and it was a way to hold onto him, even though that had not worked for Hadley. At least having a child by Ernest gave Pauline the same leverage that Hadley had to keep him always in her life. Once Ernest arrived in Wyoming, Pauline shipped his manuscript and followed up with a letter letting him know it had been insured for $1,000, the highest insurance she could get, rather than an insult to his literary endeavor. "It cost me $2.38—almost what a baby costs," she told him. "And about babies—Patrick is an angel, enormously healthy and strong, and *good*. Not at all the baby I expected we'd have. He's really remarkably little work."[30]

Patrick fared well with a house full of women, including Mary, Pauline, Virginia, and Lillie. Lillie usually took the 5 P.M. feeding, since that was when the family had its dedicated meal together. Later, after Pauline joined Ernest in Wyoming, Lillie also took over when Virginia and Mrs. Pfeiffer left the house. If Lillie took the baby out for fresh air, it had to be on the upper balcony of the house. "At first I couldn't figure that out," she said. "But later when the Lindbergh kidnapping took place, I realized they must have been concerned about such things."[31]

With Ernest's approval Pauline decided to have Patrick baptized in the chapel at her parents' home before her departure for Wyoming. The baptism took place on August 14, and Pauline pronounced it a great success: "He didn't make a noise until the priest said 'Patrick, do you renounce the Devil with all his works and prophets,' and he gave a little groan and a little whine of protest. Ernest, he is an *angel* child. He has never had the colic once, and hardly ever cries. He smiles all the time, especially at Mother, and he weighs 13 lbs. Jinny was cutting out the two o'clock feeding because the doctor said he gains too fast, and he has started on orange juice. I think we may like him very much."[32]

After Patrick's baptism, Pauline left him in the care of her mother and sister and headed to Wyoming. Despite having just given birth, she determined to join Ernest for as much hunting and fishing as she could stand. It was the first of many times in their marriage where Pauline had to choose between the famous writer and their children. She usually chose the writer, leaving their children to the care of others.

Well before Pauline left Piggott, Ernest sent her a telegram saying he would ship "wading pants" for her use when they fished in Wyoming. Pauline had trouble understanding the telegraph operator and thought the message said "wedding pants," which became their ongoing joke. Once on her way, Pauline wrote Ernest that she looked forward to spending a glorious month with him, dressed in her "wedding pants" day and night. Never mind, she said, that they made her look like a duffle bag with feet.[33] Thus, the *Vogue* woman became a *Field and Stream* wader to suit Ernest.

Pauline stopped in St. Louis for some dental work and heard all the gossip about writer Ernest Hemingway, who had recently married his second St. Louis wife. By then, wags who had read *The Sun Also Rises* noted similarities between the fictional Jake Barnes and Hemingway. They also speculated that Barnes's free-spirited love interest, Lady Brett Ashley, must be based on Ernest's new wife, who had stolen him from Hadley. Pauline chose not to point out that it was Lady Duff Twysden who had captured Ernest's attentions during the hedonistic summer in Spain that inspired the book.[34]

By the time Pauline arrived in Wyoming, Ernest needed only a few days to finish his novel. After getting his hero through the retreat at Caporetto, Ernest reunited Frederic and Catherine at Stresa, Italy, where they escaped by rowing across Lago Maggiore into Switzerland. On the same day Pauline departed for Wyoming, Catherine's labor pains began in Switzerland. Ernest left his fictional characters in the hospital delivery room while he took two days off to spend time with Pauline, then finished the novel in a three-day frenzy of writing.

He knew how the novel would end after Patrick's birth "almost killed his mother" earlier that summer in Kansas City. He gave Pauline's Caesarian delivery to Catherine, but his novel played out the alternative scenario that had scared him during the entire time he spent with Pauline in the Kansas City hospital. After Catherine suffered all day in labor, delivery resulted in a stillborn boy, strangled by the umbilical cord. A defeated Frederic Henry left the hospital briefly, only to return and find Catherine dead.

CHAPTER 10

Family Matters (1928–1929)

With the first draft of his World War I novel behind him, Ernest needed a break to recover from the stress of writing, so he and Pauline hunted and fished their way through Wyoming for the next month. Pauline found the trip somewhat grueling, but the fresh air had a therapeutic effect, and she enjoyed being with her husband. They established one of their base camps at a ranch called the Wigwam on the eastern side of the Bighorn Mountains near Sheridan.

Elsie Byron, who helped her father operate the Wigwam, recalled that Pauline had a great sense of humor. One day as Ernest and his wife sat in the car with Elsie's father, they encountered a sheepherder who began swearing. Her father quickly chastised him about swearing in front of a lady. The sheepherder glanced over at Pauline and said, "I don't see no lady."[1] In her overalls and denim shirt, with her hair cropped like a boy's and wearing a French cap, Pauline hardly looked like a former *Vogue* fashion writer.

Elsie and others at the ranch admired Pauline's spunk, although they wondered why she tolerated Ernest's boorish behavior. "I've never seen anybody act like Ernest did," Elsie recalled. "He snatched papers and photos from Pauline while she was looking at them. She'd be looking at something and he'd grab it right out of her hands and look at it first, and then hand it back. I used to get mad at him over that, but you couldn't be mad at him for long no matter what he did."[2]

While Ernest and Pauline stayed in Wyoming, Virginia concentrated on getting Patrick "raised" by the time his parents returned from their trip. She sent detailed reports on her progress to Pauline and Ernest and told them Patrick had everyone in the house well trained. He had settled into a routine and made sure everyone followed it precisely. If not put out on the swing for his amusement hour at 4 P.M., for example, the baby wailed until he got his way. Virginia bragged about his handsome eyes, his mouth like Bumby's, and his beautiful skin that browned in the sun. "And I keep him KLEEN," she said. "I have found a little Dutch Cleanser a great help for the knees."[3]

Virginia also recruited friends to assist with Patrick's care, including Ayleene Spence, who recalled, "Virginia loved babies; she loved children; and she loved her family. She wanted Pauline to go with Ernest when he wanted her to go."[4] Virginia and Ayleene passed many afternoons pushing Patrick's baby carriage around the Piggott square, showing him off to merchants and townspeople. The trips inevitably included stops at Reve's Drug Store on the north side of the square and Potter's Drug Store to the east. Both had soda fountains, famous for cherry cokes, and both served as gathering spots for ladies of the town in the afternoons. Virginia and Ayleene timed their trips to make sure everyone had the opportunity to fawn over young Patrick.

When Ernest and Pauline returned to Piggott in September, they found that Patrick had doubled his weight in three months, hardly ever cried, and thrived on his new formula. "Patrick is a fine kid," Ernest crowed to his sister Sunny. "I am thinking of advertising as a male parent—Exceptional children for All Mothers—are your children deformed, underweight, rickety: E Hemingway son of Grace Hall Hemingway the Paintress—perhaps He can help You."[5] Ernest told Sunny he planned a drive to Oak Park in about two weeks, but for the time being had to stay in Piggott to help with the baby. When his mother-in-law and sister-in-law departed on a two-week trip, Ernest and Pauline shared parenting responsibilities for the first time.

With the first draft of his yet-unnamed novel completed more than a month earlier, Ernest determined to delay revisions until they returned to Key West. Pauline and Ernest had agreed while on their western trip to winter in Key West, rather than immediately return to Paris, where they were likely to encounter miserable weather and attendant colds and sore throats. In Key West Ernest could revise without interruption and would be closer to his publisher. Ernest worked for much of the remaining time in Piggott on short stories, including a story started on the Pfeiffers' front porch about a French bootlegger and his wife. He based the story, later titled "Wine of Wyoming," on a French couple he and Pauline had met in Wyoming, but it had elements of the Pfeiffers as well. Like the couple in his story, the Pfeiffers drank in moderation, supported Al Smith in the upcoming presidential election, and dealt daily with being a Catholic family in Protestant country.

When on break from writing, Ernest often tried trap shooting with help from locals, including eighteen-year-old Otto (Toby) Bruce. Bruce sometimes threw clay pigeons for Ernest all afternoon out by the Pfeiffer barn. He loved putting Hemingway to the test, never throwing the targets in the same pattern twice, but Ernest rarely missed the mark. The author took a particular liking to Toby, or "Tobes" as he called him, and the two formed a friendship that lasted throughout Ernest's life. Some who hunted with Hemingway in Piggott were not as quick to praise his skills. Long after his first visit, locals continued telling tales about how the men who hunted with Hemingway always got their limit in a short while. Rather than wait all day on Hemingway, they started shooting at the same time, letting him believe his shots brought the birds down.[6]

Piggott residents also recounted the story of Hemingway going quail hunting with the owner of Reve's Drug Store. The two drove out to Big Slough Ditch near Piggott in Hemingway's Model A touring car. The pair shot so many quails they barely had room to sit in the car. When they returned to town, both men proud of themselves, Hemingway's father-in-law expressed displeasure. Like Clarence Hemingway, Paul Pfeiffer believed hunting a fine sport, provided you killed no more than you could eat.[7]

About mid-October, Ernest loaded up the Model A and headed to Oak Park to see his family, leaving his 652-page manuscript in a bank vault in Piggott. In the previous six months, Ernest had put 9,000 miles on the new car, and the drive north to Oak Park added another 550 miles. "The only trouble is that after a trip I do not know whether to put the car in a garage or simply touch a match to it," he told his sister Sunny.[8] Pauline and Patrick remained behind in Piggott to enable Pauline to assist Virginia. After a bout with tonsillitis, Virginia had decided to have her tonsils out in Jonesboro, 50 miles south of Piggott. Pauline sat with her at the hospital until Virginia had recuperated sufficiently to return home.

Once her sister recovered, Pauline again left baby Patrick with her mother and Virginia and took the train to join her husband in Chicago. Ernest insisted on meeting Pauline there and staying at the Whitehall Hotel, rather than taking her to Oak Park or even letting his parents know she had arrived. He did not want to explain to his parents why they had not brought their new grandson to see them. Nor did he want to take Pauline to the family home in Oak Park, where he had just stayed a week, having enough of his family's company. After a quick two days in Chicago, Pauline and Ernest left the Model A and took a train to the East Coast to make the rounds of friends. They shared time with the MacLeishes, who now lived in Conway, Massachusetts, then headed to New York to take in the fights at Madison Square Garden and conduct business with Maxwell Perkins, including negotiating the serialization of Ernest's novel.

While the Hemingways visited New York, Herbert Hoover defeated Al Smith for the presidency of the United States, and the election ended several months of good-natured arguing in the Hemingway and Pfeiffer households. Paul and Mary Pfeiffer favored Al Smith, and their son-in-law agreed. Not only a Democrat and a Catholic, Smith had a German father and an Irish mother, like the Pfeiffer children. Though Paul preferred not to put religious or political labels on himself and actually possessed great admiration for Republican president Abraham Lincoln, he believed that Al Smith would make a "safe" president. Gus Pfeiffer, on the other hand, remained a staunch Republican and touted a Hoover presidency from the day of his nomination. He took great delight in expressing his views to the rest of the family, including Ernest, telling him a few weeks before the election that he couldn't accept Smith's position that Prohibition was a foolish attempt to legislate morality. "Maybe you can convert me," Gus told Ernest, " or perhaps I can convince you or, maybe, after we have cussed and discussed it, you will continue to think as you now do and I will be on the same side as I now am."[9]

With the political contest over, Ernest, Pauline, and Mike Strater took the train from New York to join F. Scott Fitzgerald at Princeton for another highly anticipated contest—the November 17 football game with Yale. Strater and Fitzgerald, both Princeton alumni, celebrated the twelve-to-two win with their friends and had a boisterous time on the train to Philadelphia before heading on to the Fitzgeralds' Ellerslie Mansion on the Delaware River. When Ernest and Pauline boarded the train for home the next morning, Ernest was suffering from an acute hangover.

Before leaving the East Coast, Ernest sent a letter to his sister Sunny in Oak Park asking her to have the Model A serviced for him and inviting her to quit her job in the dental office and come to Key West. He offered to match her salary if she typed his recently completed manuscript and helped Pauline look after Patrick. Sunny agreed, and when the train pulled into Chicago, Pauline boarded a train to Piggott, while Ernest met his sister, retrieved the car, and drove to Piggott with her to pick up Pauline, the baby, and the manuscript.

Ernest drove during the day, and Sunny drove at night. Their conversation on the trip focused largely on their parents. Ernest worried about their father's health and erratic behavior during his visit, and Sunny let him know that some of their father's problems stemmed from financial setbacks. Clarence's investments in Florida had gone south, and when he asked his wealthy brother to help him out, his brother refused.[10] As they approached Piggott, Ernest became excited about getting there, and Sunny felt apprehension, particularly since she wondered if Pauline knew of Ernest's plans for her to assist with the book and the baby in Key West and perhaps accompany them to Europe. "As I looked back on it all later," she said, "I realized she [Pauline] didn't have the whole picture."[11]

The Pfeiffers did their best to make Sunny feel at home, and Ernest insisted on taking her on a sunrise duck hunt: "I remember—still with fright—the overloaded, small boat that took us to the blind. Ernie wanted me to have a good time, but I really felt unwanted by Pauline from the moment I entered her life. It didn't help any when I shot a live decoy by mistake."[12]

After several days in Piggott, they loaded up for the trip back to Key West. Ernest and Sunny drove from Piggott to Jacksonville, Florida, where they met Pauline and Patrick, traveling by train. Sunny joined Pauline and Patrick on the train, while Ernest drove the rest of the way alone. Pauline's behavior on the train surprised Sunny, which she later attributed to her own inexperience and naiveté. As they left the dining car, a male passenger invited Pauline to join him for a nightcap in the club car. Pauline accepted, leaving Sunny to look after Patrick. Sunny waited for her for what "seemed hours. . . . She finally appeared. She told me nothing, and I told Ernest nothing about our 'get-acquainted' evening."[13]

When all arrived in Key West and Ernest wrote his mother-in-law regarding the trip from Piggott, he could not resist adding a note for her to pass on to his father-in-law. Rather than the six days it had taken to drive from Key West to Piggott with Paul Pfeiffer's assistance, Ernest had made the trip from Piggott to Miami in only three days, driving a grueling 527 miles on the last day of the trip.[14] Thus, Ernest won at least one competition with his father-in-law.

During the Hemingways' time away, Lorine Thompson had found them a place at 1100 South Street that suited their growing family. As soon as they arrived at the house, Sunny received instructions on the care and feeding of Patrick. They placed his bed in her bedroom at the opposite end of the house to keep the noise down for Ernest. They also relocated the typewriter and table to Sunny's room so she could make manuscript changes.[15]

Anxious to concentrate on his revisions and tired of travel, Ernest learned shortly after their return to Key West of Bumby's expected arrival in New York for a visit to his second family. Bumby had celebrated his fifth birthday in October, and Ernest sent money for his party and presents, along with a suggestion that Hadley send him to Key West for six months. Hadley first declined a six-month stay as too long for him to be away. When Bumby developed a chest cold in the miserable November Paris weather, however, she decided that extended time in the Key West climate might be good for him. Hadley wrote Ernest that unless she heard differently from him, they would depart on the *Ile de France* November 28.

By the time Ernest got her message in Key West, he barely had time to board the train back to New York. Bumby and his mother stayed a few days in New York visiting friends before meeting Ernest at Pennsylvania Station to make the exchange. After a brief visit with Hadley to catch up on Paris happenings, Ernest took his son for some Christmas shopping before reboarding the Havana Special back to Key West. The train made stops in Newark and Trenton, New Jersey, before a porter arrived at Ernest's berth with a telegram from Oak Park passed down the line, informing him that his father had died that morning.

Ernest departed the train at Philadelphia, where he could make connections for Chicago, and entrusted Bumby to the porter to see that he arrived safely in Key West. He cabled his wife and sister in Key West, as well as his ex-wife, still in New York, to let them know what had happened and inform them of arrangements for Bumby. Pauline cabled back, "WILL MEET BUMBI SATURDAY SUNNY GREATLY RELIEVED YOU WENT HOME LOVE AND SYMPATHY TO YOUR MOTHER = PAULINE."[16]

Upon arrival in Chicago, Ernest learned that Clarence had committed suicide. Though concerned about his father's health when he visited Oak Park, Ernest did not know that his father suffered from diabetes and angina. As a doctor, Clarence knew what lay ahead for him and refused to discuss his health with family members. Nor did Clarence discuss with his family the unpaid bills piling up on his desk. Ernest blamed both himself and his mother for not recognizing the depths of his father's despair. He stayed in Oak Park long enough to tend to funeral arrangements, tidy up his father's affairs as best he could, and get the family back on its feet. He also remained long enough for a falling out with his sister Marcelline over who should make many of the decisions—the oldest child or the oldest son.

Pauline did what she could from Key West, and it relieved Hadley's mind to receive a telegram from her that Bumby had arrived safely. Pauline then turned her attention to Sunny, the only Hemingway sibling who could not get to Oak Park in time for the funeral. "For a few days, in Ernie's absence, Pauline was very kind and considerate of me and I appreciated it," Sunny recalled. "She even called in a doctor to quiet me down—for I was terribly distraught."[17]

When Ernest returned to Key West, a letter from his mother-in-law was among the condolences: "It was with deep regret that we heard the sad news of your father's tragic death. Poor man, what he must have suffered. No doubt his mind gave way under the constant nerve strain to which he had been subjected for so long a time. God knows everything and His mercy is above all His works. He will not hold him responsible for the rash act of a disordered mind. I have prayed for him that his spirit may have rest—and will have a mass offered for the repose of his soul. Please accept and extend to your sister our heartfelt sympathy in your sad affliction. Lovingly yours, Mother Pfeiffer."[18]

Ernest wrote to Mary Pfeiffer, admitting, "I was awfully fond of my father. . . . Pauline probably wrote you all about everything but I wanted to send just a line to tell you that I want to write and I will write—but just now I feel so very bad that I can't write a letter."[19] He then added a postscript much longer than the letter. Though ostensibly written to his mother-in-law, it seemed more an attempt to organize his thoughts and come to grips with the nature of his father's death and Ernest's sense of guilt and loss. Ernest emphasized how he had written a long letter to his father about his family finances en route to New York and assured him not to worry because he could always send him a cash advance from Scribner's. According to Ernest, the letter had arrived at the house twenty minutes after his father shot himself. He grappled with his belief that his father might still be alive if the letter had arrived sooner. Ernest's brother Leicester remembered the situation a bit differently, however, indicating that a letter had arrived from Ernest that morning, but their father had placed it unopened on his bedside table, along with other unopened mail.[20] Even so, no one who saw the letter later recalled it having anything to do with finances, but rather Ernest's schedule in New York.[21] For Ernest to agonize that he or anyone else could have made a difference was futile.

Uncle Gus sent condolences as well, adding that he would have helped Ernest's father with financial aid, if only he had known. "Alas the opportunity is now gone," he wrote. "I know as you that temporarily your Father lost his mental control. May I hope the memory of past happy associations & time, the comforter of all our sorrows, will help you to bear your grief. How tragic your letter arrived late."[22] While the death of his father drew Ernest closer to some members of the Pfeiffer family, it appeared to make it even harder for him to develop a comfortable relationship with Paul Pfeiffer. Looking upon Mary Pfeiffer as a second mother came easily, but he apparently did not want to dishonor his father's memory by calling anyone else "Father." Ernest's first letter to both Pfeiffer in-laws after losing his father was awkwardly addressed "Dear Mother Pfeiffer and Patrick's Grandfather."[23]

Ernest found concentration on his book difficult after his father's death, but he completed pencil edits by January 4, and Pauline and Sunny finished typing about one-third of it. At that rate, Ernest hoped to be done by the end of the month. He wrote Maxwell Perkins and suggested that he come to Key West to pick up the manuscript personally and enjoy some fishing. Max arrived on the first of February, read the manuscript, and thought it the best book Ernest had written to date. Ernest told his mother-in-law the book finally had a name as well: "The book—so far and I hope so good—is called A Farewell To Arms. . . . I've read the book so many times and the title so many that I'm not an authority on either. . . . It is written in the first person. I wish I could write a novel in the 3rd person but haven't enough skill to yet. But is not autobiographical."[24]

No one expressed more pleasure over completion of Ernest's novel than Uncle Gus, who suggested that Ernest must feel great relief, even though he had yet to face the reaction of publishers and the public. That hardly mattered, though, Gus told him, because "popular or not popular the book still remains an expression and part of yourself. Through it you express your observations, your judgment of a condition and to a greater or less extent yourself, and I know it's honest all the way through and that's what's important."[25]

In appreciation for his financial and moral support, Ernest determined that the dedication should be to G. A. Pfeiffer. He explained to Max that Pauline's uncle had come to Paris to check on her when the family learned that she planned to marry "a citizen who had been married before, hailed as a drunk and a man of bad associates by the critics, etc."[26] Ernest recalled that Gus came to the dreadful bachelor apartment where he lived, stayed about ten minutes, apologized for disturbing his work, then cabled the family that Pauline had picked a fine man and the family should be proud and happy: "So I owe him a couple of books on that anyway."[27] Flattered by Ernest's proposed tribute, Gus suggested a dedication to someone more deserving, indicating he already felt more than repaid for the support he provided. "Suppose we leave it this way," he wrote. "You dedicate it to the one you would most enjoy dedicating it to. . . . If it happens you choose my name, I'll of course feel proud. But if it's some other name I'll take equal pride in the success of your book."[28] Hemingway considered his advice and then later wrote to Max, "The dedication stands to G. A. PFEIFFER. There couldn't be a less graceful name, nor a much better man. I would use the full name but it happens to be Gustavus Adolphus."[29]

With the book complete, Ernest began a month of fishing with cronies. Along with Maxwell Perkins came visits from Mike Strater, Waldo Peirce, John Dos Passos, and Katy Smith. This time Dos Passos remained long enough to develop a relationship with Katy that resulted in their marriage later that year. Even Gus joined Ernest and his friends for a few days of fishing. To his delight, he caught a sunfish that Ernest mounted and sent to Gus's New York apartment, along with photos of the event captured by Waldo Peirce. It thrilled Hemingway and his fishing partners that Gus took to the fishing experience. With Gus in the crew, they most likely would not have to worry about daily expenses or a suitable craft. "I know damned well he would get us a boat next time and that is what we really need," Hemingway told Peirce. ". . . I think it will make a hell of a lot of difference. I know Uncle Gus would stake us to one."[30]

Prior to one of the spring fishing expeditions, Sunny had an accident in the Model A Ford after driving Ernest and his fishing partners to the dock. The car required substantial repairs, but Gus felt it was time for a new car anyway. The Model A, not quite a year old, had more miles than many cars accumulate in a lifetime. He sent Ernest a check for the purchase, telling him that anything left could be spent on something of his choosing. He jokingly added, "If Pauline is good, give her $1.00."[31] During his Key West visit, Gus also gave Sunny a one-hundred-bill toward her trip to Europe. "It was the first hundred-dollar bill I'd ever seen, let alone held," she recalled. Unsure whether or not to accept it, she asked her brother's advice and heard that she should "accept it with grace and dignity."[32]

By spring Ernest's reputation as both a writer and a sportsman appeared solidly established. A February front-page headline in the *Key West Citizen* proclaimed, "Visitor Lands Large Sailfish: Ernest Hemingway Successful in Hauling in Big Monster." The article went on to say that Ernest had landed an eight-foot sailfish, along with kingfish, groupers, bonitos, and other varieties. A month later the *Key West Citizen* printed another front-page article, this one written by New York columnist O. O. McIntyre, reportedly the highest-paid columnist in the country. The lengthy column began:

> NEW YORK—New York had a visiting novelist this winter who made no effort to be a bright boy at the tea table, spurt epigrams or comment on crude American manners. He was Ernest Hemingway who has a cherubic moon of a face and a cocoonish mustache and, although a product of Chicago, lives in Paris and made his reputation there.
>
> Hemingway is one of the fabled writing geniuses in real life who cares nothing for financial rewards of his trade. Since his sudden success he has been besieged with offers from magazines and book publishers, but dodges them to slip off to Florida on fishing expeditions.[33]

His disregard for money did not apply to the support from Uncle Gus that enabled him to "slip off to Florida on fishing expeditions." The column went on to say that Hemingway appeared to live life on his own terms, writing during breaks from fishing and bullfights. By the time this article appeared, Ernest longed for a return to Spain for the bullfights. Pauline wanted to go back to Europe as well. She missed their spacious apartment with all its fine antiques. She missed Virginia as well, who had returned to Paris in January. The Hemingways wrote to Pauline's parents that they would be leaving the first week of April. The Pfeiffers did not share their enthusiasm, but knew they had faint hope of keeping them in the country. "We sure will miss you folks but little Patrick most of all," Paul Pfeiffer wrote. "Mother and I often think of him. How he always expected his piggy back ride when I came home."[34]

Ernest assured his in-laws that they would be back the following year, and Patrick would be even better by the time they saw him again. He began shipping all his hunting gear to Piggott for the Pfeiffers to "store as hostages" until they returned in time for quail and duck hunting.[35]

Shortly before the couple's departure, Mary Pfeiffer penned a letter that awaited them when they arrived in Paris. "I hope you are both returning feeling that your visit was a success," she said. "I really think you ought to feel that way when you look at Patrick quite perfect in every way—and when you think of your finished book, Ernest, also quite perfect in its own way."[36]

CHAPTER 11

Return to Paris (1929)

The *Yorck* steamed out of Havana Harbor on April 5, 1929, with the Hemingway entourage, including Ernest, Pauline, Bumby, Patrick, and Sunny. Ernest and Pauline shared a stateroom; Sunny and the children berthed on a lower deck. The strain of the past year had caught up with Pauline, and she remained in bed during most of the voyage, leaving primary care of the children to Sunny. If Sunny wanted a break while the children napped, a steward stood guard and let her know if they awakened. Pauline revived in the evenings while the children slept and joined festivities aboard ship—perhaps out of self-defense.

Ernest enjoyed conversing with all the passengers, men and women, in English, French, Spanish, and German. Pauline knew better than to leave him totally alone, lest he find females on board charmed by more than his language skills. Ernest particularly delighted in playing big brother to his sister, who had never sailed before. Along with the new experiences of a captain's party and playing dominos in the lounge with a Frenchman, Sunny observed a man soliciting on behalf of two beautiful females. Watching the maneuvering proved amusing, as well as "educational," Sunny recalled.[1] After a sixteen-day voyage, they arrived at Boulogne, stayed the night, and went on to Paris the next day. Fortunately, Virginia Pfeiffer and Clara Dunn, who had arrived three months earlier, were staying in the apartment at rue Feron to ensure that everything was in working order by the time Pauline and Ernest arrived. Their thoughtfulness helped Pauline, who by then felt much worse.

Soon after the marriage, Pauline had learned that to satisfy Ernest she had to forego her needs and desires. During the previous year, after suffering the difficult birth of their first child, she had to rough it on hunts with Ernest in Wyoming. After nursing her sister through a tonsillectomy, she had to transform herself into a socialite for rounds with East Coast friends. She took on Bumby's care and assisted Ernest through his father's death. Pauline supervised Sunny's typing of Ernest's manuscript, managed a full household in Key West, and kept things relatively quiet so her husband could complete rewrites. Her part was a balancing act that became more precarious with each year of their marriage.

Some relief arrived when Virginia and Clara moved to a hotel, Bumby returned to his mother, a nursemaid was hired for Patrick, and Ernest found a place for Sunny to stay while she awaited the arrival of a friend from Oak Park to accompany her on her European tour. In the meantime Ernest showed his sister the sights of Paris, including museums and galleries where she admired paintings previously known only through books.

When Pauline's health did not improve, she visited a doctor, who diagnosed exhaustion and a sinus infection. Doctors surgically drained her sinuses, which required several trips to the hospital. To make matters worse, Patrick came down with the flu. Ernest, never comfortable around anyone with the flu, found the environment increasingly difficult for work on revisions requested by Scribner's. So once his sister left, he deserted his sick wife and son for Hendaye, returning to Paris with revisions only after Pauline and Patrick improved.

The Pfeiffers worried about Pauline, knowing that as a child she had gone into delirium any time she ran more than a couple degrees of fever. Mary wrote to her daughter, insisting she summon the willpower to take whatever measures necessary to get back to normal, even if it meant going away by herself. "If you lose your health your life will be miserable," she warned. "Turn the children and the household over to Virginia and go quietly away for a time where you can rest and have no responsibility."[2]

Unsure if his mother-in-law knew he had stayed away during Pauline's illness, Ernest explained his departure for Hendaye by telling her they might have to vacate their apartment in December and had to be ready to show it any day of the week between 10 A.M. and 2 P.M. That wreaked havoc with his writing, and he had to relocate to finish rewrites. Now back, he had things under control, he assured his mother-in-law, even though Pauline had endured a pretty rough time.

Though he had deliberately left his wife alone in her sickbed, Ernest lamented, "It is such hard luck for her to be sick. She's never had anything really the matter with her before and so doesn't realize that she must rest and get strong or there is no end to it. Just getting up thinking you are well and then relapse after relapse."[3] Ernest claimed he would have taken Pauline south with him to Hendaye, but it would have meant Virginia staying in the apartment with Patrick. He had decided against asking her because Clara Dunn had criticized him for imposing on Virginia. Clara thought it unfair to always expect Virginia to look after Patrick, get the house in shape, and run errands. Ernest now took the opportunity to complain to "Mother Pfeiffer" about Clara and her influence on Virginia: "Jinny has made some good friends of her own age and I have been lining up the finest I can for her to meet and I know sooner or later she would hit it off with someone but Clara will kill all that in a week. She conducts this constant propaganda against Pauline and me and especially against marriage and all men."[4]

Ernest also told his mother-in-law he would gladly give up ever having any help from Virginia to see her healthy and happily married, "but marriage is one thing that Clara is determined shall never happen." Rather than put up with Clara's compliments to his face and sneers behind his back, and watch her turn Virginia from a young woman into an old maid, he suggested perhaps the simplest thing would be to shoot her. His greatest fear, however, was that Clara would turn both Pauline and Virginia against him.[5] Five years later, when writing *Green Hills of Africa*, Hemingway again vented his frustrations toward Clara Dunn by specifically mentioning her in the book. Sitting around the base campfire one evening, the couple in the book discusses a literary acquaintance, George Moore. The female character in the book (Pauline) indicates that she had seen Moore while visiting in Dublin with Clara Dunn. After a pause, the male character (Ernest) says, "I hate Clara Dunn."[6]

By the first of July Ernest looked anxiously toward Spain and the bullfights at Pamplona. With characteristic spin, it became an opportunity to take Pauline south for her health, since the new nursemaid was working out well and Patrick could be left totally to her care. Though Pauline did not feel up to the frenzied activities of the Pamplona festival, she agreed to join him afterward. That gave her a chance to consider household duties that had been neglected while she was ill—getting Ernest's clothes in order, paying bills, and purchasing things requested by Ernest. Meanwhile, their nursemaid, Henriette, made arrangements to take Patrick on her holiday with family in Bordeaux.

Ernest traveled to Pamplona in the new car purchased with Uncle Gus's funds, accompanied by Virginia and his friend newsman Guy Hickok. Impressed with his first bullfights, Guy admitted to being equally impressed with Virginia. Though happily married, he chided Ernest for putting temptation in his path. "I didn't expect Jinny to look so good without Pernod glasses," he told Ernest later. "I'll bet a bull I don't get her out of my head inside a year."[7] When the Pamplona festival ended, Guy returned to Paris by train, Virginia went on to other destinations, and Pauline joined Ernest for bullfights throughout Spain. Along the way, they befriended Sidney Franklin, a new bullfighter from New York who became a star of the Spanish circuit.

While on their Spanish sojourn, Ernest and Pauline received word that their friends John Dos Passos and Katy Smith had married, an announcement that prompted Virginia to lament rather facetiously that she had lost her chance to get together with Dos Passos. Pauline wrote Virginia not to worry since another man surely would come along. Ernest added, "You could have married Dos if you would have come to Key West last winter. It's in those hot climates that marriages are made—there and in heaven."[8]

The trip to Spain rejuvenated Pauline, and Ernest experienced his typical mood swings after finishing a major work and while waiting for inspiration to start the next. Pauline understood this behavior from previous occasions and took it in stride. They swam every morning and relaxed every afternoon in excellent weather. Two months in Spain with Ernest also meant two months without Patrick. Mary Pfeiffer's concern about Pauline being away from her son that long was tempered by great relief about Pauline's improved health, and she wrote her daughter: "I think you must have had a pretty hard time for I felt it as I always do when anything is very wrong with you. It comes in the air, not like the radio communications, more like static—has about the same effect on my mental faculties as static has on the nerves. I am very glad you have recovered."[9]

Mary's suggestion that Pauline go away for some rest did not cover traveling through Spain, and she could not understand why Pauline and Ernest did not stay in any one place for more than a month. Mary preferred a much simpler lifestyle. Her travels consisted primarily of a trip to Arizona during winter months with Paul to help his asthma and to relax between crop seasons. Mary also attended an annual religious retreat in St. Louis and occasionally visited relatives around the country. Other than that, life in Piggott satisfied her. She wondered, however, if perhaps her children's wandering lifestyles held more promise. "Even at the best we are but pilgrims and why become too attached to any one spot," she mused. "It probably only makes it all the harder to go when the summons comes from on high."[10]

Mary's Catholic faith brought Ernest's joking conclusion that she had enough religion for all of them. On weeks when the priest did not come to her home, she rose early on Sunday mornings and took the train to mass thirty miles away in Paragould. Mary always walked to the station to have time for reflection before the town awoke. "I imagine myself Mary Magdalene on the way to the Holy Sepulcher," she told Ernest and Pauline. "I have been doing this now for fifteen years but have never had any visible manifestations but comfort myself with the words that Our Lord said to Thomas—Blessed are those who have not seen and believe."[11] Mary also found pleasure in nature: "We have the birds in the early morning and the radio at night and all the fruit trees are in bloom and the sun rises bright and shining and your father does the same. He is a veritable child of nature—needs only the sun to make him happy."[12]

Paul never once regretted choosing the Piggott countryside when his brothers moved on to Philadelphia and New York, and he looked forward to each planting season as a personal renewal. Though he typically was a plainspoken man who said exactly what he thought, in as few words as possible, he could be quite eloquent when extolling the beauties of nature and the virtues of living in the country, as evident in a letter he wrote that spring to Ernest and Pauline:

> Beautiful day. The fruit trees & Lawn at their best. Asparagus peeping out of ground and pleading not to cut them too soon. Finest prospects in years for fruit & crops. Farm tenants best spirits for last 3 years & we are all busy getting ready to again plant in the bosom of Mother Earth, whose bounty is never-ending. The saucy wren, the retiring thrush, Billy the aristocrat, and all the hosts of birds are again here with us, each busy in his own affairs singing, wooing and building domiciles. The frog toads not yet shown up but we know they are here as we hear their orchestra evenings. In spite of all this beauty and interesting activity of the country in the spring time people flock to the cities.[13]

Through a regular exchange of letters, Ernest settled into a comfortable relationship with both Mary and Paul Pfeiffer. Despite some awkwardness between Ernest and his father-in-law, the developing writer enjoyed and appreciated their parental support. Mary wrote many of her letters strictly to Ernest, signing them "Mother" and referring to Paul as "your father." In one letter to Ernest she wrote, "Your father has purchased several thousand more acres of land. I will not tell you how many for you would find it hard to believe, but there is now enough to give each of the relatives unto the 4th degree of kindred at least a quarter section [160 acres]."[14] She told him the property also included a fishing resort, for which they had already received an offer five times more than they had paid. "But we turned it down. That is to be yours when you get old and are no longer equal to the strenuous fishing of Key West."[15]

Paul's letters remained somewhat formal and came addressed to "Dear Ernest & All" and signed "Your Father." Quite newsy, they conveyed the latest word about federal agricultural policies, price stabilization, highway paving, and the stock exchange situation. Ernest attempted to cement the relationship by taking an interest in things he knew were important to his father-in-law, commenting on the road paving going on between Piggott and Corning, the status of the cotton crops, and concern for whether the St. Francis River levee would hold during flooding. Ernest also exchanged reading notes, and both Paul and Mary regularly wrote to Ernest and Pauline to share their thoughts on books. During 1929 Mary read *The Story of Philosophy*, *A Preface to Morals*, *Ultima Thule*, *The Life of Christ*, and *The Art of Thinking*. Regarding *The Art of Thinking*, she told them, "I . . . find that I have never done any real thinking. It is too late to begin now so will, as the English say, just muddle through to the end."[16]

When Mary received her first Book of the Month selection, *A Preface to Morals*, she noted that the preface warned, "This book is written only for those who have left the religion of their forefathers." Mary did not send it back but read it anyway. "How much trouble they do go to to find a substitute for religion, and fail miserably," she told them. "It was nevertheless quite interesting."[17] Their favorite reading that year, however, became the new book by their son-in-law. *A Farewell to Arms* was published September 27, but unable to wait, Mary had started reading the May *Scribner's Magazine* serialized version. "You have put us right back into the war atmosphere," she told Ernest. "Everything reeks with it. If you had not told me that it was not autobiographical I would think you were mistaken. The hero acts so like I would expect you to act under similar circumstances."[18]

Paul Pfeiffer enjoyed the book as well and told Ernest the favorable reviews pleased him: "Personally, I think that *The Sun Also Rises*, *Farewell to Arms*, and *All Quiet on the Western Front* are the three greatest books written covering the sacrifices and sufferings, and demoralization of the Great War." Having just read *All Quiet on the Western Front* as well, Paul praised the novel for its details about the common soldier, his sufferings, his disappointments, and his efforts at self-preservation. He appreciated Ernest's books on an entirely different level. "I think in *The Sun Also Rises* and also *Farewell to Arms* you have brought home as no other writer the psychological effect of the Great War on the generation that played the major part in it," he told Ernest. "Brother Gus feels as I do that *The Sun Also Rises* and *Farewell to Arms* are your two best and greatest works."[19]

Ernest's friends agreed as well, and Archibald MacLeish went so far as to say, "I am afraid you are not only a fine writer which I have always known but something a lot more than that & it scares me."[20] Even Ernest's alienated friends praised the book. In spite of his fallings-out with many of them, they could not deny that he had written a fine novel. "It got everyone over here," Sherwood Anderson wrote from the United States to a friend in Europe. "He's just about the big shot over here now and should be sitting on top the world."[21]

One person especially impressed with *A Farewell to Arms* was Morley Callaghan, a young writer Hemingway had befriended at the *Toronto Star.* Callaghan, a great Hemingway admirer, went to Paris with his wife, and Ernest assisted him in getting his stories published in Paris literary magazines. By summer 1929 Callaghan had had a novel published by Scribner's, and the publisher's promotions linked his name with Hemingway's. Just as Ernest and Pauline had resented Hemingway's earlier linkage with Sherwood Anderson, the comparison with an aspiring young writer also did not sit well. When Callaghan and his wife, Loretto, called on the Hemingways at their home on rue Feron, Callaghan immediately sensed that Pauline questioned their purpose in coming. While polite and courteous, she obviously disliked the association.

Callaghan recalled that Loretto wore a fashionable silk suit that she had made herself and a Paris hat acquired in the United States. Pauline commented about her stylish outfit, expressing surprise she had not bought the outfit in Paris. The trick in Paris, she told Loretto, was to pick up hats from unknown milliners with great style. Pauline knew of an especially good milliner, she said, and offered the name to Loretto. Apparently Loretto lacked sufficient enthusiasm, because Pauline stopped in the middle of writing the name and address and asked if Loretto really wanted to use this milliner. If not, she would not bother giving her the name. Loretto quickly assured her that she would.

After the Callaghans left, Loretto said to her husband, "Isn't that Pauline a blunt one? Just imagine. Her time is so valuable she can't write down the address of a milliner unless I take an affidavit I'll use it. What's the matter with her?" Callaghan responded, "Well, she liked your own hat anyway." Loretto recognized that Pauline did not approve of the Scribner promotion and resented Callaghan trying to get too close. "Nobody's edging in on Ernest while she's around," Loretto speculated. "It's a very big thing for her to be Ernest's wife, you know."[22] Later that summer, F. Scott Fitzgerald asked Callaghan what he thought about Pauline. When Callaghan responded that she seemed to be a nice woman, Fitzgerald introduced his theory "that Ernest needs a new woman for each big book. He had one for the stories and *The Sun Also Rises*. Now Pauline. *A Farewell to*

Arms is a big book. If there's another big book I think we'll find Ernest has another wife."[23] Over the years Callaghan became convinced of Fitzgerald's prescience.

A Farewell to Arms certainly was a big book. By the end of October, more than thirty-six thousand copies had sold, thrilling Ernest's publishers. "No book could have been better received than his, and it has been the outstanding seller ever since it appeared," Maxwell Perkins told Fitzgerald. "It has been pre-eminent."[24] While the Hemingways basked in the book's success in Paris, Paul and Mary hosted the first Pfeiffer reunion since 1906 in Piggott. George Washington Pfeiffer had died during World War I in Lugano, Italy, and Rose Pfeiffer Nadelhoffer had died in 1922, but the seven living Pfeiffer brothers and one living sister gathered with their spouses during October 1929.

Mary prepared for weeks, lining up menus for fourteen guests and ordering a special consignment of fruits and perishables from St. Louis. Memories of being together in Piggott later became especially poignant for the family since two of the Pfeiffer brothers, Jacob and Leonard, died unexpectedly the following year. With the cotton harvest under way, Paul reveled in showing crops to his brothers and sister. After all his relatives left, Paul wrote to Ernest on October 14: " Last week was our most busy week in the cotton game. . . . A good many of the tenants will make a little money this year and pay up their accumulated old debts, which of course gives us great pleasure. I really believe that the farm condition is a little bit on the mend and look for a steady though a small improvement in the grower's condition during the next few years."[25]

Just ten days later, the stock market crashed in New York, plowing under any prospects for continuing improvement in the farm economy. The crash seemed to have little effect, however, on curtailing any of Gus Pfeiffer's international activity. By the end of October, he made another trip through Europe to check on his company's holdings and to open another Richard Hudnut branch. He scheduled Paris as one of the first stops on his itinerary and lodged two days with Pauline and Ernest. Impressed with Pauline's decorating in the apartment that he had helped finance, Gus wrote to his wife: "Many New Yorkers would envy Pauline and Ernest their antiques, furniture and special pieces, also their pictures. I learned what I did not know before—that Ernest is an excellent judge of pictures. . . . Ernest not only knows pictures, but he knows who are the good artists. How he finds out all he knows is a mystery to me."

He also reported that grand-nephew Patrick was "a solid, strongly built boy with broad shoulders, big chest, and short neck. He is good-natured and speaks cute French, of which I understand not a word. He already shows signs that he likes games and sports."[26]

When Gus departed for Berlin a few days later, Ernest accompanied him to do research. They occupied the first day making the rounds of family holdings, including Gödecke & Co., the Pfeiffers' oldest pharmaceutical business in Germany, and the offices and laboratories of Gustav Lohse, one of the oldest makers of cosmetics and toiletry goods in Germany. The company dated to 1830, when Gustav Lohse, then barber to the king of Prussia, made and sold cosmetic preparations for ladies at court.

Leonhard Kluftinger, a nephew of Barbara Kluftinger Pfeiffer and her bachelor brother Leonhard Kluftinger, ran Berlin operations. Though a first cousin to Gus, Leonhard was six months younger than his second cousin Pauline and a rising star in the company. Gus admired this cousin, who had volunteered for military service at age seventeen and lost a leg during the retreat at the First Battle of the Marne. Captured by the Russians in 1915, he had escaped a year and a half later and somehow made his way across Siberia back to Germany. Mary Pfeiffer told Ernest before his trip that Leonhard "has been weighed in the balance, burned in the furnace etc. and not found wanting and now stands as a living monument and a shining light and all that testifying as to the excellent effects of adversity upon the moral character."[27] Ernest became well acquainted with Leonhard, and the two shared experiences of entering World War I as boys and coming out as men. While Ernest admired his wartime heroism, he found Leonhard's blind loyalty a bit hard to take. Ernest considered him "a grand boy and as square as a square peg in a round world."[28]

While in Berlin, Gus incorporated the new Richard Hudnut Co. and checked on other W. R. Warner & Co. operations and holdings. When not observing Pfeiffer family operations in Berlin, Ernest passed the five-day trip sightseeing, looking up acquaintances, visiting galleries, purchasing a few paintings, and writing. The author assured Gus he was accomplishing as much writing in Berlin as he would have in Paris. Gus, pleased to have the time with Ernest, wrote his wife, "He undoubtedly has a fine mind, one that almost instantly analyzes, absorbs and remembers the key-note of things and individuals."[29]

Virginia traveled as well during fall 1929 and stopped off to visit the Murphys at Cap d'Antibes. Earlier in the summer, the Murphys had thought their son Patrick had bronchitis, and later their daughter Honoria had become ill as well. By the time Virginia arrived, Patrick's illness had worsened. "We have everything here but pep," Virginia wrote to Ernest and Pauline. "Gerald and Sara are very worried about the children. . . . You would almost say they are all suffering from too much care—except of course what might have happened if they hadn't had it."[30] While Virginia stayed at the Murphys' Villa America, Gerald and Sara made a trip to Paris with their son. Doctors diagnosed tuberculosis, with rest at a sanitarium his only chance of survival. Gerald took Patrick to a facility in Switzerland, while Sara waited in Paris for Virginia to bring the Murphys' daughter for testing. Fortunately, Honoria checked out fine, and the Murphys relocated to a six-room suite at the residential sanitarium, where many of their summer people joined them, including Virginia and Dorothy Parker.

The Murphy family greatly appreciated Virginia's help during their tribulations. Sara wrote a letter to Pauline about how much they relied on her, adding, "We feel dreadfully about Jinny's visit having fallen on such a gloomy time—& only *hope* the slight change of air she's had has done some *slight* good—She really is so sweet, & we all like her *so* much."[31] Gerald appreciated Virginia as well, though she remained a mystery to him. He told Ernest and Pauline that he and Sara found her haunting, as if there were something out there that was just beyond her reach, and they worried about her "for no good reason."[32]

Perhaps the something just beyond her reach was the relationship she might have had with Ernest, had he not married her sister. While it was not necessarily a relationship she wanted, she no doubt thought about how things might have been different.

Virginia and Dorothy Parker remained with the Murphys at the sanitarium. As the holidays approached, Ernest, Pauline, and John and Katy Dos Passos joined them. For Christmas dinner Ernest shot a goose, which Sara roasted and served with chestnut puree and flaming plum pudding topped with a sprig of holly. While they all sang carols and pretended to be having a wonderful time, everyone knew that a tuberculosis sanitarium was no place to spend Christmas—particularly for someone as afraid of illness as Ernest. But he stayed with his friends, an unusual act of sacrifice by the author, before returning to the United States.

CHAPTER 12

A Place to Call Home (1930–1931)

The Hemingway party—Ernest, Pauline, Patrick, and his nurse Henriette—departed France on January 19, 1930, aboard the *La Bourdannais,* bound for Havana and Key West via New York. Gus Pfeiffer had left one week ahead of them, having completed his extended business trip to Europe, and planned to meet them at the dock in New York. Gus and Ernest had schemed about the future while together in Berlin, including a possible African safari, and agreed to resume discussions in New York. Gus hoped to have time as well to show off the Homestead, his new family retreat in Aspetuck, Connecticut. "We can also plan a lot of other things," he wrote Ernest. "Building air castles was always a favorite pastime with me. I remember how in 10 minutes while plowing corn I'd change from a farmer's boy to the highest pinnacle of success and then maybe I'd find I plowed out a good hill of corn, and back I was a farmer's boy."[1]

One issue Gus settled while in Europe was financial security for Ernest's widowed mother. With money from Pauline and Gus and proceeds from *A Farewell to Arms,* Ernest set up a trust fund of approximately $50,000 to take care of his mother and his two younger siblings, Carol and Leicester. The trust provided approximately $2,700 in annual income. At the death of Ernest's mother, $10,000 each from the trust principal went to Leicester and Carol; $5,000 each to Sunny and Ursula; and $20,000 back to Pauline.

Unfortunately, Grace Hemingway was less grateful than Ernest expected. She raised the issue of Carol's college financing and suggested that justice demanded that her younger children have the same opportunities as the older. A livid Ernest shot back that she could hardly bring up the issue of justice, since he had left home after high school, made his own living, and received neither money nor moral support from his family. Instead, all he had gotten from them was that they would "rather see me dead and in my grave than writing as I am."[2] Ernest wrote his mother that he did not appreciate the fact that if you gave someone ten dollars, they thought you had a million. He likened the comparison in his case to giving ten dollars when you had only thirteen. Ernest suggested that if his mother deemed his assistance insufficient, she should contact Marcelline, who not only had money but had benefited more than he from the family largesse.

Gus Pfeiffer crossed the Atlantic on schedule aboard the fifty-thousand-ton *Bremen,* considered the finest ship afloat, but the Hemingways' twelve-thousand-ton transport fared poorly in the unusually rough January seas. Several days late getting into New York, they had only two days before the ship continued on to Havana. So the trip to Gus's Aspetuck Colony went on hold, and they had just enough time to meet with Maxwell Perkins; make a few business calls; and visit Ada MacLeish at the hospital, where she was recuperating from a hysterectomy. Ernest went directly to her room, rushed over to her bed, and grabbed her. "I thought I was breaking in two," she recalled. Archibald MacLeish deplored Ernest's insensitivity.[3]

When the Hemingways arrived in Key West from Havana, they rented a large frame home on Pearl Street, located for them by Lorine Thompson, and settled in with Patrick and his French nurse. By this time, Patrick spoke nonstop, but in French. Ernest told his in-laws that Patrick's fluent French included *grandmere* and *grandpere,* but he could say "I don't know" and "hobo" in English. When they traveled to Piggott in June, Ernest assured them that Patrick would learn "all the English you will teach him."[4]

Paul and Mary, delighted that their grandson no longer lived an ocean away, suggested that the Hemingways "get a good strong anchor and sink it deep and stay put for awhile."[5] The Pfeiffers' annual excursion to Phoenix took a backseat to their attempt to save the Bank of Piggott after the stock market crash. While the institution appeared to be back on solid footing by the time the Pfeiffers finally headed to Arizona in mid-January, a run on the bank in early February forced its permanent closing. At that time, small banks all over the state were failing, leading Ernest to refer to Piggott as the "heart of the ex-banking belt."[6] Sixty-six Arkansas banks closed on one day alone (November 19, 1929), followed soon thereafter by forty-six others.

Within days of the Piggott bank closing, a group of businessmen planned a new bank, to be named Piggott State Bank, and they elected Paul Pfeiffer as president. He made it clear that he would serve with his wife's help and that the appointment would be temporary. On March 20, Paul wrote to Ernest and Pauline that the bank had opened its doors the previous morning, had received more than $30,000 in deposits the first day, and had paid up capital and a surplus of $27,500 on the balance sheet: "They have elected us as president which office, however, we will surrender to younger shoulders as soon as the bank is nicely organized and started. Everybody seems to be pleased in being able to get banking facilities again in Piggott."[7]

The Pfeiffers restructured their personal affairs as well. With profits dwindling from large tracts of land dependent on tenant farmers, Pfeiffer established the Piggott Land Company, with himself as president and Mary as secretary-treasurer, and moved all his real estate assets into the company. In their attempt to sell off properties, the company letterhead became a public relations tool. Directly under the masthead came the phrase: "Owners of over fifty thousand acres highly improved and cut-over lands in rich St. Francis, Cache and Black River valleys. Well drained. Located in Clay County, Northeast Corner of Arkansas, two hundred miles due south of St. Louis, Missouri."

The bottom left side of the stationery stated, "These lands grow fine Clover, Corn, Cotton, Wheat and Truck Crops. Mild winters and fine pastures make this an ideal Hog, Cattle and Poultry Section. Served by both the Cotton Belt and Frisco Railroads." The bottom right side added, "Near to good roads, schools and markets. State highways adjacent and through these lands, built and maintained by State of Arkansas through gas and auto tax, free of any cost or direct tax on lands."

Like his brother Gus, Paul was a shrewd businessman who was able to profit during the Depression. He sold much of his land to the federal government for resale to young farmers. Other land he typically sold in plots of forty acres or more to individual farmers, with down payments and deferred terms for those strapped for cash. Gus Pfeiffer recalled later that his brother Paul transformed Piggott "from a small backwoods town to a prosperous city and influential trading center . . . not at the expense of the inhabitants of Piggott and the surrounding country, but with genuine benefit to them." He added that Brother Paul never sued to collect a debt, cancelled the obligations of many of his debtors, and provided financial aid that "started many persons and families on the road to success."[8]

Despite Paul's financial success and willingness to help others, Gus remained Ernest's most important benefactor. In addition to dedicating *A Farewell to Arms* to G. A. Pfeiffer, Ernest gave him the manuscript in appreciation for his help with the trust fund for Grace Hemingway. A flattered Gus wrote that he would keep it for the author. Ernest could have it back whenever he wanted it. Ernest responded that he would rather give it to him, knowing he could see it any time he wanted: "It is no more than a gesture for nothing we could ever give would equal your generosity. So please consider the mss. yours. I will be so pleased if you will accept it."[9]

During that spring Ernest worked to become an expert on African rifles and equipment to take advantage of Gus's latest generous offer to finance an African safari. He also began what he anticipated would be the definitive book on bullfighting and enlisted Uncle Gus once again to assist in tracking down anything ever written on the subject. The author's request to Gus launched an exhaustive search for every book and magazine on Ernest's list. The manager of the Warner laboratory in Barcelona received the following instructions from the New York headquarters: "Undoubtedly, there is at least one book store in Barcelona that specializes in bull fighting books. Sometimes there are ads in the paper or bull ring programs announcing that some afecionado is selling bull fighting library. Such ads, of course, are excellent leads. It might be advisable for you to run some ads—both in Barcelona and Madrid—listing the books and magazines that Mr. Hemingway wants. Please send me the bill for all expenses which you may incur by reason of this request."[10]

With the search on in Spain for research materials for his next book, Ernest and friends began another round of fishing off Key West. Archibald MacLeish, Mike Strater, and Charles Thompson accompanied Ernest on a fishing expedition that culminated in an invitation for the four men to reunite the following year for the three-month lion-hunting safari in Africa being financed by Gus. "You won't have to spend a sou after we leave N.Y.," he promised MacLeish.[11] In May Ernest went fishing in the Tortugas with Maxwell Perkins and others for nearly three weeks, amid a major storm at sea. He never ate or drank better in his life, Ernest told his friend Waldo Peirce, who missed the adventure. "All wives worried sick except Pauline," he proudly informed Peirce. "She's never worried yet, damned good trait in a woman, love you and not worry about you."[12]

While Pauline waited for Ernest's sporadic appearances in Key West, Virginia remained in Europe, where she frequently saw both Bumby and Hadley. In March Virginia reported that "Bumbi went to a movie with me Thursday and he looks fine although he has his winter cough. . . . He is crazy to come to America." She added, "I am having dinner tonight with Hadley . . . had asked her out but she wished to change it and eat in." The next day Virginia expanded the letter to say the dinner was grand, and Bumby had received papers back from school that showed progress, according to the teacher's note: "He was quite delighted and asked me to put it in my letter to you and I think he would be even more delighted to have a little praise from Papa."[13]

Through the correspondence, they worked out plans for Bumby to return with Virginia to the United States and accompany his father and stepmother on their next trip west. Since Bumby's school term ended in June, Virginia booked passage to New York for the two of them in mid-June. Pauline went on to Piggott with Patrick and his nurse, Ernest took the train to New York, and Virginia with Bumby sailed on the *Lafayette,* with an expected arrival in New York on June 22. The ship docked a day and a half earlier than expected, however, requiring Ernest to cut short some of his planned activities, including a visit to Archibald and Ada MacLeish in Massachusetts. The three traveled nearly half the journey to Piggott in Virginia's car, shipped with them on the *Lafayette,* then picked up Ernest's car in Cincinnati, where it had been driven by a friend from Key West. At this time, Ernest and Pauline still drove the second car purchased for them by Uncle Gus—another Model A Ford. Gus sent them a check to buy a third car on their return to Key West, but Ernest assured him that the existing car performed well and that they could use the money for other purposes. Gus agreed, telling Ernest, "So long as your present car is giving satisfaction, I can see the wisdom of taking it, and not a new car, on your western trip."[14]

Piggott welcomed Bumby, and he quickly learned that Pfeiffer family membership had its advantages. He recalled in his memoir: "From Grandfather Paul Pfeiffer I learned that being a step-grandson of the bank president and owner of the cotton gin, as well as the largest landowner thereabouts, was a privileged position which entitled one to the luxury of 'charging' sodas and sundaes, and any number of wondrous goodies that had not existed in France, at the local drugstore."[15]

Ernest, Pauline, and Bumby headed to Wyoming on July 2. Before setting out, Ernest sent a note to MacLeish, apologizing for missing him and suggesting he join him back in Piggott in December for quail hunting season. "It has been very dry here—bad for crops but wonderful for quail. Have spotted any quantity of coveys and we'll shoot them in Dec. Season opens Dec. 1. Am storing up local wines, moonshine, etc. You'll come and we'll have great shooting."[16] Though the trip westward typically seemed a monotonous drive, Bumby recalled it being great fun. His father frequently picked up riders who could not afford their own transportation and pressed them for their stories as they traveled. Their hard-luck Depression tales fascinated the family and could have come straight from the pages of John Steinbeck's *Grapes of Wrath.*

Another family tradition probably originated on this trip. To avoid the habit of swearing or telling off-color stories and jokes all the time, they set aside one hour each evening during their travels with nothing off-limits. It got particularly wild in later years, Bumby recalled, when he and Patrick shared the rumble seat and they could really let fly with some colorful language.[17]

On this trip, however, two-year-old Patrick stayed behind in Piggott, or "Baggott," as he called it, with Henriette and the adoring Pfeiffer family[18] "I have to report that your son is in excellent health and spirits and grows more interesting daily," Mary Pfeiffer wrote almost a month after his parents' departure. While everything in Piggott wilted in the heat, Patrick thrived on it from morning to night. His grandmother told the parents, "He says his mother is in Mon tan-a, and his papa is in an auto in Wyoming."[19]

Patrick had their location just about right. The Hemingway home base remained L-Bar-T Ranch, owned by Lawrence and Olive Nordquist, just over the Montana line in Wyoming. When Ernest broke from writing, he and Pauline generally packed a picnic lunch, saddled their horses, and rode until they found a good fishing spot—sometimes in Montana, other times in Wyoming. Occasionally Bumby accompanied them or went riding with Pauline or fishing with his father, but he soon found friends his own age and discovered plenty to do on a ranch. Before joining his friends each day, Bumby had two chores: putting logs on the fire first thing in the morning to warm up the cabin and gathering wild strawberries in the woods nearby. Each morning he filled two glasses with strawberries, and "Pauline would then crush the strawberries into the bottom of the tumbler and add gin for their first-of-the-day 'ranch cocktails.'"[20]

Ernest displayed great kindness toward his son during the trip, and Olive Nordquist recalled one occasion that she found especially touching. With all sitting in the lodge when Bumby's bedtime approached, Ernest knew that Bumby feared walking across the ranch alone at night, but father did not want to embarrass son in front of everyone. Instead, he jumped up and proclaimed, "Damn! I forgot something at the cabin. I'll have to walk back with you, Bumby."[21] It showed a sensitive side of Ernest, attuned to the needs of others, that few people got to see.

In mid-September, Pauline and Bumby left the ranch for New York to get him back to Paris for a new school year, while Ernest stayed on to work on his bullfighting book. Pauline and Bumby traveled via Piggott to pick up Henriette to accompany the boy aboard ship and return to her family in France, leaving Patrick in Piggott with the Pfeiffers. Prior to Pauline's departure from Wyoming, she and Ernest signed new wills, leaving everything to each other and then to the two boys. Ernest narrowly escaped his will being probated less than two months after it was signed. John Dos Passos joined Hemingway at the ranch for ten days of hunting and sightseeing, and after they started for Piggott on November 1, Ernest lost control of the car when blinded by oncoming headlights. He went off the gravel road, and the car flipped upside down. Dos Passos walked away from the accident, but Hemingway landed in a hospital in Billings, Montana.

This incident marked the third in a series of injuries that year for the accident-prone writer. Less than six months earlier he had cut his right index finger to the bone on a punching bag in Key West, requiring six stitches. Before Pauline and Bumby had left the ranch, his horse bolted into the woods, which brought a gash in his face that required another six stitches. In this more serious accident, Hemingway fractured his right arm just above the elbow, a particularly painful break and one difficult to heal.

Dos Passos immediately telegraphed Pauline in Piggott, where she awaited Ernest's arrival after delivering her stepson and Henriette to the ship in New York. On learning the news, Pauline took the first train to Billings, arriving Tuesday evening to find her husband in great pain and heavily sedated with morphine. After four days of unsuccessful attempts to maneuver the bones back into place, his doctor recommended surgery. Typical of Ernest, he later provided graphic descriptions of the procedure to his friends, noting that the repair required boring a hole through the bone and fastening the ends together with kangaroo tendons. The inside of his arm "looked like the part of an elk you have to throw away as unfit for human consumption when you butcher it out."[22]

Clearly his goal of completing the new book by Christmas had become impossible. On December 6 Pauline wrote to Ernest's mother that for more than four weeks he had not changed positions, but that he had sat up that morning for the first time. Along with keeping his mother informed, Pauline took Ernest's dictation to all his friends. Quail hunting in Piggott went out the hospital window, and he alerted Archibald MacLeish and Mike Strater that the African safari might be postponed as well.

When Pauline suggested in her own note to MacLeish that he send Ernest a card to cheer him up, his friend did better than that. He flew to Montana and arrived at the hospital to find Ernest "surrounded by nurses and looking rosy and fine with a magnificent, glossy, black beard." Never one to accept kindnesses gracefully from his friends and family, Hemingway glared at MacLeish and growled, "So! You've come to see me die, have you?"[23] Ernest lived, however, and by December 21 he had recovered enough to be released and travel to Piggott for convalescence. Pauline and Ernest took a train from Billings to St. Louis, where Paul Pfeiffer met them and got them to Piggott on Christmas Eve.

During the holidays Ernest regained some strength and began walking downtown to build up stamina after being immobilized for so long. On one occasion, as he trudged up Cherry Street hill, children pelted him with snowballs from the schoolyard across the street from the Pfeiffer home. The bearded stranger, with his arm in a sling, looked so scruffy that the children assumed him to be one of the hobos who periodically showed up at the Pfeiffers' door asking for a handout. The children were attempting to do the Pfeiffers a favor by chasing him away. Ernest hurried to the house and never quite forgot the incident.

The Pfeiffer family rallied around Ernest throughout his stay in Piggott, but once again, he proved unable to graciously accept their kindnesses. Ernest wrote a self-pitying letter to his mother-in-law upon return to Key West. In response to learning that Virginia had supposedly made a comment about all the trouble he caused, Ernest apologized to his mother-in-law for "inflicting" himself on them and assured her that it would never happen again. "Can't promise, of course, not to go in the ditch again," he told her, "but will try to see that the car is one of the kind that kills you when it turns over on you instead of merely making you a nuisance to friends and relatives."[24]

Mary Pfeiffer would not allow her son-in-law to get away with such childishness. In her response she asked where he had gotten the impression that his short stay caused any trouble for the family and asserted that he certainly was not trouble in the sense of the family being inconvenienced. "Don't you know, Ernest, if you don't know now you will in time, that the troubles of our children are always our troubles," she chided him. "In that sense your great trial and long-suffering was a trouble and a grievance to us. We expect to share in your joys and your sorrows the same as in Pauline and Karl and Virginia's."[25]

Long over her inhibitions about what to say to Ernest Hemingway the writer, Mary viewed Ernest as just another child in the family who needed to be straightened out and reassured every now and then.

Back in Key West, the January sunshine melted the Hemingways' resolve to return to Paris, and they settled into a rental house at Whitehead and United streets, with the first order of business being household help. Pauline had her hands full with a son who tried to do everything and a husband who could do nothing. Given the Hemingways' change in plans, Henriette could not return from Paris to Key West until mid-February. Though Virginia traveled from Piggott to Key West with the Hemingways, she could not stay, having previously agreed to look after her brother's children, Barbara and Paul.

As Karl Pfeiffer and his wife, Matilda, planned their first trip to Europe, they got help from Ernest. Prior to their departure he sent an eleven-page

letter, dictated through Pauline, that included a definitive primer on European wines, liquors, and liqueurs. His assessment of each included how,
when, and where to drink it and how they would feel afterward. Ernest
instructed them on the education of the wine palate, which went from sweet
to dry. And they should start with cheaper wines and proceed to the more
expensive, he advised.

The Bordeaux, he suggested, were the best to drink with most meals,
because overall they cost less and had lower alcohol content. White
Bordeaux could be consumed with oysters, fish, or chicken, and the red
with everything else. "You can't get tight on either of these wines, but don't
try to prove me a liar," he warned.[26] Drink Burgundy, the most noble and
full-bodied wine of all, only when you are getting lots of exercise, he added,
"because otherwise it can put the liver on the bum and make you billious
and ruin your capacity to drink all other fine things."[27]

Quite likely Karl and Matilda did not need as much education as Ernest
provided. They lived near New York City and socialized at events ranging
from Warner-Hudnut company parties to gatherings with friends at
speakeasies. Nevertheless, they graciously accepted the advice, particularly
since it had taken a lot of effort to dictate the lengthy epistle to Pauline.
Later Karl recalled, "Hemingway was the greatest authority on wine I ever
met. He taught me all I know about wines and he was the only American I
know who was ever invited to the Wine Tasters Convention in Paris."[28]

While Karl and Matilda traveled through Europe, wine tasting and
socializing went on in Key West as well. Ernest's injuries rendered him
unable to write or work on his book, so he lifted many a glass with friends
and relatives. His youngest sister, Carol, was attending Rollins College in
Winter Park, Florida, and became a frequent visitor. Ernest's mother came
for a few days to see Carol and meet her grandson Patrick for the first time.
She had not seen Ernest since he came to Oak Park for his father's funeral.

Pauline was still feeling her way with her mother-in-law, having met her
only once. She had started by writing to her as "Mother Hemingway," then
determined that to be too formal—particularly since her own grandchildren
called her "Gracie." She finally settled on "Mother Grace."[29] During Grace's
two-day stay at the Casa Marina, she entertained Ernest and Pauline over
lunch, and Pauline managed to develop a bond of sorts with her.

Patrick hit it off with his Grandmother Hemingway. He still spoke primarily in French but picked up some English from his parents and on the
trip to Piggott. His favorite English expression at the time, addressed to his
father, became "Whatchasay, Papa?"[30] Grace thought Patrick delightful,

although Patrick recalled his Hemingway grandmother as a "large, strange woman whom his father disliked."[31]

When a bout of unseasonably cold weather warmed up, Ernest started fishing with his friends. Maxwell Perkins arrived for his annual excursion, as did Mike Strater. Lawrence and Olive Nordquist came down from their ranch in Wyoming, along with Chub Weaver, who drove Hemingway's car back from Billings after repairs. The W. P. Sidleys of Chicago, also frequent guests at the Nordquist Ranch, took advantage of Ernest's invitation to try Key West. Writers John Hermann and his wife Josephine Herbst arrived for a second season, having lived the previous year in the house now being occupied by the Hemingways.

Hemingway limited his fishing somewhat, thanks to his injured arm. While he could cast and set the hook, someone else had to reel in any fish. Thus, Pauline pulled in a record sailfish that season—a seven-foot, one-inch beauty. An article in the *Key West Citizen* carried the headline, "Mrs. Hemingway Is Newest Holder of Fish Record Here."[32] Pauline also pulled in something else that spring. Within a month, she hit the front page again after rescuing Mrs. Sidley from a near drowning at a Key West swimming pool.[33]

Generally, however, the headlines belonged to Ernest, and the town took note of a well-known author enjoying his fourth season in Key West. With the town suffering from the Depression, Hemingway's personal endorsement helped boost the economy, particularly whenever Gus Pfeiffer came to town. This time he arrived at the end of February, accompanied by his wife, Louise. After a brief sightseeing trip to Havana with Pauline, Aunt Louise returned to New York, while Gus joined Ernest's fishing expedition to the Dry Tortugas.

The Tortugas, first discovered by Ponce de Leon in 1513, included seven coral-reef and sand islands about seven miles west of Key West. Ernest found the area to be an excellent fishing spot, and Gus's beginner's luck from his previous fishing trip with Ernest continued when he caught the biggest fish on the trip. They stayed longer than intended because rough seas prevented their small boat from making it back across the Gulf. Word spread of them marooned on an island, but they fished and dined on "fine cakes for breakfast with stewed prunes, home baked bread, fresh fish, lettuce, oranges, apples and other things, so we never suffered and are not entitled to sympathy," Gus later reported to his family.[34]

They also used the time to soak up the history of the main island. The Union had utilized a partially built fortress, started on the island before the

Civil War, as a base for raids during the war and as a prison after the war. Its most famous inmate became Dr. Samuel Mudd, the physician who set John Wilkes Booth's leg after Lincoln's assassination, imprisoned there for twelve years for complicity in Booth's escape. In the years after the war, the fort became a coaling station, but by 1931 it lay in ruins.

The greatest advantage of the trip for Gus became an additional opportunity to spend time with Ernest. Gus found him to be a man who took pleasure in simple things and shunned pretense. "To understand Ernest you must know him, to know him is to admire his simplicity, his honesty and his understanding," Gus wrote to his family. "Ernest not only has a great fund of knowledge, but he has that which is far more desirable and precious— understanding and wisdom. I wish I could be with him more."[35]

While Gus and Ernest fished, Pauline looked all over Key West for a suitable home, aided once again by Lorine Thompson. Pauline knew she was pregnant again, with a due date in November confirmed by a local doctor, so finding a permanent residence became important. By then Paris had lost its luster in Ernest's eyes, since many of the American literary set had returned home, and newcomers filled his favorite places. Spain and bullfights continued to capture his interest, but war loomed on Spain's political horizon. Gus promised to purchase a home for Pauline and Ernest, as he had for other nieces and nephews, so Ernest promoted a Key West location. Pauline preferred returning to Paris, or perhaps a big city in the United States, but by that point in the relationship Pauline almost always gave in to whatever Ernest wanted.

She searched for a secluded location, with a European flavor for her fine Spanish and French antiques; an ample master bedroom; and bedrooms for the two children, a visiting older son, and household help. Pauline also wanted a yard with plenty of space for the children to play and opportunities for gardening. They looked all over the island and eventually selected a home Pauline had seen a year earlier and dismissed. She referred to it as the "haunted house" because on her first visit she had gotten ceiling plaster in her eyes as soon as she stepped inside. After further consideration, she recognized the house's advantages.[36]

The Spanish colonial-style mansion, located at 907 Whitehead Street, had been erected in 1851 by shipping tycoon Asa Tift. A solidly built structure constructed primarily of white coral stone, the house featured heart of pine throughout that came directly from Tift's Georgia property. Black wrought-iron balconies surrounded the upper and lower floors, and long graceful French doors with old shutters opened onto the balcony from virtually every room. Open fireplaces warmed several rooms. A staircase opened onto an upper central hall that separated a master bedroom suite from children's rooms. Additionally, the structure sat on a piece of property that included a large yard, a twenty-thousand-gallon cistern, and a carriage house that could be made into a secluded studio.

On the negative side, the house badly needed repairs to the roof and had crumbling plaster, peeling paint, warped doors, and ancient plumbing. Windows needed reglazing, floors sagged, tile needed replacing, and some walls needed removal to open up rooms. The Hemingways also needed a second bathroom and a new kitchen. The lawn consisted of a few scraggly palms and would require a lot of care.

When Gus returned from the Dry Tortugas trip, Pauline took him to see the house, and he thought it a good buy. Gus provided the eight thousand dollars purchase money, which included three thousand dollars owed in back taxes. The Hemingways closed the deal on April 29, 1931, and the next day, a local newspaper noted that they had acquired "one of the most ideally located homesites in the city."[37] The paper commented that it would require an estimated five hundred dollars in repairs—not even close to the real costs.

Charles and Ernest celebrated that evening by getting drunk at Sloppy Joe's. Lorine and Pauline toasted with drinks at Pena's Garden of Roses, as they discussed their next steps. Both Thompsons expressed elation that the Hemingways would become permanent residents of Key West. Pauline shocked Lorine the next day, however, by telling her they would delay most work on the house for the next eight months because Ernest had decided to return to Europe to finish his bullfight book. "Besides," Pauline told her, "you have to live in a house for a time before you really know what to do with it."[38]

Pauline and Ernest figured that if they went to Europe in May, Ernest could work on his book, while Pauline closed the Paris apartment. Also, they could attend the bullfights at Pamplona, make their usual Spanish tour, and still be back in the United States by the first part of October to await the birth of their second child. If violence in Spain accelerated, Pauline could remain in Paris. Just weeks earlier, Spain's monarchy had been overthrown and a provisional government installed amid growing reports of disturbances. Despite the unrest, Ernest left for Spain aboard the *Volendam* three days after becoming a homeowner, sharing passage with seven Spanish priests exiled from Mexico.

Pauline stayed behind long enough to take care of details on the house that could not be delayed and to contact her doctor in Kansas City to make sure that he approved her travel plans and that he would do the delivery when she returned. "Things seem to be going very well so far—as such things go—with my full share of nausea (tho no vomiting) combined with large appetite," she wrote to Dr. Guffey. "I've gained seven pounds already."[39]

Finally en route to Europe in mid-May, Pauline, Patrick, and Henriette stopped in New York, where Uncle Gus put them up at the Brevoort Hotel. Aunt Louise accompanied Pauline to the top of the Empire State Building, which had opened officially on May 1, less than two weeks earlier, when President Herbert Hoover pushed a button from the White House that turned on the lights. Gus also showed her his new Hudnut building, which opened later in the week, and she received word from her lawyer cousin Matthew that Uncle Gus had added fifteen thousand dollars to her trust fund, though Gus had not mentioned it.[40] The Depression that wracked America did not seem to affect the Pfeiffers in New York. As Gus told Ernest, "Fortunately, our problems do not include success or failure. They only include (up to now) the size of our success. . . . So in a way we are sitting as some would say 'quite pretty.'"[41]

Pauline, Patrick, and Henriette sailed May 20 aboard the *President Harding* and made it to Cherbourg, France, by May 28, then arrived in Paris at midnight. Two days later Henriette and Patrick departed for her family home in Bordeaux; Pauline stayed on in Paris to pack the apartment furniture and ship it to Key West. When they all reassembled at Hendaye in June, Pauline stayed with Patrick and Henriette, while Ernest took Bumby to Pamplona for his first bullfights. Ernest had conceived the idea for the trip earlier that spring, when he visited Hadley and Bumby in Paris. On that occasion, he had arrived at Hadley's apartment with a gift of animal skins, which she later made into a stole.[42] It was the first time all three—Ernest, his ex-wife, and his son—had come together since the divorce, and they seemed almost like a family again. By this time, however, Hadley had fallen in love with Paul Mowrer, foreign editor for the *Chicago Daily News,* and they were awaiting his divorce from his first wife. Hadley had met Paul and Winifred Mowrer the same fall that she and Ernest separated, and she became friends with Winifred. From the start, a strong romantic attraction existed between Hadley and Paul, and she found herself again in the midst of a romantic triangle, but this time she was the other woman.

By 1931 Hadley and Paul talked about marriage, but Hadley retained some emotional ties to Ernest. Since he and Pauline planned a permanent move to the United States, Hadley felt perhaps she could now move on with her life. She contacted Ernest later in the month, after his first visit, and asked him to meet her again so she could sort things out and seek his advice about Paul, particularly since marrying him would place Paul in the position of helping raise Bumby. Ernest encouraged her to marry Mowrer, calling him a fine man. When he left her apartment several hours later, Hadley watched from the balcony as he walked permanently out of her life and disappeared into the crowd. She would see him only once again in her lifetime.[43] With Hadley about to remarry, the Paris apartment vacated, a new home in Key West, and Ernest about to become a father for the third time, it seemed to the Hemingways that nothing would ever be the same. And indeed, it would not.

CHAPTER 13

Chaos Abounds (1931–1932)

Along with personal changes for Ernest and Pauline, the world economy was disintegrating so rapidly that it was difficult to judge the soundness of their decision to return to the United States as homeowners. Relatives in America reported that business conditions continued their downward slide across the country.

Though farm prices throughout the country had hit their lowest levels in thirty years, things did not look quite as bad in the Pfeiffers' Piggott household. Pauline's father wrote that although cotton acreage had fallen 20 percent in Clay County, acreage devoted to corn, wheat, and oats had increased. The weather had provided needed rain, with "all fields well cultivated and clean, and the present crop and fruit prospects very good."[1] At least one family member fared poorly, however. Virginia had entered into a financial venture with Clara Dunn that fell to only 20 percent of its original value, and the Pfeiffers liquidated Virginia's account with Clara on Virginia's "solemn promise that she would in the future avoid debts like she would the plague."[2]

Virginia then turned her attentions to a family project. She and her parents had celebrated the Fourth of July at the Homestead, Uncle Gus's home at the family compound in Aspetuck, Connecticut. Gus had had his barn remodeled, inspiring Virginia to attempt a similar miracle with the barn in Piggott. She figured it could be a place for her to entertain friends, as well as a more comfortable writing haven for Ernest when he visited Piggott.

By the end of August, Ernest and Pauline began to formulate plans for delivery of their second child. They decided to bypass Piggott and go directly to Kansas City, then from Kansas City back to Key West, to minimize Pauline's travel. That left the question of what to do with Patrick, as well as how to get the household shipment from Paris unpacked and installed in the Key West house. Pauline would be in no shape to move furniture, but she hesitated asking Virginia's help since her sister already had done so much that year for Karl's family, as well as for Ernest and Pauline.

Ernest wrote to his in-laws to put out feelers on both concerns. He suggested perhaps Patrick could come on to Piggott via train when Ernest and Pauline traveled to Kansas City, provided they could find a suitable nurse for Patrick "so he will not be an unmitigated nuisance."[3] Ernest also floated the idea that perhaps Virginia might enjoy going to Key West and doing some interior decorating after she returned from a trip to Mexico with Clara Dunn. He went on to say that Virginia certainly possessed talent for decorating, and she had the advantage of knowing the arrangement of things in their Paris apartment.

Paul Pfeiffer immediately wrote back with the support Ernest sought. Of course they wanted whatever proved best for Pauline's health, and the family would adjust to whatever needed to be done. Yes, they would make room for Patrick and his nurse, and it would be a joy to have them around. As for Virginia, she planned to return to Piggott in October, and he felt certain the Key West trip would not be a problem. "She loves to fix up places and takes pleasure in helping others and I think your plans will suit her very nicely," Paul told his son-in-law.[4]

Henriette did not wish to return to the United States on a long-term basis, but she found a replacement named Gabrielle, whom Ernest later characterized as specializing in "child care, veterinary surgery, cooking, and brewing."[5] The Hemingway family departed Europe toward the end of September on the *Ile de France*. Fellow travelers included Hemingway's old friend Don Stewart, along with his pregnant wife, Beatrice, and their attractive friend Jane Mason, wife of George Grant Mason, an officer for Pan American Airways who resided in Havana. With Pauline and Beatrice both pregnant and uncomfortable through most of the trip, Ernest and Don spent much of their time with Mrs. Mason on what Ernest described later as a "merry and drunken crossing."[6]

After arriving in New York and checking in at the Brevoort Hotel, Ernest went to Massachusetts to see Archibald MacLeish. The two men in turn headed to Cambridge to meet Waldo Peirce and take in a football game at Harvard. Back in New York, Ernest stopped by Maxwell Perkins's office long enough to drop off photos gathered in Spain during the summer, then boarded the Kansas City–bound *Spirit of St. Louis* at Penn Station with his family.

Patrick and Gabrielle went on to Piggott; Ernest and Pauline once again moved in with the Lowrys until time for their friends to close up the Kansas City house for a vacation in California. Upon arrival in Kansas City, Pauline immediately checked in with Dr. Guffey, who pronounced the pregnancy on schedule. Dr. Guffey took pleasure in his involvement once again because of his admiration for Ernest's writing skills. With the Caesarian surgery in *A Farewell to Arms* drawn from Pauline's earlier Caesarian delivery, Dr. Guffey proudly displayed not only an autographed copy of the book but a framed copy of Ernest's cancelled check for Patrick's delivery.

He asked Ernest about the possibility of purchasing the original manuscript, but Ernest explained to him that he had given it to Uncle Gus to do with as he pleased, so ownership issues needed to be discussed with him. Dr. Guffey wrote to Gus and learned it was not for sale. Gus appreciated Dr. Guffey's high regard for the Hemingways but stressed that no price would induce him to sell, since he intended to keep it until Hemingway's death and pass it on to Patrick.[7]

On Armistice Day the Hemingways moved from the Lowry home to the Riviera Apartments, at 229 Ward Parkway, and Pauline went into labor. Dr. Guffey hoped that she could have a natural childbirth, but after more than twelve hours of labor and much suffering on Pauline's part, he performed another Caesarian. By 8 A.M. on November 12, the Hemingways had a nine-pound boy, large and lean, with all organs in the proper place, wide shoulders, and a big head.[8] Dr. Guffey told Pauline the shape of her pelvis had made it impossible for the baby to descend for a normal childbirth. He also told her that a third pregnancy might kill her.[9] They named the boy Gregory Hancock Hemingway, the "Hancock" in honor of Ernest's maternal grandmother's family. "We would have called him Max but it seemed bad luck maybe," Ernest wrote to his mother-in-law. "You can call him Max if you want."[10] Mary Pfeiffer must have been taken aback by such an insensitive reference to the earlier deaths of Uncle Gus's son Max and Paul and Mary's son Max.

Pauline remained in the hospital for about a month, while Ernest went to work on the last two chapters of his book. During the hospital stay, Pauline told her mother-in-law that Gregory did not resemble anyone in either family.[11] Ernest, on the other hand, told his in-laws that the baby had Pauline's forehead, his ears, and an Eskimo nose.[12] The new parents celebrated Thanksgiving Day in the hospital with turkey and fruitcake, and on December 1 Ernest headed to Piggott for a week of quail hunting. When he arrived, he found a note from Pauline tucked into his suitcase. Although the author's heroine in *A Farewell to Arms* died after a Caesarian birth, Pauline told Ernest she did not plan to die. If anything happened, however, she wanted him to know she would always be with him. Probably he should marry someone else after a while, since he needed the steady routine of marriage and a good environment for his children. "We've had a lovely, lovely time together," she told him. "Lovelier than anyone, and you have made me very happy, and I was never lonely with you and I love you more now than I ever did and always will."[13] Ernest may have felt some twinge of remorse at leaving Pauline and Gregory alone at the Kansas City hospital after reading her note, but not enough to give up the hunting trip.

Ernest arrived in Piggott a day ahead of Karl, traveling from New York to meet him, and hunted on his own without much luck. Once Karl arrived and put the Pfeiffers' two bird dogs to work, however, things changed dramatically. Karl's dog Dan and Virginia's dog Hoolie pointed Ernest and Karl each toward their limit of twenty quail within an hour.[14]

Virginia hunted a few times with her brother and brother-in-law before departing for Key West to get the Hemingways' house in shape, and Karl introduced Ernest to some of the locals. These included Mark Hopkins, part Indian and one of the region's best hunting guides. A blacksmith by trade, with a shop just off the Piggott town square, Hopkins had a reputation for being able to shoot quail in flight with a rifle.[15] He also could match Hemingway drink for drink. Karl recalled that Hemingway and Hopkins could "split a quart of gin and then get up and act like they hadn't had a drink."[16] Long-time local newspaper editor Laud Payne, who hunted with Hemingway, recalled that during this trip Hemingway began a practice that he continued each time he hunted in Arkansas. He traded shells to his hunting partners in return for the game they had killed, then put the quails in packages of six and the ducks in packages of two to send to his friends as Christmas presents.[17]

Ernest also found time to write while on the Piggott trip, and he became a difficult, darker person when he switched from hunting. His sister-in-law Matilda Pfeiffer remembered that it would take him a while to wind down after a full day of writing: "The word was 'Pay no attention to Ernest 'til he has had his drink.' . . . Then everyone would be happy."[18] By the time Ernest returned to Kansas City, he had finished the last chapter of his bull-fighting book. Pauline, released from the hospital on December 8, returned with him to the rented apartment for several days of rest. They left their newborn son at the hospital until the day of departure, then retrieved Patrick and his nurse and continued on to their new home.

When they arrived back in Key West, Virginia Pfeiffer and Carol Hemingway had things in fairly good shape. Carol, on holiday break from school, had arrived the week before Christmas to help out. The Hemingways moved in on December 19, and later that week a local newspaper headline announced that Key West had inspired "Love at First Sight" for the

Hemingways, now permanent residents.[19] But none of Ernest's romances proved permanent.

Pauline began restoration and renovation work immediately, even though still recuperating from childbirth. From morning until evening the house swarmed with carpenters, painters, plumbers, and electricians. A net placed over Gregory's crib kept plaster from falling into his eyes, but it did not keep his brother from dousing the baby with mosquito spray as a prank. With workmen around, keeping three-and-a-half-year-old Patrick out from under foot became a full-time job, but he slowed down after swallowing an arsenic-laced rodent tablet and vomiting for two days.

Instead of helping Pauline, Gabrielle needed attention herself. She became ill almost immediately after arrival and swore to the Hemingways that she could not imagine why, as she had never had a sick day in her life. During a visit to the doctor, however, he pointed out evidence of several surgeries and missing organs. Gabrielle then admitted she had been ill prior to taking the job with the Hemingways and that her French doctor thought the Florida climate might be good for her. Given her hefty weight, Ernest posited that her problems stemmed from overeating.[20]

With a new baby, an active older son, an ailing nurse, a house in need of attention, and no help from her husband, Pauline did too much lifting and running up and down steps and ended up in bed. Having been through two Caesarian surgeries with Pauline, Ernest considered himself knowledgeable on childbirth recovery and told his in-laws, "There is no way a woman can be more completely and utterly ruined than by not being careful for eight weeks after a baby is born, until the placental site is healed."[21] He assured the Pfeiffers that he was nursing everyone in the ailing household and supervising craftsmen. Despite his upbeat report to the Pfeiffers, the atmosphere choked his writing, and Ernest complained to his in-laws that if his book failed, he doubted readers would care about his parenting skills or his wonderful house. Thus, though he was good at giving advice, he was not much help with either parenting or home renovations.

As soon as Gabrielle and Pauline became well enough to travel, Gabrielle received a ticket back to Paris, and Pauline headed to New York in search of a new nurse. Ernest remained to run things with the assistance of a newly hired household staff, which included Isobel, the cook; Jimmy Smith, the gardener; Ida Hepburn, the laundress, and a houseboy named Bobby. Given the economic situation, Pauline had no trouble finding and training a household staff, but she wanted someone with more experience to look after her boys. The search paid off when she located Ada Stern, a middle-aged spinster from Syracuse, New York. Ada seemed to be the no-nonsense, take-charge person the Hemingways needed. She balanced firmness around the children with flexibility regarding the Hemingways' ever-changing plans and quickly became a part of the family.

Shortly after Pauline's return to Key West, her parents paid a visit to check out their newest grandchild. They vacationed in Miami, rather than their usual winter sojourn to Phoenix, to coincide with their expected attendance at Henry and Annie Pfeiffer's fiftieth wedding anniversary in Palm Beach. Mary, disappointed that they had missed Gregory's baptism on January 14 at St. Mary's Star of the Sea Catholic Church, celebrated with Paul by setting up a bank account for him. Mary mused that Gregory, already teething when they first saw him in March, seemed to be "in a big hurry to get thru with the things he has to do. I imagine he will be like that always."[22]

With crops in the field, Paul and Mary headed back to Piggott as soon as the Pfeiffer celebration ended in Palm Beach. The anniversary event apparently proved too stressful for Henry, who suffered a mental breakdown the next day and never fully recovered. Though Henry remained president of the family business enterprises, Gus took over many of Henry's responsibilities. First, however, Gus went to Key West for another round of fishing with Ernest.

During this second fishing trip of the season to the Tortugas, Ernest, Gus, Archibald MacLeish, Mike Strater, and Charles Thompson began serious discussion of an Africa trip. Gus displayed his passion for research and suggested they check out the African exhibit at the American Museum of Natural History. He conferred with a curator there, who indicated that many of the museum's specimens came from an area where the Hemingway party intended to hunt, and staff members would be happy to provide information even though they were not in the market for new specimens.

Not long after the Tortugas trip, Ernest found a new passion—marlin fishing in waters around Havana. Ernest went to Havana with his cousin Bud White, Joe Russell, and Charles Thompson aboard Russell's boat, the *Anita,* on what started as a ten-day excursion. The trip stretched into two months, with various wives and friends coming and going while the men mostly remained on the boat. The Ambos Mundos Hotel near the docks provided a place for wives and friends to stay when they visited and a quiet spot where Ernest could read galley proofs.

Though taking care of the boys and tending to household improvements limited Pauline's time, she managed two Havana visits in May for a week each time, perhaps to monitor her marital property. Part of the allure of Havana, particularly for Ernest, was the presence of their new friend Jane

Mason, who often fished with them. Pauline enjoyed Jane's company as much as Ernest, though she detected Ernest's infatuation with her. Beautiful, charming, a good sport, and a great admirer of Hemingway, Jane fed his insatiable ego. She enjoyed fishing with Ernest and the crew, and whenever Pauline came to town, Jane and her husband, Grant, showed them Havana nightlife.

If the relationship between Ernest and Jane became too close, Pauline hardly had time for it to register. She served as Key West dispatcher for her far-flung family, and attempting to coordinate everyone's schedules for the summer and fall was a logistics nightmare. The Hemingways' fifth wedding anniversary came and went on May 10 almost without notice, except for the telegram Pauline received from Jane Mason extending congratulations and letting her know that to mark the occasion two flamingoes awaited her in Havana. Pauline picked them up on her next trip and turned them loose to roam in the Hemingways' Key West yard, along with the peacocks Ernest had sent several weeks earlier.

Throughout Ernest's two months in Havana, whatever he needed or wanted became Pauline's top priority. And since Ernest did not want to be pinned down to a schedule with the marlin running, it made her tasks almost impossible. Clearly the trip to Africa originally planned that fall had to be postponed. Along with enjoying marlin fishing and reading galley proofs for his book, now titled *Death in the Afternoon,* Ernest wanted to hunt in Wyoming that fall, fearing it might be the last time for any really great hunting because of a new road planned through the area. Additionally, while in Havana he generated a number of short story ideas to develop in the fall. Gus agreed to postponement of the safari and assured Ernest that timing would not affect his willingness to finance the trip.

Toward the end of May, everyone's plans began falling into place. Virginia returned from Europe and headed straight for Piggott to finish the barn restoration, and Pauline sent the boys to Piggott with Ada, escorting them as far as Jacksonville to catch the train. When the children arrived in Piggott for what became a six-month visit, Ada impressed the Pfeiffers, even though they remained concerned about what little time the children seemed to have with their parents. Mary wrote to Pauline that they especially liked Ada's handling of Patrick, still at an impressionable age and needing "an understanding person to deal with him as he is intelligent beyond his years and resents wrong treatment more strongly than most children."[23]

By the first week of June, school let out for Carol Hemingway, so she and Pauline departed Key West for Havana. After a couple of weeks there, and with Ernest still not ready to leave, Pauline returned to Key West to inspect work in progress on the house. Two days later, she took the train to Piggott and found both boys thriving under the watchful eyes of their grandparents, Aunt Virginia, and Ada. Gregory displayed two new front teeth, and Patrick had friends and admirers all over Piggott.

Virginia had transformed the drafty barn into a cozy guest apartment, getaway spot, and writer's haven. The two lofts converted nicely to a room for writing and entertaining and a step-up area for sleeping. Pine floors now covered the loosely nailed cypress boards that had gaps wide enough to see into the stalls below, meaning Ernest no longer had to straddle the cracks with his chair and typing table. Walls paneled in beadboard had new windows cut in to allow plenty of light. Electricity, running water, and a wood-burning stove made the barn an ideal retreat. Pauline pronounced the project "grand" and began sleeping in the barn with Virginia, since a simultaneous visit from Karl's family filled the main house.[24]

After an additional week of fishing in Havana, Ernest and his sister Carol left for Key West so that he could finish the set of galley proofs for *Death in the Afternoon* that needed to be returned before they headed to Arkansas. A case of bronchial pneumonia, contracted during a rain squall on the eve of their departure from Havana, slowed his work considerably, but by July 2 they were on the road to Piggott. As soon as they arrived, Ernest went straight to bed.

Carol paid her respects to the Pfeiffers, visited her nephews, and then headed to Michigan for the remainder of summer with her brother Leicester before going to Europe to study at the University of Vienna. Within days of Carol's departure, Pauline and Ernest once again said goodbye to their sons and migrated west to Wyoming and another season at the Nordquist Ranch. Pauline basked in the time alone with Ernest, who appreciated the attention and wrote to Guy Hickok that Pauline was "cockeyed beautiful," her figure was lovely after Gregory's birth, and she had never looked or felt better.[25]

Though things seemed idyllic on the surface, their time together was marred by the fear that Pauline once again might be pregnant. Ernest wrote to Dr. Guffey that because Pauline's religion prevented her from taking precautions, he had been extra careful and "have either practiced withdrawal or used Havana's best Safeties and withdrawal. However, a certain amount of semen gets splattered around and this of mine seems very virulent."[26]

Pauline had taken Smith's ergoapiol capsules and other similar drugs in an effort to bring on her menstrual period, Ernest related, but in spite of successful use as prescribed by Dr. Guffey on other occasions, nothing seemed to be working.[27] Apparently, however, the pregnancy scare was a false alarm, perhaps brought about by the change in altitude when they headed west to Wyoming.

In September Gerald and Sara Murphy arrived at the Nordquist Ranch with two of their children, Baoth and Honoria. Son Patrick, still recovering from tuberculosis, stayed behind at the family's Hook Pond Cottage in East Hampton, Long Island. The two families spent three weeks fishing and camping together. While they enjoyed the reunion, they found that the warmth of their Paris friendship had cooled considerably in the intervening years. The Murphys saw unflattering changes in their old friend. Ernest seemed distant and quick to anger. After Sara criticized a meal prepared by the ranch staff one evening, Ernest snapped at her. Looking back, Gerald felt that at least Ernest had had some sort of exchange with Sara, whereas Ernest had little to say to him, critical or otherwise. He reflected to Archibald MacLeish that Hemingway was "never difficult with the people he does not like, the people he does not take seriously."[28] Gerald believed he belonged in that category.

As soon as the Murphys left, Charles Thompson arrived to hunt with Ernest, and Pauline departed on September 22 to return to Key West. Along with checking on restoration progress, Pauline had to meet Bumby, arriving for an extended stay to be tutored in math and other subjects by Ernest's friend Evan Shipman. The day after Pauline's departure from Wyoming, the publication of *Death in the Afternoon* brought less than stellar reviews. Most critics speculated that readers of this latest work would fall into two distinct categories: those wanting to know more about bullfights and those wanting to know more about Hemingway. As a treatise on the art and science of bullfighting, reviewers found it the most comprehensive book ever written on the topic. Some ranked the material among his best writing, and others deemed it overly romanticized. Those who read it to find out more about Hemingway, according to pundits, would be disappointed at the contrived and banal manner in which the author inserted his views into the book.[29] Nevertheless, Maxwell Perkins expressed pleasure with the book's start and stressed positive aspects of the reviews. Uncle Gus sent a telegram stating, "Scribner made good—the book was delivered on time. I ordered copies for the family, both in the U.S.A. and Europe, so I can assure you that at least sixty copies were bought."[30]

At the time of the reviews, Ernest was too intent on besting Thompson in his hunting exploits to worry about the criticism. Thompson had managed to shoot a bear, and there was no way Hemingway was going to be outdone. Finally, after tracking and killing his own bear, Hemingway was ready to leave. They departed Wyoming on October 16, driving through snow and ice to return to the warm Key West climate. Like Pauline, they stopped in Piggott long enough for Ernest to see his sons, go hunting with Karl, and make plans with Virginia for a group duck-hunting trip in south Arkansas in December. Virginia assured him that she would make all the arrangements. When Ernest arrived back in Key West, Pauline and Bumby hosted a welcome-home dinner consisting of green turtle steak, black beans, and yellow rice, accompanied by a good French wine.[31] Pauline looked forward to all three spending time together before Ernest departed to take care of business in New York.

Everything changed abruptly, however, when Pauline got a frantic call from Piggott telling her that both Patrick and Gregory had whooping cough and that the boys had become more than the Pfeiffers and Ada could handle without Pauline's help. She boarded the train for Piggott, leaving Bumby to go with Ernest to New York. Pauline wrote Ernest about Bumby's care, urging him to be careful about his eating, drinking, and sleeping and reminding him that Bumby needed "good *plain* food, no meat at night, not much between meals. Don't want him to get sick. Don't let him dress up too warm."[32]

Bumby made it through Ernest's New York business trip without getting sick, but he and his father arrived in Piggott during Thanksgiving weekend to find Pauline and Virginia both down with the flu. Soon Bumby succumbed as well. One morning while Bumby was ill, Ernest checked in on him before leaving to quail hunt with his brother-in-law Karl. After being gone all day, he returned to find Bumby acting strangely. In France, where temperature is measured in Centigrade degrees rather than Fahrenheit, Bumby had learned that a person could not live with a temperature above 44. Having discovered his temperature of 102, he had lain awake all day in the Pfeiffers' upstairs bedroom, waiting to die and trying to be brave about it. Ernest later turned the episode into a poignant short story titled "A Day's Wait."

Another story idea evolved from Ernest's drive from New York to Piggott with Bumby. As Ernest drove through the countryside, observing coveys of quail in the fields, he periodically glanced over at his son sleeping beside him in the front seat. His thoughts wandered to his own father, who had committed suicide nearly four years earlier. As he reflected on his role as both father and son, remembrances sowed the seeds for his short story "Fathers and Sons."

Adding another burden to illnesses in the Pfeiffer household, one of the worst ice storms on record hit Piggott, bringing everything to a standstill. Ernest used the time to work on short story ideas prior to the duck-hunting trip scheduled on the White River near Watson, Arkansas. The location, close to the confluence of the White and Arkansas rivers and just above where the two emptied into the Mississippi River, attracted many ducks migrating along the Mississippi Flyway. Virginia booked the houseboat *Walter Adams* for a party of four, and its owner assured them it would be well stocked when they arrived.

As the trip got closer, Pauline and Virginia became unsure whether they would be recovered sufficiently to go, and Ernest contacted Maxwell Perkins to join the party. On the morning Ernest was to leave to pick up Max at the Memphis airport, disaster struck when Virginia's newly remodeled barn caught fire. The Hemingways slept each night in the barn, and Pauline's father had arranged for a high school student, Rex Carter, to stop by early each morning on his way to school across the street to stoke the fire. When the student had it going, he routinely awoke Pauline to let her know, so that when the barn warmed up they could get up and shut off the damper. On that particular morning, they went back to sleep, only to be awakened by fire leaping at the windows in the next room.

Laud Payne, for many years editor of the local paper, saw the blaze when returning from an early-morning hunting trip and raced to help Ernest throw manuscripts and other belongings out the window. By the time firemen arrived to douse the flames, Ernest had lost his hunting clothes, his new clothes purchased in St. Louis, and a few guns, books, and manuscripts.[33] His most important papers and manuscripts survived, although they were wet from the fire hoses. Payne helped lay them out to dry but recalled he never got so much as a "thank you from Ernest."[34]

Karl recalled later that after the fire his former brother-in-law received a telephone call from a New York clothing firm, offering him a complete new wardrobe if he allowed them the use of his name in their advertising. "Go to hell," came Ernest's immediate response as he slammed down the receiver.[35] Irate at everyone but himself about the fire, Ernest focused on the student and "blessed him out," according to the version passed down in the Carter family.[36] The family story goes that when Paul Pfeiffer found out about the confrontation, he made Ernest apologize to the young man.

Regardless of actual culpability, Virginia chose to be upset with Ernest, blaming him for ruining her remodeling job by not tending the fire. Paul guessed that improper venting in the first place had also contributed. The next spring, when Virginia again undertook remodeling the structure, Paul handled the heating.

After excitement about the fire died down, Ernest met Max for the duck hunt. He borrowed hunting clothes, a gun, and shells from the houseboat owner, since his had gone up in flames, but remained in foul humor during the trip. Ernest's discomfort included pique about Paramount's handling of the movie version of A Farewell to Arms, including rumors and publicity to the effect that the movie had a happy ending. The hype supposedly justified the change with the statement that the author "had in mind a happy ending when he wrote the book."[37] Ernest said he had never contemplated any such thing.

Paramount set the movie premiere for early December, but with Ernest in Piggott, they hoped to hold off the New York showing and have the premiere in Piggott so they could include Ernest's comments in early publicity for the film. On December 2, Hemingway received a telegram from Paramount officials stating: "Two prints, unexpectedly available, make possible a private showing of the motion picture version of 'A Farewell to Arms' to your family and friends at Piggott on the night of the Broadway premiere or before. . . . Immediate reply appreciated so arrangements can be made."[38]

Ernest scribbled out several vitriolic responses, including "Use your imagination as to where Paramount can put two prints," before he finally settled on a telegram to Paramount representative Ralph Stitts that read: "Do not send here. If the book and motion pictures survive, a really great picture interpretation will be made. Meanwhile, although Paramount bought picture rights, it did not also get the right to my sanction of the picture version."[39]

The brouhaha continued when the film's director, Frank Borzage, heard that Hemingway had bashed the film because it had a happy ending. "Well, Hemingway hasn't seen the picture, so how does he know?" Borzage inquired in print.[40] He added that the film actually followed the book faithfully and held true to Hemingway's tragic ending: "The girl dies in the end, and if that is not an unhappy ending, I don't know what one is." He admitted, however, that the studio had made two endings and decided to premiere the tragic ending in New York. "Tell Borzage for me personally and not for publicity to watch his mouth," Hemingway fired off to the Paramount publicists.[41] Despite the rancor, Paramount determined to send the film to Piggott anyway in the hope that Hemingway would change his mind.

In the meantime, the New York premiere proceeded on December 7 with Gus Pfeiffer in attendance. Not aware of the long-distance dueling, he wired Ernest with glowing comments about the film and inadvertently stepped into the middle of the melee. He noted in his wire that Ralph Stitts of Paramount had telephoned him after the showing for his response and prevailed on him to intercede with Hemingway: "He does not understand how you learned picture would have happy ending. Stitts is anxious for you to see picture and solicit your suggesting changes to improve. He guarantees showing will be strictly private. Our party all felt picture quite correctly expressed scenes and spirit of book. Wire Stitts or me if when and where you will see picture or if you prefer call me long distance reversing charges."[42]

Ernest responded with yet another telegram, informing Gus that Paramount admitted making two endings and had not decided which to use until shortly before the opening. Further, after Ernest refused to preview the picture even privately, Stitts sent out publicity indicating that Hemingway had invited everyone in Piggott to see it as his guests. While Ernest sympathized with the need for publicity, he wanted no part of it and ridiculed the notion that Paramount would make changes at his suggestion at this late date.

"If picture is good am happy but will not approve it or disapprove it until see it sometime paying my own admission," he concluded, "and then would probably be wiser to keep my mouth shut. Glad you and Aunt Louise liked it."[43] The next day he received a simple telegram from Gus telling him to stick to his guns.[44] By the Piggott premiere, held nearly two weeks after the New York showing, Ernest had calmed down a bit and had other things occupying his attention, including the aftermath of the fire and the duck-hunting trip to south Arkansas. The favorable packet of reviews Gus sent from the New York premiere may have helped soften his attitude.

The *New York American* raved that the film "filled the hearts of a hard-boiled audience with emotions that welled to its throat and came from its eyes in hot, scalding tears."[45] The *Daily News* called it "heart-rending and throat-hurting. It moves you so deeply that it is often difficult to see the screen, for the haze which mists your tear-filled eyes."[46] The *New York Daily Mirror* went so far as to call it Borzage's masterpiece, with an "exquisite quality, a noble simplicity, a shining beauty which make even his previous lovely pictures seem insignificant."[47] Only the *New York Times* took issue, leading its review with "Bravely as it is produced for the most part, there is too much sentiment and not enough strength in the pictorial conception."[48]

Despite the overwhelmingly positive reviews, Ernest stood by his refusal to attend the Piggott showing. Several explanations covered his absence. One version said he purposely went to St. Louis that weekend to legitimately be able to say he was out of town and not available. Another story claimed he stayed in Piggott but refused to go, even though the rest of the family attended. His brother Leicester, who arrived in Piggott that week to quail hunt, recalled Ernest telling him to go and take Virginia. When Ernest pumped them afterward regarding treatment of different scenes, Leicester asked why he didn't go see it himself. "Nope, bad luck to see the picture now," Ernest replied.[49]

Virginia apparently had a slightly different recollection. She supposedly told a friend years later that Ernest had gotten over being mad, especially after the favorable reviews, and intended to go. The afternoon of the premiere, however, he went to the town square to hear all the buzz about the upcoming premiere from women gathered at the soda fountain at Reve's Drug Store. After he overheard two women expressing displeasure about *Tarzan the Ape Man* being preempted for the special showing, Ernest became furious. He stormed up the hill to the Pfeiffer home and retreated to the barn with a bottle of scotch and got drunk. The family found him in no shape to go anywhere and went without him.[50]

Whatever happened, the version about the women being more interested in *Tarzan* fit with the treatment given to the premiere by Piggott's newspaper. The day after the first showing, a small article at the bottom of the front page led with the fact that few towns the size of Piggott could boast a movie world premiere, pointing out that Paramount had brought the film to Piggott because of Ernest Hemingway's presence, that the film would not be seen outside of New York or Piggott until after the first of the year, and that box office proceeds would benefit the Community Fund. But the next paragraph went on to say: "'Tarzan,' the picture which scored such a tremendous hit in its one-night stand two weeks ago, has been called back and will be shown Friday and Saturday. This picture is one of the most interesting ever filmed, with beautiful scenery, numerous animals, and the pygmies making a background for a thrilling plot. This is not the same type of picture as the shows 'Bring Em Back Alive,' or 'Congorilla,' but is much more exciting and has a fascinating love story all the way."[51]

The same page gave far more prominence to two local items of interest than to the premiere. One item reported that Paul Pfeiffer had purchased and installed a Christmas tree on the northeast corner of the court square and led in cash contributions toward gifts for Piggott children who might not otherwise have a Christmas. The second article reported that Mrs. Virgil Smith, a tenant on one of P. M. Pfeiffer's farms, had set a record by selling $237 worth of chickens, eggs, and cream during 1932 through her own efforts, as well as assisting her husband with ninety acres of cotton and corn.[52]

With most of Piggott deeply impacted by the Depression, perhaps many people preferred a fanciful escapism about an ape man, rather than a story about war with a tragic ending. Those who attended the premiere, however, remembered it as a gala event with standing room only. John H. Jones, son of one of the town's doctors and then a young boy, recalled being awestruck by the searchlights that lit up the night sky around the theater and watching the Pfeiffers, who "arrived in a car like they knew how to do. . . . That made quite an impression on the town."[53]

Noel Berry Burton, a high school sophomore at the time, recalled that guests, motion picture people, and newspaper critics from St. Louis, Memphis, and Little Rock filled the town's small hotel and rooming houses. He felt fortunate to have a seat and remembered the aura of the evening and the community pride that lasted for days, marred only by a derogatory report in one of the major dailies that conveyed the rural nature of the town by describing "the round, pot-bellied wood stove that half-warmed the theater."[54]

By the time the Hemingways left Piggott, Ernest longed for winter to be over and wanted to forget his troubles with the movie, barn fire, ice storms, and family ailments. Almost a year later, however, some of the events in Piggott found their way into a book. After reading "A Day's Wait" in Ernest's book of short stories *Winner Take Nothing*, Mary Pfeiffer told Pauline that it stayed true to the facts, even though they had not given it much thought at the time. Instead, everyone was too busy grappling with "plague and fire and cold and all the evils attendant thereon. But it is past; we will forget it."[55]

CHAPTER 14

In Good Times and Bad (1933)

After the holidays, Pauline returned to Key West by train with the boys. Ernest drove as far as Roanoke, Virginia, where he put the car in storage and went on by train to New York. Having just been with his editor in Arkansas, Ernest probably had little business, but after all the turmoil of the previous months, he needed some time on his own away from family. This was despite the fact that he had spent less than four months total with his sons and about six months with his wife during the previous year.

While in New York, he made arrangements for a trip to Spain in the fall for follow-up work on *Death in the Afternoon,* and he met Thomas Wolfe, another of Scribner's literary lions. Ernest admired Wolfe's writing ability and called *Look Homeward, Angel* one of the two finest novels Scribner's had ever published—second only to *A Farewell to Arms,* of course. After becoming acquainted with Wolfe over lunch, Hemingway decided that he had "a great talent and a very delicate fine spirit," but believed the author's intelligence limited.[1] He had the opportunity to visit with other writers in Scribner's stable as well, including a disastrous evening with his old friend F. Scott Fitzgerald and the literary critic Edmund Wilson. Fitzgerald was drunk beyond coherence and had to be put to bed, causing Hemingway to write later to Perkins that Scott needed to grow up and sober up, two things that were not likely to happen.

When not conducting business or resurrecting old friends, Hemingway made social rounds with his sister-in-law Virginia. After two weeks in the city, Ernest returned by train to Roanoke, retrieved his car, and drove on to Florida. Pauline met him in Jacksonville to provide company on the last leg of the trip. Once back in Key West, things settled into a normal routine. The leisurely environment suited Ernest, providing a comfortable atmosphere to write in the mornings and a great place to fish in the afternoons.

The population of Key West had dwindled from thirty thousand inhabitants before the Depression to about eight thousand by 1933. All the cigar factories had closed, as well as the naval station, which had once employed about four hundred people.[2] Even maritime traffic out of Key West had decreased, due substantially to increased air travel. Most people flew from Miami to Havana, a two-hour trip that avoided waiting in Key West and possible rough waters in the Gulf. Despite the slower pace, the three Hemingway boys kept things lively in the household. Bumby's tutoring went well, and Pauline got him involved with the Boy Scouts to meet boys his own age.[3] Patrick referred to himself as "Old Bull Strength" and dubbed his little brother "Gregory the Unafraidest." A hammer became Gregory's favorite toy, and he could break nearly anything.[4]

Despite those who later questioned Pauline's maternal instincts, Bumby recalled his stepmother being a great storyteller and keeping them entertained for hours. One story in particular was an ongoing tale involving a fictitious boy who talked to fish and lived in the lighthouse across from the Hemingway house. As they passed by each day, Pauline expanded on the story, and the boys eventually added their own twists to the little boy's adventures. In later years, Bumby regretted not writing a children's book to capture the story.[5] When the boys grew bored with storytelling, Pauline always kept plenty of family pets around for excitement, including dogs, cats, goldfish, peacocks, and flamingoes. Sometimes non-pets stopped by, such as alligators, raccoons, and possums. The previously neglected yard became a showplace. Pauline loved working on the grounds with Jimmy the gardener, and the two planted and babied the palms, the eucalyptus, and the orchid tree.

With major renovations largely completed on the Key West house, the interior looked beautiful and livable. A great living room extended the entire length of the first floor on the north side of the house, with shuttered screen doors on three sides. Furnished with Pauline's antique furniture and modern paintings from Paris, the room had a spacious elegant look. Opposite the living room, separated by a central hall and stairs, the dining room, butler's pantry, and kitchen complex awaited completion. During the previous year, Pauline had remodeled the kitchen, originally separated from the main house by a breezeway, and connected it directly to the butler's pantry. Renovating the dining room and turning the butler's pantry into a children's dining area remained on her list of major projects for the main house, and Pauline launched into them immediately after returning from the holidays.

A studio set up in the small carriage house insulated Ernest from family commotion, and his writing went well. By the end of March, the author had completed four short stories and more than fifty pages of a new novel that never quite materialized. In addition, he had agreed to submit an article for a new men's magazine debuting in the fall.[6] Arnold Gingrich, its editor and a big Hemingway fan, assured him that this magazine, ultimately called *Esquire,* would be for men what *Vogue* was for women.[7] Ernest thought the magazine's name a bit high-toned for the Depression era; nevertheless, he became a major contributor.

After three highly productive months, including another trip to New York to work out details of his Spanish trip, Ernest rewarded himself by spending the next three months fishing in waters near Havana. Pauline's uncle Gus and her brother, Karl, became some of the first guests of the season. Ernest played the perfect host on the memorable Pfeiffer trip. Fishing started off slow when Gus became ill for three days. He recovered, however, and reeled in a seven-foot marlin on his first day back. On his final day of fishing, Gus recalled that "the Gulf seemed to change: the waters became animated and full of life." Watching the marlins "jump seven feet in the air, their heads shaking to throw out the hook, their whole bodies quivering, their brilliant colorings gleaming in the sun," created a vision he never forgot. Two of the biggest marlins got away—one breaking the line, the other shaking loose—but the struggle itself thrilled him. "I really could not feel badly or weep about losing them," he wrote to his family. "It was a fight between fish and man—the fish fighting for his life, the man fighting for the fish. One can hardly feel bad when the fish win some of the battles."[8] Ernest later captured this tension in his novella *The Old Man and the Sea.*

Karl shared some of the same thrills described by Gus and returned with a wonderful record of the trip on 16-millimeter film. The adventure had exceeded his expectations, he wrote Ernest, with highlights that he would never forget, such as "the first time I saw a Marlin jump, Uncle Gus landing his fish, your fine fight with the big one."[9] Gus's admiration for Ernest grew on the Havana trip. He found the writer great company and a genuine sportsman who relished a good fight but accepted defeat gracefully. "I cannot say too much in praise of Ernest," he wrote the family. "I have always stated that he is one of the few who are mentally honest. . . . He deserves all his success, and all the admiration and respect he has from those who know him.[10]

Although family members refrained from public comment about it, Pauline contributed significantly to Ernest's success, choosing not to pursue her own writing career. What she lacked in personal ambition she more than made up for when it came to assisting in developing her husband's literary reputation. Along with being his best editor and critic, she made sure during their marriage that he remained free of any responsibilities that might hinder his writing. As soon as he left for Havana on this particular trip, she organized his paperwork, as he saved virtually every scrap of paper from whatever source. Pauline enlisted Evan Shipman, after tutoring Bumby, to sort and classify Ernest's letters and papers. At one point, the house looked like a snowfield, with yards of pages laid end to end on the floor. Pauline shuddered to think what might happen if a hurricane came along.[11] With Ernest gone, she also used the opportunity to create a real office space for him above the carriage house, which became known as the "little house." Pauline wanted a room somewhat larger than their master bedroom, with lots of bookcases, two cupboards, a large storage closet, picture space, and a bathroom.[12] She anticipated having it completed by July, then acquiring furnishings while she and Ernest traveled in Spain.

Despite her busy schedule, Pauline wrote to Ernest nearly every day, reminding him to do his Easter duty, asking him to pick up tiles for the studio, and offering opinions regarding his appearance. "About your hair, don't know how to turn red to gold," she wrote. "What about straight peroxide—or better what's the matter with red hair. Red hair lovely on you, and you lovely yourself, and it will be so nice to have you again."[13] She visited Havana as often as possible. Though the pair generally devoted evenings to Havana clubs before retiring to the Ambos Mundos Hotel, they passed their days on the water, with Ernest showing her everything he knew about the sport. Ernest loved playing teacher, and when Pauline departed Havana, others awaited tutorials, including Jane Mason. Rumors abounded about goings-on between Ernest and Jane, but Pauline believed them to be just mutual admirers and generally tried to ignore gossip.

The rumors must have registered, however, since in one letter she enclosed an ad from a plastic surgeon and joked about having her "large nose, imperfect lips, protruding ears, warts and moles all taken off" before her next trip: "Thought I'd better. Mrs. Mason and those Cuban women are so lovely."[14] She concluded that same letter with a parting shot: "I can't wait to come to Cuba. . . . Will bring reels, bathrobe, slippers, etc. Found woman's hdkcf [handkerchief] in your woolen bathrobe pocket when putting it away. Have put away coat—found an extra button and sewed it on. Love from your wonder woman Pauline."[15] It was her not-so-subtle way of letting him know that she was not totally blind to his attentions to other women.

Bumby, Patrick, and the boys' nurse, Ada Stern, also made frequent visits to Havana for the boys to fish with Ernest. As an adult looking back over that summer, Jack (Bumby) Hemingway surmised that an affair took place between his father and Jane. He knew his father never carried on in front of the crew or on the boat, but later Ernest bragged to him that Jane liked climbing through the transom to his room at the Ambos Mundos Hotel.[16] Whatever happened that summer, it ended badly when Jane suffered two accidents. In the first, as she drove Bumby, Patrick, and her own son, a passing bus forced her onto the soft shoulder. She lost control of the car and slid down an embankment. Though the car landed upside-down, she got all the boys out, and no one was seriously hurt. Not long after the car accident, Jane broke her back under cloudy circumstances. Gossip had it that she either fell or jumped from the balcony of her home in a suicide attempt. Sent to the States to recuperate, she laid in a back brace for more than a year. Ernest commented about the episode that Jane was the only woman who ever truly "fell" for him.[17]

Though Ernest's behavior that summer appeared questionable, he could not have been more puritanical when it came to his younger sister Carol. Earlier in the year, John Gardner had contacted Ernest while in New York. Gardner, who attended Rollins College with Carol, wanted Ernest to know that he loved his sister and planned to marry her. Ernest, the protective big brother and male head of the Hemingway household, informed him that Carol could not marry without his permission, and she certainly did not have it. Undaunted, Gardner left for Europe to meet Carol where she studied at the University of Vienna. An infuriated Ernest tried to enlist help from his sister-in-law, still skiing nearby in Austria. Virginia declined and told him she thought Jack was a likeable guy. Both seemed a lot smarter than most twenty-year-olds, and even if they made a mistake, she told Ernest, it seemed better to make it and move on. "Perhaps they won't make any," she added. "The odds seem at least fifty-fifty. There is also a possibility that if Pauline had married Mr. Herold [her cousin Matthew], she would still now be Mrs. Hemingway isn't there?"[18]

Ernest even tried to convince his mother-in-law of the correctness of his position through a lengthy letter. He expressed disgust that Virginia seemed to be taking Gardner's side, partly because she liked Gardner and partly to irritate him. "From a man's standpoint he is about as bad as they come," Ernest insisted, "but from girls who have not had much experience with men he is simply wonderful."[19] With her usual patience, Mary pointed out that strong opposition to someone often made those involved that much more determined. "I have seen almost unsurmountable barriers swept away by two hearts that beat as one," she told him. "Haven't you? Oftentimes those things turn out better than one expects. Let us hope it will be so in this case."[20] Mary obviously saw parallels with the difficult days when Pauline pined in Piggott awaiting Ernest's divorce from Hadley.

Despite Ernest's protests, Carol and Jack married on March 21 in Kitzbühel, Austria. Ernest never spoke to his sister again, although she tried many times to contact him and patch up their relationship. "I always felt close to him anyway," Carol recalled. "It was as though, you know, I wasn't in his life, but he didn't really hold it against me. I didn't feel terrible animosity there. We didn't see each other again, but I often thought of him and I imagine he did of me."[21]

When Virginia returned that spring from Europe, she had a beau of her own—a blond German count. She introduced him first to Uncle Gus as they passed through New York. When her uncle asked about their marital status, Virginia replied, "Not yet."[22] By the time they reached Piggott, however, her ardor for the count had cooled. Mary Pfeiffer's message to Pauline and Ernest noted that the count "sojourned with us for a week and then went on his way, but not merrily. He was very much cut up that Virginia was not of a mind to continue with him to the journey end. Yes even on thru life."[23] In Mary's opinion someone always got hurt when two people traveled together in such an unconventional way.

Though the count interested her, Virginia opted for independence rather than involvement. After she sent him packing, Virginia apologized to Pauline about not coming to Key West before heading to Piggott. The problem was, she said, "I let somebody else step in and run my plans for awhile and it didn't take him long to make a bigger mess of it than I usually do."[24] Once rid of the count, Virginia went back to work on the barn and writing studio, this time opening up the main room, installing steps to the upper area, putting in extra windows, and building a brick flue to eliminate fire hazards. Virginia's father took great interest in the project as well, particularly in making it fireproof. When it was completed, Paul congratulated his daughter on a finished product much nicer than it had been before.

During the summer of 1933, Karl left Uncle Gus's employ in New York and moved back home to assist his father. By then many of Piggott's farmers had defaulted on crop loans and could not pay their rent, leaving Paul Pfeiffer strapped for cash. To infuse additional money into the operation, Paul suggested that his son move to Piggott with his family and invest his considerable savings in the Piggott Land Company. Mary wanted her son and daughter-in-law in Piggott as well, so that the Pfeiffers could help look after young Paul, whose physical handicaps became more difficult for his parents to deal with as he grew older. Karl and Matilda moved in with his parents while building their country manor on eleven acres just north of the home place. Matilda, who had always wanted to work on Hollywood sets, designed and supervised the English Tudor–style home and surrounding grounds.[25]

In the throes of the Depression, Pfeiffer building projects and activity helped feed numerous hungry Piggott workers and their families. Mary also canned fruits and vegetables from their orchard and garden to share with the community, and Paul's efforts to find work for those in need sometimes went far beyond expectations. Whenever anyone showed up at his door looking for work, Paul hired him to paint his house. Almost as soon as one man finished, another came along, and Paul assigned him to the same task. By the end of the Depression the Pfeiffer house had more than forty coats of paint. Paul also let it be known around town that his family needed quilts, resulting in tenants' wives bringing quilts from miles around. He bought them all, regardless of workmanship, and consigned them to an upstairs storage closet.

One day Mary wrote to Ernest, "Your father—following our dynamic President—has started a little forestation plan of his own. He is planting one hundred Catalpha trees. He says they are for posts for coming generations, but I know it is to give employment."[26] In spite of the Depression, Piggott's prospects looked up after Roosevelt took office and implemented the Agricultural Adjustment Act. Under this federal program, farmers received cash payments to set aside acreage, thus reducing supply and increasing price. The Piggott Land Company in 1933 plowed up 1,328 acres, or about 40 percent of that year's acreage planted in cotton.

"It all seems very strange and confusing," Mary reflected. Her husband worked all spring to plant crops, "and the last two weeks he has been working like a fiend to get the greatest possible number of acres plowed up."[27] By the end of July, the price of cotton had gone up by six dollars a bale. The reduced supply caused prices to double in one year, and the financial situation for farmers began to turn around. The plow-up also saved operational costs, such as planting, cultivating, and picking. "The President keeps opening one new avenue after another towards speeding recovery," Paul wrote to Ernest and Pauline. The success of the program, however, depended on how his plan was carried out: "If a bunch of politicians control the levers, I am afraid it will prove a big fiasco."[28] Paul approved of the president's plan, though revolutionary in many ways, since strong emergency measures would harvest timely results.

The Depression did not affect Uncle Gus as it did Piggott farmers. From New York he wrote Ernest that fall still seemed as good a time as any to make the Africa trip. Gus added that "we happen to have a surplus of funds and are more than pleased when somebody offers our First Preferred Stock for sale. Frankly, in these days investing money safely is not easy and not being speculators we do not wish to buy common stocks of other companies."[29] The Pfeiffer brothers made it a principle to avoid speculation, Gus told Ernest, and purchasing their own preferred stock met this principle. He first suggested that Ernest cash in the preferred stock he had given him earlier for trip expenses, but ultimately recommended that Ernest borrow against the stock. This approach allowed Ernest to have his money and continued ownership of a sound investment in uncertain times.

By Pauline's and Ernest's birthdays on July 21 and 22, plans had developed to tie Ernest's Africa trip with his fall business trip to Spain. When Gus sent birthday greetings, wishing them another year of good luck and good health, he concurred with their latest plans, praising them for always seeking experiences to broaden their lives. Relishing life provided sound insurance for happiness, he told them, so for an added measure of happiness, "please wave the magic wand of your imaginations over the enclosed checks and transform them into something you will enjoy having."[30]

The Africa trip shaped up much differently than originally envisioned when Archibald MacLeish and Mike Strater both canceled out. MacLeish backed out ostensibly due to financial difficulties, but in truth he had lost interest after his last fishing trip with Ernest. Following lengthy delays due to a storm that blocked their trip home, the two men squabbled over petty issues, and both hurled hurtful words that damaged their close friendship. Upon his return home, MacLeish wrote to Ernest, "I know that you do not believe in trusting people but I thought I had given you about every proof a man could of the fact of my very deep and now long lasting affection and admiration for you."[31] Though the two remained superficially friendly, the wounds inflicted during the fishing trip never healed.

Strater backed out for family and professional reasons, including a pregnant wife and a one-man show of his paintings scheduled before Ernest finally announced a definite date. Strater got the impression that Ernest had his nose out of joint over Strater putting his wife's condition ahead of the trip. As for the one-man show, "for Hemingway that was unimportant," Strater reflected. "He had a low opinion of his friends' achievements. He wanted to be a star that shone alone."[32]

Charles Thompson, the only man remaining, harbored reservations about whether he could play in the same league with Ernest. Pauline knew that Ernest would not be happy with only Thompson to share in his exploits, so she decided to go. While much more comfortable shopping and socializing than shooting, Pauline knew Ernest needed an audience in Africa.

Pauline, Ernest, Virginia, Bumby, and Patrick departed for Spain via Havana on August 4. Gregory stayed behind to travel with Ada Stern to her family home in Syracuse, New York. During their three-day layover in Havana, the Hemingway entourage witnessed the final throes of Cuba's

Gerardo Machado regime from their hotel room window. In the wake of growing economic and political unrest, the Cuban dictator was forced out of office in early August. Less than a month later the new provisional government was toppled by military forces led by Fulgencio Batista. The continuing instability and violence in the country resulted in the closing of the Pfeiffers' Hudnut branch in Cuba, one of only two unsuccessful branches in the world, the other in Chile.

Upon arrival in Spain in August, they went straight to San Sebastian and met Henriette, who took Bumby and Patrick back to her home in Bordeaux. Hadley seemed pleased that Henriette had agreed to look after Bumby, as well as Patrick, until Bumby's return to Paris for school. Hadley and Paul Mowrer had married during July in London, where he was covering the World Monetary and Economic Conference. Without having to worry about Bumby's welfare, she traveled on to Geneva with Paul for the World Disarmament Conference.

During his sojourn in Spain, Ernest abandoned the novel started earlier in the year. In the unfinished work, a writer in Paris is separated from his wife and in love with another woman, who happens to be in the United States. In the manuscript fragment, Ernest resurrects many of the feelings and experiences expressed in his actual letters to Pauline during their time apart. The fictional work differs in that the divorce is speeded up when the writer learns his first wife is in love with another man, freeing him to pursue his new relationship. With Hadley's actual remarriage, the fictional piece might have served as an excellent catharsis, but it was going nowhere as a novel.

With no major work in progress, Ernest used his time in Spain to edit galley proofs for *Winner Take Nothing,* take in bullfights, and work on his "Spanish Letter," one of a series of magazine articles regarding his trip promised to Arnold Gingrich for upcoming issues of *Esquire.* He also agreed to help his friend the bullfighter Sidney Franklin by editing his 422-page Spanish novel for English publication through Scribner's. Ernest thought the piece trashy, but Franklin remained a dear friend, and Ernest felt he owed him.[33] After nearly two months in Spain, Pauline and Virginia headed off to France; Ernest remained in Spain to read final proofs of his book and be fitted for safari boots.

Soon after Pauline arrived in Paris, Hadley returned from Geneva and invited Pauline to go with her to visit Bumby's school, just a half hour out of Paris. Pauline liked the school, which had only seventeen pupils and seemed a lot like her old convent, and she greatly appreciated the invitation from Hadley.[34] Pauline reported to Ernest that Hadley liked the decorative plates the Hemingways had sent as a wedding gift. She sported a new mink coat and looked very happy.

With Ernest in Spain by himself, without the company of his wife or any of his hunting or fishing companions, he and Pauline wrote letters to each other almost daily. Pauline knew the kind of funk Ernest could get himself into when alone, so her letters stayed bright and cheerful, full of news and assurances, such as "I miss you very much and in such surprising places, such as crossing the streets in traffic and when I've eaten too many chocolate peppermints, and especially when I get in bed at night."[35]

Ernest had trouble being in bed by himself as well and tried sleeping on Pauline's side, but wrote to her, "Your side is no better than mine. . . . I just sleep in it now to remember you by."[36] He liked Pauline's idea of antique tiles for his studio and took a day to go through about four hundred tiles to pick out twelve that he thought Pauline would like. Though they were expensive, Ernest felt justified since he had received a refund that day on overcharges for the Africa trip.[37]

Despite her concern about higher prices in France, Pauline bought four old Morrocan rugs for less than fifty dollars each, cheaper than similar rugs she had purchased on previous trips. Two appeared perfect for Ernest's studio, and the others would fit somewhere in the house. The two not in her studio budget could come out of her clothes budget for the Africa trip, she rationalized.[38]

Everyone seemed to be in a buying mood. News from Piggott told of climbing cotton prices under the new government programs, and many cotton farmers got out of debt for the first time in years. Though other farmers around the country faced ruin, Paul Pfeiffer remained optimistic that Roosevelt's plans could work if allowed continued implementation without interference from big business.

While things were looking up financially at home, letters back and forth from Pauline's family expressed growing concern over politics in Germany. With Ernest in Spain, Pauline in Paris, Gus in New York, Paul in Piggott, and numerous Pfeiffer relations in Germany, viewpoints varied regarding a new German leader named Hitler, who had come to power earlier that year. Family members agreed that the Western powers had contributed to Hitler's rise through punitive features of the Treaty of Versaille. "A peace treaty should never be written by the military leaders," Paul Pfeiffer told his son-in-law. "They are too much dominated by revenge to write a treaty that will stand *seasoning*."[39] Paul held a wait-and-see attitude with regard to Hitler, due to conflicting news out of Germany and lack of clarity on Hitler's specific plans. "Hitler himself, as is usual with dictators, is employing dramatics and the German people have about decided not to let England and France wipe their feet on the face of Germany any longer, and I don't blame them," he told Ernest.[40]

Pauline agreed. When Hitler withdrew Germany from the League of Nations and walked out of the World Disarmament Conference, Pauline told Ernest, "Germany had a point in resigning from the League. I do think she had a humiliating position."[41] Ernest assured his wife and in-laws that Hitler worked for only one thing—war. "He says one thing with his mouth and does another with his hands," he wrote to Mary Pfeiffer. "War is the health of the State and anyone with his conception of the state has to have war or the threat of war to keep it going."[42]

At the time, however, safari plans rather than world politics preoccupied both Hemingways. Ernest joined Pauline in Paris after stopping in Bordeaux to pick up Patrick. They tied up loose ends for the Africa trip and revisited their favorite spots in Paris, but the Paris they knew was gone, along with most of their Paris friends. The Murphys lived in New York and were tending their ailing son. Archibald and Ada MacLeish and John and Katy Dos Passos lived in Massachusetts. F. Scott and Zelda Fitzgerald resided in Towson, Maryland, with Zelda in and out of mental clinics. Lady Duff Twysden and her husband, Clinton King, could barely make ends meet in New York. In "A Paris Letter," written for the February 1934 issue of *Esquire* during Hemingway's visit, he wrote, "Paris . . . was a fine place to be quite young in. . . . We all loved it once and we lie if we say we didn't. But she is like a mistress who does not grow old and she has other lovers now." Ernest wrote that he had other new loves as well and preferred life "out on the ranch, or in Piggott, Arkansas in the fall, or in Key West, and very much better, say, at the Dry Tortugas." [43]

One of the few early friends remaining in Paris was Gertrude Stein, the last person Ernest wanted to see. Stein's memoirs, published earlier in the year as *The Autobiography of Alice B. Toklas*, made unflattering references to Ernest. She infuriated Ernest with her statement that she and Sherwood Anderson had created him, and he resented her description of him as "fragile" and her suggestion that "whenever he does anything sporting something breaks, his arm, his leg, his head."[44] Though Ernest had fallen down a flight of stairs before heading to Paris and suffered from strep throat as his most recent malady, he disparaged her notion.

His new book of short stories, *Winner Take Nothing*, came out the day after he arrived in Paris. Reviews disappointed him, as was often the case, but sales went well. His father-in-law wrote before publication that he thought it had a fine title and sounded as though it covered a lot of territory.

"We are all anxious to get the copy that Brother Gus has promised us," he told Pauline. "Mother and I have great faith that it will be a fine book. You know we have always given Ernest credit for brains and of course we know he has plenty of action."[45]

After such high praise from his father-in-law, Ernest became concerned about some of the book's themes and tried to prepare his mother-in-law for its complex relationships and unconventional topics, such as castration, prostitution, and lesbianism. "I am trying to make, before I get through, a picture of the whole world—or as much of it as I have seen," he told his mother-in-law. "These stories are mostly about things and people that people won't care about—or will actively dislike. . . . Sooner or later as the wheel keeps turning I will have ones that they *will* like."[46] Mary responded tactfully after the book arrived by writing to Pauline, "Ernest's book came last night. Have had time to read but one story as the other members of the household wanted to see it."[47] She had read only "A Day's Wait," Ernest's story of Bumby's illness while in Piggott the previous year.

As the Africa leg of the Hemingway trip approached, Virginia and Patrick departed for New York, stopping first in Syracuse to check on Ada and Gregory before going to Piggott for the Thanksgiving and Christmas holidays. Though the Pfeiffers wanted their youngest grandson in Piggott for Christmas as well, Ada had made plans for him to be with her family in Syracuse for the holidays, and the Pfeiffers chose not to push the issue. The Pfeiffers were somewhat surprised to learn that Pauline intended to go with Ernest to Africa, rather than remain in Paris as they had originally thought. "And so you are to journey to Africa in the near future," Mary wrote to her daughter. "What part please? Just Africa is pretty indefinite. I have been looking at it on the map. Have also purchased a globe the better to keep you located."[48]

CHAPTER 15

On Safari (1933–1934)

Charles Thompson arrived in Paris to join the Hemingways for the trip, and on November 22, 1933, they boarded the *General Metzinger,* bound for their next great adventure. Ernest assured his mother-in-law he would take good care of Pauline on the trip. The seventeen-day journey took them from Marseilles down the Mediterranean to Egypt, where they went ashore at Port Said for dinner and sightseeing. The ship passed from the Suez Canal into the Red Sea and through the Indian Ocean before disembarking at the African port of Mombasa. Coincidentally, the same port shipped chilies to the Pfeiffers' pharmaceutical company for their Sloan's Liniment.[1]

After freshening up, the party went on by train the 330 miles to Nairobi, where they checked into the New Stanley Hotel. Jane Mason, who had been on a previous safari, insisted they needed Philip Percival as their guide, but he remained unavailable until December 20. That gave them almost two weeks to become acclimatized to the higher altitude, enjoy the sights, and get in some practice shooting in the immediate vicinity of Nairobi. It also gave them the opportunity to strike up friendships with two wealthy, avid sportsmen, Winston Guest and Alfred Vanderbilt, with introductions provided by Jane Mason. Vanderbilt and Guest also were waiting on their safari leader, Percival's partner, Bror von Blixen, whose ex-wife Karen had written *Out of Africa* under the pen name Isak Dinesen. Hemingway, impressed with Von Blixen's reputation as the best white hunter in East Africa, found himself equally taken with Percival, the guide company's director.

With Percival in charge, they headed toward the Tanganyika border across rolling plains and bush country. Two days into the trip, they spent one day at a luxurious hotel in Arusha, a treat Pauline missed over the next two months. Leaving Arusha, they pushed on across the Rift Valley, up over the rim of the Ngorongoro Crater, and out onto the vast Serengeti Plain.

Magnificent scenery, unlike any that Ernest and Pauline had seen in all their travels, stretched across the horizon. They admired herds of all manner of game, including giraffes, zebras, antelopes, kudus, buffalo, and as many as thirty lions in one group. Regrettably, the view came amid heat so intense at midday that the color faded out of Pauline's nail polish within a few hours.[2]

Ernest started off poorly, spending an entire morning shooting and missing a prize gazelle, but Percival assured him that everyone shot off the mark at first. Ernest almost became the first major kill. They spotted their first lion on Christmas Eve, and after shooting two zebras to bait the lion, Ernest put his gun on the top rack of their vehicle to begin pursuit. Not long after, Pauline heard a huge explosion and looked in Ernest's direction to see that the supposedly uncocked gun had fallen to the ground at his feet and fired. Pauline found Ernest alive but shaken. Later the experience found its way into Hemingway's short story "The Short Happy Life of Francis Macomber."

Pauline did not take to big-game hunting the way Ernest did, but she acted like she enjoyed it for his sake. In truth, she did not like killing and feared animals bigger than herself. Whenever Pauline shot and missed, the guide assured her of a splendid shot, but it just needed to be a little higher, a little lower, or a little more to the right or left. To make matters worse, she felt plagued by the heat, dust, fleas, night noises, and far too many men around, including assistant hunters, gun bearers, drivers, cooks, and others in the party of forty.

Pauline's spirits picked up, though, on Christmas Day when Ernest presented her with the dustproof, waterproof watch she wanted, which he had purchased while in Paris. Being away from their children on the holiday tempered Pauline's pleasure, but the boys were in good hands. Gregory celebrated the day with Ada Sterns's family in Syracuse; Patrick stayed in Piggott with his grandparents and Aunt Virginia. Patrick came down with chicken pox over the holidays, "but he took very good care of himself and didn't scratch," Virginia assured his parents, "so I don't think there are any marks that will last."[3] After the holidays, the two brothers reunited in Key West, with Gregory arriving from Syracuse with Ada, just ahead of Virginia and Patrick. In addition, Ernest's sister Ursula, now the author's "best sister," moved in with her daughter Gale to help house-sit.[4] Virginia and Ursula fished with some of the locals until Virginia left for New York to see relatives.

For her relatives in Africa, the hunting became more intense after the holidays. By the end of the first week in January, Ernest and Charles each had animal trophies for four of the five animals on their most dangerous list—lions, cheetahs, leopards, and buffalos. Only the rhinoceros remained to check off the list. Pauline had had some success with lesser game, but she preferred cheering for Ernest's success when it came to bigger game. The gun bearer assigned to the Hemingways, known as M'Cola, took a liking to Pauline and remained extremely protective of her throughout the hunt. He referred to her as Mama and believed that others on the hunt "were simply a lot of people who interfered and kept Mama from shooting things."[5] M'Cola's protectiveness resulted in an incident that was somewhat embarrassing for Pauline. Everyone had decided that Pauline should have the honor of killing the first lion, but when her first shot missed, Ernest fired off a shot that brought it down. M'Cola did not believe that Pauline had missed and sent the word out among all the others in camp that Mama had killed her lion. When they returned to camp, Pauline wrote in her Africa diary that she was "greeted by all the boys clapping and chanting and carried on their shoulders to my tent. Very splendid; wished I had shot the lion." As was the custom, Pauline gave a shilling to everyone in camp.[6]

Ernest pushed himself throughout the entire hunt, even though by mid-January he clearly had dysentery and was flown to Arusha for treatment, while Pauline and Charles continued the hunt with Percival. Four days later Pauline and Percival drove into Arusha to surprise Ernest, only to find that he had been taken on to Nairobi, where a doctor put him in bed at the Hotel Stanley and began a series of shots. The shots helped, and after exchanging telegrams, Ernest assured them that he had recovered and would meet them two days later in Arusha to return to the field. On her first morning in Arusha, Pauline awakened to the sound of Sunday-morning church bells and felt bad about not being able to go to mass. But with no stockings to cover her bare legs, her only alternative was to wear pants, which she could not bring herself to do inside a church. Even though Pauline had veered far afield from her Catholic teachings by marrying Ernest, she clung to church rituals and dress protocols. For Pauline, practicing the rituals of the church became more important each year as a way to atone for the major sins and guilt resulting from her early relationship with Ernest, including premarital sex, the breakup of his family, and possibly even an abortion.

Hemingway rejoined the hunt on January 24 with gusto. He and Thompson both got rhinos, though Hemingway displayed chagrin that Thompson dropped the best specimen. When Hemingway saw Thompson's rhino, he wrote later in his safari account, "He had made my rhino look so small that I could never keep him in the same small town where we lived."[7]

Thompson, not attempting to outhunt his host, did so anyway. As each impressive prize was credited to Thompson, Hemingway grew more jealous. His competitive nature caused so much irritation that Percival began keeping the two men totally separated, taking the Hemingways out himself and sending Thompson into the field with his assistant.

In the final days of the safari, they searched for kudus, the African gazelles with spirally twisted horns that made such great animal trophies. By this time, weary of the hunt, Pauline generally remained in camp. They went several days without either man spotting or killing a kudu, the last animal on their list, and Pauline wrote in her diary each evening, "No kudu."[8] On the fifth day of their search, Thompson finally killed one, although not a great specimen. Ernest brightened at the thought that it would not be difficult to find a better specimen, but several additional days passed with no luck.

Percival, worried because they needed to start back to Nairobi, did not wish for his client to be disappointed. But the rainy season was approaching, and after the rains the roads would become impassable. Nevertheless, he decided to remain as long as possible. Six days after Thompson's kudu, with Ernest still out in the field, Pauline learned that Thompson had killed another kudu, this one a magnificent specimen. With the advent of dismal weather, Pauline knew they had to turn back, and it appeared there would be no kudu for Ernest.

Feeling bad for him, she turned in early, only to be awakened around 10 P.M. by loud singing and dancing outside. She rushed out in her pajamas to find Ernest back in camp with two kudus and a sable. An elated Ernest and Pauline spent the evening celebrating. After he saw Thompson's second kudu in the morning, however, with what appeared to be the biggest pair of horns, Ernest wrote, "I did not want to see mine again; never, never."[9] With their trophy lists completed, the party declared the safari officially over, and they broke camp and headed back to the coast. There Ernest arranged for a two-week fishing expedition with Percival, Thompson, and Vanderbilt, while Pauline relaxed at the Palm Beach Hotel on a white sand beach in Malindi.

The successful fishing trip took the sting out of not being the star of the safari for Ernest, and they boarded the *Gripsholm* during the first week of March for the long trip home. The ship stopped in Haifa, where Lorine Thompson joined them, bearing pictures of Patrick and Gregory. Lorine recalled Pauline being moved nearly to tears. "Poor little lambs," she commented. "I can see they miss Mummy."[10] Their father remained unmoved, however, and uninterested in heading straight home. After a picnic on the banks of the Sea of Galilee, the two couples reboarded the ship and went on to Villefranche, where they disembarked for Paris. Ernest and Pauline gave Lorine a quick tour of the city before the Thompsons headed back to Key West. The Hemingways remained in Paris for nearly two weeks.

On April 3 they arrived back in the States—eight months from when they had started. Uncle Gus had a gathering at his apartment a few days later to welcome them home, and the Hemingways showed reels of film and photographs and regaled guests with their adventures, insisting they could not wait to go back—a sentiment probably shared by Pauline only to the extent that she wanted to be with Ernest, wherever that might be. The Hemingway party returned from the safari with four lions, two leopards, three cheetahs, two rhinoceros, and four buffalo. Their trophy kills also included gazelles, wildebeests, impalas, klipspringers, zebras, oryx, bushbucks, reedbucks, waterbucks, roan antelopes, topi, elands, sables, and kudus.[11]

Impressive results, but Pauline undoubtedly preferred the trophies she had acquired before the safari and shipped from Spain to Uncle Gus for safekeeping until her return. Containers waiting for her in New York held primarily eighteenth-century antiques, including a sideboard; two tables; an armchair; a stool; a seventeenth-century chest; an 1810 carpet; a variety of lamps, bowls, jars, and vases; and the sixteenth-century earthen tiles picked out by Ernest.[12] Between animals and antiques, both Hemingways felt good about the trip.

One thing remained to do before they returned to Key West. Ernest longed for his own fishing boat, and they looked at a thirty-eight-foot cabin cruiser at Wheeler Shipyard in New York. Thanks to a three-thousand-dollar advance from *Esquire,* he made a down payment. Modifications Ernest wanted included additional gas tanks, the transom lowered twelve inches for pulling in big fish, a live fish well, a second deck chair, and an auxiliary motor. The hull was to be painted black with the name *Pilar* in white letters and "Key West" below the name.[13]

After sending Pauline ahead to Key West, Ernest met with natural historians at the Philadelphia Academy of Science. Through Gus Pfeiffer, the historians had become interested in Ernest's theories on marlin, particularly his idea that fewer species existed than originally thought. Ernest attributed differences to the same fish at various stages in the life cycle and made arrangements for the men to join him on his new boat later that spring for firsthand research.

A welcoming crowd greeted Ernest back in Key West, including Pauline, Patrick, Ada MacLeish, John and Katy Dos Passos, the Thompsons, his brother Leicester, and a local jazz band. His return was a major marketing opportunity for area businessmen. In the Hemingways' eight-month absence, Key West had begun its transformation into a tourist haven, luring travelers en route to Havana. Thus, the town celebrated the return of its favorite son, the great writer, fisherman, big-game hunter, and all-around adventurer Ernest Hemingway.

Early in May many of the same faces waited at the Key West navy submarine base, now mooring luxury boats, for arrival of Hemingway's *Pilar*. Looking regal, she cruised into the harbor with Ernest at the helm. Beside him stood Bra Sanders, who had assisted in bringing the boat down the inland route between Miami and Key West, and a boat company representative, along for the shakedown cruise to take care of any necessary adjustments.

The respect demonstrated for the Hemingways upon their return from Africa did not extend to their own household. With Ernest and Pauline away for so long, Patrick and Gregory no longer viewed them as "the bosses."[14] Ada Stern's continuing domination over their daily lives made it especially difficult for the boys to accept parental authority. One visitor in the Key West household that summer, Arnold Samuelson, recalled that it appeared hard to tell that the children belonged to Pauline since she rarely accompanied them. Samuelson, a young writer from Minnesota, had come to Key West early in the summer hoping to meet his favorite author. Not only did he get to meet his literary hero, but Ernest put him to work for the summer helping take care of the *Pilar*.

When in port, Samuelson often visited the Hemingway home and noted that the boys ate their meals in a separate room with Ada, who taught them table manners and etiquette. She accompanied them on afternoon walks downtown for ice cream and supervised play in the backyard. They rarely had playmates over with Ernest at home, partly because none of Pauline and Ernest's friends had children, but mainly because the noise disturbed Ernest's writing. Instead, they played quietly with their toys, ignoring everything else going on around them. A garage full of toys kept them occupied, including tricycles, cars, wagons, rocking horses, and an assortment of castoffs from their father's hunting and fishing expeditions. "They played with their toys as oblivious to spectators as animals in a zoo," Samuelson remembered. "No laughter, no anger, no excitement. No stress of any kind."[15]

Though the boys had to be quiet in the mornings while Ernest wrote, things became less rigid in afternoons, particularly when Ernest left to fish aboard the *Pilar*, now almost his real home. On the boat the author came and went as he pleased and took full advantage of being in command. Pauline caught the first marlin aboard the *Pilar*, and Ernest reeled in a record sailfish. Father Magrath, a Catholic priest out fishing with Ernest, actually set the hook but turned him over to Ernest when he was unable to bring him in. Ernest garnered the glory, however, and the *Miami Herald* ran a story crediting him with the record, including a photo of Hemingway posed by the fish on the dock. Ernest quietly explained to his friends that the Jesuit priest did not want his name in the papers.[16]

As usual, Gus Pfeiffer praised Ernest's role in the feat. "I was delighted and enthused over your bringing in the huge, record Atlantic sail fish," he told him. "I can appreciate how pleased you would be if you had, besides bringing him in, hooked him. Actually, however, the honors of landing the fish are yours. Most any one can hook a sailfish, the real achievement is bringing him in."[17]

With an African safari under his belt, his own boat, and a record fish added to his triumphs, Hemingway began to believe the larger-than-life image of himself created in the press. He became an insufferable bully and a self-righteous know-it-all, according to some of his friends. Archibald MacLeish attempted another fishing trip with him upon Ernest's return from Africa, only to have it disintegrate once again into an argument. After the trip, Hemingway wrote to Waldo Peirce, calling MacLeish "righteous, fussy, and a bloody bore. . . . But he kept asking for it and asking for it. I only like the people I like. Not the bastards that like me."[18] MacLeish expressed more charity toward Ernest. "He was fed up with the world and I was fed up with him," he recalled years later. "It was a simple conflict of over-exposure. He was a wonderful, irreplaceable, but an impossible friend; a man you couldn't get along with, a man you couldn't get along without."[19]

Mike Strater found himself in a similar situation when he fished with Ernest for the first time aboard the *Pilar*. During the trip Ernest acquired a Thompson submachine gun for keeping sharks away from their fish. When Strater hooked a twelve-foot marlin and tried to reel him in, Ernest's shots at nearby sharks put blood in the water, resulting in a feeding frenzy. The blood drew more sharks to the area, and by the time Strater got his marlin on board, little remained.[20] Strater, furious at Hemingway for ruining what would have been the biggest marlin he ever hooked, remembered, "We were friends, but he was a goddamned thankless friend."[21] Strater, not invited to fish with Hemingway again after catching the big fish, figured some of Ernest's animosity toward him stemmed from his refusal to go to Africa. "I would have been a fool to go," he believed. "He would have tortured me in every way possible."[22]

F. Scott Fitzgerald also felt tortured by Hemingway. Though they had not been close for years, Fitzgerald still admired and envied Hemingway's writing, while Hemingway saw him as a drunk whose crazy wife, Zelda, had ruined his literary career. When Fitzgerald's *Tender Is the Night* came out in 1934, with Dick and Nicole Diver patterned after the Murphys, he waited anxiously for Ernest's opinion. Rather than providing encouragement, Ernest berated him for taking liberties with the Murphys, resulting in "faked case histories," rather than real characters. "You're a rummy and Zelda does not help," Hemingway told him. "All you need to do is write truly and not care about what the fate of it is."[23] Upset by Hemingway's rebuff, both personally and professionally, Fitzgerald turned down an offer to fish with him in the fall of 1934. Cowed by Ernest's success and his own perceived failures, Fitzgerald could not face Ernest in person. Instead, he devised a story about his mother being ill and needing to tend to her.[24]

Throughout summer and fall of 1934, Hemingway worked on what he expected to be his next major success. His Africa book had elements of a novel and a travelogue. Ernest prided himself on writing a true and honest account of their safari, but he gave fictional names to participants for a novel-like quality. Pauline became P.O.M. (Poor Old Mama), Charles was Karl, and Philip Percival was Jackson Phillips or Pop. If Pauline sacrificed personal comfort to be with Ernest on the safari, she got her reward in the fictional treatment. "The only person I really cared about, except the children, was with me," Hemingway wrote, "and I had no wish to share this life with any one who was not there, only to live it, being completely happy and quite tired."[25] Even in the hot safari country, Ernest described Pauline as "very desirable, cool, and neat-looking in her khaki and her boots, her Stetson on one side of her head."[26]

While Ernest concentrated on the Africa book, Pauline and Patrick departed for Piggott on May 31, and Gregory stayed with Ada Stern. Pauline could manage only one child at a time without Ada along to help. After she departed, Pauline sent Ernest a pair of dark blue fishing trousers purchased in Jacksonville and a note that read, "Patrick is a fine boy, but not, I am learning, you. . . . Hope you don't miss me as much as I miss you."[27] By the time Pauline arrived in Piggott, she had spent all but $6 of her travel money. Once in Piggott, however, her father alerted Pauline to a childhood savings account with a balance of $2,308. She immediately sent $400 of the nest egg to Ernest. "I'm sure all my life I was saving for a time like this," she happily informed him. "Pay yourself a *good* salary. To hell with the bills. Can bring along some more if you wish. Have no end of this filthy money. Just leave me know and don't get another woman."[28]

To guard against that possibility, Pauline watched her weight. After a week in Piggott, she weighed only 113 pounds. "Far from gaining here I am thinning up and shaping out," she wrote Ernest, "and I'm kind enough to think that I look like a better wife & more for the money and at the same time less." She signed it, "Your white wench."[29] To be in perfect shape upon return to her husband, Pauline spent her nearly three weeks in Piggott playing tennis in the mornings with Virginia on their brother's new court and swimming in the afternoons with Virginia and Patrick. While his mother exercised, Patrick played with cousin Paul, canoed on the St. Francis River with Aunt Virginia, and visited his grandfather at the bank, where Paul often loaded his grandson's pockets with coins to be spent in the local drugstores.

Pauline's letters to Ernest during this period possessed the same qualities found in her correspondence almost eight years earlier, before they were married. "The days are very long here. Wish you were in them," she wrote shortly after arriving. "Please keep on missing me, for I miss you very much and X X X X to Gregory and you really do miss me don't you? Don't know why I can't write better letters—maybe too much exercise and not enough Ernest."[30] Ernest's letters to Pauline sounded equally reminiscent of earlier days, causing Mary to reflect to her son-in-law, "My observation Ernest, is that Pauline reads your letters with as much pleasure and complete absorption as she did the ones that came before you were married. That is interesting and quite exceptional after seven years."[31]

At the end of the Piggott visit, Pauline and Patrick headed to St. Louis to pick up Bumby for the summer. Bumby now lived in Chicago with his mother and stepfather, and Pauline arranged with Hadley to meet him at the St. Louis train station before returning to Key West on June 21. Pauline with the two boys arrived in Key West to find Gregory in good spirits and Ernest so deeply engrossed in his book that even fishing visitors had worn thin, particularly when not guests of his choosing.

Although Pauline cheerfully entertained Ernest's guests, the reverse proved not always true. Thus, when she invited her cousin Ward Merner to stop in Key West en route to South America on business for Uncle Gus, the invitation displeased Ernest, and he let Pauline know his resentment of the intrusion. Part of his attitude developed because Ernest was prepared before the visit to dislike Ward. Prior to Ward's arrival, Mary Pfeiffer wrote to Ernest, "Ward will always be at a disadvantage on account of his stature. People seem to resent the housing of such a mammoth intellect in so small a space."[32]

Likewise, Gus wanted Ernest's opinion of Ward, since Ward represented him at some of the South American plants. "Ward has in mind doing many, many things," he commented. "More I feel than he can hope to accomplish in one man's allotted time on earth. However, there is some advantage to having many things ahead of you to do."[33] Such praise did not sit well with Ernest, who felt threatened by such high praise of others. After meeting Ward, Ernest could not see why the family made such a fuss over him. He decided that Ward had a good mind and a wealth of general information, but nothing remarkable.[34]

Some of this same attitude toward the talents of others occasionally crept into his treatment of Pauline. Ernest valued Pauline because he did not have to worry about competition from her, and she had the skills to edit and improve his work. He enjoyed, even if he did not fully appreciate, the fact that she had dropped her career to help make his. As the Hemingway legend grew, however, Ernest downplayed her role. On one occasion, aboard the *Pilar,* Arnold Samuelson recalled a conversation when Ernest told Pauline, "You threw away a novel that was better than Main Street."

"Could I write as good as Sinclair Lewis?" she volleyed.

"Much better."

"Could I write as good as Ernest Hemingway?"

"Now don't start that, Mummy," Hemingway quickly responded. [35]

On August 13, Ernest departed once again for an extended trip to Cuban waters. With the world in turmoil and deep into the Depression, Ernest had qualms about being gone for any length of time. Uncle Gus supported him, however, in his rationalization that fishing off the coast of Havana fulfilled a public service, since it gave people jobs. "The fishing you do in Cuban waters will result in spreading some good all around—to those in Havana and other parts of Cuba who are hungry and need food and by giving compensation to those whom you employ," Gus wrote. So rather than contribute to charities, Ernest fished to help feed the poor.[36]

During the more than two months that Ernest fished near Cuba, Pauline made frequent visits and wrote letters almost daily when not with him. Jane Mason returned to Havana, and though Pauline considered Jane a friend, she also knew Ernest's need for intimate female companionship and the likelihood that Jane would continue to provide it. To compete with Jane, Pauline experimented with her hair. Throughout their marriage, Pauline's hair held erotic qualities for Ernest, particularly because of its cut and feel. Pauline decided to take things a step further by going blonde, like Jane. In mid-September Pauline told Ernest that her hair had reached a deep gold shade, with no pink, and she intended to "just jockey it along" and not do too much else besides keeping the roots light. "Wish you were here to watch it and to advise me," she wrote.[37] "I'm trying to avoid peroxide as I think that's the most texture destroying, but I may have to come to it," she reported three days later.[38] Two days after that she delayed her trip to Havana to see him, partly because she wanted her hair "a little golder before showing off to friends in public demonstration—certainly wish you were here for the process."[39] Finally, she had it the right color and headed off to Havana. Ernest pronounced all her efforts a success.

While Ernest's fishing trips took him away from his boys for long periods of time, Pauline alternated her time between the boys and Ernest. With Patrick turning six and Gregory approaching three during the summer of 1934, the two displayed wide disparity in their abilities to communicate, putting Patrick in much better favor with his mother. Ernest apparently shared his wife's sentiments and found everything he did of interest. "How do you like Patrick?" Ernest asked his mother-in-law after she saw him in Piggott. "He's my favorite. Gregory is still too young to tell much about but he may turn out to not be as dumb as he seems."[40] In a similar comment to Waldo Peirce, Hemingway noted, "Patrick is getting to be a good kid. . . . Gregory is too big and dopey yet to tell anything about."[41] Though he never made such remarks directly to Gregory, the boy probably noticed differences in the way his parents responded to their sons. Gregory's efforts to win the favor of his parents would haunt him the rest of his life.

Patrick entered his first year of school in the fall, and once more Gregory went to New York with Ada, not returning until just before his birthday in November. With Gregory in Syracuse and Ernest in Havana, Pauline devoted time to Patrick's adjustment to school. Pauline's tendency to treat her sons more like companions than children surfaced when she wrote to Ernest about Patrick: "He's a nice companion, at times rather demanding, but he wants to please and tries to control his demands, tho, and the days pass fairly successfully with house and yard work, but from about five on is the difficult time. Then I'm TIRED of Patrick."[42]

Pauline devoted evenings to adult company, including Lorine and Charles Thompson. Several new clubs had opened in Key West, including Raoul's, one of the most popular with locals. On one occasion, after spending the evening there with the Thompsons, she wrote to Ernest the next morning, "All together I must have had about six or seven gins and tho apparently perfectly sober all my subconscious missing you took the form of friendliness to all. Not a trace of that splendid aloofness that has stood me good in the face of many a threatened engagement."[43] As best she could remember, Pauline told him, she had made a dinner engagement for later in the week with people she didn't particularly care for, asked a musician to contact her about arranging a musical evening, may have joined the bicycle club, and perhaps made about fifty other contacts of the worst kind.

In the same letter, however, Pauline told Ernest that she had attended confession and First Friday communion and decided she talked about people too much. "More christian charity," she vowed, and "less active animosity."[44] When their African trophies and skins arrived in Key West, Pauline added another household project to her list—building a trophy room. Gus Pfeiffer assumed the cost of the mountings and told Ernest, "I feel a good trophy merits the best of mounting. My view on this is that the best is none too good.[45]

Uncle Gus also sent Ernest several $1,000 advances over the summer to tide him over until his book came out. He wanted to make life easier for Ernest so that he could concentrate on writing. Despite his largesse, Gus always made sure that those around him fulfilled their financial obligations, including Ernest. After returning from one of their later fishing trips, which included Baron von Blixen, he gently reminded Ernest, "Also note that Blix gave you the $100 I advanced him. Check mentioned by you was not enclosed in the letter. Please feel free to defer sending it until it is convenient for you."[46]

Although Ernest took and spent the money, financial dependence on the Pfeiffers began to wear thin, and he resented anyone calling attention to it. His pique showed when he wrote what he intended to be a nice note to his in-laws, thanking them for the fifty-dollar check they had sent for his birthday. Along with the gift, Mary Pfeiffer had sent a breezy message, perfectly innocent in her mind, saying, "Happy birthdays have come again. . . . Please accept our congratulations and the enclosed checks. Make merry with the latter and don't forget to count your blessings. They are many and great. A happy union, lovely children, a fairy godfather, etc."[47]

Her reference to "a fairy godfather" apparently set him off. At this point, Ernest grew irritated at any reminders of his financial dependence on the Pfeiffer family. True, he had just returned from a twenty-five-thousand-dollar Africa trip financed by Gus, but after all, he earned good money as well and had purchased the *Pilar* with an advance from his *Esquire* articles, not a loan from Gus. Thus, when he wrote back to his mother-in-law, the author added, "As usual when I am writing a novel I am making nothing and am probably regarded by the family intelligence service as a loafer. On the other hand when I am all through with a novel I make plenty of money and then, while I am loafing, am regarded with respect as a Money maker."[48]

When Ernest returned from fishing in Havana in late October, he received an invitation from Gus for the entire family to spend Thanksgiving with him and Louise in New York and Aspetuck. The invitation included five hundred dollars for expenses. Ernest sent the money back, saying he had reached a critical point in his book. Gus expressed disappointment that they could not come but again sent the check, saying it could be used for a future visit or for something else they would enjoy. He considered it bad luck to redeposit his own check, once written. This time Ernest kept the money.

Though they passed on the invitation to spend Thanksgiving in New York, the Hemingways responded differently when a message arrived from Piggott inquiring, "May the grandparents expect you all at the home on the hill for Christmas?"[49] The Hemingways loaded up the children and headed for Piggott. Paul assured his son-in-law that even though the warm, dry fall had reduced the number of quail, good hunters still bagged their daily limits.

Among Christmas gifts that year, Gus sent everyone in the family an article on love, titled "The Greatest Thing in the World," which he had had privately printed and bound. He had been inspired to send the article, written by well-known Scottish theologian Dr. Henry Drummond, by a conversation around the Pfeiffers' dining room table in Piggott several years earlier. At that time, Gus indicated that he thought truth the greatest thing in the world. Pauline disagreed with him, insisting that love was the greatest. "Before our discussion proceeded very far I began to doubt my belief," he noted in the cover letter, "and before it was over, I agreed that love includes truth, and that love, not truth, is the supreme virtue and the inspiration of man's good deeds."[50]

Pauline, who had everything she wanted in her husband, sacrificed all else for love. She loved him after seven years of marriage as much as when they first fell in love in Paris. For Ernest, however, both love and truth seemed secondary to his art, and often he appeared to need neither.

CHAPTER 16

More New Places (1935)

When the Hemingways returned to Key West in early January 1935, little remained of the sleepy town they had fallen in love with in 1928. During the previous year, the city and county governments had declared bankruptcy and, in a bold move, turned the town over to the Federal Emergency Relief Administration (FERA). That agency created a Key West Authority that attempted to breathe life into the dying town through a variety of measures, including a strong emphasis on tourism. Volunteers began a clean-up, fix-up campaign, and a promotional brochure printed in December identified town attractions for tourists.

The Hemingways' home was labeled number eighteen in a list of forty-eight places to see, sandwiched between Johnson's Tropical Grove and the Lighthouse and Aviaries. In the April 1935 issue of *Esquire*, Ernest wrote facetiously: "Your correspondent is a modest, retiring chap with no desire to compete with the Sponge Lofts (number 13 of the sights), the Turtle Crawl (number 3 on the map), the Ice Factory (number 4), the Tropical Open Air Aquarium containing the 627 pound jewfish (number 9), or the Monroe County Courthouse (number 14). . . . This is all very flattering to the easily bloated ego of your correspondent but very hard on production."[1]

The Hemingways soon hired Toby Bruce to build a six-foot brick fence around three sides of their property to maintain privacy, a move that created controversy in a city gearing up for tourists. One city commissioner, though without legal authority to do so, used his influence to prevent access to the city's brick piles, the source for Hemingway's fence materials. Undaunted, Ernest arranged with the naval station's commanding officer to purchase bricks stored at the base. Toby made numerous trips in a borrowed, dilapidated truck to haul off three thousand bricks at a time to finish the project.[2]

International news, however, soon would capture everyone's attention. After the death of German president Paul von Hindenburg in August

1934, Chancellor Adolf Hitler assumed the office of reich president. By March 1935 Hitler denounced disarmament clauses of the Versailles Treaty, which had ended World War I, and began to rearm and enlarge the German military.

When Gus Pfeiffer made a two-month visit to Europe right after the holidays, he expressed relief to have cousin Leonhard Kluftinger at the helm of the Warner-Hudnut factories in Berlin. Leonhard kept up with European politics and had a good mind and sound principles, Gus wrote to Ernest. "He's just the same as always—not the kind of man you would care to face in battle. He is outspoken in his views regarding political situation . . . and is combative if things done do not conform to his views of what is right & what is wrong."[3] Though they eventually wound up on opposite sides of the approaching war, Kluftinger sent greetings to Ernest and extended an invitation through Gus for him to visit. "That is if they will let you in Germany," Gus joked. "I don't know if you are one of the not wanted. I believe they burned your books."[4]

While Gus visited family throughout Europe, the Hemingways received guests in Key West. Virginia arrived for her usual stay, and John Dos Passos with his wife, Katy, moved south for the winter in November. Dos Passos, recovering from a bout with rheumatic fever, could not take the cold winter at their home in Massachusetts and found Key West more to his liking.

Additionally, Sara Murphy and Ada MacLeish arrived together for a visit, primarily to give Sara an opportunity to relax after a difficult fall and winter. Shortly after Gerald had assumed leadership of the family's Mark Cross business the previous fall, their fourteen-year-old son, Patrick, had experienced a relapse. Throughout the holidays Sara stayed at his side in the hospital, and when Patrick's condition improved, his exhausted mother gratefully accepted the offer to head south with Ada. About two weeks into the Key West trip, however, she got totally unexpected news from Gerald. Their fifteen-year-old son, Baoth, attending prep school at St. George's in Newport, Rhode Island, had developed a double mastoid infection and needed surgery. Ernest took Sara and Ada to Miami in the middle of the night aboard the *Pilar* to catch a plane out of Miami. Problems during the surgery developed into meningitis, and within a few weeks Baoth died. His death stunned the Hemingways and John and Katy Dos Passos. Ernest, perhaps closer to the Murphy children than anyone outside the family, had difficulty bringing himself to write Baoth's stricken parents. After two days of grieving, he wrote: "You know there is nothing we can ever say or write. . . . It is not as bad for Baoth because he had a fine time, always, and he has only done something now that we all must do. He has just gotten it over with . . . and he is spared from learning what sort of place the world is. It is your loss more than it is his so it is something that you can, legitimately, be brave about. But I can't be brave about it and in all my heart I am sick for you both."[5]

The Murphys' ordeal affected Pauline deeply as well, leading her to reflect on friendships and the importance of various people in her life. When Lent arrived she gave up cigarettes and drinking and decided to do a better job of staying in touch with friends. She wrote one of the first letters of her new resolve to New York writer Dawn Powell, telling her how much she had enjoyed her latest book, *The Story of a Country Boy*. Getting back into the habit of writing would not be easy, Pauline told Dawn, so she was "writing first to the people I've always wanted to write to and working up to Ernest's sister Marcelline to whom I have written one a year for five years without yet meeting her."[6]

By 1935 Ernest rarely saw any of his siblings, though Leicester popped in and out to hunt and fish with his brother, and Ursula had stayed for a time with the Hemingway children the previous year. He unequivocally refused to see Carol after she married Jack Gardner against his wishes. Ernest also shunned Marcelline after a falling-out at their father's funeral, which had started as the typical dissension when families under stress try to make decisions. It grew as Ernest came to resent putting more money into their mother's financial support, when he believed that Marcelline possessed more money and had benefited more financially from family resources while growing up. Though he occasionally sent perfunctory letters, more often than not Ernest communicated to Marcelline and others in the family through their sister Sunny, who became the liaison between high-strung family members.

Pauline also attempted to keep things smoothed over as best she could, making sure that Ernest sent Christmas gift checks to family members each year, including Marcelline and her family. Marcelline also sent holiday presents to Ernest's family, and the gift exchange and thank-you notes between Marcelline and Pauline became an annual ritual. They did not meet in person, however, until Marcelline and her husband, Sterling Sanford, visited Key West in January 1949, well after the two women's sister-in-law status had ended.

Over the 1935 Memorial Day weekend Ernest's mother, his siblings, and their children gathered in Oak Park, with even Bumby in attendance, since he lived nearby in Chicago with his mother and Paul. Ernest wanted no part of any reunion, and besides, by then the discovery of new fishing grounds had diverted his attention to other pursuits when not writing.

With the Batista dictatorship unsteady in Cuba, Ernest wanted a safer spot and found it in Bimini, a small, quaint island with an environment largely untouched by the outside world. Only forty-five miles across the Gulf Stream from Miami, the island even had an aura of mystery about it. Myths claimed the Fountain of Youth sprang forth from the ocean passage between North and South Bimini. Another legend made Bimini the gateway to Atlantis, based on an ancient underwater layer of stones just a quarter-mile off North Bimini's Paradise Point. By 1935, the island's primary contact with the world came via seaplane or private boats that arrived to fish its pristine waters.

Ernest's first Bimini trip in early April began auspiciously. With John and Katy Dos Passos on board the *Pilar,* along with Mike Strater and the crew, Ernest managed to shoot himself in both legs. With a shark on a gaff in one hand and his .22 Colt Woodsman pistol in the other hand to finish the shark off, a final thrust by the huge fish broke the gaff pole. As it broke, the gaff hit his gun, causing a discharge that struck both legs. His legs covered with blood, Ernest diverted the *Pilar* back to Key West for a trip to the hospital, postponing Bimini for another day. Katy, mad at Ernest for his carelessness and for ruining their trip, expressed no sympathy whatsoever. By the following week, Ernest had recovered sufficiently to reach Bimini without further mishap.

With Ernest and Dos Passos usually off fishing in Bimini, Pauline invited Katy to move in with her at the Hemingway home. At first Pauline enjoyed playing social director, including organizing an Easter breakfast for Katy, but she valued her independence too much for the arrangement to last long. The visit ended earlier than expected when Katy developed medical problems that required surgery. Pauline volunteered to take her to Miami and introduce her to doctors there, but Katy insisted on returning to her doctor at Johns Hopkins in Baltimore. When Katy and John Dos Passos returned to Key West from Baltimore after a period of recuperation, they moved back into their own quarters. Pauline found the arrangement more comfortable and told Ernest, "Katy has been lovely, and I have liked having her with me, and she is a lot like me in lots of ways, but please dear good Papa, when you hear again of my asking a girl friend to come and live at my house behave very badly and stop me." Pauline valued her friends but wanted "to be able to swing a bat without hitting them."[7]

With no houseguests around, and Ada tending to the boys, Pauline made frequent trips back and forth to Bimini for time with Ernest, who rarely returned to Key West. Both Patrick and Gregory took great notice of their parents' extended absences. On one occasion Patrick remarked to Ada,

"I don't know WHAT to make of it. My father says he is going away for two weeks and he stays two months. My mother says she is going away for four days and she stays four weeks. I don't know WHAT to make of it." Gregory chimed in with a resigned air and a shrug: "That's the way it goes."[8]

Pauline, who never liked separations from her husband, sent daily letters to Ernest when she had to be in Key West, occasionally including a sprig of white oleander or gardenia petals from the garden. Still a blonde, she lightened her hair even more to an ash blonde shade, causing Ernest to reflect to Jane Mason, "She looks simply marvellous; sweller looking all the time . . . can't think of herself as ever haveing been anything but a blonde. Me I can think of her plenty of ways and all marvellous."[9]

Uncle Gus arrived in late May after returning from Europe, and during their fishing trip Ernest brought in a record tuna weighing 381 pounds. Gus could not have been more ecstatic if he had caught it himself. He pronounced the trip "well above what one could hope or expect" and opined that just being in a boat when a new record is established is a rare thrill.[10] He continued talking about the adventure when he arrived to host relatives at the Aspetuck Colony the next week. After fishing in Bimini with Ernest, Gus stopped by to see Pauline and the boys in Key West and check out the suitability of the backyard for the pool that Pauline and Ernest wanted to install. Always enjoying a challenge, Gus worked on a strategy for digging a test well to determine the best procedure for draining the pool. From Aspetuck he wrote Ernest: "Regarding the swimming pool, you and Pauline of course both know that having a part in providing you with this gives Aunt Louise and me much pleasure. I feel it is much worth while and almost a needed addition to your Key West home."[11]

Pauline did not start on the pool right away, however, and instead headed to Piggott for a brief visit with family, this time taking Gregory. The trip provided an opportunity to assure the grandparents that Gregory really did exist, despite several trips to Piggott without him. Pauline timed her schedule to meet Bumby in St. Louis and bring him to Piggott, then to Key West and Bimini for the summer.

Virginia arrived in Piggott as well, having just returned from her own visit with Hadley and Bumby in Chicago, where she had found Hadley looking beautiful and in wonderful spirits.[12] Family members in Piggott agreed that Hadley was doing a fine job raising Bumby, and Pauline pronounced him "a LOVELY child, not spoiled or self-centered or silly, but a handsome, considerate, well-mannered intelligent fellow with a fine sense of humor."[13]

During the Piggott visit Pauline convinced her sister to join them for the summer. "Jinny has been grand and lots of fun for poor old mama," Pauline wrote to Ernest, "Don't think I could stand life without her."[14] Thus, after five days in Piggott, Pauline, Virginia, and the two boys departed Arkansas, picked Patrick up in Key West, and took a sea plane to Bimini. Before their arrival, Jane Mason had come to Bimini at Ernest's invitation to fish for tuna. The great personal attraction between the two of them apparently belonged in the past. Prior to the Bimini visit, Ernest had not heard from her in months. Jane let it be known that on a recent trip to Africa, she had become greatly enamored of her friend Dick Cooper.

Placing further strain on Ernest's relationship with Jane, her psychiatrist, Dr. Lawrence Kubie, had written a series of magazine articles applying psychoanalysis to the works of well-known authors, including Hemingway. When Kubie sent a draft of the article for him to read, an infuriated Ernest threatened to sue if the article came out. Caught in the middle, Jane feared that Ernest thought she had shared information about him with her psychiatrist. Though Kubie insisted he had used nothing Jane told him, Ernest prevailed upon *Esquire* editor Arnold Gingrich to prevent publication of the article. Though Ernest accepted Jane's assurances that she had said nothing to Kubie about him, no doubt Ernest questioned her judgment in telling Kubie her problems in the first place.

Once Pauline arrived in Bimini, Ernest moved off the *Pilar* and into comfortable quarters with the family, away from sand flies and mosquitoes. He occasionally broke from fishing and writing to box with locals, successfully challenging everyone from conch pickers to boat captains in three-minute, bare-fisted rounds at the Bimini dock. When not fishing with their father or being regaled with stories of his adventures, the boys explored the island, while Pauline and Virginia swam or collected shells with John and Katy Dos Passos. Each evening when the *Pilar* came back into port, Pauline waited dockside with the mixings for evening cocktails.

After an idyllic summer, the Hemingway family returned to Key West in mid-August. Ernest planned to go from there to Havana, but his boat developed problems, and he put it in dry dock for needed maintenance and repairs. It proved a fortuitous change in plans, since the weather turned ominous at the end of August. By Labor Day weekend a major storm loomed on the horizon, and after securing the *Pilar,* Ernest and family boarded up the house. The storm barely skirted Key West, unleashing its full force on Upper and Lower Matecumbe keys, where veterans employed through the Civilian Conservation Corps worked to build a highway and a bridge. Rescue efforts came too late to evacuate workers and others from the area, resulting in about five hundred deaths. Fortunately, approximately half of the more than seven hundred government workers were in

Miami attending a Labor Day baseball game, or the devastation would have been greater.

Ernest joined the approximately two hundred volunteers attempting to collect and bury the dead. Outraged at the federal government for leaving workers there during hurricane season and housing them in flimsy work-camp shacks, he wrote an article, "Who Murdered the Vets? A First-Hand Report on the Florida Hurricane," that appeared in *New Masses* magazine just weeks after the tragedy.

To divert his thoughts from death and destruction in the Keys, Ernest agreed to cover the Joe Louis–Max Baer boxing match for *Esquire* in mid-September and planned a side trip from New York City to Gus and Louise Pfeiffer's family colony at Aspetuck. The compound consisted of more than twenty homes, ranging from historic 1700s structures to new construction, on the Aspetuck River in Fairfield County, Connecticut. Louise had supervised renovation and construction of each house, followed by furnishing each, down to kitchen utensils and bathroom towels. The houses varied in size from country manors to smaller cottages, with completed houses given names and assigned to family members and friends for their use as summer homes, weekend retreats, or year-round residences.

George Washington Pfeiffer's son Robert, for example, occupied "Harvard House" in recognition of his position as professor of Old Testament, ancient history and ancient Semitic languages at Harvard University. Gus and Louise lived at the primary residence, the Homestead. Thanks to Gus, Helen Keller and her assistant, Polly Thompson, also had a permanent residence at Aspetuck, known as Arcan Ridge. Gus, who served on the board of the American Foundation for the Blind from 1932 until his death, had provided 4.5 acres and a home built to meet her special needs after the death of her teacher, Anne Sullivan Macy. When Helen and Polly moved in, Gus presented a symbolic golden key and a model of the home so that she could feel its contours.

"How wonderful it all is!" Helen told Gus and Louise. "There is no counting the treasures to which the key symbolically opens the door. It means a home in New England, to which affection and memory have ever bound me . . . a sanctuary where rural solitude will again sweeten my days."[15] When the original home burned, some ten years after Helen and Polly moved in, Gus ordered Arcan Ridge II built on the same spot, and it remained Helen Keller's home until her death in 1968.

Though the Pfeiffer colony at Aspetuck encompassed vast acreage, and its homes dotted the ridges and hollows near Easton, Connecticut, along the Aspetuck River, few people in the area knew much about the Pfeiffers. A

1930s article in the *Bridgeport Post* gave some indication of their reputation: "Quietest and most retiring of the grand families of the Fairfield countryside are the almost baronial Pfeiffers, of Easton, though if you dubbed them that they would seriously demur. They are the drug and patent medicine kings, manufacturers of Sloan's liniment, among other mendicants, and the Hudnut perfumes."[16]

The article went on to say that even though they lived quietly and shunned publicity, the Pfeiffers did much for charity in their quiet, inconspicuous way, including major contributions toward building the town hall in Easton, Connecticut.

During their visit in the fall of 1935, Pauline and Ernest stayed in Brook Cottage, directly on the Aspetuck River, next to an old mill. Set apart from most of the other houses, the cottage provided privacy for writing, and the Pfeiffers left Ernest alone at his request. He rarely ventured out, even to enjoy communal meals, and few adult residents recalled meeting him or being aware of his presence. He was less reclusive with children, however, and one young girl recalled a funny man who invited her to play "bullfight" and seemed to enjoy taking turns rushing at a make-believe cape.[17] Though Ernest appreciated the colony's peace and quiet, his thank-you gift of two white peacocks made so much racket that Gus had them done away with shortly after the birds arrived.

Ernest became more sociable after arriving in New York, even treating all the Pfeiffer women to dinner at the Hollywood Restaurant. With Mary Pfeiffer and her daughter-in-law Matilda both in town for Christmas shopping with Pauline and Virginia, Ernest played the perfect host. "When he was good he was very very good," Matilda recalled. "But when he was bad, he was a son of a gun. He was a man who had to be number one because he wanted to be perfect. When he wasn't perfect to his own satisfaction, that's when he was a son of a gun . . . but the rest of the time he was a charmer."[18]

While in New York, Pauline entertained her cousin Ward Merner and his friend Jay McEvoy from San Francisco. Jay had become a friend of the Merner family in 1930, when he assisted with a European tour that included Ward's younger sister Mary Louise. Eventually the Merners moved from St. Louis to the San Francisco area, and their friendship with the McEvoy family continued. After Mary Louise married in August 1935, with both Ward and Jay in the wedding, the two young men decided to strike out cross-country in Jay's Plymouth convertible.

They stopped first in Piggott and stayed ten days with Paul and Mary Pfeiffer. Jay did not want to intrude, but Ward called ahead, and the Pfeiffers insisted they both come. As a Roman Catholic, Jay hit it off especially well with Pauline's mother. Though the house had a chapel, the priest held services elsewhere that Sunday, so Jay accompanied Mary, along with Karl and Matilda, to services in Missouri, while Ward stayed home with Pauline's father.

It took the pair three weeks to get from California to New York. The first day in the city, Ward had an appointment to see Pauline and insisted that Jay come along. When they arrived at Hotel Westbury, where Pauline had a suite of rooms, Jay recalled that the maid fed Patrick and Gregory in a small pantry area, while he and Ward had drinks with Pauline in the living room. In a great mood and happy to see her cousin, Pauline sparkled in the eyes of her guests. Things became even livelier when a Hemingway friend, American bullfighter Sidney Franklin, burst into the room carrying all sorts of gifts.

Franklin's brother owned a dress factory nearby, and he brought women's and children's clothing in all shapes and sizes. Pauline tried many of them on, adopting her most serious tone to convince Franklin that her wardrobe would not be complete without a blue knit dress that she modeled for them. In the midst of it all, Ernest arrived, and the entire mood changed. Pauline became quiet and subdued, suggesting that Ernest might find her previous behavior unbecoming. Jay recalled Ernest being "just full of life, full of beans. I doubt if he even remembered meeting me at that time—he was so full of his own ideas and himself."[19]

Part of Ernest's bluster possibly resulted from nervousness over the anticipated publication of his Africa book. Normally not in New York during release of a book, Ernest hoped to bask in accolades after the late October publication. The book got mixed reviews, however, causing Ernest great consternation. Already upset at receiving only five thousand dollars from Scribner's for serialization, he now had to endure reviews that criticized him for writing a hybrid book instead of a novel. Ernest decided that three problems had ruined his book: too steep a price tag, insufficient advertising by Scribner's, and the realization that he had antagonized critics before its publication by almost daring them not to like the book.[20]

When F. Scott Fitzgerald weighed in with his own well-meant critique, Ernest responded snidely that Scott remained a poor judge of good writing. "Was delighted from the letter to see you don't know any more about when a book is a good book or what makes a book bad than ever," he railed at him. "You are like a brilliant mathematician who loves mathematics truly and always gets the wrong answers to the problems."[21] Ernest's personal attack elicited a beaten-down response from Fitzgerald, causing

Ernest to lay on the abuse a little thicker. If Scott wanted to kill himself, Ernest suggested he could take him to Cuba and get him knocked off by a revolutionary.[22]

In truth, however, Ernest wallowed in his own self-pity. Despite invitations to spend Thanksgiving and Christmas in Piggott, the Hemingways remained in Key West throughout the holidays. Not even a letter from Karl with the prospects of an excellent quail season, plenty of scotch, and a roaring fire could lure Ernest to Piggott.[23] With his melancholia worsening, Ernest backed away from family connections altogether.

The problem, he decided, resulted from not getting enough rest and exercise and the stress of needing to write what people wanted to read. Though Ernest experienced extreme highs and lows throughout his life, generally his extreme lows, or what he called his "black-ass moods," came when alone and separated from the woman he loved, whoever that might be.[24] Now, however, he found himself in a deep funk, even though surrounded by those he supposedly loved. Ernest could not remember ever being so blue and claimed that at least it "makes me more tolerant of what happened to my father."[25]

CHAPTER 17

More New Faces (1936)

Though 1936 started with Ernest stalled in the doldrums, Pauline entered the New Year in great spirits. Ernest told his mother-in-law that she had "the same energy as always and manages to put in a good eight-hour day every day and then in the evening is suddenly very tired and goes sound asleep at nine o'clock and sleeps like a child all night."[1] Ernest, on the other hand, slept fitfully and often got up before dawn to write. He was easily angered by distractions and belligerent toward family and friends, so Pauline and the boys avoided invoking his wrath as best they could.

His sister Ursula learned about his volatility firsthand. While visiting early in the year with her daughter, she found herself at a party with poet Wallace Stevens, who vacationed each year at Key West. Having had a bit too much to drink, he proceeded to make uncomplimentary remarks about Ernest, sending Ursula back to the Hemingway household in tears. As soon as Ernest heard what had occurred, he stormed out into the rain to find Stevens. The men fought, and Ernest knocked the rather large man to the pavement, breaking Stevens's hand in two places. Later, when Stevens sobered up and Ernest calmed down, they vowed never to tell anyone what had happened, but each immediately spread the tale.

Ernest inflicted pain on himself as well as others. Unbeknownst to Ernest, Pauline locked the front gate of their home one afternoon to prevent tourists from flocking into the yard to see visiting film star Nancy Carroll. On leaving the house, Ernest attempted to kick open the gate, broke his big toe, and limped back into the house. Ernest's anger probably stemmed from his writing slump, exacerbated by negative reviews. He told Sara Murphy that he was "going to blow my lousy head off."[2] Pauline worried about his growing preoccupation with death and thoughts of suicide. Earlier she had considered accompanying her mother on Mary's annual St. Louis religious retreat in March, but dismissed the idea to stay home with Ernest. Fortunately, much of his dark mood passed in a matter of weeks when he began writing well and mixing his work with fishing and exercise. To most winter visitors Ernest appeared as charming as ever.

Gus Pfeiffer missed his spring visit to Key West, opting instead for an extended trip to Europe early in the New Year to inspect their pharmaceutical branches. On this trip he acquired another new plant in France, approved designs for a new building in the center of London, and purchased an additional chess collection with more than one hundred complete sets. Pauline's cousin C. Leonard Pfeiffer stirred Gus's interest in chess by presenting him with an unusual set in 1928. This latest acquisition, considered the finest chess assemblage in England, increased his total sets to nearly three hundred, making it the largest private collection in the world.[3] The pieces ranged from wood and ceramic to gold, silver, ivory, jade, and amber, with many representatives from ancient civilizations. Designing a space in his Manhattan apartment to display the sets became Gus's next major challenge upon return from Europe.

C. Leonard, who also worked at Warner-Hudnut, traveled with Uncle Gus on the European trip, using it as an opportunity to see sisters Anna and Dora and their families, since both lived in Italy and were married to Italian men. After visiting Dora and Enrico Zappala in Catania and Anna and Ettore Leonardi in Bologna, Gus and Leonard made the rounds of relatives in Munich on the Kluftinger side of the family. The situation in Germany differed significantly even from Gus's visit the previous year. By this time, Germany occupied the Rhineland, and Hitler's intentions seemed apparent. Gus told Ernest that even cousin Leonhard Kluftinger had withdrawn his support: "Leonard K. asked to be remembered to you. He's still the same Leonard. No longer a Hitler enthusiast, quite the contrary. Further he makes no apologies. He never hangs out the Swastika flag on the Nazi Gala days. He does pay his dues for he believes in National Socialism but he doesn't believe in dictators or self power seeking individuals. Instead he believes in sacrificing self for a cause—always has done so & still doing so."[4]

Despite the emergence of Germany's ruthless leadership, the region remained an attractive spot for American visitors. Virginia Pfeiffer and Ward Merner visited Germany early in the year in conjunction with a ski adventure in Austria. The mountain air in Kitzbühel, Austria, must have cleared their heads, since both arrived at plans for their next moves. Virginia determined to rent an apartment in New York near Uncle Gus, while Ward decided to try his hand at writing. When Ernest heard this, he grew even more skeptical of Ward than during the earlier Havana fishing trip.

"I swear that Ward has no more talent for being a writer than I have for playing the violin and I could not make a nickel playing the violin (even as a blind violinist) if I should work at it 15 hours a day for the next 2000 years," Ernest wrote to his mother-in-law. "Why couldn't he have picked out something else to fail at without dragging in our old craft?"[5] Writing is no different from anything else, he insisted. One must first have a basic talent for it, then work hard to develop that talent. He doubted that Ward had such talent but believed the opposite of Virginia. "Jinny has as much talent or more for writing than I have, only she has no confidence and won't work at it," Ernest told Mary. "She really has talent and has been around enough so that she has something to write. I wish she would."[6]

On Virginia's return from Austria, she went to Piggott in late April to meet her sister, who had arrived once again with Gregory. Not yet five years old, Gregory, the family believed, already had his grandfather Pfeiffer's acumen for numbers. He could add large numbers in his head and count by fives and tens. Used to being away from his parents, Gregory thought of himself as grown-up and independent. During the Piggott trip, he confessed to his mother that as a baby he had feared the dark. Now that he was big, however, he knew that "the dark was just the dark."[7] While Pauline and Gregory visited in Piggott and Ernest fished in Havana, Patrick celebrated his First Communion without family present. Pauline sent him a prayer book and rosary with his name on it and wrote Lorine Thompson to assist Ada in looking out for him. "I think he will be alright," Pauline told Ernest. "He is very self reliant. Don't YOU forget your Easter duty."[8]

Though Ernest seemed to embrace Catholicism primarily because of his marriage to Pauline, he nonetheless participated in church rituals and sometimes drove for miles when on vacation so that they could attend holy day masses. Years later, Gregory surmised that his father did not truly believe in any organized religion: "We were brought up Catholics, but he made it clear he didn't believe in an afterlife. He did, finally, believe in a superior being."[9]

Both Patrick and Gregory received Catholic educations, and while Pauline worked at making them good Catholics, Ernest worked at making them good fishermen. By 1936 Patrick had become a great deck hand on the *Pilar*. Like Pauline, Ernest preferred his children one at a time and usually had only one on the boat with him. "It is only this last year," he told his mother-in-law, "that I have gotten any sort of understanding or feeling about how anyone can feel about their children or what they can mean to them."[10] Ernest confessed that he always thought of his career as the most important thing and did not want to "be fond of anything I could not lose."[11] Now, however, he recognized that he needed to take pleasure in his family while he had them, instead of placing so much emphasis on work. In spite of such sentiments expressed to his mother-in-law, he passed the spring deeply engrossed in work, yet fearing his talents might be waning.

Ernest's mood grew dark again when F. Scott Fitzgerald wrote about his own mental breakdown in an *Esquire* article, "The Crack-Up." Rather than being empathetic, Ernest felt anger that his so-called friend and fellow writer would lay himself bare to the reading public. Fitzgerald acted, he believed, as a coward who went directly from youth into senility without passing through manhood.[12] Ernest attacked him by name in his short story "The Snows of Kilimanjaro," printed in the August 1936 *Esquire*. When Fitzgerald read the story, which suggested that his ruin resulted from worshipping the rich, he wrote his colleague to insist that his name be removed in any future reprints of the story. Just because he wrote about his problems, Fitzgerald said, he saw no reason for "friends praying aloud over my corpse."[13] Ernest thought it a strange reply for a man who had just totally exposed himself to the world. The business with Fitzgerald merely increased his resolve to write about whomever he pleased, using whatever material furthered his story, hurt feelings or not.

Ernest's remaining Africa material, with several other stories, finally came together to form a novel. The work included identifiable references to Jane Mason and her husband, Grant; Sara Murphy; Philip Percival; John Dos Passos; Arnold Gingrich; the Pfeiffers; and a host of new wealthy friends, whom he believed were ruining his writing abilities by causing him to go soft. Despite his acceptance of Pfeiffer largesse over the years, the author seemed especially to resent Pauline's family wealth. In his Africa story "The Snows of Kilimanjaro," the dying writer Harry reflects that "in yourself, you said that you would write about these people; about the very rich; that you were really not of them but a spy in their country; that you would leave it and write of it and for once it would be written by some one who knew what he was writing of."[14]

Harry does not write about them, however, because every day of living in comfort among them has dulled his sensibilities. He blames his fictional wife because "your damned money was my armour."[15] When the fictional character lashes out at his wife, "this rich bitch, this kindly caretaker and destroyer of his talent," Hemingway was aiming right at Pauline.[16] When Harry curses her "bloody money," his wife fights back: "That's not fair. . . . It was always yours as much as mine. I left everything and I went wherever you wanted to go and I've done what you wanted to do."[17] Even more revealing, perhaps, the dying writer reflects that while his wife "loved him dearly as a writer, as a man, as a companion and as a proud possession; it was strange that when he did not love her at all and was lying, that he should be able to give her more for her money than when he had really loved."[18] It should have been a clear signal to Pauline that Ernest no longer needed her, now that he was an established writer with a good income.

Stories woven together to create Hemingway's novel *To Have and Have Not* also contain bitter references from the female's point of view. Much of the confrontation between writer Richard Gordon and his wife, Helen, seems taken right out of the early pages of his relationship with Pauline: "You wouldn't marry me in the church and it broke my poor mother's heart as you well know. I was so sentimental about you I'd break any one's heart for you. My, I was a damned fool. I broke my own heart, too. It's broken and gone. Everything I believed in and everything I cared about I left for you because you were so wonderful and you loved me so much that love was all the mattered. Love was the greatest thing, wasn't it? Love was what we had that no one else had or could ever have. And you were a genius and I was your whole life. I was your partner and your little black flower."[19]

Though Hemingway's fictional dialogue may not have reflected exactly his experience—past or present—such passages provide insight into his state of mind at the time, including his growing disdain for the rich and for anyone who tried to make things easier for him. If such thoughts and resentment toward Pauline and her family simmered underneath, none had reached the surface by summer 1936. And if Pauline saw any warning signs buried in Ernest's fiction, she chose to ignore them. Ernest appeared attentive to Pauline, and no woman around seemed to pose a threat. Even though Jane Mason fished again with Ernest and his friends while Pauline visited Piggott, and periodically spent time with both Hemingways throughout the summer, Jane's romantic interests appeared to lie elsewhere.

Part of Ernest's underlying dissatisfaction with his marriage may have been lack of a suitable woman around to relieve Ernest's sexual frustrations. After the spontaneity of Ernest and Pauline's initial passion, a carefully orchestrated sexual relationship had emerged after Gregory's birth. Pauline's doctor had warned her that another pregnancy might kill her, and when she thought she was pregnant just months after his birth, she became even more cautious. For a repentant Catholic who now strictly adhered to church doctrine, including opposition to birth control, that left abstinence, careful scheduling, or coitus interruptus. None suited Ernest, but the rigid sexual regimen with Pauline could be tolerated as long as he had other outlets. Sara Murphy picked up on Ernest's restlessness when she visited Havana with John and Katy Dos Passos before Pauline came back from Piggott. Their return flight to New York coincided with Pauline's arrival from Piggott, and the friends made arrangements to meet in the Miami airport. After the visit Sara wrote to Ernest that Pauline looked "like a delicious and rather wicked little piece of brown toast."[20] As if to encourage him not to throw all that away, she added, "Oh Ernest, what wonderful places you live in and what a good life you have made for yourself and Pauline."[21]

Upon Pauline's arrival back in Key West, the family headed for another summer in Bimini, moving into the most luxurious house on the island, even as Ernest complained about the trappings of the rich. The house at Cat Cay belonged to Mike Lerner, one of their wealthy new friends in Bimini, who offered it since much of the island had yet to recover from the previous year's hurricane. After Ernest, Pauline, Patrick, Gregory, and Ada settled in, Virginia joined them, bringing Bumby when he got out of school. Among friends who showed up, Arnold Gingrich came to spend a week. Less than enthusiastic about fishing, he decided to cut the week short. But as he prepared to depart, Jane Mason arrived, and they began secretly seeing each other over the summer. Nearly twenty years later, after several affairs with and marriages to others, Gingrich and Jane married in 1955.

Pauline left Bimini with the boys on July 5 to supervise household projects in Key West, leaving Virginia with Ernest, perhaps a dangerous thing to do given Ernest's state of mind. Being around Virginia reinvigorated Ernest, since she reminded him of the earlier, more spontaneous Pauline who did not have to carefully plan everything in their lives. While like her sister in some ways, Virginia remained a free spirit, who argued and took issue with Ernest and called his bluff when necessary. Pauline, on the other hand, shaped her life around making Ernest comfortable and happy as best she could, a docility that began to irritate him. When he returned to Key West for his thirty-seventh birthday on July 21, Ernest realized that he missed Virginia. The only people he really cared about, he told Gingrich, were Pauline, Virginia, and his sons.[22] For Virginia, however, the time with Ernest in Bimini seemed to mark a turning point in her high regard for him, due perhaps to inappropriate behavior or complaints about Pauline that Virginia did not want to hear.

By the end of summer the Hemingways moved westward. They had not been to the Nordquist Ranch since before their Africa trip, and Ernest yearned for more big-game hunting. Leaving Gregory with Ada, the rest of the family drove as far as New Orleans, where they stayed several days waiting for Virginia to arrive from Bimini. Ernest left a letter for Jane, who was meeting Virginia there to start an Acapulco trip, telling her to look after Virginia for him because it was "always very hard on me when she goes away." Of all the things he did not have and would never have, he told her, he valued Virginia the highest, even though she "cares nothing for me." He added as a postscript, "In regard to shipment [Virginia] see she gets a lot of swimming and is never too drunk to take her calcium."[23] Some of his comments about Virginia may have been intended to convince Jane he was over his infatuation with Jane and did not care about her new relationship with Gingrich. He had professed similar feelings about Virginia when she left Bimini the previous summer, however, telling Jane, "She always leaves a big hollow place when she goes; not to be filled by food nor drink"[24]

After depositing Virginia in New Orleans, Ernest and Pauline stopped for the state fairs in Dallas and Fort Worth to treat Bumby and Patrick. Once in Montana Ernest read an article in the July issue of a national magazine, *Country Gentleman,* that focused on tenant farming and featured his father-in-law as a successful example of landowner-tenant relationships. At that time, Paul Pfeiffer had 126 tenant families farming thirteen thousand acres in the Piggott area, with another fifty thousand acres in woods, pastures, and wetlands. The article noted that Pfeiffer had no particular use for formal or written contracts, believing that any contract depended on the goodwill of parties involved.

"If it thrives at all, a plantation thrives on tenant loyalty," Paul said in the article. "Why try to make tenants into serfs? All matters of scruples and honor aside, it would be the worst business in the world, a very nasty way of cutting one's own throat."[25] Ernest wrote to his mother-in-law that the article "made me admire Pauline's father even more. You both have given our kids a fine heritage. It's a good thing to try to breed some of the suicide streak out."[26]

Since they had missed Piggott earlier, the Hemingways stopped by on their return trip, after sending Bumby back to his mother. Virginia, in Piggott ahead of them after her Acapulco vacation, departed before their arrival to move into an apartment in New York. She left behind a request for Pauline to join her and help furnish the apartment, giving them time for a sisterly chat about men and marriage. With Pauline going to New York, Ernest did not wish to drive back alone from Piggott with Patrick, so he needed a driver. Toby Bruce, who had assisted the Hemingways with other projects, presented himself at the Pfeiffers' door, dressed as he thought a chauffeur ought to look after he heard about the job. Ernest agreed to hire him, provided he never wore that getup again. From that point forward, Toby became Ernest's "driver, secretary, man Friday, getaway-money-holder, and drinking companion."[27] When Ernest and Patrick left the Pfeiffer home in November 1936 with Toby Bruce at the wheel, none dreamed that Ernest would never see Piggott again.

Along with helping her sister, Pauline's trip to New York provided an opportunity for Christmas shopping and visiting friends, including Dawn Powell. While Dawn considered both Pfeiffer sisters dear friends, she could be caustic in her treatment of even close friends. A particularly biting attack on Virginia in her diary during that period indicates that she had picked up on Virginia's unusual relationship with Ernest: "Virginia Pfeiffer is an odd person. . . . Bitterly envious of her sister's position as wife of a world-recognized writer and in touch therefore with the social and rich far more than the artistic, she believes in a bond between herself and the husband—I shouldn't be surprised if he occasionally gave her reason to believe this."[28]

Whatever set Dawn off, she probably wasn't too far off base when it came to the bond between Virginia and Ernest. If Virginia bitterly envied her sister, Pauline never sensed it. Dawn added her belief that Virginia sought fame and recognition but refused to exercise the discipline required to achieve such status: "I cannot understand why—when a person cares so obviously about Name—why, with her time and money, she doesn't study her own patter; read art and music news, some political, a few books; observe; maintain a decent balance about celebrities, since that is her obsession. At least study her own stuff—give something. . . . A worthless woman who should marry and support some worthy gigolo."[29]

It was a rather low blow from a supposed friend. While Virginia remained unsettled about what to do with her life and experienced more than her share of wanderlust, she could always be counted on to give 100 percent of herself to friends and family who needed her—hardly a worthless trait.

By the time Pauline left Virginia in New York for the return to Key West, Walter Winchell's gossip column suggested that Ernest Hemingway would soon be leaving to check out the situation in Spain. Throughout that entire fall, radios broadcast news of the civil war in Spain, which had broken out the last week of July as the Hemingways drove to Montana. Anxious to see the conflict for himself, Ernest's opportunity came when John Wheeler of the North Atlantic Newspaper Alliance contacted him on November 25 to cover the war for that news service. Ernest wrote back expressing his interest.

Since he had a novel to finish before leaving, Ernest redoubled his efforts to bring To Have and Have Not to completion. He mailed off a draft manuscript to Arnold Gingrich for his review, since Gingrich was familiar with the material, but he became chagrined when Gingrich responded strongly that whole sections needed to come out unless Ernest wanted to be sued for libel. Ernest suggested that they meet in Bimini to discuss changes and that he would contact his lawyer, Moe Speiser, to come as well and "check the checker."[30] Ernest, Pauline, Speiser, and Gingrich argued for days over what could stay and what had to go. Gingrich recalled it being a strange week: "It was like those Paris riots, where the rioters and the cops would lay down their brickbats and nightsticks respectively, and adjourn two hours for lunch, then come back and pick them up again. . . . Ernest and Pauline and Moe and I would 'riot' all morning, then Ernest and I would go out fishing for the afternoon, then in the evening we would 'riot' again."[31]

When Gingrich insisted that certain passages libeled Jane and Grant Mason, Ernest hit him with, "Goddamn editor comes down to Bimini and sees a blonde and he hasn't been the same since."[32] Pauline tried to gloss over Ernest's obvious reference to Gingrich's affair with Jane by pointing out that Gingrich had a blonde wife, but Gingrich realized that they must all know of his dalliance. Later Gingrich alerted Jane about his intervention on her behalf. "Ernest's new book seemed to me to have six recognizable characteristics of yours," he told her, "and I took it upon myself to suggest that these be eliminated since the character's other characteristics combined to spell bitch in capital letters."[33] Ernest agreed to tone down the more obvious references, but friends still recognized the fictive Helène Bradley, a rich socialite and consummate hostess, as Jane Mason. The author painted an unflattering portrait of Helène when another female in the book reflects, "The bitches have the most fun but you have to be awfully stupid really to be a good one. Like Helène Bradley. Stupid and well-intentioned and really selfish to be a good one."[34]

Pauline undoubtedly recognized herself in the book as well, particularly as Helen Gordon, whose writer husband cheats on her, but she knew Ernest always took liberties with his characterizations. Often his characters became composites of several friends and acquaintances, taking on a life of their own. Thus, while unconcerned for herself, Pauline worked with Ernest to eliminate any libelous references to friends. After Ernest made agreed-upon changes, the Hemingways returned to Key West, and Pauline tried to establish a normal routine. Ernest continued work on the book, with plans to deliver it to Maxwell Perkins in New York after the first of the year. Pauline and Ernest avoided talking about Spain, since he knew she opposed such a trip.

One evening in December, Pauline invited Charles and Lorine Thompson to their home for a crawfish dinner. After a round of drinks without Ernest, Pauline suggested that Charles find him and bring him home. Charles dutifully set out for Sloppy Joe's but returned alone. "He's talking to a beautiful blonde in a black dress," Thompson reported to Pauline and Lorine, adding that Ernest said he and the blonde, along with her mother and brother, would meet them for drinks after dinner at Pena's Garden of Roses.[35] None of the three thought much about it and dined without him.

It wasn't the first time Ernest Hemingway got detained by a beautiful woman or an adoring literary fan. This time, however, the beautiful woman turned out to be Martha Gellhorn, and she arrived at a time in Ernest's life when he was especially susceptible to her charms. Frustrated with the lack of excitement in his marriage, and anxious to turn out another big novel, he needed a new muse for inspiration.

Like Hadley and Pauline, Martha Gellhorn had grown up in St. Louis. An alumna of Bryn Mawr College and a successful writer at age twenty-eight, she had a novel and a book of short stories to her credit by the time she met Ernest. A social activist almost from birth, Martha produced work investigating human suffering during the Great Depression that brought her to the attention of Eleanor Roosevelt and ultimately of President Franklin Roosevelt. Her short stories, based on impoverished people she met throughout the country, endeared her even more to the First Lady, and the two became friends.

When Ernest met Martha at Sloppy Joe's, she had just returned from Germany after completing research for her third book. Martha was in Florida on vacation with her mother and younger brother, and the three had traveled to Key West on a whim after tiring of Miami. Over the next few days, Ernest happily toured with the Gellhorns, introduced them to Pauline, and invited them into the Hemingway circle. When Martha's brother returned to medical school and her mother went back to St. Louis, Martha stayed on in Key West. Flattered by the attentions of an admired author, she sought Ernest's views on the Spanish Civil War, particularly since the experience and knowledge she had gained in Europe made her sympathetic to the plight of the Spanish people.

Martha's tall, blonde good looks and literary reputation intrigued Ernest. Pauline noted how well they hit it off, but Ernest's fascination with beautiful women stayed constant throughout their relationship. Her friend Lorine Thompson, more leery of the situation, recalled, "Pauline always tried to be very tolerant of Ernest and any of the girls that sort of made a play for him, or that he seemed entranced with. I don't think he fell in love with other women. He was nice and maybe a lot of women thought he was giving them more attention than what there was; his was in a kidding way. And I think Pauline had a feeling that Ernest's interest in other women sometimes was as a writer, not just as a man."[36]

Though Martha and her family supposedly came to Key West and walked into Sloppy Joe's by chance, Lorine remained unconvinced of the event's coincidental nature. Martha had previously studied Hemingway's style and patterned much of her writing after his, including borrowing his phrase "Nothing ever happens to the brave" as an epigraph for her novel, *What Mad Pursuit*. The likelihood that she had just run into one of her favorite authors by chance seemed remote.

In Lorine's view, Martha set out to win Ernest. "She said she came to see Ernest, she wanted him to read a book she had written, she wanted to know him," Lorine recalled. "There was no question about it; you could see she was making a play for him. Pauline tried to ignore it. What she felt underneath nobody knew."[37]

Ernest and Pauline's wedding photo, May 10, 1927. *(Ernest Hemingway Photograph Collection, John F. Kennedy Presidential Library and Museum)*

Archibald and Ada MacLeish (left) and Sara and Gerald Murphy in Vienna.
(Photo © Estate of Honoria Murphy Donnelly/Licensed by VAGA, New York, NY)

Ernest and Pauline on the beach in San Sebastian-Hendaye area, ca. September 1927. *(Ernest Hemingway Photograph Collection, John F. Kennedy Presidential Library and Museum)*

Clarence, Ernest, Grace, and Pauline Hemingway in Key West, 1928. *(Ernest Hemingway Photograph Collection, John F. Kennedy Presidential Library and Museum)*

Ernest and Pauline Hemingway at a bullfight in Pamplona, Spain, 1929. Virginia Pfeiffer and Guy Hickok at left. *(Photograph by "Rodero," Ernest Hemingway Photograph Collection, John F. Kennedy Presidential Library and Museum)*

Pauline at the L-Bar-T Ranch in Wyoming, 1930. *(Patrick Hemingway Papers, Department of Rare Books and Special Collections, Princeton University Library)*

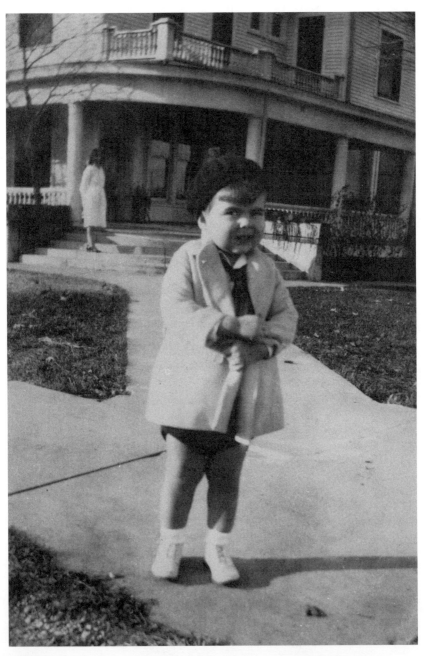

Patrick in front yard of Pfeiffer home in Piggott, 1930. *(Patrick Hemingway Papers, Department of Rare Books and Special Collections, Princeton University Library)*

Key West house not long after purchase by Uncle Gus for Ernest and Pauline.
(Wright Langley Archives)

Pauline with Charles Thompson, left, and Joe Russell, 1933. *(Wright Langley Archives)*

Jane Mason, with Carlos Gutierrez, aboard Joe Russell's boat *Anita*, 1933. *(Ernest Hemingway Photograph Collection, John F. Kennedy Presidential Library and Museum)*

Katy Smith Dos Passos aboard the *Weatherbird*. *(Photo © Estate of Honoria Murphy Donnelly/Licensed by VAGA, New York, NY)*

Pauline on safari, with gazelle, 1934. *(Ernest Hemingway Photograph Collection, John F. Kennedy Presidential Library and Museum)*

Baron and Eva Von Blixen with Pauline and Ernest Hemingway in Bimini, 1935. *(Ernest Hemingway Photograph Collection, John F. Kennedy Presidential Library and Museum)*

Pauline cutting Ernest's hair. *(Ernest Hemingway Photograph Collection, John F. Kennedy Presidential Library and Museum)*

Sara Murphy and Pauline Hemingway (with friend Ellen Barry at left), in Key West, 1935. *(Photo © Estate of Honoria Murphy Donnelly/Licensed by VAGA, New York, NY)*

Ernest, Pauline, Jack, Patrick, and Gregory in Key West yard. *(Patrick Hemingway Papers, Department of Rare Books and Special Collections, Princeton University Library)*

Gus Pfeiffer aboard the *Pilar*, 1935.
(Ernest Hemingway Photograph Collection, John F. Kennedy Presidential Library and Museum)

Ada Stern with Gregory, ca. 1936. *(Monroe County Library)*

Sidney Franklin and Ernest headed to the Spanish Civil War, 1937. *(Ernest Hemingway Photograph Collection, John F. Kennedy Presidential Library and Museum)*

Martha Gellhorn during the Spanish Civil War, ca. 1937–38. *(Ernest Hemingway Photograph Collection, John F. Kennedy Presidential Library and Museum)*

Pauline entertaining on Key West patio shortly after her divorce, 1940. From left: Lorine Thompson, Esther Chambers, Jane Mason, Pauline, James B. Sullivan, and Virginia Pfeiffer. *(Wright Langley Archives)*

Ernest and Mary Hemingway outside Sun Valley Lodge, Idaho, ca. 1947. *(Ernest Hemingway Photograph Collection, John F. Kennedy Presidential Library and Museum)*

Mary Hemingway and Pauline Pfeiffer shopping in San Francisco, 1947. *(Hemingway-Pfeiffer Museum and Educational Center)*

Laura Archera, Pauline Hemingway, Ward Merner, Virginia Pfeiffer, and Jay McEvoy in Europe, late 1940s. *(Patrick Hemingway Papers, Department of Rare Books and Special Collections, Princeton University Library)*

CHAPTER 18

Trouble Ahead (1937)

About the time Martha decided to leave Key West, Ernest's planned trip to New York took on newfound urgency. Fortuitously, he heard from Virginia Pfeiffer in New York regarding a place to stay. After wiring her several times from Key West and receiving no answer, Ernest finally received a telegram on January 7, in which Virginia apologized for a migraine that had prevented her from responding and letting him know that he would be a welcome guest at her new apartment. Martha left on January 9, and Ernest departed the next day, catching up with her for dinner in Miami with boxer Tom Heeney as a chaperone. Martha and Ernest went on by train together as far as Jacksonville, where he continued on to New York and Martha entrained for St. Louis.

During Martha's return home, she wrote to Pauline, thanking her for the hospitality in Key West and for not minding her "becoming a fixture, like a kudu head, in your home."[1] She also let Pauline know that she had had a lovely steak dinner in Miami with Ernest, whom she now called Ernesto. The letter bore a strange resemblance to Pauline's letters to Hadley some ten years earlier. No doubt Pauline recognized the irony. When Arnold Gingrich mistakenly received word of Ernest having a serious illness, she wired back: "*SECONDHAND REPORT ABSOLUTELY BASELESS ERNEST IN MIAMI ENROUTE TO NEW YORK IN SHALL WE SAY PERFECT HEALTH THANKS FOR SOLICITUDE.*"[2]

Pauline shipped Ernest's cold-weather clothes via special delivery to New York, since his quick departure from Key West had left no time to pack. Upon his arrival, the author began a round of meetings to wrap up his novel, get things organized for Spain, and assist a young novelist with narrative for a Spanish documentary film. Maxwell Perkins counseled against the trip, since Hemingway had a book in the works, but Ernest assured him he would get back in time to finish rewrites and read proofs. Additionally, he worked out terms with John Wheeler of the North American News Alliance (NANA) to receive five hundred dollars for each cabled story and one thousand dollars for each mailed feature, with payments sent to Pauline in Key West.

While in New York, Ernest and Virginia, along with Sidney Franklin, made a trip to Saranac Lake in upstate New York to see sixteen-year-old Patrick Murphy, whose health had gradually deteriorated. When Ernest came out of the boy's room, he wept openly at how sick Patrick appeared. Later in the day, the sick boy shakily wrote in his diary, "Ernest came in to see me for a few minutes before I went to bed. He is giving me a bear-skin for a Christmas present, but it is not ready yet."[3] Virginia stayed on to help Sara and the family and made arrangements for her cousin Ward Merner to bring her car from Manhattan the following week. Aside from concern for the Murphys, Virginia may have remained at Saranac Lake to avoid more time with Ernest. The two had gotten into a serious argument at her apartment in New York. Each accused the other of changing drastically since they first met. Virginia criticized Ernest about his infatuations with other women, the way he abused and berated his friends, his lack of appreciation for Pauline's total devotion to him, and his plans to leave his family and go to Spain. It concerned her as well that Ernest assumed his relationship with Virginia could be the same as in the beginning, before he married her sister.[4]

Their arguing continued at the Murphys, prompting Gerald to write to Pauline, "There was, it seems, a certain amount of conversational sniping going on between Ernest and Ginnie. . . . Someone won on points, I suppose."[5] Virginia compared Ernest to a porcupine, which sticks anyone who gets too close. Ernest declared Virginia to be the one sticking in the barbs. Caught in the middle, Pauline wrote to Ernest on his return to New York, "I *am* sorry about the Jinny situation. You are probably both to blame, but that doesn't help *me* any, the middleman."[6] After Ernest returned to Key West the fighting continued by mail, and Virginia reminded him, "The quills on a porcupine are pointed out and not in and intended to protect the porcupine by jabbing anyone who comes in contact with him anywhere. That is how I used the simile. . . . I'm sorry to have changed so much that you feel the way you do."[7]

Despite Ernest's displeasure with his sister-in-law, the Murphys' affection for Virginia had continued to grow from the day Patrick first became ill, nearly eight years earlier. On the day Virginia left Saranac Lake, Gerald wrote to Pauline, "We *love* that girl. There's no one *like* her. She not only says things that no one else does, she *feels* different things than any one else—and what's more she has learned the most endearing way of communicating them to people."[8]

On January 30, a week after Virginia left, Patrick Murphy slipped into a coma and died. The next day John Dos Passos arrived to comfort Gerald and Sara and their daughter Honoria, and a letter from F. Scott Fitzgerald arrived with the message, "The whole afternoon was so sad with thoughts of you and the past and the happy times we once had. Another link binding you to life is broken." He could see hope, however, in "another generation growing up around Honoria, and an eventual peace somewhere, an occasional port of call as we all sail deathward."[9]

Pauline prayed for Patrick's soul every day during the week after his death, even though she knew the Murphys did not believe in prayer. "But I cannot help feeling that when a little boy goes alone to another place it is good to have prayers follow him," she wrote. "As for understanding why a boy so richly and uniquely endowed to live in this world happily should have been taken from it, I don't . . . and I do not know why such things happen to two people like you who did not need to be refined by suffering."[10]

When not thinking about the Murphys, Pauline worried about Ernest's proposed trip to Spain, fearing for his safety as well as the impact this trip would have on his writing. She felt somewhat better about it, however, when Ernest asked their friend Sidney Franklin to accompany him. When Franklin asked him why he didn't just pick up and go if it was so important, Ernest replied to the effect, "That's easy for you to say. I've got a wife and kids. Pauline doesn't like the idea. She says I shouldn't go. But I know it would be all right with her if you came along with me."[11]

Franklin happily complied since another proposed venture with Ernest appeared to be in limbo. Some months earlier, Ernest had come up with a scheme to build a bullfight ring in Cuba. According to Ernest, Gus Pfeiffer had agreed to put eight hundred thousand dollars into the deal, and Ernest believed he could get seven hundred thousand dollars from other investors to provide adequate funding to purchase the land, build the ring, and cover bullfighters' contracts for the first two seasons.[12]

With Franklin's help he drew up plans for a twenty-thousand-seat arena modeled after the new bullring in Madrid, but with some improvements. They set their sights on a plot of land about a ten-minute walk from central Havana. The two would-be entrepreneurs met with Colonel Fulgencio Batista, then nominal head of Cuba, and received his blessing for their scheme. Plans went awry, however, when the time arrived for the Cuban legislature to adopt a law permitting and governing bullfighting in the country. The evening before a vote in the lower chamber, three senators got word to

Ernest that their price for going along with it, as well as squelching opposition, would be ten thousand dollars each. Ernest had passed on the deal and decided to try again later, but conflict in Spain diverted his attention.

With his wife, his sister-in-law, and his publisher not wanting him to go, Ernest also had some explaining to do in Piggott. When he wrote to thank the Pfeiffers for stocks and checks sent over the holidays, Ernest added: "I hate to go away but you can't preserve your happiness by trying to take care of it or putting it away in moth balls. And for a long time me and my conscience both have known I had to go to Spain. Can usually treat my conscience pretty rough and even make him like it but it catches up with you once in a while."[13]

Having friends on both sides of the Spanish conflict, Ernest first declared himself neutral, but his politics eventually turned him to the left of his inlaws and the Roman Catholic hierarchy, which supported Franco's forces. Ernest disregarded reports of Loyalist forces killing Catholic priests and tiptoed around the Pfeiffer position, referring to himself in a letter as "the leader of the Ingrates battalion on the wrong side of the Spanish war."[14] The author assured his relatives that for his peace of mind Pauline needed to stay in Key West. "This is the dress rehearsal for the inevitable European war and I would like to try to write anti-war correspondence that would help to keep us out of it when it comes," he told the Pfeiffers. As a postscript, Ernest added, "I'm very grateful to you both for providing Pauline who's made me happier than I've ever been."[15]

After completing preparations and telling his family goodbye, Ernest returned to New York and showed up unannounced at Virginia's apartment as she prepared to leave for dinner with Jay McEvoy, who now worked for Uncle Gus. Jay recalled that he, Virginia, and Ernest went out to dinner together, and Ernest, acting as if nothing had ever happened between him and Virginia, "was very, very amiable, entertaining." His ship sailed at midnight, and Virginia went to see him off. Ernest did not want her to leave the ship and asked her to go with him to Europe, possibly because he knew she would refuse. Later Virginia told Jay she should have taken him up on the offer because "if I had done it, perhaps I could have saved Pauline's marriage."[16] Jay always assumed that Virginia had a more intimate relationship with Ernest that she let on: "I think it's why she didn't want to stay on the ship with him the night he was sailing to the Spanish War. . . . I could tell that night more than any other in my memory that he was very fond of her and very close. . . . Being on the ship, I don't know that she meant she would have carried on an affair with Hemingway, but I don't think she wanted to behind Pauline's back."[17]

Ernest sailed aboard the *Paris* with Sidney Franklin and Evan Shipman on February 27, and after ten days in Paris he went alone to Spain, leaving Franklin in Paris to work out problems with his visa. He established headquarters at the Hotel Florida in Madrid with other journalists covering the war. In addition to sending back his NANA dispatches, Ernest became directly involved with Dutch filmmaker Joris Ivens and others shooting scenes for a new documentary, *The Spanish Earth*. Prior to arriving in Spain, Hemingway had joined with John Dos Passos, Archibald MacLeish, and Lillian Hellman to form a group called Contemporary Historians to handle fund-raising and distribution for the film.

While Ernest settled in Spain, Martha secured war-correspondent credentials through *Collier's* and got her papers in order. From the time she left Key West and returned to St. Louis, Martha and Ernest had exchanged letters and telephone calls, and she had soon decided to abandon her novel and check out the situation in Spain firsthand. In one of her letters to Ernest before his departure she wrote, "I hope we get on the same ark when the real deluge begins."[18]

Martha arrived in Valencia about the same time as Franklin, who resolved his visa issues, and the two rode in the same government vehicle to Madrid. Franklin disliked Martha from the start, given his loyalty to Pauline. Though Ernest and Martha attempted discretion as their relationship developed, the affair became common knowledge when the two emerged from the same room after a shell struck the hotel in the middle of the night.

Pauline attempted not to think about what might be going on in Spain. In response to a letter from Maxwell Perkins, inquiring as to whether she needed anything, Pauline wrote, "I am told that when I was a very young baby I could be left alone on a chair and would never fall off. I seem to be still on it." She assured him that all was well on the "widow's peak," with "little reason to think such a state won't continue."[19]

Pauline's efforts to keep busy included bicycling with a young writer, Jack Latimer, and she offered to proof the manuscript of his newest mystery novel. Latimer readily accepted her help, knowing how much Ernest thought of her editing skills. It delighted Pauline when *Collier's* serialized Latimer's book. Latimer later remembered her as "not pretty, but very winning, very bright. Her face was not beautiful, but so intelligent and alert that she became attractive."[20]

After assisting with the book, Pauline passed the time playing tennis with friends, playing Parcheesi with her children, and starting work on the swimming pool. Gus Pfeiffer sent along a diving board, with blueprints for Toby Bruce on how to set it up. Pauline also traveled some, and everywhere she went she wrote long letters to Ernest about how much she missed him. In mid-March she toured Mexico with a friend, Esther Chambers, and wrote en route to Vera Cruz that she hadn't been on a ship with anyone but Ernest for so long that she felt lost and missed his jokes and "the way we pass the time."[21] By the time they reached Mexico City, Pauline loved the country and suggested that she and Ernest take the boys to a Mexican bull ranch during the summer as an alternative to heading west. Upon returning home, she complained to Ernest of being "sick and tired of all these people in Key West and I wish you were here sleeping in my bed and using my bathroom and drinking my whisky."[22]

In late April Pauline heard from Jane Mason, hospitalized again in New York for continuing back problems. Jane conveyed her boredom and asked Pauline to send a copy of Ernest's manuscript to read. Pauline stalled, saying she could not do so without Ernest's permission, and suspected correctly that Gingrich had said something to Jane about the book being highly libelous. Even though Gingrich had convinced Ernest to remove some of the most offensive passages, Jane remained identifiable as Helène Bradley.

The book still needed work, and Maxwell Perkins wanted Ernest to return home and tend to necessary revisions. By the end of April, with film footage for the Spanish documentary also completed, editing the documentary in New York became the next step toward its completion. Ernest cabled Pauline in Key West with the message "Everything Marvelous" and indicated that he would be home soon. Ecstatic over the news, she immediately threw a party for "nineteen of my intimate friends" to celebrate. They dined on the patio and danced and drank until 4 A.M., Pauline told Ernest, but the next afternoon found her "cold sober and missing you just as much as ever."[23]

When Ernest arrived in Paris from Spain in May, he told reporters that he planned to head home to revise a novel but would return to Spain with his wife once he had completed his book and galley proofs. After four days in Paris with Martha, Ernest departed on the *Normandie* for New York and then went directly to Key West to gather his wife and children for the summer in Bimini.

Shortly after arriving in Bimini, Ernest received a wire from Gus letting him know that he could not make the fishing trip they had talked about earlier. Concerned about Ernest's rushed schedule and citing the need to stay close to his office, Gus suggested that perhaps things would be more favorable for a trip the next year. When Ernest replied that he would not have come home, except for making good on their fishing trip, it totally floored Gus. Even if meant facetiously, it could not have been a more inappropriate statement to make to Pauline's uncle, of all people. After recovering from his shock at the insult, Gus wrote, "I hope . . . the happiness your return gave to Pauline and the boys is worth the trip back."[24] Gus was beginning to see Ernest in a different light.

The Bimini trip did not prove to be the leisurely summer vacation Pauline had hoped it would be. During the first six weeks Ernest made three trips to New York, each time meeting Martha and then returning to Pauline. After a quick trip on June 4 to address the American Writers Congress, he made a second trip to deposit his book with Max and oversee recording the narrative for *The Spanish Earth*. As Ernest and Joris Ivens worked toward completion of the documentary, Martha convinced her friend Eleanor Roosevelt to schedule a White House screening for the president in July.

Though upset over his departures from Bimini and his unwillingness to take her along, Pauline resigned herself to his trips and took a different tack once Ernest arrived in New York. She suggested that he not worry about rushing home, his work there being too important to rush: "So you go ahead and do what you can and to hell with getting back on a fixed date." She informed Ernest that his family, all in wonderful shape, would find amusements. Pauline also expressed support for the final product of their earlier editing marathon, telling him, "I'm really crazy about the book." With the substance already perfect and the writing "lovely and hard and full of juice," she suggested that after leaving it with Maxwell Perkin, he should perhaps "let it lie a little to perfect the form." She signed the letter "Remember me to the comrades, and remember me yourself."[25]

During another New York trip, Ernest met Joris and Martha for the leg to Washington, D.C., and a July 8 screening with President and Mrs. Roosevelt and others. Afterward, Hemingway wrote to his mother-in-law in Piggott that he liked the Pfeiffer home on Cherry Street hill much better than the White House. The White House had no air-conditioning, except in the president's study, and its food was "the worst I've ever eaten. . . . I wished Karl could have been there to eat the meal." Referring to Martha Gellhorn as "the woman who had made the arrangements," he told them, "She has stayed there a lot. Me, I won't be staying there any more." Nevertheless, he thought "it was damned nice of the Roosevelts to have us there and to see the picture and I appreciate it."[26]

The Roosevelts liked the film and made several suggestions, including making the Loyalist case even stronger and toning down the overly dramatic narration. The trio agreed with the changes, and several days later Hemingway and Ivens left New York for Hollywood to show the film and raise money for ambulances. Pauline indicated to Sara Murphy a few days before the trip that she planned to come to New York and accompany

Ernest to Hollywood and San Francisco, but accounts of the trip do not mention her presence. The California trip raised enough money to send twenty ambulances to Spain, and Ernest returned to Bimini, via a few days in New York, in time for his thirty-eighth birthday.

By August, with proofs read and references to his friends subdued considerably, Ernest planned a return to Spain. Ada Stern flew to Miami with Patrick and Gregory, while Ernest, Pauline, and Bumby took the *Pilar* up the Miami River to secure it from possible hurricanes. Aboard the boat, Pauline pleaded with Ernest not to return to Spain or to take her with him if he chose to go. Despite her pleas and his earlier comments to reporters about taking Pauline on the next trip, he insisted on returning alone. His mother-in-law suggested pointedly that Ernest needed to stay home and take care of his sons, but the author wrote that he had no choice because "I promised them I would be back and while we cannot keep all our promises I do not see how not to keep that one. I would not be able to teach my boys much if I did."[27]

Ernest insisted that such separations bothered him as much as the rest of the family, recalling that after a few weeks in Madrid earlier in the year, he had "an impersonal feeling of haveing no wife, no children, no house, no boat, nothing." Developing such detachment was the only way to function while there, he told them, "but now have been home just long enough to lose it all; to value all the things again; and now go back knowing I have to put them all away again."[28] Ernest left for Spain aboard the *Champlain* and arrived in Paris on August 21. Martha followed aboard the *Normandie* and got into Paris two days after Ernest. Sidney Franklin decided not to go back and instead accompanied Pauline and the two oldest boys to the bull ranch in Mexico that she had hoped to visit with Ernest.

Earlier that summer the Murphys had returned to Europe with their daughter, Honoria, to establish some distance from the loss of their sons. Ernest stopped by to see them when he arrived in Paris, apparently still smarting over his falling-out with Virginia. "I've been thinking a lot about Ernest," Gerald wrote to Sara as he traveled back to the United States on business. "He dreads life becoming soft for him (or anyone he likes)—and if it threatens to he takes it in hand. . . . But Ernest's feelings about Jinny are not encouraging. He may be unreasonable in his own right—and critical and unforgiving."[29]

Virginia's was not the latest friendship ruined. His relationship with John Dos Passos had become a casualty of the Spanish civil war. The two had discovered creative differences from the beginning of their collaboration on *The Spanish Earth* documentary, but the split widened when Dos Passos attempted to learn what had happened to his long-time Spanish friend José Robles Pazos. When they learned of Robles's execution by the leftist government for treason, Hemingway accepted his guilt at face value and warned Dos Passos not to pursue the matter further. It infuriated Dos Passos that Hemingway declined to find the truth and seemed to think that any atrocity could be justified if it furthered the Loyalist cause. Thus, another Hemingway friendship ended in acrimony.

When Ernest arrived in Spain for his second tour, not much appeared to be going on. During the first three months he sent only two dispatches to NANA, along with occasional cables and a few letters to Pauline. He occupied much of his time writing a play, *The Fifth Column,* in which he seemed once again to be working out his marital difficulties in print and preparing for a break with his wife. The play takes place in Spain, where Philip Rawlings, a counterspy posing as a war correspondent, is involved in a relationship with a female war correspondent, Dorothy Bridges. Dorothy is based on Martha, but many of the places mentioned belonged to Ernest's life with Pauline. In breaking with those places, her lover and counterspy Philip Rawlings says, "I've been to all those places, and I've left them all behind. And where I go now I go alone, or with others who go there for the same reason I go."[30] Such sentiments suggested that Ernest intended to shift his life in a new direction.

While the author struggled with his play and his conscience, his book came out in October, again to mixed reviews. Critics cited superb scenes, but they complained about awkward transitions—a result of Ernest's drastic cuts without adding new bridges to tie sequences together. Nevertheless, the book sold thirty-eight thousand copies in five months, with two reprints in October and one in November.[31] In addition to the awkward transitions in *To Have and Have Not,* some people objected to its subject matter, including a description of sexual intercourse between a middle-aged married couple. When authorities in Detroit attempted to ban sale of the book, even Sherwood Anderson weighed in on Hemingway's skill as a writer, though he could not say much for him as a friend. "I want to add my word of protest against the effort to suppress Ernest Hemingway's novel," Anderson wrote to the leaders of the opposition. "Mr. Hemingway is a great writer. Nothing he writes will hurt anyone. It would be a thousand times more intelligent to fight the kind of evil he depicts than to fight him."[32]

Pauline attempted to feel connected to Ernest by keeping up with news on his book and by reading his dispatches. By late fall, however, Pauline knew she made a colossal mistake by not joining him in Spain. During the Mexican trip she had ample opportunity to pump Sidney Franklin, whose reports convinced her that she was about to lose Ernest, if not to Martha, at least to the war. When Pauline visited Piggott on her return from Mexico, her parents told her they felt that Ernest should come home to his family, rather than Pauline going to him. In mid-November Paul Pfeiffer tried to entice the author to Piggott once again for a good quail and duck hunt. "It has been a long time since we all had a visit with you," Paul wrote. "Wishing you lots of good luck and a safe journey home."[33]

Pauline also visited her friend Katy Dos Passos in the fall and found her sympathetic to Pauline's proposed trip to Europe. John and Katy Dos Passos both had seen Ernest with Martha while working on the Spanish documentary and registered the strong attraction. After Pauline's visit, Katy wrote to Sara Murphy, "Have you heard anything of the Monster of Mt. Kisco?" referring to Ernest. She added that "Pauline's visit was a great pleasure to us, but she seemed worried about Ernest, and no wonder—she was very cute and nervy, I thought—but couldn't sleep, and said she found it a little dull in Key West."[34]

By early December Pauline had decided on a trip to Europe and insisted on meeting Ernest in Paris for Christmas. Though some accounts say it surprised Ernest to learn of her arrival in Paris, he cabled Pauline twice from Barcelona to let her know he probably would be there by December 22. Ernest and Martha traveled as far as Barcelona together, and then Martha went home on the *Normandie,* arriving in time for Christmas and a cross-country speaking tour.

Pauline reached Paris on December 21 and checked into the Hôtel Elysée Park to wait on Ernest, but he did not arrive as expected. Just as he departed Barcelona, Loyalists launched a long-awaited offensive at Tereul, and he returned to the front. When Pauline learned of Ernest's delay in Spain, she approached an old friend headed back into Spain, Jay Allen, about interceding with the American consul general to get her a visa. Pauline told him she had to see for herself why the war had such a hold on her husband. Allen crossed back into Valencia and told Ernest, who "seemed amazed and flattered that his wife would risk the dangers of war in order to see him . . . and mightily displeased with me for not making it possible."[35]

When Ernest wired a story to his NANA editor, he asked him to cable correspondent's credentials to his wife in Paris so that she could obtain a visa and join him for Christmas in Spain. The visa did not get there, however, and Pauline sat through Christmas alone in her room at the hotel. Ironically, a telegram arrived for Ernest from Gus Pfeiffer on Christmas Eve: *"CHRISTMASTIDE IS SEASON DEDICATED TO JOYOUSNESS AND*

*GOODWILL. . . . LET US RESOLVE TO CARRY THE XMAS SPIRIT
OF PEACE ON EARTH GOODWILL TOWARD MEN DURING ALL
THE COMING YEAR IN THIS SPIRIT WE GREET AND SEND LOVE
AND BEST WISHES TO YOU AND PAULINE FOR A MERRY XMAS
AND HAPPY NEW YEAR.* "[36]

Things could not be less merry or less happy for Pauline, however, and
Ernest finally arrived in Paris on December 28 to a depressed and angry
wife. To make matters worse, Ernest became ill. Despite their troubles, the
Hemingways stayed in Paris for two weeks, then departed for home
aboard the *Gripsholm,* which disembarked in Nassau, enabling the unhappy
couple to avoid reporters waiting in New York for the return of the war
correspondent.

CHAPTER 19

The Marriage Unravels (1938)

When Ernest and Pauline arrived in Key West in late January 1938, Ernest began pulling together a book of all his short stories and catching up on correspondence, including a letter to Hadley with two checks enclosed from Gus Pfeiffer for Bumby's education fund. Gus sent each of the boys an additional forty shares of Warner stock with a par value of one hundred dollars per share, paying a 4 percent dividend. Home only three days, Ernest told Hadley in the letter that already he missed Spain.[1]

As days passed, he grew increasingly irritable and paranoid. *Time* magazine coverage of the Tereul offensive angered him because Herbert Matthews appeared to be the only journalist present, when in reality Ernest felt Matthews had him to thank for being there. With the Catholic hierarchy on the other side of the war, Ernest suspected that Catholics on the night desk of the *New York Times* must have thrown away his stories and deleted his name from Matthews's dispatches. The author's Key West lifestyle seemed frivolous compared to what he had experienced and accomplished in Spain, and he believed Maxwell Perkins had failed to promote *To Have and Have Not* extensively enough. To make matters worse, Ernest had conflicted feelings for Martha and guilt over his treatment of Pauline. He admitted to Max that he had gotten himself into "an unchristly gigantic jam."[2]

By mid-March Ernest had learned of a new fascist drive across Spain and welcomed the excuse to get out of Key West and return to the action. A resigned Pauline helped him pack and flew with Ernest to Newark to see him off. He boarded the *Isle de France* and headed back to Europe in time to meet Martha in Paris. After the pair arrived in Barcelona, they were virtually inseparable for the next two months. While in the New York area, Pauline had tea with Maxwell Perkins and his wife and visited Jay and Ruth Allen. Though she was reserved around others, the tears flowed when she let down her guard around her sister. Pauline resisted hearing it, but Virginia insisted to Pauline that Ernest no longer resembled the man they knew and that if the marriage ended, Pauline should not let him off the hook easily.

Gus Pfeiffer, one of the few family members unaware of the impending split, maintained his support for the author. Ernest called him from New York on the day he sailed to say goodbye, and Gus followed up with a letter reinforcing his regard. "My confidence in you started at our first meeting in Paris, and has not changed or wavered," he told him, adding that nothing he might do in the future would change that because "the background of my regard and respect for you is faith in your being honest. Also I know if you do make a mistake, it hurts you more than it will hurt those affected by it."[3] It was ironic that Ernest should receive such a letter at a time when he was not being honest with himself or others.

Pauline returned to Key West and tried to keep her letters to Ernest light and cheerful. In spite of her upbeat tone, Pauline made it clear that she did not want Ernest to come back if it meant him being as miserable as the last time. When he cabled that he might come home in May, she warned "please do not think of coming if you want to stay on for any reason, and I do not think you could be happy here with the war going on." She added that life in Key West had not changed since he left and that since he had found it so disagreeable the last time, it probably wouldn't be any different when he got back, "so if you are happy over there don't come back here to be unhappy but hope you can come back and we can both be happy."[4]

By mid-May Ernest's contract with the North American News Alliance had wound down, and NANA had little reason for continuing it. Clients such as the *New York Times* thought Ernest's stories too often duplicated those of their own correspondent, Herbert Matthews. NANA attempted to eliminate duplicate coverage by having Ernest do only human-interest stories, then only significant developments, but the restrictions severely limited his style and creativity. Ernest and Martha left Spain in May for Paris, where they enjoyed each other's company for several days before Martha headed off to assignments in Czechoslovakia, England, and France for *Collier's*. Unsure whether the affair would survive the separation, Ernest lapsed into his usual depression between relationships. His unhappiness when alone and need for an adoring woman to validate his manhood took him home.

As he left Paris, Ernest wrote to friends, "Am going home to see Pauline and the kids and take them wherever they want to go. . . . Have neglected my family very badly this last year and would like to make it up."[5] He arrived in New York aboard the *Normandie* on Memorial Day and paid a visit to Jay Allen and his wife before going on to Key West. He knew

Pauline had talked to them, and he pumped them about whether they thought Pauline would take him back. The Allens recalled that he blamed all his marital problems on Virginia, claiming Virginia had tried to turn Pauline against him.

Though he got little encouragement from the Allens, Ernest went on to Key West, where Pauline picked him up at the airport after his flight from Miami. Not knowing what to expect and wanting to avoid confrontation, she took Toby Bruce and the boys with her. The trip home from the airport provided some indication of things to come. As they neared the house, with Ernest driving, a car driven by a Works Progress Administration (WPA) worker collided with them in an intersection. Both drivers immediately jumped out and squared off verbally in front of Ernest's family and bystanders. Unable to figure out exactly what had happened, police arrested both Ernest and the other driver and took them to police court. Though the judge dismissed the case after hearing everyone's testimony, the arguing continued as they left the courtroom.[6]

Once Ernest arrived home, he acted as if everything was fine, including his marriage, and went back to work on his short stories and a series of articles for a new magazine called *Ken*. Pauline assumed, since she had made her feelings clear in her letters, that Ernest had elected to stay for good. When Paul Pfeiffer sent a letter including shares of Piggott Land Company stock as a welcome-home present, Pauline wrote to her parents, "Ernest seems very content to be home and is leading a quiet life, working, swimming, fishing and reading—with no tourists to intrude. I am beginning to wonder if he isn't TOO quiet. But it seems good to have him home again, and so far it is so peaceful we haven't made any plans for the future. . . . I hate to hound Ernest for plans when he seems so happy without any."[7]

Ernest added a postscript to the letter, thanking them for the stock, expressing the desire to see them soon, and thanking Mary Pfeiffer for the prayers she had sent his way. "That explains the whole mystery," he told her. "I knew I was having an awful lot of luck I didn't deserve."[8] His letter signaled an uneasy truce, but Virginia, in Piggott when the letter arrived, had her doubts. She wanted no part of his lies and deceits and purposely arranged to be away from New York when Ernest and Pauline arrived there in June to cover the Schmeling-Louis fight and pick up Bumby for the summer.

Paul and Mary wanted to believe the best, and the day after receiving Pauline and Ernest's letter, Paul followed up by encouraging them to make sure they put Piggott on the route when they made plans for the summer. Along with being anxious to see the entire family, they wanted to hear directly from Ernest about the situation in Spain. Though the Pfeiffers did not share their son-in-law's politics, they shared his respect for a fellow Arkansan, Frank Tinker of DeWitt, a "Flyer of Fortune" for the Loyalist cause. Tinker had eight enemy kills to his credit, earning Ernest's admiration as a hero of the Spanish Civil War. Hemingway had immortalized Tinker, along with his fellow flyer Whitney Dahl, in his short story "Night Before Battle."

The Pfeiffers followed Tinker's exploits, and when the pilot wrote an account of his experiences in a book titled *Some Still Live,* Paul and Mary read a serialized version in April issues of *Saturday Evening Post.* Though not a great writer, Tinker wrote genuinely and honestly, leading Ernest to call the articles "damn good."[9] Just one year later, Ernest learned from his mother-in-law that Tinker had committed suicide on June 13, 1939, in a Little Rock hotel, unable to cope with his despair over the plight of the Loyalists and whether he might have made a difference by staying longer, rather than ending his service out of fatigue. Ernest regretted that he had not known Tinker's state of mind and had not intervened. "Have argued myself out of that so often that I think I could have kicked the idea out of his head," he told Mary. "He was a good fellow; very brave and a truly fine flyer."[10]

Ernest also knew what it was like to want to be in the midst of the action. After relaxing in Key West during the summer of 1938, his edginess returned. While their friends usually sided with Pauline, they could see that both seemed miserable. Throughout it all, Pauline attempted to keep her dignity and prevent Ernest from destroying her already battered pride. At one point Ernest came in from fishing to go with Pauline to a costume party. When he found the door locked to his studio and the key missing, he grabbed a pistol and fired it at the ceiling, then shot the lock off the door. Pauline tried to ignore his tirade and went to the party without him. When Ernest decided later to come to the party, he found Pauline, clad in a hula costume, dancing with another man, and he punched the guy. The altercation ended in broken furniture and more humiliation for Pauline.

Unlike Pauline, some of their friends decided they would no longer tolerate Ernest's behavior. Ada MacLeish, already upset over his affair with Martha and likely divorce from Pauline, viewed an incident when Ernest berated her husband as the final blow. Ernest not only attacked Archibald MacLeish for what he considered a paltry financial contribution to the production of *The Spanish Earth,* but claimed that his so-called friend had cheated him into making a greater financial commitment than others had to make. MacLeish tried to smooth things over and make peace with Ernest, but Ada wrote, "I wish to state in writing that the MacLeish family . . . will find it entirely convenient to stay out of Pappy's way for all time."[11] Fortunately for their friendship, they had too many mutual interests to sever all ties permanently.

By the end of July 1938, with Key West temperatures as hot as Hemingway tempers, Ernest decided to take his family west. They got as far as West Palm Beach, when Ernest accidentally scratched his pupil of his eye for the fourth time. After two days in a hotel with the blinds drawn, they continued, with Ernest wearing an eyepatch and dark glasses. Gregory and Ada left them at Jacksonville for Syracuse, while Patrick and Bumby headed for the L-Bar-T Ranch with Ernest and Pauline. Patrick recalled the trip being full of bickering between his parents. Pauline attempted to give Ernest directions; he ignored them and then chewed her out if he took a wrong turn.

The happy campers bypassed Piggott since the Pfeiffers were in Aspetuck, but Ernest wrote Paul and Mary from Wyoming to thank them for birthday gifts. The author bragged that in spite of all his traveling in the last eighteen months, he had rewritten and published a novel, written and made a documentary, written a play and about fifteen magazine articles, and filed some fifteen thousand dollars' worth of newspaper dispatches. Even so, his dissatisfaction filled the letter: "If I had hired somebody to run my life badly couldn't have done a more complete job of it probably. War is a bad business for everybody that has anything to do with it. In the last one I was both wounded and frightened and so the suffering and the fear gave you a sort of humility and understanding and decency. In this one I have not been scared, nor hit, although I expected to be all the time at the start. And I know I have been intolerant, righteous, and many times ruthless and cruel."[12]

Ernest and Pauline worked two weeks in Wyoming on galley proofs for his book of short stories and discussed how to handle the play written in Spain. They agreed it best to publish the play with his short stories. After several conversations, Perkins agreed. The book, *The Fifth Column and the First Forty-Nine Stories,* included four new stories and all his short stories to date. Ernest had a lot riding on the work's success. Still smarting from the poor reception of *To Have and Have Not,* he told Perkins that he wanted to "produce something so extra good and extra big this time that there wouldn't be any question." Though he pretended that critics' views didn't matter as long as his books sold, their attacks always bothered him. "I don't think it is persecution mania or egotism if I say that there are a lot of critics who really seem to hate me very much and would like to put me out of business," he told Perkins. "And I don't think I mean it conceitedly when I say that a lot of it is jealousy; I do what they would like to do, and I do what they are afraid to do."[13]

Once Ernest finished and mailed the galleys, his desire to be elsewhere returned. Hitler provided the author's exit by provoking the next world war. The North American News Alliance wanted Ernest to cover any action, so Ernest made plans to leave Wyoming at the end of August, with Toby coming later to drive Pauline and the boys to Piggott. Not long after Ernest's departure, Pauline wrote from Wyoming that she had received his wires and missed him very much, but felt surprisingly serene about their fate. "But I do hope you won't stay away too long," she added. "A husband should not stay away from a loving wife too long. I won't say this again as I do not want to hurry you."[14]

Toby arrived in Wyoming on September 6, and he, Pauline, and the children left at dawn the next morning. They made it to Piggott in three days, even after stopping in Lincoln, Nebraska, to put Bumby on a train back to his mother in Chicago. After ten days in Piggott, Pauline and Patrick left for New York by train, leaving the car with Toby to drive back to Key West. Pauline had decided to rent an apartment in New York for the months of October and November to avoid the last of the Key West heat. Before leaving, she dropped Ernest a newsy letter with all her plans. The letter ended, "Don't forget I am following rigorously my policy of believing what my husband says in his letters. Also, if you want to keep a contented wife, see to it that she does not hear from strangers where her husband is and with whom."[15]

By then Ernest had reunited with Martha in Paris, though they saw each other only sporadically, given Martha's various assignments. Ernest started a novel incorporating his Spanish experiences and working on new short stories. He sent "Night Before Battle" to Arnold Gingrich as his final piece published in *Esquire*. Along with the story came an explanation to Gingrich that Ernest was unsure of some grammatical uses because "Pauline, whose word I take on grammar, is not here."[16]

When Pauline and Patrick arrived in New York, they went straight to Virginia's apartment and found Hadley. She had come from Chicago to enter Bumby at Storm King School in Connecticut and stayed over another day in New York to visit with Pauline. Hadley appreciated having Pauline close, where Bumby could spend weekends with her. Pauline and Patrick moved into Apartment 8C at 147 E. Fiftieth Street on September 26. The next day Ada and Gregory arrived from Syracuse to join them in the large apartment, and Pauline wrote Ernest that she would send him a golden key so he could slip in at any time.

Her relocation to New York came at a good time, with Bumby nearby and other Pfeiffer relatives around to keep her occupied. Leicester Hemingway moved to the city as well, along with his wife and baby, after landing a job at *Country Home* magazine. Pauline shopped with Virginia, visited relatives at Aspetuck, and dabbled in the New York social scene, including assisting with a large banquet for the Duchess of Atholl to raise money for the Spanish Children's Milk Fund.

Ernest's new book came out on October 14, and Pauline did her best to promote it. Perkins sent her the book a week prior to publication, and she liked the way it looked. It infuriated her on the day of publication, however, to find not a single copy of the book in Scribner's window. It angered her as well that Ernest was not there to tend to it, and she wrote to him, "Perhaps my dear fellow you should be shifting from your mistress—shall we call her War—to your master."[17] When Ernest heard about the lack of promotion, he wrote his editor, "I'm sure there must be some mistake. Is there any connection with the size of the reviews and the size of the ads?"[18]

Most reviewers took a ho-hum approach to the book, pointing out that it included only four new short stories, very much like previous short stories, and a play obviously insufficient to stand on its own. "Its grave defect," the Associated Press review pointed out regarding the play, "is that it is political and is not removed even a little from reality." As such, "it is as effective as propaganda plays ever are."[19]

Ernest made no secret of his Loyalist sympathies in any of his writing or war coverage. In fact, a French unit going into Spain offered him a staff captaincy that fall, which Ernest gladly would have accepted, but he had a commitment to the North American Newspaper Alliance and had promised Pauline he would not go to war. "So there were certain conflicting obligations," he told Perkins. "I am very sick of conflicting obligations which seems to be the product that I have the greatest supply of."[20]

One of his greatest obligations, he determined, was to his work, believing that he needed to concentrate on serious writing and finishing his novel. With the defeat of Loyalist forces inevitable, it became a matter of time before Franco took Madrid. Ernest knew he needed to move on and headed back to New York in November, leaving Martha to make one last trip to Barcelona for a visit with suffering Spanish people. Ernest arrived in New York on November 24 and stayed at the apartment with Pauline and the children until the lease ran out at the end of the month. While he looked forward to being reunited with family, once there he fell into the same emotional abyss. On one occasion he and Pauline met at Virginia's apartment for dinner. Jay McEvoy attended and found Hemingway morose and untalkative. Rather than having their evening ruined, Virginia and Jay went out to dinner on their own, leaving the Hemingways at the apartment. "When he had that attitude there was nothing in the world you could do about it," Jay recalled.[21] When the lease expired on the apartment, Pauline and Ernest returned separately to Key West, keeping up the pretense of a happy marriage.

While maintaining a public front, Pauline and Ernest both recognized their marriage was one more work of fiction. After a few less than satisfying trips out in the *Pilar,* Ernest escaped back to New York for scheduled meetings with Benjamin (Barney) Glaser, hired by the Theatre Guild to rewrite Ernest's play, *The Fifth Column,* for stage production. Ernest concluded angrily that Glaser's rewrite smacked of amateurism. His telegram to Pauline called it "absolutely appalling stupid childish ignorant sentimental silly."[22] Glaser's version opened with highlights from the third act, leaving nowhere to go. To fix it, Ernest wrote two totally new acts in what he referred to as a feverish "Old Testament nightmare" of a trip. The result "should be called the 4.95 column marked down from 5 now," he grumbled later to his mother-in-law.[23]

Only Martha's arrival in New York after the Christmas holidays saved his trip. Ernest made no attempt to hide the new woman in his life, not even from his children. When Bumby arrived in New York from school to spend a night with his father and attend the opening of *The Spanish Earth,* he was surprised to find such a gorgeous blonde on his father's arm. While he knew of Martha, Bumby did not expect her to be so young and attractive. He delighted in hearing four-letter words roll off Martha's tongue like smooth pearls and found the new woman in his father's life totally enchanting.[24]

With his work completed, Ernest flew out of New York in a snowstorm. Yet even the warmth of visiting family and friends did not take the chill off his relationship with Pauline. Gus and Louise Pfeiffer arrived in Key West just ahead of Ernest, so the Hemingways' company manners prevented major confrontations. Ernest set out with Gus for a few days fishing in the Gulf, while Pauline entertained Aunt Louise. But bad weather, Gus's exhaustion from the long car trip, and Ernest's distraction made for little enjoyment. When the lights went out at dinner during the Pfeiffers' last evening in town, it signaled a fitting end to their visit.

Shortly after the Pfeiffers' departure, Ernest's mother made a rare visit to Key West. Checking in at the Casa Marina Hotel, she stayed six days to get acquainted with her grandsons. She had not seen Patrick since he was a toddler, and she met seven-year-old Gregory for the first time. The boys recalled from the visit a rather regal-looking, strange, and distant woman, who, unlike their grandmother Pfeiffer, did not seem especially grandmotherly. At one point Grace gave Patrick a penknife, which she said had belonged to his grandfather. Embarrassed, Patrick recognized it as a trinket his grandmother had purchased that morning at a local dime store.[25] Years later he understood this as his grandmother's effort to connect with him and establish some sort of link to his Hemingway grandfather.

By this time Grace lived in a small house in the River Forest area, adjacent to Oak Park, having allowed foreclosure on the family home when it became impossible to pay the mortgage or keep up taxes. The house suited Grace, and she contented herself with painting, teaching art, and an occasional lecture. Leaving many of the trappings of her former life behind when she moved, Grace deeded Windemere Cottage to Ernest and Pauline in appreciation for their financial assistance. Her visit to Key West may have made Grace wonder if they would ever use it as a couple. Though she said nothing to her son about the state of his marriage, she surely recognized that Pauline and Ernest were only going through the motions.

Hiding the situation from Pauline's parents proved easier, since Paul and Mary knew only what they read in letters. Ernest's letters told them what he knew they wanted to hear. He wrote that their grandson Patrick's confirmation in the Catholic church had taken place in February and that he "was the pride of the Parish since no one could answer the questions the Bishop asked except him."[26] He told them that he had visited Virginia during his trip to New York, and he let them know that Pauline looked "better than ever."[27] Ernest failed to mention that visits with Virginia almost always disintegrated into arguments or that while Pauline might be looking "better than ever," their marriage looked to be over.

CHAPTER 20

The End of Something (1939)

By Valentine's Day 1939, with Ernest's heart elsewhere, he headed once again for Cuba. The author rented his usual room at the Ambos Mundos for sleeping and a room at the Sevilla-Biltmore for writing, stocking it with plenty of food to avoid breaking for meals if writing was going well. The best way to get any work done, he told a friend, is to "tell everybody you live in one hotel and live in another."[1] Relocation to Cuba helped clear his head, and he launched into a frenzy of composition. Ernest intended to complete three short stories and quickly finished the first one, titled "Under the Ridge." Though he no longer prized Pauline as a marriage partner, he still valued her as an editor. After sending the story to Key West for her review, he told Perkins, "Pauline thinks among best I've ever written."[2]

When he started on the next story, the words flowed much more easily than expected. By the time he reached fifteen thousand words, Ernest realized that, instead of a short story, he had the makings of a Spanish Civil War novel. Thus, Ernest marked March 1, 1939, as the day he officially began *For Whom the Bell Tolls*. Vowing to concentrate on the novel until it was finished, he generally started writing around 8:30 each morning and worked straight through until about 2 or 3 in the afternoon. Martha joined him in Cuba, and when he broke for the day they swam, played tennis, fished for marlin from the *Pilar*, or went into Havana and strolled along the Prado or drank at the Floridita.

Pauline's letters to Ernest from Key West remained upbeat and correct for the most part. Occasionally, however, she let her guard down, and her feelings flowed across the page. Responding to Ernest's complaints about being asked to change love scenes in his play, she admitted her helplessness in advising him, indicating that there was "a time when I might have taken a stand about love, but find I know nothing about love."[3]

In mid-March, Ernest returned to Key West for Bumby's Easter visit. While there he tried to keep up the writing momentum established in Cuba but found it virtually impossible. Pauline had developed several new friendships during Ernest's prolonged absences, and gathering around the Hemingways' pool for drinks had become an afternoon ritual. Pauline made no attempt to alter the routine after Ernest returned. Unlike in the past, when his need for quiet ranked as her top priority, Pauline no longer felt compelled to send guests away or even have them be quiet. When Ernest argued with Pauline about it, Virginia defended her.

Ernest soon headed back to Cuba, where he again became engrossed in writing. Earlier he had promised Martha that he would find a house for them, but the words flowed so well that he never got around to it. Martha took matters into her own hands and found a Spanish-style house about fifteen miles from Havana in the little village of San Francisco de Paulo. With about ten acres, the property included a guesthouse near the main house and rented for one hundred dollars per month. Though it was run-down, Martha perceived great possibilities.

When Ernest first saw the house, he immediately dismissed it, proclaiming it not worth one hundred dollars per month. Undeterred, Martha went to work on it using her own funds while Ernest went fishing. When he returned, the house pleased Ernest so much that he moved in immediately. To avoid questions from friends and save embarrassment for Pauline, he continued receiving his mail at the Ambos Mundos address, just as on previous fishing and writing trips.

Not long after Ernest returned to Cuba, Pauline and Virginia decided on a leisurely trip to Piggott by way of New York, leaving the boys in Key West with Ada to finish the school term. Their uncle Henry Pfeiffer had died on April 13, and since they had not made it to the funeral services in New York or the interment in Cedar Falls, Pauline thought visiting family might do her some good. Also, she wanted some time to herself without worrying about everyone's schedules. Pauline planned to spend May in Piggott and return to New York with Virginia, then perhaps visit friends in Nantucket and see how the summer shaped up from there.

Figuring out what to do with the boys over the summer presented a real quandary. The boys wanted to go to the ranch, but that had to wait until late summer or fall. Pauline proposed sending them to a camp in Connecticut for June and possibly July, but Ernest let her know he did not like the idea of just sticking them somewhere. Pauline assured him she had carefully checked out the camp. Similar to a farm, Camp Te Whanga provided opportunities for children to ride horses, build dams, swim, and learn about bird and animal life. With several friends sending their children and the child of another friend working as a camp counselor, Pauline thought it sounded ideal.

"Please consider this well, and also the fact, too, that I would like to have a little while to myself," Pauline wrote to Ernest. "I don't know whether it is all the people, or the time of year, or what, but I am feeling sort of over-whelmed—which isn't like me, and it won't last—and I would like a little time ahead just to do what I like."[4] As it happened, a polio epidemic broke out in Key West during the sisters' trip to Piggott, and Ernest wired Max to send five hundred dollars to J. B. Sullivan in Key West so he could send the children north with Ada to her family home in Syracuse. There they remained until time for camp. Pauline tried to keep her letters to Ernest from Piggott light and breezy and to avoid direct confrontations. She made it known, however, that she was not totally ignorant about his lifestyle in Cuba. She addressed one letter to "Dearest Husband (ha ha!)," referring to him as a great all-around guy, although "not around at all."[5]

The Pfeiffer sisters arrived in New York from Piggott on June 1, and Ada brought Patrick and Gregory down from Syracuse to be outfitted before going to camp. Bumby arrived to spend four days with his step-mother and stepbrothers before returning to his mother's home in Chicago for the summer. Pauline treated all three boys to a day at the New York World's Fair before taking Patrick and Gregory to camp in New Preston, Connecticut. The World's Fair, which opened in April, appealed to Pauline as much as the boys. She had been fascinated by such events since the day she attended the St. Louis World's Fair thirty-five years earlier, at age nine. This latest celebration promised to be one of the grandest of all time, ulti-mately attracting more than twenty-five million people. With the country just coming out of the Great Depression, audiences clamored to see the "World of Tomorrow." For Pauline, however, tomorrow looked bleak.

Pauline sent a note to Ernest letting him know that their friend and for-mer safari guide Philip Percival planned to be in New York and hoped to see them. In Florida earlier to visit the Thompsons, Percival had missed the Hemingways. Pauline suggested Ernest might want to come to New York and take Percival to the much-publicized Joe Louis–Tony Galento heavy-weight title fight on June 28 at Yankee Stadium. With Patrick's birthday the same day, the boys could come from camp, and they could have a family celebration and coordinate plans for the remainder of the summer. "I thought I was so good not to bother you about plans," Pauline told Ernest, "but it seems from recent letter of yours that I should have told you plans. Also, sweetie I didn't just shove children in camp to get rid of them as you seem to think."[6]

After finishing her letter, Pauline realized that Ernest would not receive it in time to make plans to come, so she sent a cable as well. Her first message said, "Wish you would come up to fight," which she quickly amended to "Wish you would come up to Louis-Galento fight."[7] Ernest did not show up in New York for Percival, the fight, or the birthday, indicating in a letter to Patrick that he had not gotten Pauline's letter until the day of the fight. He didn't have a checkbook, he told Patrick, but would send a birthday check as soon as he got some blank checks from Pauline. He would send a small check to Gregory as well.[8]

Amid all this activity, Pauline experienced rectal bleeding during a trip to Nantucket and feared she might have cancer. She made arrangements to see a doctor in Boston for two days of diagnostic tests and put all her plans on hold until she figured out the cause of her medical problems. At the end of the first day of tests, Ernest happened to call from Havana, ostensibly because he had not heard from her in about two weeks. More than likely, however, he telephoned to ask Pauline to send checks. She mailed five blank checks after the conversation, along with a note to "write them for any amount and I'll try to make them all good—tho good for nothing myself."[9]

When Ernest learned during his conversation with Pauline that she might have cancer, he assured her he would call the next evening for news of her test results and come to New York to help her through the ordeal, even though the interruption might wreck his book. In a portent of things to come, as Ernest hung up the telephone in Havana, a bolt of lightning shot through the wires, destroying the telephone, throwing him nearly ten feet, stiffening his left arm and neck, and rendering him speechless.

The next day Pauline learned that her tests revealed nothing wrong. When Ernest called, he was relieved to hear her good news and that he would not have to interrupt his writing. After weeks of worry about her health, and with Philip Percival still waiting in New York to see Ernest, Pauline grew angry that Ernest had failed to make even a brief visit. Even more aggravating, Ernest seemed more concerned with talking about his experience with lightning than her cancer scare.

After the telephone conversation, which escalated into a major argument, Ernest dashed off a rambling letter to Pauline about her "public" tongue-lashing. Writing a book was no easy task, he reminded her, insisting that he had never worked harder on a book in his life, that it was all for her and the children, and that he would give up everything if he needed to come and take care of her. Since no emergency existed, however, Ernest saw no reason to leave his work. He added that he would interrupt his writing if Percival wanted to come to Havana to fish, and Pauline could even come with him, provided she could refrain from cursing him. Further, he did not want to be where she could bawl him out twenty-four hours a day. Nor did he intend to let her partying friends interfere with his writing or ruin his life. "You are the finest, best, smartest, loveliest, most attractive, and all time glamourous and wonderful person that I have ever known," he wound down. "But no likem friends."[10] The diatribe ended in self-pity when Ernest suggested that perhaps the lightning should have killed him the day before, because it certainly would have made things easier for Pauline.

His comment had a familiar ring. It sounded much like his assurance to his mother-in-law after his car accident some eight years earlier that he would make sure the next accident killed him, rather than making him a nuisance to his family. Similarly, during the one-hundred-day separation before his marriage to Pauline, he had suggested that perhaps he should kill himself to remove the sin from her life and spare Hadley a divorce. By now, however, Pauline was no longer moved by Hemingway's self-absorbed pronouncements.

After conveying to Percival that Hemingway would not come to New York, Pauline sent a letter to Ernest that crossed with his in the mail and included other options for getting together with Percival. She noted that plans "would be quite simple if our lives were not so complicated and you were say a brick layer instead of woman layer and writer."[11] She asked Ernest to call Percival at the expense of the "nasty extravagant wife from rich family, who thinks money grows on trees."[12] The letter then pleaded with Ernest to do something about the current situation. Their lives could not continue this way, she told him, and the next time the two saw each other they had to work something out. "My God, Papa, but you have made things complicated with this Einhorn [Martha Gellhorn] business," she wrote in frustration. "There is something rotten somewhere."[13]

Frustrated by fighting with Ernest, Pauline impulsively decided she would head to Paris with her friends Paul and Brenda Willert. Less than a week before the *Normandie* sailed, Pauline wired Charles Thompson in Key West to go to the house and find her passport. She wired Ernest as well, followed by a letter telling of her plans, which included leaving the boys at summer camp until Ernest could make arrangements to pick them up in August. If she seemed to be spending too much money, Pauline reminded him of the ten-thousand-dollar inheritance from her uncle Henry, expected any day, which could go into the bank as soon as it arrived. Her letter concluded, "Relax and enjoy Miss Einhorn and here I am off your hands temporarily at least. Enjoy life a little."[14] On the day of her departure, with bags packed, Pauline wrote Ernest to wish him luck with the rest of his book and to assure him that "aside from a few crazy ideas you've got there's nobody like you, and nobody smarter, so you're bound to come out right in the end."[15]

Ernest thought Pauline's trip a good idea, particularly since it might be the last opportunity to see Europe before war broke out. With Pauline on her way, he wrote Patrick and Gregory the news that he would pick them up from camp at the end of August and head to the L-Bar-T Ranch, where Bumby would join them. In the meantime, he continued the book. By his fortieth birthday, on July 21, Ernest had sixty-three thousand words, making it about two-thirds complete. He took the occasion to write his mother-in-law, suggesting he would like to bring Patrick and Gregory through Piggott on their return from the ranch. The letter also served as a not-so-subtle reminder that he had yet to receive the Pfeiffers' usual birthday greeting in the form of a check.

Not knowing whether Pauline had told her parents about their troubles, but wanting to appear as the attentive husband, Ernest took the opportunity as well to provide his version of recent events. He gave his mother-in-law a rundown on Pauline's health and indicated that he had booked passage on a plane, arranged for the care of his boat, and packed his manuscript for a long siege before learning of Pauline's good medical report. As for Pauline's trip to Europe, he had wholeheartedly encouraged her to go. "There is plenty of money for a European trip as I had just deposited the proceeds of the sale of *To Have and Have Not* to the pictures," he boasted.[16] Ernest made no mention of the inheritance from Uncle Henry that more than covered her trip expenses. The Pfeiffers wrote back, sending his late birthday check along with assurances that even though they expected to head to the New York World's Fair and to the Homestead to visit family, they would be back by the time Ernest and the boys arrived.

Pauline found the trip to Europe bittersweet, since she visited many of the places she and Ernest had shared during the good times. Pauline and her friend Brenda followed the Tour de France, then went on to Switzerland, Austria, and Bavaria, where they took in art galleries, festivals, and shopping. The trip unearthed many memories for Pauline. In one letter to Ernest she wrote, "When I was unpacking yesterday at the bottom of my bag was a little fly fish hook. Don't know HOW it got there, but when I saw it—had just read your letter—I burst out crying. I hope you are happy and that the book is going well."[17] In another, in the midst of a recitation of all her activities, she suddenly shifted gears and burst out, "Oh, Papa darling, what is the matter with you. If you are no longer the man I used to know get the hell out, but if you are, stop being so *stupid*."[18]

Ernest went to Key West along with Toby in August and packed up the boys' western clothing and fishing and hunting gear. While he was in town, the local paper quoted him as saying that he planned to head north but would go to Europe if war broke out. His wife, now traveling in Europe, would come home immediately if the situation became too grave, he said. The paper speculated that its next report from Hemingway might well be news from the front.[19]

Ernest headed west by car, dropping Martha at her mother's in St. Louis, while Toby went to Connecticut to fetch Patrick and Gregory from camp. The boys and Toby would go west by train. Hadley and husband, Paul Mowrer, also vacationing in Wyoming, allowed Bumby to drive out on his own to meet them and spend some time before being picked up by his father. When Ernest arrived at the Mowrers' lodge, he learned he could find them fishing at Grebe Lake. Ernest hurried out to meet them and surprised Paul and Hadley by stepping out from behind some trees as they headed down a trail toward home. Hadley and Ernest had not seen each other in eight years. She thought he looked tired and rather sad; he thought she looked terrific. Later he wrote to her, "You and Paul were certainly a swell looking pair of people on that trail. I was as proud of you guys as though I had invented you."[20]

When Bumby caught up with the trio, it thrilled him to see them all talking so animatedly, with Ernest and Paul deep into a discussion about Germany's invasion of Poland earlier that afternoon. "It was wonderful for me to see my mother, my father, and Paul all together talking like that," he recalled. "This was the first time since the Paris days that they had been together and, as it turned out, it was the last time ever."[21]

As Paul and Hadley packed for their return to Chicago, Ernest and Bumby went on to the L-Bar-T Ranch, where Patrick and Gregory joined them. The Hemingway men had barely settled in when a telephone call came from Pauline. Back from Europe and in New York, she wanted to meet them at the ranch. Deep down perhaps Pauline thought things might be different with everyone together in an environment they all enjoyed. Even if Ernest wanted out of the marriage, she certainly did not want him going on to Piggott without her, as he planned, where he could spin his side of the story.

Despite her hopes of a happy reunion, Pauline contracted a terrible cold on the plane and went straight to bed upon arrival. Ernest tended to her as best he could, but Pauline seemed to him like a stranger who had intruded on his vacation with his sons. Ernest had soon had enough of playing nurse-maid to his sick wife and packed his things in the car. He called Martha to meet him at the Billings airport and summoned Toby to drive his family back to Key West. The three-thousand-mile trip home gave Pauline plenty of time to come to grips with her situation. While she loved Ernest, Pauline could no longer tolerate him coming home when he felt like it and leaving to be with Martha when that suited him.

Ernest did not make the final parting easy on either of them. After meeting Martha at the airport and traveling to Sun Valley, Idaho, they spent six weeks together before *Collier's* contacted Martha about taking an assignment in Finland. Two weeks later Martha departed for Europe, and once again Ernest found himself alone—a condition he could never tolerate for long. To relieve his loneliness, Ernest determined he would go back to Key West and spend Christmas with Pauline and his sons. Pauline informed him, however, that he would not be welcome if he simply planned to rejoin Martha after the holidays.

In spite of her protests, Ernest remained convinced that Pauline would change her mind and welcome him back as usual. When Toby arrived to help Ernest with the drive home, he warned Ernest that this time Pauline had vowed to abide by her decision. If Ernest insisted on returning home, Pauline relayed through Toby, she would not be there. She planned to take the boys to spend Christmas with her sister in New York. Even forewarned, Ernest was surprised to arrive in Key West and discover his family gone. Even more surprising, he found the entire house deserted except for Jimmy the gardener, residing temporarily in the pool house. Pauline had given all the other household staff a paid Christmas holiday. Not only did Ernest have to spend the holidays alone in the house, but being without a kitchen staff forced him to take his meals in town.

Pauline's actions gave Ernest an opportunity to transfer guilt and blame to her. In his view, she had behaved atrociously and thought only of herself in denying him the chance to be with his sons for the holidays.[22] Thus he assigned blame for the actual breakup to Pauline, along with Virginia. Ernest's final letter to his mother-in-law was an attempt to absolve himself: "If we could have talked I believe you would have found that I have changed less than Pauline and Virginia have. Virginia's version of my life and conduct is a very fantastic one. But she spread it sufficiently and at the right time to break up my home. So am now doing the best that I can. I do not mean that I have ever been in the right in *anything* but the true version would be very different from anything you have heard."

Ernest told her how bad he felt about not making it to Piggott with the children as planned, but that Pauline's unexpected change in plans had upset his own. The author assured Mary that he would look after Pauline's material interests and would take good care of the children. "This kind of letter is no fun to write and probably less to read," he told her. But he wished her much love and a good Christmas, adding, "If it's not merry it will be sooner or later again."[23]

In her typical fashion, Mary wrote a poignant motherly letter back to her only son-in-law, which read:

> Dear Ernest,
> Your letter received. All this trouble and misunderstanding between you and Pauline is beyond our comprehension.
> Your father and I are deeply grieved. As a member of the family for so many years I had come to regard you as one of my very own.
> This is the saddest Christmas I have ever known. A broken family is a tragic thing, particularly so when there are children.
> Sorry to send you such a message but it is the way I feel.
> I shall always remember you in my prayers and hope that we shall meet again in a fairer clime upon a farther shore.
> Sadly and Sorrowfully, Your Mother Pfeiffer[24]

It marked the end of Ernest's relationship with a woman he had often felt closer to than his own mother, whom he alternately loved and hated. Mary Pfeiffer never saw or heard from him again.

CHAPTER 21

Acrimony and Alimony (1940–1941)

Ernest stayed nine days in the Key West house, packing his belongings and attempting to work on his novel. He stored boxes of manuscripts and other papers in the basement of Sloppy Joe's bar and filled his Buick full of clothing, fishing gear, and other personal items. The day after Christmas, he drove onto the Key West–Havana ferry and said goodbye to his years as a resident of Florida.

Meanwhile, Pauline said her goodbyes to Ernest's family. Her letter to Grace Hemingway expressed deep sorrow over the breakup but admitted it seemed best for everyone involved. Ernest's brother Leicester recalled that "Pauline was as gracious and considerate as any human being could be. . . . [Her] letter expressed the kind of feeling which Ernest had long searched for in others."[1]

During Pauline's Christmas holiday in New York, she discussed events with Uncle Gus, who advised her to immediately work on a settlement and move on. Nevertheless, the process dragged on for months as Pauline grappled with conflicting emotions. On one hand, she still loved Ernest despite his relationship with Martha. "I think she felt very bad about the divorce," recalled her sister-in-law Matilda. "But by that time, she knew Ernest. And she knew when he decided he was going to marry another woman . . . there was probably nothing she could do, and there was no point in standing in the way."[2]

On a deeper level, Pauline felt humiliated and abandoned. Consequently, she vacillated from wanting a fair settlement to wanting to punish him for his disloyalty and the hurt he had caused. After all, she had abandoned a career and poured her life and energy into helping him achieve success as a writer, with her family supporting him financially all the while. In the fifteen years of their relationship, including thirteen as a married couple, Ernest had gone from an unknown writer to a legendary literary figure, producing nine books and numerous articles and short stories during their time together. She had functioned as his chief editor and critic, as well as providing financial and emotional support. But Ernest no longer saw her devotion to him as an asset. In fact, he told Edna Gellhorn, his prospective mother-in-law, that he especially valued Martha's independence and the fact that she would never be "a dull wife who just forms herself on me like Pauline and Hadley."[3]

Ernest clearly missed Pauline's editing skills, though. Back in Cuba, he had expanded his novel to twenty-three chapters by the time Martha returned from Finland in mid-January. Anxious for it to be his greatest book yet, Ernest passed early chapters to friends for review. But he preferred Pauline's opinion and complained that she would not speak to him, much less look at his book. "Pauline hates me so much now she wouldn't read it," he told Maxwell Perkins, "and that is a damned shame because she has the best judgement of all."[4] Indirectly, Pauline's refusal to read the book may have been a positive influence on its quality. Ernest later told Perkins it had become a matter of principle with him to write a book so good that anything ever written in Pauline's company would "seem slight by comparison."[5]

As to Pauline's hurt and humiliation over being abandoned for Martha, Ernest contended that Pauline had gotten what she deserved. After all, she had done exactly the same thing to Hadley, Ernest rationalized, and he took no responsibility for either split. He saw himself as an innocent bystander watching other women parade into his happy home life and break up his marriages. According to Ernest, Pauline had deliberately set out to steal him away from her good friend Hadley. "When women start on that sort of thing they can't be stopped," he told Mary "Pete" Lanham, wife of his good friend Buck Lanham.[6] He had succumbed, Ernest admitted, because Pauline seduced him with the wealth Hadley lacked. With Pauline now in Hadley's shoes, and Ernest wanting a divorce to marry Martha, he callously told Pauline, "Well my dear, those that live by the sword must die by the sword."[7]

As part of the separation agreement, Ernest paid five hundred dollars a month for the boys' support, which was to be sent to Pauline by his publisher. She did not need the money, but she considered it more an admission of guilt on Ernest's part. In spite of his assurances to her mother that he would always look after Pauline's material interests and take care of the children, Ernest resented paying the "blood money."[8] The author had cash-flow problems, with his novel still in the works and no Pfeiffer money coming in. Shortly after the breakup, Ernest asked Scribner's for a one-thousand-dollar advance on his new novel. Pauline also agreed to help Ernest pay his income taxes for that year, infuriating her friend Lorine

Thompson. "I told her she was crazy after the way Ernest had treated her," Lorine recalled. "But she said she was going to help him just the same. A promise was a promise."[9]

While Ernest dealt with settlement problems concerning his soon-to-be ex-wife, his wife-to-be presented another set of concerns. With Ernest concentrating on finishing his book, Martha grew bored. She worked on her own writing, ran the household, and played tennis with Ernest in the afternoons, but it irritated her when he unwound from mornings of writing with evenings of drinking and carousing with the boys. Though he claimed to support her independence, Ernest expressed deep hurt over Martha's growing desire to leave the Finca and return to her journalism career. By the end of May 1940, when she departed for a month-long trip to New York, Ernest wondered if she even wanted to proceed with the marriage. If not, he needed to know so that he could slow down his divorce proceedings with Pauline. Not that he wouldn't still want to divorce Pauline, Ernest explained, but perhaps he could make her "accept a decent settlement instead of giving her the entire world with a fence around it which I am cockeyed delighted to do if it is to marry you."[10] As things stood, Ernest had no problem giving in to certain concessions to speed up the divorce, he claimed, provided it meant that he would have Martha in the end. Reading between the lines, one might interpret Ernest's comments to mean that if he lost Martha, he thought Pauline might take him back.

Throughout the spring and summer, Ernest complained to Perkins and any friends who would listen that Pauline wanted to break him and "put him out of business" with her insistence on support payments. If anything should happen to him, he informed his editor, the payments should stop immediately.[11] Ernest told his friend Clara Spiegel to warn her husband "not to ever marry any rich girls next time he gets married because it is much more expensive than marrying the poorest people in the world."[12] Later in the summer Ernest told Perkins that Pauline had originally agreed to a just settlement proposed by Uncle Gus, but "she now wants more and of course will get it. . . . She's been very tricky. Accepts to Uncle Gus then tells her lawyer to do something else." He advised Perkins "to marry as little as possible but never to marry a rich bitch."[13]

In an attempt to keep Gus on his side and remain in his good graces, Ernest decided to give him the original manuscript of his new novel, *For Whom the Bell Tolls,* just as he had earlier given him the manuscript of *A Farewell to Arms.* In late August, he wrote Gus, "I am forwarding the original Mss. to you from Key West. I give them to you not to be preserved for the children, nor as any sort of a meaningless gesture, but because they are the only thing I can give to you that I know neither you nor anyone else can buy. I only wish they were chess sets."[14] Later Ernest penned a note to include with it, indicating that the book, written in Cuba and Sun Valley between March 1939 and July 1940, was for G. A. Pfeiffer "in appreciation of his unfailing loyalty, tolerance, understanding and generosity and to Uncle Gus in friendship."[15] Upon receipt of the gift, Gus wrote that he considered himself merely "custodian of the manuscript and will discuss with you whom you would wish to have it."[16]

Some of the Hemingways' friends wondered if Gus's respect for Ernest the writer outweighed his disappointment in Hemingway the man divorcing his niece. New York novelist Dawn Powell wrote in her diary, "E. H. . . . has played on present wife's rich uncle's cultural passion, so that uncle upbraids niece for not holding him and is set to receive the supplantee of his niece and thus add to the cruelty."[17] In truth, Gus probably never met Martha, and from that point forward correspondence between Gus and Ernest went through Pauline.

The atmosphere in Key West during the spring and summer of 1940 remained no more pleasant than in Cuba. Gregory, then nine, recalled in his memoir, "I can't remember much of the divorce period, just shouting in other rooms, doors slamming, Mother scurrying out of their bedroom crying—the usual 'amicable' divorce."[18] Though Pauline attempted to hide the hurt from family and friends, they could see that she harbored great bitterness toward Ernest. Pauline told friends she had had eight wonderful years with Ernest—a telling remark given their thirteen-year marriage. Gregory recalled his mother saying, "I don't mind Ernest falling in love, but why does he always have to marry the girl when he does?"[19]

To get away from Key West and the publicity surrounding her separation, Pauline took the boys to San Francisco for the summer. Aided by her sister, Virginia, Pauline found an apartment on Telegraph Hill overlooking San Francisco Bay and put the boys in a summer camp north of San Francisco. Her friend Jay McEvoy remembered Pauline's distress upon arrival: "When she came to San Francisco with the two little boys, they looked like rag-a-muffins off the street, and she looked desperate. . . . She didn't want to go to Reno. She didn't want any publicity. . . . So she put Patrick and Gregory in boys summer camp and stayed here."[20] After the boys returned from camp toward the end of summer, they left for the fall hunting season with their father and Martha in Sun Valley. Pauline wrote to her friend Lorine, "So I am alone at last and having a wonderful time. Will probably stay through this month, and hope to get divorced before I leave, but it's a slow business even though the settlement is about drawn up. It will be fine to be a free woman. How do you suppose it will feel?"[21]

On November 5, 1940, the *Key West Citizen* carried a headline announcing, "Divorce Granted Mrs. Hemingway: Key West Author Charged with Desertion; Suit Uncontested."[22] The accompanying article reported presentation of the divorce petition the previous day on Pauline's behalf by her lawyers, Henry H. Taylor Sr. of Miami and his son Henry H. Taylor Jr. of Key West. Actually, the terms of the divorce had become final on Labor Day, more than a month earlier. A *Miami Herald* bureau chief in Key West had withheld news of the divorce until November at Ernest's request. When the bureau chief first looked into rumors of a split between the Hemingways, Ernest agreed to send him a telegram and report of the final decree in return for the editor not releasing the news on Associated Press wires until after publication of the author's new book.

During the divorce hearing, Charles and Lorine Thompson stood in for Ernest and Pauline "in absentia." The Thompsons' appearance caused quite a bit of consternation for Circuit Court Judge Arthur Gomez, a former resident of Key West and a friend of the Thompsons. Prior to their arrival in chambers, the judge knew only that a couple had asked for a hearing on the holiday to avoid publicity. It startled him when the Thompsons entered, since he considered his good friends to have a happy marriage. The judge expressed great relief to learn that they represented the Hemingways.[23]

A one-hour proceeding gave Pauline custody of Patrick, twelve, and Gregory, nine. Ernest retained parental rights regarding education. Neither Pauline nor Ernest appeared in court. Ernest remained in Sun Valley with Martha; Pauline surrounded herself with family in New York. Under terms of the settlement, the five-hundred-dollar-per-month payments continued, and Pauline received 60 percent of the house on Whitehead Street, paid for by Uncle Gus. She held the right to remain in the house or lease it, provided she paid the real estate taxes and insurance. If she chose to sell the house, Ernest had first purchase rights to Pauline's 60 percent share. If he did not exercise his option, Ernest received 40 percent of sale proceeds. In the event of Pauline's death, Patrick and Gregory shared equally in their mother's 60 percent.[24]

With the divorce behind him, Ernest prepared to enjoy the success of his book, published October 21 with the dedication "This book is for Martha Gellhorn." Selected as the October Book of the Month, *For Whom the Bell Tolls* received widespread praise and quickly became a best-seller. Ernest obtained the highest price ever paid for film rights to a book and agreement that the starring role would go to his friend Gary Cooper.[25]

In the novel, Ernest uses his Spanish Civil War experiences to create a bigger-than-life hero, Robert Jordan, an American teacher who joins the Loyalist forces. Jordan is sent behind fascist lines to blow up a bridge with the help of a small guerilla band, including Maria, who becomes his love interest. The story takes place over an intense three-day period, with Jordan succeeding in blowing up the bridge but failing in his efforts to get out alive. "This is a book about love and courage and innocence and strength and decency and glory," Dorothy Parker wrote in her review for *PM,* a New York newspaper. "It is about stubbornness and stupidity and selfishness and treachery and death. It is a book about all those things that go on in the world night and day and always; those things that are only heightened and deepened by war."[26] It helped the review that Dorothy and her husband, along with Gary Cooper and his wife, had vacationed with Ernest and Martha at Sun Valley the week prior to the book's publication. Though their reviews were not as glowing, other critics declared the novel a triumph for Hemingway.

Anxious to get to New York and soak up the praise, Ernest and Martha left Sun Valley on November 20, stopping the next day in Cheyenne long enough to marry in a quiet civil ceremony in the Union Pacific Railroad dining room. Thus, Martha became Ernest's third wife from a prominent St. Louis family. As he told Hadley prior to the ceremony, "If one is perpetually doomed to marry people from St. Louis, it's best to marry them from the very best families."[27] When Ernest married Pauline thirteen years earlier, he professed guilt for several years over leaving Hadley. Before marrying Martha, however, he had had nearly four years before his actual divorce from Pauline to work through any guilt. During that time, he had managed to assign blame to everyone but himself. Pauline and her family money had allowed his writing to go soft. Her fragile health and Catholic principles had prevented him having the daughter or the active sex life that he wanted. Ernest even blamed Pauline for not following him into Spain, claiming that "while he was risking his life, Pauline was frolicking on the Riviera, so naturally he fell in love with the brave, lovely correspondent."[28]

A few days after his marriage to Martha, Ernest received a letter from Pauline thanking him for the pheasants sent with the children when they returned home and letting him know that Toby had packed up his books for him. She gently chided Ernest about his suggestion to Uncle Gus that Gus give Patrick a gun for Christmas. Pauline proposed instead that Ernest discuss splitting the cost with Uncle Gus, "and then we wouldn't be asking [for] such a big present for a little boy from his uncle even though he is rich." She added a final note saying, "Just heard that you and Mart are married. Best wishes and much happiness."[29]

While in New York, he received a letter from his former father-in-law, addressed to "Friend Ernest," sent "according to advice received from brother G. A. [Gus] today." Despite all the civility, it did not take long for the Pfeiffers to make Ernest's position with the family quite clear. The enclosures included papers to be signed for cancellation of twenty-five shares of Piggott Land Company stock issued in Ernest's name in 1935, along with two substitute Piggott Land Company stock certificates, assigning fifteen shares to Patrick and ten shares to Gregory. The formal letter contained a brief handwritten note: "Please sign all 3 copies. Keep one for your files and return 2 copies to P L Co., PMP."[30]

After divorcing his second wife, marrying his third wife, and topping the best-seller list, all within less than a month, Ernest became fair game for newspapers such as the *New York Daily News*. On December 8, 1940, the paper ran more than two pages featuring photos of his first, second, and third wives and the headline, "Love Collaborates with Hemingway: Once Again Author Weds His Latest Inspiration." The story proposed that Hemingway needed a new female inspiration for each new book, as well as a new set of friends, since his books included unflattering and easily recognizable characterizations of "former" friends.

The reporter quoted someone "who knew him in Paris," commenting that "Hemingway loses old friends and makes new ones with every book." His new wife had recently visited his first wife, the article pointed out, and the two of them got along exceedingly well because Hadley "could ill conceal her feminine feelings at learning that Pauline had lost Ernest, even as she, Hadley, had lost him 15 years before."[31]

Ernest may have miscalculated this time, the report suggested. Hadley and Pauline had abandoned any ambitions of their own in favor of making Ernest their career. Martha, however, had tasted personal fame and found it to her liking. She would not likely give that up for Ernest. After seeing the article, Ernest told Hadley that the paper had sent reporters all over to dig up lies and half truths, and he hoped she hadn't read it. It disgusted him, and he believed his former sister-in-law, Virginia, had collaborated in the story.[32] He made no mention of F. Scott Fitzgerald, who more than ten years earlier had theorized that Ernest needed a new woman for every major book.

While in New York, Ernest and Martha received assignments to the Far East after the first of the year to cover war in China, with Martha writing for *Collier's* and Ernest sending dispatches to *PM* newspaper. Before their departure, the newlyweds returned to Havana via Key West, where Ernest stopped off to see his children over the Christmas holidays. Once more the headlines followed him. The Key West paper of December 21, 1940, carried the news, "Hemingway Here; Going to China." Ernest had to dispel rumors that his return to Cuba meant he planned to give up his American citizenship. "That's a merciless lie," he told a reporter. "You can't keep a good American down, and I have no intention of letting America down." He said the rumor stemmed from a facetious remark made to a Cuban woman and subsequently picked up by Walter Winchell.[33] Though Ernest did not renounce his American citizenship, he used royalties from his latest book to purchase the Finca for $12,500 as a wedding present for Martha. Thus, his permanent address for nearly twenty years became Finca Vigia, San Francisco de Paula, outside Havana, Cuba.

With divorce final and settlement issues behind them, Pauline began adjusting to single parenthood. The new role required major changes. After her star turn as Ernest Hemingway's wife, she now turned to the role of Patrick and Gregory's mother. Pauline readily admitted that she had never had much maternal instinct, and marriage to Ernest had allowed little opportunity for development of what instincts she might possess.

Having had no funds to hire a nurse for Bumby while married to Hadley, Ernest had enjoyed having someone around to tend to his children with Pauline, suggesting later that "everyone is bitched" when you let your life revolve around a baby. He pointed out that "anybody *good* you hire can take better care of them at the start than I can and no reason to have the drudgery wear out husband and wife or split them apart and no sense ever have baby drive you crazy."[34]

His sons might have taken issue with the notion of Ada Stern doing a better job. While Ernest and Pauline always appreciated the discipline imposed by Ada and believed her an efficient and loyal employee, her sons saw a different side of their nurse. This included an unpredictable temper, secret drinking, and methodical efforts to turn Gregory against his mother by playing on his fear of being unloved. When in the household, Bumby generally got around Ada by bribing her with liquor liberated from the pantry. Patrick was old enough to avoid being intimidated and understood Ada's role in their lives. "My mother was my mother and Ada was simply a woman whom I hated," Patrick recalled. He prayed regularly for her to burn in hell.[35]

Gregory, on the other hand, became emotionally dependent on Ada. He went through childhood feeling his parents' disappointment that he was not a girl and believing their frequent absences meant they did not love him. Ada made him obey by constantly threatening that she, too, would abandon him if he did not do as she said. Gregory recalled in his memoir that as a child he tried everything to get his mother's attention, but to no avail. He attempted imitating his older brother, but that didn't work. He tried imitating his father, an even less successful endeavor. That really surprised him because he saw how much his mother loved his father.[36] On one occasion when Pauline admired a photograph of Ernest as a child, Gregory suggested that perhaps he looked a little bit like his father. She dismissed the idea with "You don't look at all alike," then continued her reverie on Ernest's handsome good looks.[37] His futile efforts to get his mother's attention led him to conclude that the best thing his mother did for him was hire a good nurse.[38] When he was older, Pauline admitted to Gregory: "Gig, I just don't have much of what's called a maternal instinct, I guess. I can't stand horrid little children until they are five or six—they're still pretty awful then, but at least I can communicate with them on a semi-rational level. That is why Ada always took care of you. But I loved you, darling, I really did, though I guess I didn't always show it."[39]

Ernest expressed similar sentiments, pointing out that babies can be extremely dull for the first few months or year of their lives, "and I like to keep away from them much as possible," but "nobody puts more time in on them than I do once they are ready for it. Maybe people love their kids more but I love ours plenty."[40]

His child-rearing views aside, Ernest's constant desire for travel, coupled with his hatred of being alone, had forced Pauline to make one-sided choices from the very beginning of their relationship. She could go with him and leave their children behind with nurses and relatives, or she could stay with the children and risk Ernest finding another woman to assuage his loneliness. Invariably she chose Ernest, though in the end she lost him anyway. Now she had to build new relationships with her sons.

Patrick was old enough to handle the divorce without too much difficulty, but Gregory had major problems with it. He continued to feel guilty for not being the daughter his father had wanted and his mother had hoped to provide. He also believed Patrick to be the clear favorite and harbored resentment at having to spend more time with his nurse than with his parents. His father considered Gregory an enigma. "He has the biggest dark side in the family except you and me," Ernest wrote to Pauline, "and I'm not in the family. He keeps it so concealed that you never know about it."[41]

Pauline performed her single-parent duties as best she could, including running the household and getting everyone to appointments on time. From the beginning of the separation, the boys typically joined their father in Cuba for spring break, an end-of-school visit, and a later summer trip. Pauline attempted civility with Ernest for the boys' sake but could not bring herself to be around him. Thus, arranging the boys' itineraries meant arranging her schedule to avoid seeing him. During his time with the boys in Key West over Christmas holidays, she visited her family in Piggott and did not return until after his departure for Cuba.

The awkwardness became clear right after Christmas when Ernest headed to New York on the first leg of his trip to the Far East. He contacted Pauline about stopping by Key West on the way to see the boys and to go through papers that remained in their joint safe-deposit box. Pauline, in the midst of redecorating the living room, suggested that she sort through the contents and move his things to another box. If Ernest had questions about specific papers, she could find them and let him know. As for the children, they could take the Friday bus to Miami, spend the night with him, and return late Saturday afternoon. "Now please understand me," she told him. "If you think it is absolutely necessary that you come here, I can arrange to leave, but I would rather not as I have plumbers and tile setters and plasterers to oversee and the home is most unattractive."[42] She congratulated him on the great reviews of his book and said she thought it would be good "for you and Marty to go away together out of the tumult and the shouting for awhile." Pauline also suggested that he needed to take it easy after working so hard on his book.

Ernest delayed the Key West stop until he came back from the Far East three months later. The visit to pick up the *Pilar* and his sons generated nostalgia for the good times. He sat in Sloppy Joe's, exchanging sea stories as bar owner Joe (Josie) Russell put things in order to depart with Ernest for their usual summer marlin fishing trip. Not long after arriving in Havana, Josie had to be hospitalized for minor surgery. Ernest stayed in the hospital with him until he appeared out of danger. The day after surgery, however, Josie hemorrhaged and died. Ernest took it extremely hard and wrote Pauline that "losing Mr. Josie was no fun for Mr. Josie and I . . . should have protected him better and truly. Though he always had so much sense and judgment and so I didn't worry."[43]

Josie's death came on the heels of the deaths of several literary acquaintances, but Hemingway took the news of most of these in stride. In fact, when Ford Madox Ford died in 1939, Hemingway simply shrugged and quoted his friend Josie: "People dying this year that never died before."[44] Thomas Wolfe died in 1938, followed by F. Scott Fitzgerald in 1940 and Sherwood Anderson and Virginia Woolf in 1941.

Fitzgerald's death of heart failure on December 21, 1940, in Hollywood came not long after Ernest sent him a copy of *For Whom the Bell Tolls* inscribed "To Scott with affection and esteem, Ernest." In his last communication with Ernest, Fitzgerald thanked him for the copy and told him the book was "better than anybody else writing could do . . . and I envy you like hell." In his own journal, however, he called it a "thoroughly superficial book."[45] Fitzgerald died with his current book unfinished, one that Maxwell Perkins believed could have reinvigorated his career. Even though the last one-third remained to be written, ultimately the publishing house made the decision that Edmund "Bunny" Wilson would edit and comment on the manuscript. It would be issued as *The Last Tycoon, An Unfinished Novel by Scott Fitzgerald* and include other Fitzgerald works.[46] Ernest opposed publishing any writer's unfinished work and wrote Perkins, "It is damned hard on Scott to publish something unfinished any way you look at it but I suppose the worms won't mind. Writers are certainly dying like flies. It is a damned shame about old Sherwood. He always liked living very much."[47]

By the time Ernest wrote to Pauline of Josie's death, she had retreated to her apartment in San Francisco, leaving the boys in Key West long enough to see their father. Key West did not seem the same without Josie, causing some melancholia for Ernest, but he and Martha visited his sons and then put them on a plane to meet their mother. Pauline wired to report their safe arrival, leading Ernest to write back thanking her for the wire but chiding her for signing it "Regards." He claimed to miss her, saying "so will sign this letter with love if you know what I mean."[48]

Despite Ernest's peace offering, Pauline remained combative. After receiving a letter from Ernest detailing complicated arrangements for getting the boys to Sun Valley at the end of the summer ahead of him and Martha, she lamented, "It is a pity you can't be with them yourself. Can't you arrange that?"[49] The remark sent Ernest into a tirade about how he could not get there sooner, thanks to the necessity of having to maintain six months' nonresident status (three months in the Far East and three months in Cuba) to avoid paying everything he made to the government and to be able to afford his "blood money" payments to her. Ernest told her, "I have to have a little money of some kind to run things you see. I pay over $15,000 in tax on the $6,000 you get tax free. . . . If anyone asks the children what their father did in Mr. Rooseveldts [sic] war they can say 'He paid for it.'"[50] Pauline responded by telling him that her five-hundred-dollar July 1941 alimony payment was in arrears, and the acrimony continued.

Ernest complained to Maxwell Perkins about Scribner's delinquent deposits and made the payment himself. Perkins wrote back, "I must get it straight about Pauline. I am not making excuses, which I hate, but I did not understand that we were to make a deposit every month, and I can't find anything in your letters specifically to that effect." He informed Ernest of one thousand dollars being deposited into Pauline's account to cover August and September.[51] While Perkins helped clear up financial matters, Bumby arrived in San Francisco to assist with travel plans. After celebrating high school graduation by fishing their way across the country, Bumby and two friends camped out on the floor of Pauline's guest room. Bumby remained after his friends' departure to await his brothers, coming from summer camp in Northern California. After a week with Pauline visiting relatives and touring, the three boys headed for Sun Valley with Bumby in charge.

Despite upheaval over the divorce, Ernest's three sons appeared to adjust well to his new wife. Bumby considered it history repeating itself. He had accepted Pauline, who always remained like a mother to him, but he quickly made room for Martha as well. Her young, blonde good looks made this an easy sell, and the younger boys had a crush on her as well. She proved to be a great companion, and they all enjoyed a glorious few months in Sun Valley. Before returning to Cuba, Ernest and Martha set off on a trip through the Southwest. As they crossed the Texas border on December 7, 1941, on their way to San Antonio, news of Pearl Harbor came over the radio.

CHAPTER 22

War on the Home Front (1942–1945)

With the United States now in the war, Ernest longed to be in on the action. Initially regulations did not allow war correspondents at the front, so Ernest came up with a scheme that allowed him to remain in Cuba and still claim to be serving his country. He organized a private intelligence network, endorsed by the American embassy, to provide Washington with reconnaissance reports on German submarine activities off the coast of Cuba.

To carry out this mission, Ernest recruited a band of cronies, which he referred to as the Crook Factory, and outfitted the *Pilar* with arms and special equipment to patrol nearby waters. The project appealed to Ernest's sense of romance, intrigue, and adventure. When his two youngest sons arrived in Havana in June 1942 to stay the summer, Ernest immediately recruited them for his merry band. Adventures with their father and his friends in Sun Valley always turned out to be great fun for the Hemingway boys, but spending the summer on patrol with their father exceeded their expectations. Martha considered the entire Hemingway clan maladjusted and believed Ernest's patrols a ruse to get rationed gasoline and continue fishing. To escape from the "Crook Factory," she convinced *Collier's* to send her on assignment.

When the summer in search of enemies came to a close, Patrick headed off for Canterbury School in New Milford, Connecticut, and Gregory stayed on with his father in Cuba. The time alone with Ernest boosted Gregory's fragile self-esteem. With Martha on assignment until the end of October, Hemingway devoted afternoon breaks from writing to Gregory, who learned to shoot and became a champion marksman during their time together. In the meantime, Pauline got Patrick situated at boarding school and took up residence at the Hotel New Weston in New York for several months to be close in the event Patrick needed anything. During that period friends and family tiptoed around the dissolution of her marriage and her volatile relationship with Ernest. Cousin Louise Pfeiffer recalled her embarrassment when Pauline caught her reading *A Farewell to Arms* beside the pool at Aspetuck. "It's a darn good book," Pauline assured her. "Don't apologize."

Louise also recalled how attractive Pauline looked on that occasion, having just had her hair done at Elizabeth Arden's on Fifth Avenue. "She had a certain style. I think Jinny didn't care so much how she looked, but Pauline did."[1] Not all of Pauline's friends considered her preoccupation with appearance a virtue. Novelist Dawn Powell, who had made an earlier caustic diary comment about Virginia, added another entry after lunch with Pauline: "Pauline seemed sharp-edged, too eager, brown and desperate. Her confessionals, her rosaries, that kept her head up during the bad years (so that she amazed everyone with her poise) do not after all fill the major gap in her life and give it a frittering quality that does not flatter. She should have a cause, beyond Saks-Fifth Avenue, and a philosophy, instead of a religion."[2]

While in New York, Pauline visited Uncle Gus regarding disposition of Ernest's manuscripts. Earlier that summer Gus had reminded Pauline that Ernest had given him manuscripts of *A Farewell to Arms* and *For Whom the Bell Tolls* and that he intended to present them to the boys: "In each case I told Ernest I was happy to accept as custodian. . . . I shall let you decide which to give to Patrick and which to give to Gregory. When you let me know your decision, I will mark each manuscript to indicate who is to receive it, and when doing so, clearly indicate that I am only acting as the custodian."[3]

He added that if Pauline wanted the boys to have them immediately and had a safe place to keep them, he would send them at once. Otherwise, he would store them in his safe. Pauline wrote back that she couldn't be more pleased with his decision and that it was "awfully nice of you (and very like you)."[4] Agreeing that Gus needed to hold them for safekeeping, she suggested that during her trip to New York they could talk about which manuscript should go to whom. After meeting with her about it on September 14, Gus made a note the next day: "Discussed with Pauline last evening. Pauline stated she would consider and advise later."[5]

By the time Pauline returned to Key West, the town showed the war's impact on its leisurely lifestyle. Residents had to stand in line at the post office, the butcher shop, the grocery, the rationing board, and restaurants, thanks to the burgeoning number of military personnel at the naval air station on the island. Some of the greatest excitement came during a training exercise for forces at the base. A mock invasion with ships, planes, and parachuting troops interrupted the daily lives of civilians, and "Nazis" won the contest. "Finally it was decided the island was in Hitler's hands," Pauline told Patrick. "Several spies got into the Navy Yard in express and cocoa [sic] cola trucks, and one truck labeled plainly *dynamite* got in and has never been located, although an electric company truck on its routine of reading meters was held up and Mr. Lucas (practically our only electrical repair man) was put in jail and held there for an hour and a half of his busy life."[6]

With so many men away in the service, Pauline did much of the major household maintenance, including putting shingles on the house, repairing walls, mending furniture, laying tiles, and painting shutters.[7] She also worked two days a week at the hospital and regularly spent time at the USO "cheering up the fighting forces."[8] Pauline made friends among officers and their families attached to the Seventh Naval District, and occasionally she dated, although her heart was not in it. Pauline had the misfortune of still being in love with Ernest, despite her claims to the contrary. A Commander Campbell became her close friend, and he visited often. Though they seemed fond of each other, Pauline apparently never gave any thought to a long-term relationship. In fact, each time she saw him, Pauline assumed it to be the last. In a letter to Patrick, she joked, "Mr. Campbell is down here now on his series of farewell tours (this is the third), and it is getting to be just like picking caterpillars off the oleanders—I pick them off every day and just as many are back—not that Mr. C. is at all like a caterpillar. He is very handsome, as you know."[9]

Gregory also lacked serious enthusiasm for Campbell. Later in life he recalled that when his mother asked what he thought of her suitor, he "quickly made a big face and objected strenuously."[10] Gregory's objections stemmed partly from hero worship of his father, but probably more from his resentment of any man who got too close to his mother, since he hungered for her attention himself. Patrick, on the other hand, later regretted that his mother never remarried, particularly since she enjoyed running a household and caring for a husband. It appeared to him, though, that she really had little interest in any sexual relationship.[11]

Pauline occasionally tried to break out of her pattern. At one point she vented to Patrick about her dull social life and her idea of buying a bright red 1940 Packard convertible being sold by a friend. "I think I NEED something new in my life," she told her son. "Perhaps my spirit of adventure is not so dead as you think."[12]

She also found that spending time with Gregory could be especially entertaining. While Gregory gained self-confidence from time alone with his father over the summer, time with his mother had beneficial effects as well. Gregory always believed Patrick was his mother's favorite. With just the two of them at Key West, Gregory told her at dinner one night, "Mother, I guess you will be pretty bored eating dinner with me nights. I am not a good talker. Patrick is the good talker. He is the one who is interesting to listen to. I am not."[13]

Despite Gregory's opinion, Pauline found him interesting and enjoyed watching his imagination at play. Just as Gregory searched for kudu in the backyard after his father's safari, now he embellished Ernest's wartime experiences. "Gigi has a couple of his friends over this morning (Sunday) and they are playing with powder," Pauline wrote to Patrick. "The whole place smells like an arsenal and is I think apt to blow up at any minute, but they all seem so happy I hate to stop their innocent bomb making."[14] It wasn't too long, however, before Gregory replaced his Sunday morning bomb-making activities with serving as an altar boy at Catholic mass.

Over time mother and son experienced several adventures together that brought them closer, including weathering a major hurricane that took down seventeen trees in the yard. Pauline and Gregory holed up for two days in their home, along with four neighbors who sought refuge. Without electricity through much of the ordeal, they played poker by candlelight and told ghost stories. They also found a practical use for a portrait of Pauline, placing it over a bedroom window that broke out.[15]

Pauline regarded Bumby as a son, too. Now called Jack, after a stint at Dartmouth College, he entered the army in February 1943. Following graduation from Officer Candidate School, the twenty-year-old left for overseas in command of a military police platoon just before Christmas 1943. Pauline wrote Ernest, "Had been expecting such developments, but just the same it was a shock when it came. But maybe the actual fighting over there will be over soon."[16]

The war affected other members of Pauline's family as well, including Virginia. Because of it, Virginia encountered Laura Archera, who became a lifelong companion. The young violinist from Italy had met Virginia briefly in Berlin and renewed the acquaintance through mutual friends when she played a concert at Carnegie Hall in 1936. After graduation from Philadelphia's Curtis Institute of Music in 1940, Laura became stranded in the United States when Italy entered World War II. "I put my hand in my pocket and I had exactly three cents," Laura recalled.[17] Virginia Pfeiffer took her in, and the pair headed to Hollywood to go into the movie business together.

Along the way, Laura got her first taste of staying with an American family when they stopped off to visit Virginia's parents in Piggott. Laura recalled being unaware of American customs and learning a lesson about the Pfeiffers that she included in her book *You Are Not the Target*. She noticed that everyone wore immaculately white shoes, and it was a great mystery to her how everyone managed to keep their shoes so clean: "In the evening I had put mine outside the door, as is customary in Europe, expecting to find them clean in the morning. Nothing happened. The shoes were just put back in my room." The pattern repeated itself for several days. One afternoon while talking to Virginia, she was lamenting the situation in Italy and blurted out, "And now, on top of everything else, my white shoes are getting blacker and blacker!" Not long afterward, her shoes appeared back in her room whiter than new. When Laura asked how much she should pay or tip the person had done the cleaning, Virginia laughed and replied, "There is no one to pay—I did it," adding nonchalantly, "Didn't you know that I love to clean white shoes?" Laura recalled that this was her introduction to the Pfeiffer habit of giving for pure enjoyment.[18]

Upon arrival in California, they spent fifteen hundred dollars, provided by Virginia's father, to purchase equipment for their movie studio. Laura worked as the sound technician; Virginia served as photographer. They began by filming movie tests for aspiring actors and actresses: "At the time . . . when actors made a screen test, they had their own script, and they had to read it and perform it. And we would do the directing and sound and organize the whole thing."[19]

The pair also completed a prize-winning film about war bonds, as well as some experimental movies on animals and more controversial pieces on social and civil rights issues. On the side, they raised and sold poodles. Though the kennel and movie businesses did not seem to match, Virginia viewed selling dogs as a good entrée to studios. "When some poor struggling unknown actor wants to contact some untouchable casting director or Mr. M.G.M. himself, I make him special agent to sell a poodle and the gates are wide open," Virginia told her family.[20]

Being of German descent, the American Pfeiffers had family, friends, and business associates fighting on both sides of the war, but their allegiance was clear. At least seven of Pauline's cousins served in the U.S. Army or Navy. They could not help worrying, however, about Leonhard Kluftinger, Pauline's cousin and manager of Gus Pfeiffer's Warner-Hudnut operations in Berlin, who now served in the German S.S. After the German surrender, Kluftinger's war service placed him in jeopardy, and Hemingway used his considerable influence and credit with the U.S. Army to protect his former friend as a favor to Gus.

Another close Pfeiffer friend, Alfred Bachschmid, was interned in a German prisoner-of-war camp in Fort Meade, Maryland. Bachschmid wrote Gus, "You will be surprised to learn that I am again in the United States. Unfortunately, this time I am a P.W. I would be very glad to see you, but I don't know yet if it will be possible."[21]

When Gus paid a visit to Piggott during the 1943 Christmas holidays, the war occupied everyone's minds. Unable to sleep at 4:30 one morning, he wrote: "As I lie here, reveling in the peace and comfort of this lovely home, war seems very remote. Yet, I realize all too well that we are living in the tragic period of the greatest and most destructive war of history. While we on the home front are called upon to make some sacrifices in pleasure and comfort, our sacrifices are infinitesimal compared with those of our men and women on the far-flung battle fronts."[22]

Though the war raged on, Pauline and Ernest kept their fighting personal. Ernest grew increasingly impatient with Martha's independent spirit, and much of his frustration found its way to Pauline, an easier target to locate. He wrote to Patrick criticizing her lack of consideration and "the way things are managed" in Key West. Ernest told Hadley he hoped to have some things shipped to Jack from Key West, "but that is not the headquarters of co-operation."[23] Further, writing to Maxwell Perkins, Ernest called Pauline a "hell of a wonderful woman" before she turned mean.[24] Perhaps, he surmised, a man ought to shoot any woman he planned to leave, even if it got him hanged. On the other hand, a less drastic solution might be to get to the point where no one could hurt you. But by then, as a rule, one was usually dead.[25]

Paying alimony to his rich ex-wife continued to be his greatest source of irritation. Ernest told Perkins that Pauline's "blood money" kept him broke between books, but he figured that to be her intent all along—to make it so that it would be impossible for him to write. Even worse, he told his editor, Pauline behaved "abominably about the children; really wickedly. I think perhaps she is off her rocker as women often are at such times. But women who are that way continue to do their damage for years."[26]

As a result of Pauline's behavior, Ernest claimed, he and Martha were broke, and it meant that Martha had to go off to war. Thus, it became Pauline's fault that Martha planned to leave him again: "It is a damned fine thing she likes it because Pauline has the cards stacked so she has to do it whether she likes it or not."[27] He made no reference to the fact that his gross income for 1941, the first year after publication of *For Whom the Bell Tolls*, amounted to more than $137,000, a hefty sum at that time.[28]

The early 1940s proved particularly profitable for Paul and Mary Pfeiffer, with many farmers paying off their loans and purchasing land from the family's Piggott Land Company. The Pfeiffers shared their good fortune with family members, including Pauline, through additional shares of stock in the land company. Gus Pfeiffer found Paul and Mary in good physical shape as well during his 1943 Christmas visit. Despite being long past middle age, "we were not depressed," he recalled. "On the contrary, we felt jubilant that we septuagenarians were enjoying good health, had no rheumatism or other aches, took a lively interest in world affairs, were always ready to give advice, and ever-receptive, we hoped, toward taking advice when we thought it good."[29]

Just one month later the situation changed dramatically, and Paul entered St. Bernards Hospital in Jonesboro in a semiconscious state from which he never recovered. Pauline rushed home, and the end came quietly eight days later, on January 26, 1944. "He just breathed softer and softer and finally stopped," Pauline wrote to Patrick.[30] A portion of the tribute written by his brother Gus the previous year on Paul's seventy-fifth birthday could have served as his eulogy: "While great changes have occurred in the world during these seventy-five years, the motivating principle of Brother Paul's life, namely, always to do right, has never changed. . . . I wish to express my deep felt gratitude to Brother Paul for the advice and encouragement he has given me through the years, and for the inspiration and help I have derived from his example. His influence and example, like Mother's, have guided me in right thinking, have helped me to overcome temptations, and have schooled me in ways of kindness and consideration to my fellows."[31]

Content to live a life in Piggott, Arkansas, out of the limelight shared by his more worldly brothers, Paul Pfeiffer left behind a town much changed from his arrival there in 1913. By 1944 Piggott was an agricultural hub with paved roads, a hospital, a library, and numerous other amenities that the Pfeiffers had made possible. After Paul's death, his son Karl took over Piggott Land Company operations and learned the true extent of his father's generosity. Unbeknownst to the rest of the family, Paul had been handing out ten- or twenty-dollar bills every month to most of his farmers. "He's been giving it to us for years . . . for no reason," several farmers told Karl.[32] Though he eventually phased out the practice, Karl continued a version of the tradition by walking to the town square every Christmas Eve and handing out ten-dollar bills to everyone shopping or working in downtown businesses.[33]

Pauline placed her inheritance from Paul's estate in government bonds and AT&T stock on the advice of her brother and bought National Airlines stock on her own. She wanted an investment that would add some excitement to her life, and a friend tried to convince her to invest forty thousand dollars in his worldwide export business. Karl talked her out of it, however, and she wrote to another friend: "The money from my father's estate is coming through in driblets, and I now have seventeen thousand dollars (and more at the drop of a hat) in old drawers and socks, in checks, that I don't know WHAT to do with, and my brother keeps writing me and keeps writing me to cash these checks because they keep his books open, which it seems is very untidy in a business."[34]

While Pauline pondered financial matters, Ernest considered whether to head for Europe or sit the war out in Cuba. Off on assignment since October 1943, Martha came home in March to help with his decision. Tired of being alone, Ernest accepted an assignment with *Collier's* and went to New York with Martha to make preparations. In May, Martha left by ship for London, and Ernest departed several days later by plane, thus arriving ahead of her. While waiting on arrangements for his assignment, Ernest renewed old friendships and made new ones. The new acquaintances included Mary Welsh, a journalist from Minnesota and the wife of Noel Monks, an Australian reporter for the *Daily Mail*. Mary worked for the London Bureau of the three Luce magazines, *Time, Life,* and *Look,* and studied politics and economics in her spare time.

When Martha arrived in London she found Ernest in the hospital. After a night of drinking, he had accepted a ride with revelers in a car that crashed into a steel water tank. Ernest's head had gone through the windshield, resulting in a deep head wound and concussion. Martha, disgusted with such behavior during wartime, burst into laughter when she first saw Ernest in the hospital all bandaged up. This reaction did not sit well with her husband, who preferred fawning women who nursed him back to health. So Ernest turned more and more to his new friend Mary for compassion and adulation. Their relationship deepened during his two months in London and continued after an assignment took him to France. Meanwhile, he saw little of Martha, who left for Italy shortly after the D-Day invasion in early June.

Typical of Ernest, accounts of his adventures in France overflowed with bravado and derring-do. Letters home to his sons, generally a mixture of highly embellished fact and fiction, regaled them with stories about narrow escapes, harrowing adventures, and enemy action. Pauline seemed to accept

Ernest's version of events. She wrote to Patrick, "If the war in Europe is won, I am inclined to think Papa will do it."[35] Pauline speculated as to whether Ernest might be prevailed upon to bring back some wines and perhaps even some new French bicycles, but she thought better of asking him: "He might think I was just a gold digger and not interested in the noble work that takes up all his time if I think he has time to run errands for people in America the land of plenty."[36]

Little did Pauline know that while she praised his noble work, military authorities were conducting a formal inquiry as to why he had violated the Geneva Convention. Ernest had assumed command of a rag-tag band of French partisans outside of Paris, against regulations that prevented war correspondents from being armed or participating in combat. Despite that and a litany of related allegations, Ernest managed exoneration after some fast talking.

Pauline took pride in Jack's service, as well as Ernest's perceived contribution. After receiving a top security clearance, Jack transferred into an Office of Strategic Services (OSS) unit. She grew concerned, however, when she received no answers to her letters and could not find a valid address. On a trip to the Mayo Clinic for a checkup, Pauline contacted Hadley on her way through Chicago, and Hadley gave Pauline a new address in France. Unbeknownst to either of them, by then Jack was a prisoner of war. Badly wounded in the arm during a reconnaissance mission along the Rhone River, he had been captured and taken to German headquarters for questioning, where fate stepped in. After Jack recited his name, rank, and serial number, the officer looked at him quizzically. Further questioning established that the officer's girlfriend had taken care of Jack in 1925 when Ernest, Hadley, and then two-year-old Bumby (Jack) vacationed in Schruns, Austria. The Germans sent him to a hospital and later to a POW camp, where he remained until liberation of the camp in April the following year.[37]

Meanwhile, Ernest's behavior grew bizarre. NANA correspondent Ira Wolfert told Hemingway biographer Carlos Baker of an incident when Ernest and Martha happened to be in the same town, and Ernest invited Martha to dinner. When she arrived at Ernest's door, he greeted her totally naked and pretended to attack her. Martha fled to her room.[38] Journalist Bill Walton witnessed a similar incident in which Ernest went to Martha's door with a pail on his head and a mop over his shoulder.[39] Others verified his strange behavior. General C. T. "Buck" Lanham related to Baker that he and a friend had visited Ernest at the Ritz Hotel in Paris and presented him with a pair of German machine pistols. Ernest, pleased with the gift and slightly intoxicated, loaded one of the pistols and prepared to shoot holes through a photograph of Mary's husband. When convinced not to open fire in the crowded room, Ernest retired to the bathroom, where he put the photograph on the commode and riddled it with bullets. He shot up the toilet as well, sending water pouring everywhere.[40]

In November Martha formally sent word that she wanted a divorce, and when they actually saw each other on Christmas Eve, both knew there was nothing left of the marriage. By then, Ernest was convinced that Mary would be the next Mrs. Hemingway.

Despite Ernest being smitten by her, they fought often. At one point, as Ernest relaxed in her bathtub after a brutal war of words, Mary suggested that perhaps he should go back to Pauline. Mary believed Ernest still cared deeply for Pauline because he talked at length about their marriage, her education and intelligence, and how she ran a shipshape household. "You must be still very attached to her. You're a bloody fool not to go back to her," Mary told Ernest as he soaked in the tub. "You could start again more or less where you left off. Your children would have their own mother instead of a phony. It seems merely good sense to me. And I'm easily disposable. I had a good life before I met you."[41] She recalled that Ernest looked thoughtful, then responded, "We made too many cruelties to each other. We couldn't erase them." Mary did not let up and countered, "Why don't you try, at least?" Ernest responded, "There are things you don't know, Pickle. And from this tub I can't explain them to you."[42]

Pauline expected Ernest back in the States for Christmas with the boys. They had missed their usual summer with him and gone with Pauline to a new place instead—a camp in the Smoky Mountains. Ernest did not make it back by Christmas, but by the end of the holidays, he missed his boys and was anxious to get home to the Finca and to prepare for a life with Mary.

He made arrangements for passage back to the States in time for Patrick's spring holiday, and his relationship with Pauline fell into the same old pattern. This time the sniping began when he went by Canterbury School and retrieved Patrick for spring break without consulting Pauline. When he aggravated things even more by contacting her to make arrangements for picking up Gregory in Key West, she informed him that Gregory could not come until later.

Thus, Ernest arrived in Cuba with only one boy in tow. A letter from Pauline arrived suggesting that in their conversations the previous week, they had come close to being the monsters they determined never to be—two parents fighting over their children. There wasn't much point in arguing over blame, she noted, because they both had acted pretty pathetically, and their squabbling had upset the children. "Can't we wipe out last week, and continue to regard each other with the respect due one parent from another and not behave like two righteous pigs fighting each other for their JUST due? " she asked him. "If you will try to be considerate of me and I of you, it will surely make for a more comfortable relationship. After all you and I trusted each other pretty thoroughly for some ten years. We SHOULD have some sort of basis for trust that I think we would be fools to destroy."[43]

Since she had not expected his return and had already made other plans for the boys, Pauline suggested that in the future they check with each other before making commitments to the children. Once she had her say, Pauline informed Ernest that she would be sending Gregory on March 24 on the noon plane: "Try to see that he gets a certain amount of sleep as he has been working pretty hard. The children have been looking forward to seeing you so much. They've missed you and having wonderful time with Papa very much. So be very happy and have a good time all of you." She concluded by wishing him "Happy Easter, Egg."[44]

Shortly after their blowup, Pauline ran into Hadley at the Algonquin Hotel in New York. Hadley's husband, Paul, had accepted a new job in France and gone on ahead while Hadley remained in Chicago to sell the house. With that task completed, she stopped at the Algonquin en route to meeting him in Europe. While checking out, Hadley spotted a small, exquisitely dressed woman sitting in a chair in the lobby and immediately recognized Pauline. The two ate lunch together, and Hadley recalled Pauline dominating the conversation with her complaints about Ernest. "She kept telling me how she begged him not to go to Spain," Hadley recalled. "Then, all of a sudden she said, 'Well, I hate him now.'" Her venom shocked Hadley: "I never hated him. I couldn't hate somebody like him. Even in the bitterest moments of pulling apart, I sometimes was pretty mad at him but I didn't hate him."[45] In truth, Pauline's venom came from a woman still deeply in love with the man who had rejected her.

Hadley also ran into her son Jack on that same trip. Released from a German prison after more than six months, he had raced home to his mother in Chicago, only to find her not there and the house sold. Jack learned that she had left for France via New York, and by pulling strings he managed to get an immediate flight. He knew her favorite hotel, and his appearance at the Algonquin came as a wonderful surprise and great reunion for Hadley.

Once Ernest's younger sons had come and gone, he returned to preparations for Mary to become mistress of the Finca. She arrived on May 2, and when Patrick and Gregory returned to Cuba again for summer vacation, they took an immediate liking to their new soon-to-be stepmother. An unplanned circumstance, however, led to delay of the marriage. On June 20,

1945, Mary left for Minnesota to inform her parents of plans to divorce Noel Monks and to start the legal process. As Ernest drove her to the airport, he lost control of the car and plowed into a tree, suffering four cracked ribs and other minor injuries. Mary received a deep cut on her left cheek and abrasions across her forehead. Yet again, Ernest's self-inflicted injuries forced a change in everyone's plans. Mary's trip, the divorce proceedings, and arrangements for the marriage had to be postponed.

CHAPTER 23

New Beginnings (1946–1948)

Pauline Hemingway turned fifty in July 1945 and felt every day of it. She had stiff joints and a touch of bursitis and told Ernest that she felt "old and angry."[1] Pauline took some satisfaction from Ernest's split with the young, attractive Martha Gellhorn, even though he had taken up with the thirty-seven-year-old blonde Mary Welsh. Since Mary was not the one who had broken up her marriage to Ernest, Pauline sent them her sincere congratulations when they officially wed on March 14, 1946. Even Pauline's sister, Virginia, tried to be cordial. While on a trip to Italy with Laura, Virginia learned that Ernest and Mary might take a trip to Europe as well. Virginia wrote to Mary, "I am on the look out for gold hatchets and enough gold dust to bury them, should you come here, which you should."[2]

While Ernest chose a woman to keep him young, Pauline picked a Bantam convertible. This sports car, a vehicle produced for only a few years, was best known as Donald Duck's vehicle in Walt Disney cartoons. Pauline loved the car and refused to trade it in, even when it required constant repairs. In January 1946, she and a friend were headed home from dinner one night, with Pauline at the wheel of her Bantam, when the lights malfunctioned. In her confusion, Pauline took a wrong turn and tried to turn around in an area that looked like black asphalt but turned out to be a six-foot shaft. After the Bantam slid completely into the hole without ill effects, a bystander offered to fish it out with a block and tackle. Pauline watched her car rise twelve feet above the shaft, dangle briefly, then slam headfirst back into the shaft when the rope broke. Undaunted, Pauline replaced smashed fenders, lights, the top, and the windshield, putting the Bantam back in business for another few months.[3] When finally forced to acquire a new car, a Mercury that drove "like an angel," she found it completely boring. "I'm just another driver in another car, instead of a lovely weasel," she complained to Patrick.[4] It wasn't long before she switched to an MG Tourer convertible.

With both Gregory and Patrick now at Canterbury School, Pauline played tennis on a regular basis and took a part-time job in the local bookstore. She enjoyed the association with books and referred to them as "a woman's best friends after her Mother."[5] Pauline's mother stayed the winter with her, and they often entertained at night around the pool. By this time, Mary Pfeiffer experienced constant memory lapses but retained her sense of humor. When asked about her health, Mary invariably said something to the effect of, "[I'm] just fine . . . my mind's failing something wonderful."[6] As Mary's senility increased, her bank account decreased. She wrote checks to virtually every charity and church that approached her until her children put limits on their mother's check writing.

In the spring of 1946, Pauline made arrangements to rent her house for six months and take a fishing trip to California with Patrick and Gregory. The trip was partly a gift to Patrick, who graduated from Canterbury School in June. Ernest did not like the idea of Pauline driving that far, even though she planned to take her mother's car instead of the Bantam. Nor did he like the idea of his boys going on a fishing trip without him there to offer his advice. In fact, Ernest worked himself into quite a state over it. He asked Patrick, "How good a driver is mother? How far has she ever driven? How much in towns? How many long hauls?"[7] He finally admitted that much of his irritation resulted from Pauline being able to take off any time she wanted and for as long as she wanted, while he remained desk-bound, working on his newest book.[8] Ernest's selective recall omitted all the times he had taken off for months of fishing in Havana, leaving Pauline in Key West to tend to the house and boys. As his writing progressed slowly, Ernest took out his frustrations on Pauline.

To ease his concerns, Ernest persuaded Jack to join the family trip and do much of the driving, as well as lend his fishing expertise. The arrangement delighted Pauline, since it meant she got to be with all three boys. After visiting Piggott in early June, Pauline, Patrick, and Gregory met Jack in Shoshone, Idaho, so the boys could fish while Pauline went on to San Francisco. Eventually the boys met up with Pauline for sightseeing in California, taking up residence in Virginia's Los Angeles house while Virginia and Laura toured Europe. Ernest fumed that the boys' adventures left him out, and it did not help when they failed to write or provide any information about plans to meet him for their later trip to Sun Valley. By the end of June Ernest wrote to Patrick, complaining that their atrocious lack of consideration had caused his writing to suffer from worrying about them, and he intended to impose some discipline: "I wish to hear from you and Giggy and Bumby on the first and the fifteenth of each month throughout the year. The letters are not to be hurried, nor sullen, nor forced, but are to be as good letters as you can write at bi-monthly intervals. These letters will total 24 a year."[9]

Ernest warned that if he did not receive these letters for any reason other than illness, there would be consequences. Further, he wanted each of them to initial his letter to Patrick, indicating that they had read it and understood it. In a follow-up a few days later, Ernest said that they could change their letter-writing obligation to the first and third Sundays of each month if coupling it with their religious duties would help them remember. "But there are going to be 2 letters per month per man. So learn to like it."[10] Two days after his birthday in July, Ernest wrote to thank them for the "really fine letters" and the birthday cable. He concluded his letter with "Much love and keep on writing. Will have to give a trophy for Finest Letter of the Year—with points for penmanship, humor, spelling, readability and accuracy."[11] The letters quickly fell by the wayside after the initial correspondence, but Ernest and his sons managed at least to coordinate plans for Sun Valley.

The boys met Ernest and Mary at the end of August, while Pauline remained in California to visit Virginia and Laura upon their return from Europe. During Pauline's absence from Key West her friend the poet Elizabeth Bishop rented the house. A graduate of Vassar College who later taught at Harvard University, Bishop first visited Key West in 1937 and fell in love with the island. "One of the reasons I like Key West so much is because everything goes at such a natural pace," she told a friend. "If you buy something and haven't any money and promise . . . to bring it around in ½ hour, and then forget for 2 weeks, no one even comments."[12] Key West became Bishop's primary home between 1938 and 1943, and she joined Pauline's circle of friends. In spite of her widely recognized talent, Bishop often experienced self-doubt and benefited from Pauline's encouragement. Pauline's comments about her friend's work sometimes sounded like the feedback she had once given Ernest. After reading the poem "At the Fish House" in the *New Yorker,* Pauline wrote, "I am enchanted with this poem. Can't see a thing wrong with it, except perhaps the word gloaming, and am not sure about that. . . . I am indeed proud to know you."[13]

Ernest's opinion also carried clout with Bishop. Pauline asked him to read the poet's work, and his positive comments provided a major boost to her morale.[14] Despite her recognition of Ernest's literary stature, Bishop did not care much for him as a person and expressed doubt about his creativity as a writer. While on a fishing trip before she met Pauline, the poet had coincidentally gotten Ernest's good friend Bra Saunders as her guide. When Bra told them a story about an experience he had once had with salvaging a shipwreck and seeing a woman's blonde hair floating through the port-hole, Bishop recognized it as the source of a Hemingway short story, "After the Storm." The poet later told a friend she doubted that Ernest had even put it on paper. Rather, Pauline had probably listened to Bra's oft-told story and written it out for Ernest.[15]

With encouragement from Bishop and other friends, Pauline invested some of her inheritance in a decorator fabric shop. She bought a house on the corner of Caroline and Ann streets in Key West and remodeled the front as "The Caroline Shop."[16] The back became an apartment for one of her business partners, Marjorie Stevens, who ran the shop and kept the books. Pauline's long-time friend Lorine Thompson also became a partner. In addi-tion to fabric, they carried various decorative accessories, and the high-end inventory gave Pauline an opportunity to go to New York and the West Coast on buying trips that doubled as visits to relatives. They expected to open the shop in November 1946, but when Pauline arrived back in Key West from her visit with Virginia and Laura she found the project delayed by difficulty getting laborers to finish renovations. The three women worked frantically and managed to have the shop open for Christmas.

During 1947 Pauline made an unlikely new friend—Ernest's fourth wife, Mary Hemingway. The two women's lives intersected when Patrick suffered a serious illness. After Christmas with Ernest and Mary in Sun Valley, Patrick had decided to move into the guesthouse at the Finca for six months to study for the Harvard College Board exam. On a visit back to Key West in March to see Gregory, home from Canterbury for spring break, the two boys had an automobile accident in Pauline's old Bantam. Gregory received a minor knee injury, and Patrick suffered a cut on his chin and a slight headache. When he returned to Cuba the next week, however, his headaches grew worse.

Ernest realized Patrick had symptoms of a concussion but still believed his son could take his college boards the next day. After he returned from exams, Patrick's behavior grew more erratic, including spells of violence. Two days later he suffered delirium, and Ernest alerted Pauline, who imme-diately flew to Havana. By the time Pauline arrived, Mary Hemingway had departed to tend to her father in Chicago, undergoing surgery. Pauline moved temporarily into the guesthouse at the Finca, and Ernest moved Patrick to the main house, where he personally tended his son around the clock. Upon her arrival, Pauline wrote to Mary, "I am over here in Cuba and staying at your house. I hope you do not mind. . . . I was very worried about Patrick when he was in Key West. . . . This is the first real trouble I've ever had."[17] Mary wrote back that she had clean shirts and shorts in the bottom of her chest of drawers, and Pauline could use whatever she needed. She also insisted that Pauline move into her bedroom in the main house so she could be closer to Patrick.

Pauline and Ernest got along well during the ordeal. Ernest orchestrated Patrick's care, and their mutual concern kept them from discord. Not initially pleased with Pauline's arrival, Ernest recognized that he could not discourage her and that she needed to be there since the illness appeared to be life threatening. He wrote to Mary that Pauline actually helped a little, but he could not resist adding, "She is used to not doing things but willing to do anything."[18] Pauline apparently agreed that Ernest let her do very little. She told a friend, "I'm not of much use here but I can plan the meals and mix the drinks. . . . and spread feminine lack of charm where it will do the most harm."[19]

When Patrick showed signs of improvement, Pauline returned to Key West on May 10 to take care of a few things. She planned a return to assist with whatever treatment the doctor thought best for Patrick—either leaving him there to convalesce or moving him north. When she arrived home, Pauline immediately wrote to Ernest about how much she admired his performance and added, "I shall never forget what a source of strength and kindness you were to me while I was in Cuba and how unremittingly kind and considerate you were in every way. If I behaved at all well it was due to your splendid example. . . . I think the way you kept up the morale of the troops, never sparing yourself and never beefing, had to be seen to be believed. You were WONDERFUL, and you still are."[20]

Mary did not return home from Chicago until a week after Pauline's departure from Cuba, but when Pauline returned the next week, Mary met her at the airport. Somewhat surprisingly to both, they took a liking to each other. The light bantering and giggling between the two of them about being graduates of Hemingway University helped relieve the gravity of Patrick's situation. Throughout their superficial conversations, neither seemed particularly uncomfortable, and Ernest certainly did not seem to mind once again having two women in the household.[21] Nevertheless, the awkward nature of their relationship appeared in a letter written to Ernest and Mary immediately following Pauline's first trip to their home. Pauline's effusive praise of Mary had a strained quality reminiscent of the praise she had once given Hadley. From Key West she wrote: "It always cheers me to visit a happily married couple; and I derived great satisfaction from seeing with my own eyes the high grade wife Mr. Hemingway brought back from the war. I think she is tops as to looks, charm, intelligence and general appeal. She certainly appeals to me. Lovely girl."[22]

On another occasion Pauline wrote, "Our Miss Mary is just naturally breath-taking wonderful. I am sure she *is* Miss Most Popular and Most Loved Human Being Out There. She's got looks, charm, intelligence, consideration for other people, and perhaps the sweetest nature extant."[23]

Patrick's doctor decided the young man should stay in Havana to convalesce, so Pauline's entire summer consisted of flying back and forth between Key West and Cuba. Each time she made the trip, Pauline attempted to transfer bits and pieces of Ernest's former life in Key West to his current life in Cuba. She made each flight with about five of the two hundred hampers of Ernest's letters and other papers at Key West, along with four or five trophies from the African safari.

On one trip Pauline managed to bring back more than she took. Mary Hemingway came down with the flu and required bed rest and quiet. Given the commotion at the Finca, and knowing Ernest's aversion to the flu, Pauline insisted that Mary come to Key West for recuperation. Thus, while Ernest tended to Patrick, Pauline took responsibility for Mary's care. Mary greatly appreciated Pauline's attentiveness, and while running a high fever she even jotted down a will on a brown paper bag giving the contents of her London flat to Pauline.[24]

Before becoming ill, Mary had started thinking about building a watchtower at the Finca to provide a hangout for the cats, an office for Ernest, and a place for her to sunbathe. Pauline used her design expertise to assist Mary with the plans during her illness and then helped work out the details on trips back and forth to Havana.

Ernest appreciated Pauline's care of Mary, and at least on one occasion they recaptured a bit of the past. One afternoon in early July, while Mary remained in Key West recuperating, Ernest and Pauline relieved the stress of the twenty-four-hour care for Patrick by spending a day on Ernest's boat.[25] The day fishing along the coast and swimming near a deserted beach undoubtedly reminded both of happier days they had shared. Ernest's work on *Garden of Eden* must have triggered memories as well. His characters resembled Hadley, Pauline, and Ernest, with a bit of Mary thrown in, and the story took place where Ernest and Pauline had honeymooned almost twenty years earlier. A major erotic game for the characters in his manuscript included experimenting with hair colors and styles, a fetish that Ernest indulged in his relationship with Pauline and then with Mary.

While Mary tended her father earlier that summer in Chicago, Ernest wrote that she might have a salon there do her hair a bit lighter as a surprise for him—perhaps an ash blonde or a smoky silver. If she really wanted to surprise him, she might consider coming back a redhead. "You can tell I've been a long time without my kitten," he added parenthetically, "but with so much awful lately is okay to talk about all our jollities and secrecies."[26]

The next day Ernest wrote Mary to say he had passed an entire afternoon reading the Roux color booklet and gotten "spooked" about whether she should do anything to her hair other than what they always did. He found that the colors he had suggested earlier were dyes, and while they probably would not hurt her hair, perhaps she should try going as light as possible with the Roux combination they always used. The couple could try different rinses when she got home.[27]

While awaiting Mary's return, Ernest received an unexpected telegram from Charles Scribner alerting him that Maxwell Perkins had died of pneumonia on June 17. Ernest cabled a brief response but could not convey the enormity of this loss. Perkins had tolerated Ernest longer than any of his wives and deftly handled his highs and lows for twenty years. In a follow-up to his cable, Ernest wrote to Scribner, "I hadn't figured on him dying. I'd just thought he might get so completely damned deaf we'd lose him that way." Ernest called him "one of my best and most loyal friends and wisest counselors in life as well as in writing."[28]

By Ernest's birthday in July, Mary had recovered enough to leave Key West and return to the Finca. She and Pauline planned a birthday luncheon for Ernest around the pool, with elaborately wrapped packages, music, champagne, Morro crab, and roasted ham. At the last minute, Mary discovered that Pauline's birthday fell on the next day, so she extended the festivities by baking a cake that said, "We love Pauline."[29]

September brought news of another loss for both Pauline and Ernest. Katy Smith Dos Passos, whom Ernest had known since she was eight years old and Pauline had known since Journalism School at the University of Missouri, had died in an auto accident in Massachusetts on September 12. Her husband, John Dos Passos, blinded by the sun, had driven their car into a parked truck and lost an eye in the crash.

Not long after news of Katy's death, Patrick seemed well enough to travel, and everyone needed a break from Havana. Ernest and Toby Bruce left in mid-September to drive Ernest's new roadster cross-country from Key West to Sun Valley. Though Toby had served as Ernest's right-hand man during his marriage to Pauline, Martha disliked having him around, and Ernest had discontinued his services. Mary more than appreciated his assistance, however, so Toby once again went on the payroll. Pauline and a rehabilitated Patrick left on October 2 to join Virginia in San Francisco, where they sublet a flat, and Mary flew out the next day to join Ernest in Sun Valley.

While in San Francisco Pauline received a letter from Uncle Gus alerting her that Yale University wanted him to donate Ernest's manuscripts to its library. He reminded Pauline of his preference to give the documents to Patrick and Gregory and suggested that she and Ernest discuss the situation and advise him.[30] Pauline responded: "About the disposal of Ernest's manuscripts, I am inclined to agree with you and think they should be left to Patrick and Gregory, and I would think Ernest is of this opinion too. However, I forwarded your communication on the subject to him, asking that if he differed he write to you about the matter. If you should not hear from him therefore, it will mean he agrees with you too."[31]

Ernest did not agree. In fact, he did not want the manuscripts left to Yale University or to his sons. Instead, he wanted them back so he could convert them to cash, keep them himself, or pass them along to his sons as he deemed appropriate. In explaining Ernest's sentiments to Uncle Gus, Pauline wrote, "Of course you are free to do as you please, as these mss. were a gift to you. But I am inclined to think that you will agree with me in thinking that Ernest's wishes in the matter (as after all he produced them) carry a certain weight."[32]

When Gus received Ernest's response through Pauline, he asked his secretary Adele Brockhoff to seek advice from his attorney and cousin Matthew Herold. She reported back that Matthew believed he should proceed as originally desired, "inasmuch as your interest is primarily in Pauline and Patrick and Gregory."[33] Gus essentially settled the issue with his last notation to Miss Brockhoff on the matter: "Read and fully agree with you that it would be logical for me to deliver manuscripts to Pauline to preserve for Patrick and Gregory."[34] Gus Pfeiffer's loyalties were clear. The person that he had once admired, as both a man and a writer, could not begin to compete with family ties and blood relations.

Despite family lines drawn against Ernest, Pauline continued her relationship with Mary Hemingway, insisting that Mary join her around Thanksgiving for some Christmas shopping in San Francisco. Mary welcomed the opportunity to get away from Sun Valley activities for a while and departed for a week of shopping. The stay gave the two women a chance to spend some time with Jack, who had dropped out of school in Montana and now shared an apartment in San Francisco with George Pfeiffer, son of Pauline's cousin C. Leonard Pfeiffer.

George, who clerked in a law firm, recalled that "Jack was at loose ends. He was tying trout flies and selling them to make some money. We had a room, one room with two bunks in it, couple of bureaus, in the lower floor of an old wooden hotel in San Francisco."[35] Jack's primary purpose in being there, however, centered on a young widow named Byra "Puck" Whitlock. Totally smitten, Jack had met her when she worked for a time in Sun Valley, and he had pursued Puck when she took a job at the ticket office of United Airlines in San Francisco.

During Mary's visit to San Francisco with Pauline, they celebrated Thanksgiving dinner with some of Pauline's relatives. As they prepared to enter the house, Pauline referred to their hosts as practicing Catholics. When Mary asked if "practicing" meant the "'do unto others' kind of stuff," Pauline declared, "More than that. If I hadn't been such a bloody fool practicing Catholic, I wouldn't have lost my husband."[36] For the first time, perhaps, Mary realized just how deeply resentful Pauline remained about her divorce from Ernest.

Nevertheless, Pauline seemed happy to be involved again in Ernest's life and even went to Havana in January to check on progress of the watch-tower since Ernest and Mary planned to be away until February. Ernest did not share Pauline's comfort with such personal closeness. On their trip back from Sun Valley, Mary and Ernest stopped to visit Pauline in Key West, and Ernest felt ill at ease being a guest in the castle he had once ruled. Pauline, noticing his discomfort, could not resist salting old wounds. "Nice little place I have here, don't you think?" she said and hastened to add, "Of course, you know a woman really can't run a place properly by herself. Needs that wonderful authority of a man. There's nothing in this world to match the male prerogative. His right to come and go . . . especially go." Mary attempted to change the subject, but Pauline pressed on. "These animals on the floor. They were my partner's idea," she jabbed at him. "Lovely word, partners. Lovely idea . . . until it blows apart."[37] Fortunately, Charles and Lorine Thompson appeared at the door, and Pauline quickly returned to being the charming hostess.

Had they not been aimed at him, Ernest might have appreciated Pauline's needles. He had once told a friend, "If a good woman isn't a little bit Bitchy sometimes, it is just as though Dijon mustard didn't have any taste.[38] Mary's taste in friends, however, specifically Pauline, had grown increasingly difficult for Ernest to stomach. He suspected both women of being less than honest in how they felt about each other. The two had very little in common, except for Ernest, and probably would not have liked each other under different circumstances, he believed.

Pauline's approach to money also continued to be a source of irritation for Ernest, whose temper again flared as they attempted to work out their sons' schedules for the summer of 1948. Patrick had attended Stanford University for the spring semester, and it pleased his parents that he had done well and seemed entirely recovered from his illness. Since he had received no high school graduation present from his parents and no vacation the previous summer, Ernest and Pauline now determined to send him to Europe. They talked first about him going with Pauline and Gregory but decided Patrick should experience Europe on his own. Acknowledging Ernest's expertise about Europe, Pauline wrote, "About the trip, he [Patrick] has organized all he knows about very well. He is anxious to talk to you about details, such as present conditions in France, the best trip to take on a bicycle, hotels, etc., all the dope you are so well qualified to give."[39] She gave Patrick express checks amounting to eight hundred dollars and asked Ernest to augment the sum if necessary.

With both boys coming home from school, then going on to Havana to visit their father, followed by travel to New York and Europe for Patrick, Pauline carefully documented round-trip expenses for the summer. She wanted to make sure that she and Ernest each paid exactly half. The practice always galled Ernest, especially after peeking in Pauline's checkbook while she was at the Finca the previous summer and finding her balance to be $9,068.43.[40]

Later that summer, Mary Hemingway made another trip to visit Pauline in Key West and get away from the crowd at the Finca. When Pauline returned with her to Havana, Ernest expressed great displeasure. He disliked Mary spending time with Pauline, and he particularly resented Pauline's presence when it prevented Mary from accompanying him on fishing trips. One day he left a note for Pauline, asking her to change the day she planned to leave. Her scheduled departure day would cause Mary to miss a fishing derby they had looked forward to for a long time. "I know you'll understand and help on this no matter what she says trying to be good hostess," the note said.[41] Pauline apparently adjusted her plans. Ernest decided to take Mary further away from Pauline, so on September 7 the Hemingways set sail for Italy and did not return until the following May.

Even while in Europe, Ernest's skirmishes with Pauline continued, and his oldest son provoked Ernest's anger as well. Jack had returned to active military duty after quitting a job that Ernest had landed for him on the West Coast, and he was now assigned to an intelligence unit in West Germany. Angry that Jack had given up his job after Ernest called in favors, his father also disapproved of Jack's plan to marry Puck. After a farewell weekend with Puck in New York, Jack departed for Europe. While in New York, he saw Pauline, who loaned him money to buy army uniforms, with the understanding that he would pay her back from his allotment.

In January Pauline wrote Ernest a breezy letter, telling him she had seen Jack and Puck in New York and had loaned him money for uniforms. She would write Ernest more fully later, Pauline said, since she had guests.[42] Ernest went through the roof and fired off a vituperative letter, wanting to know the exact amount Jack had borrowed so he could repay it. Also, he had heard that his brother Leicester was paying back money borrowed from Pauline. If repayment lagged, he wanted her to advise him so he could repay that as well. "I am sick of hearing about money you have loaned to my brother or my oldest son," he told her. "If you do it either bill me or keep the transaction quiet. The only valid news you write me about Mr. Bumby is that you loaned him money and that Puck came to N.Y. You will write in a later letter. Did anyone ever receive any one of your later letters?"[43]

Other frustrations spilled out as well. He complained that she did not write often enough or in sufficient detail to keep him informed about the boys, "either from sloth and drunkenness; or perhaps because of the cost of postage stamps." As a parting blow he told her, "People are no longer as naïve as I was when I married you and believed what you said nor as you were when you married me and believed the same. But you were not beaten by Miss Martha. You were beaten by coitus interruptus imposed by the church. Burn a candle for me."[44] It would not be the last time Ernest complained about his unsatisfactory sex life with Pauline. In fact, for some reason he even felt it important for his sons to know, as if it absolved him of guilt for the adultery. Some years later, after Patrick had married and Pauline had died, Ernest told him: "It is true that I was an unfaithful husband and was divorced as such with punitive alimony. But I was faithful for seven years under a regime which would not permit any form of birth control (none; period) and with six years of imposed coitus interruptus. . . . I loved Mother and admired her and loved her truly more than I ever loved anyone in all my life. But I think I was beaten by a system and my own inability to stick it out."[45]

Pauline, long past becoming upset by Ernest's tirades, sent another letter to relieve his "mind some more. I had so much luck the last time."[46] She told Ernest not to worry about Jack's debt because they had worked out a payment schedule, and Leicester's credit was good with her. He always paid back every cent. She concluded the two-page typed letter by cutting certain sentences out and enclosing the fragments in the envelope to be pieced together, obviously just to agitate him.

Ernest's original letter, triggered in part by his continuing resentment over alimony and constant money reminders, had also resulted from his distress about Pauline knowing more about his own son's life than he did. After sending her his return dig, which included her pasted fragments plus revisions reiterating sentences from his first letter, he determined to attempt a rapprochement with Jack. Getting Jack's address in Berlin from Gregory, Ernest wrote to apologize for interfering in Jack's life. He pointed out, however, that Jack had brought his father into his business in the first place by asking his help getting a job. If Jack had hurt feelings over his father's advice about marrying Puck, Ernest still thought he had a right to offer his opinion, just as Jack had a right to accept or reject it. After all, Ernest told him, he did know a little bit about women and marriage: "I made a horse's ass of myself with Miss Martha. But did marry Mother [Hadley], Paulinose, and Miss Mary. That is hitting .750."[47]

By that time Ernest had yet another romantic interest. While vacationing in Italy with Mary, Ernest had participated in a private duck hunt in early December 1948, where he encountered Adriana Ivancich. Not quite nineteen years old, the dark-haired beauty came from an old Venetian family that had suffered great personal and financial losses at the end of World War II. Along with injuries incurred by her brother Gianfranco and the bombing of her family estate during the closing months of the war, Adriana's father had been found murdered in an alley. Ernest found Adriana's young life of hardship and innocence an irresistible combination, and he immediately began calling her "Daughter." As they began seeing more of each other, Adriana considered it an innocent friendship, but Ernest's growing infatuation with her consumed him. "Ernest was weaving a mesh that might entangle and pain him, I felt," Mary recalled later. "But I was sure that no cautionary phrases of mine could arrest the process."[48]

CHAPTER 24

Last Rites (1949–1951)

By the time Ernest and Mary left Italy in April, the author had begun playing out his fantasies about Adriana Ivancich on paper. Eventually called *Across the River and Into the Trees,* this new work told the story of an aging, battered fifty-year-old American colonel, Richard Cantwell, who falls in love with a nineteen-year-old Venetian countess named Renata. Hemingway's hero in the book has been through World War I, observed the Spanish Civil War, and survived World War II, even having a war correspondent ex-wife whom he considers a shrew. Knowing he is dying, the colonel comes to Venice to spend his last days with his young mistress.

As Ernest continued working on the book back in Havana, he could not stop thinking of Adriana, and he corresponded with her regularly. Though gentle and respectful of Adriana in his letters, Ernest became surly and short-tempered with Mary. He often humiliated and embarrassed her in public the way he had Pauline when in love with Martha Gellhorn.

Ernest took a break from his Adriana book in June 1949 for a celebratory trip to the Bahamas with his sons. Patrick had successfully completed his first year at Harvard University after transferring from Stanford, and Gregory was now a graduate of Canterbury School. During Ernest's absence, Mary planned a stay with Pauline in Key West. Pauline could not have helped Mary's frame of mind when she wrote, "How pleasant it will be to see you and hear all about the old country and those Italian Women, those Sexy Italian Women."[1]

Pauline made her own return trip to the "old country" that summer, this time with both Patrick and Gregory. After arrival at Hendaye, France, near the border with Spain, Pauline dropped a postcard to Ernest saying she found no trace of the little villa or small hotel where they had once stayed, but the coast remained as beautiful as ever. She closed with "Affectionate souvenir to Mary."[2]

The trip included a visit with Hadley, who lived near Paris with her husband, Paul Mowrer. Patrick recalled later being surprised at how friendly his mother and Hadley appeared and told biographer Bernice Kert, "Perhaps it was because they were well out of the running and could relax."[3] Pauline and her sons also then went on to Venice and met Adriana Ivancich. Ernest was concerned since Martha happened to be in Venice at the same time, fearing that the various Hemingway women might get together and compare notes.[4] Despite such reservations, Ernest wanted Adriana to see his boys, warning her that their mother was "a lovely woman but very difficult at times."[5]

Pauline stayed on in Europe after Patrick and Gregory returned to the United States in time to begin the fall semester, with Patrick returning to Harvard and Gregory entering St. John's University in New York. Before departing Europe, Pauline spent a week with Jack and Puck in Berlin. They had married June 25, 1949, in Paris, and though Ernest did not attend, he sent his congratulations. It touched Jack for Pauline to visit, the only family member who braved the flight to Berlin to do so.[6]

While Pauline traveled through Europe, Virginia and Laura took up summer residence in Aspetuck to help Uncle Gus, who had become increasingly senile after Aunt Louise died the previous fall. Gus needed help hosting guests at the family compound, since his mind seemed to come and go. He became confused, for example, when family members scattered Louise's ashes in the Aspetuck River, running alongside their homes. When told that Louise's ashes were being scattered as she wished, he seemed relieved, but did not recognize they were referring to his wife.[7] On another occasion before Louise's death, when approaching the driveway of a summer home they owned in Fort Lauderdale, Gus commented, "My, the man who lives here must be very rich."[8]

During that summer of 1949, Gus's secretary, Adele Brockhoff, made the mistake of sending a letter to Ernest inquiring about how to appraise the manuscripts still in Gus's possession. Though Gus's last written comments on the matter indicated that he wanted them given to Pauline to hold for Patrick and Gregory, the transfer had not taken place before his senility. Had Miss Brockhoff known what a state Ernest had worked himself into earlier in the year about Pauline and her family money, she probably never would have sent the letter seeking advice on the manuscripts.

Ernest seized this opportunity to vent and stress that he owed the Pfeiffer family nothing. He told her that Uncle Gus had given him many wonderful gifts, and he had taken them because he respected Gus and knew he could afford to make them. In return, he had given Gus his manuscripts, the only things he had of value and something money could not buy. In regard to her specific questions, Ernest told her he had provided this information to Pauline several years earlier to forward to Gus, but she had apparently neglected to send it. Pauline might be trying to get the valuable manuscripts for herself, Ernest suggested. He contended that his other manuscripts had been "eaten by rats and roaches during the war when she decided that those filing cabinets were more useful for her decorating and upholstering business than to house my very valuable papers."[9]

Brockhoff got to hear all about his sacrifices during Patrick's illness, how he had to work continuously to pay Pauline's punitive alimony, and how he no longer wanted to hear all the stories "about how Pauline supported me and I was some kind of fortune hunter who moved in on the Pfeiffer family."[10] He may have been poor when he came into the marriage, Ernest informed her, but only because he refused to sell out. He made plenty of money during the marriage, but Pauline wasted most of it or got it in the divorce settlement. Ernest suggested, "If Uncle Gus wishes to leave those manuscripts to me in the event of his death (which he wrote me many times he was doing) I will have them taken care of by Scribner's rare book department . . . and it will be a heritage I can leave for my children."[11] Ernest's tirade spilled over into his letter to Charles Scribner that same month, when he wrote: "I note that you are still takeing 50% of the re-print rights of my life's work and Miss Pauline, who is a lovely girl and who I love dearly, (and who owns one third of 70,000 acres of good cotton land in northern Arkansas, and a good share of Richard Hudnut, Sloan's liniment, Dr. Bell's Pine Tar Honey and other products and enterprises) takes most of the rest."[12]

Ernest exhibited similar sentiments upon receiving a previous six-month royalty report showing $3,000 of $7,271 going to Pauline for alimony payments. That report prompted him to jot in the margin that it was "not a bad take for a woman you slept with last in 1937."[13]

Pauline returned from Europe in mid-October expecting to relieve Lorine at their Key West shop, but Virginia's health problems changed her plans. Virginia had experienced severe pain after leaving New York to return to California. So instead of going home, she and Laura had gone directly to the Mayo Clinic in Rochester, Minnesota. Pauline worried about Virginia, who all her life had had more than her share of migraines and illnesses, and joined Laura at her sister's bedside. When Laura learned that Virginia had cancer, she insisted that Virginia not be told, and Pauline agreed. They both knew Virginia well enough to know that if she found out, she would just accept the inevitable consequences and not fight. "I knew the character of Jinny," Laura explained. "With another person, being told you are going to die would be a spur. But she would say, 'Oh, that'll be allright. . . . It's just a door you go through.' [D]eath was not such a tragedy for her, as it would be for me."[14] Despite a gloomy prognosis from doctors, Virginia survived almost twenty-five years beyond her initial diagnosis.

Virginia had not yet recuperated from surgery at Mayo Clinic when she and Pauline received word of their mother's illness in Piggott. Along with her memory, Mary Pfeiffer's general health had deteriorated drastically the previous year, and a niece had moved in to assist her. Though not able to remember much, Mary retained her sense of humor. Virginia once wrote about her mother's wonderful Irish wit and her Piggott experiences in a play called "Life with Mother." All copies of the play burned, however, when Virginia's Hollywood home caught fire some ten years later. Mary had finally reached the point where she could not go up and down steps, and her son, Karl, made the decision to move her upstairs and arrange so that she did not have to come down for anything. As they carried her upstairs in a chair, she exhibited her typical good humor, waving at each item downstairs, saying "Goodbye Piano. Goodbye Lamp. Goodbye Radio."[15]

When Mary's failing health became worse, Karl called both of his sisters to come home. Virginia arrived first. Whenever her mother slept, and to the extent her own health allowed, Virginia cleaned the house and barn, which still held many of Ernest's manuscripts and papers that no one had bothered to remove. She called on a local man, Ken Wells, to assist with heavy lifting. Wells ran a grocery story and came to the house frequently to deliver groceries to the Pfeiffers. A year younger than Patrick, Wells recalled playing with the Hemingway boys when they came for visits.

One afternoon after Ken and Virginia finished their project for the day, Virginia broke open a bottle of wine. Well into the wine, she began complaining about Ernest and how it looked like she still had to clean up his messes. For some reason, that led to the early days in Paris and the fact that she had gone out with Ernest first. She never told her sister, Virginia said, because Pauline remained too much in love with Ernest to want to hear that. Virginia insisted that now she hated Ernest for taking advantage of the family and its money.

Fascinated by Virginia's comments about her own earlier relationship with Hemingway, Wells asked her, "You mean you could have been the second Mrs. Hemingway, instead of Pauline?" Virginia replied flatly, "I had an Uncle Gus, didn't I?"[16] When Pauline arrived in Piggott a short time later, she was nursing a bad cold and went immediately to bed. Ken Wells encountered her the day after her arrival, standing at the kitchen sink when he came in the back door to deliver groceries, and said, "You must be Pauline." She quickly spun around and told him, "People I don't know address me as Mrs. Hemingway!" Wells never quite forgot her rebuff.[17]

The day after encountering Wells in the kitchen, Pauline felt better, and Mary experienced an unusually good day. The sisters decided to throw a party with their mother upstairs, similar to a scene Virginia had written in her play, even down to having their good friend Ayleene Spence join them. They passed the evening laughing, carrying on, and remembering earlier days. At the end of the evening, Virginia said, "Mother, you are doing so well, perhaps tomorrow you can go downstairs." Mary looked at her and said, "No, tomorrow I go up."[18] She died the next day, January 29, 1950.

Mary's funeral took place two days later, and after the service, Pauline and Virginia rushed their preparations to get out of Piggott before becoming stranded by a forecasted blizzard. They quickly went through the house, selecting a few things they wanted to keep and placing them on separate blankets in the middle of the living room floor. Karl agreed to pack up their selections and ship them later. Within a few months of Mary's death, the Piggott house sold to Tom and Beatrice Janes, a Piggott family that owned a department store on the town square. The sale included nearly all of Mary's household possessions, down to the dinnerware and pictures hanging on the wall.

Virginia did not get home with the few things she managed to actually carry out of Piggott. She reported a robbery to police at the Los Angeles airport, claiming a thief had apparently taken all her mother's jewelry and negotiable stock certificates. A few days later, however, police contacted Virginia to return a gray box containing the approximately one hundred thousand dollars in valuables. An aircraft worker had spotted the box along a road near the airport entrance and turned it in to police. The box had apparently fallen from the luggage compartment of the airport limousine taking Virginia to Hollywood after her flight from Memphis.[19]

Though Virginia later bought farm property in Piggott with some of her money, the town no longer seemed like home for either her or Pauline with both parents gone. Not long after their mother's funeral Virginia wrote to Elizabeth Bishop, her friend who had been raised by relatives: "Now I know how it feels to be an orphan and can better sympathize with you for having had this feeling so long. . . . I always looked upon Piggott as home, and the fact that it is no longer is glooming."[20]

Virginia and Pauline sought investments beyond their Piggott Land Company and Warner Company stocks and with their family friend Jay McEvoy became backers of a movie titled *Cry Danger*. The movie starred Dick Powell as a framed ex-con who goes after the real culprit upon release from prison. The film also starred Rhonda Fleming, its plot leading Powell through a dark world of deceptive dames and double-crosses. Released in 1951, the picture met with moderate success, although Jay recalled, "It got the money back but didn't do much."[21] Though not an investment success, the film gave Virginia a project to keep her mind off health problems. She periodically visited the set to lunch with producer Sam Wiesenthal or to observe the work in progress by Academy Award–winning director Robert Parrish. "I enjoy making an occasional visit," she told Bishop that spring, "as I am treated with the respect accorded a gold brick, which I haven't been since I was Hemingway's sister-in-law."[22] It is impossible to know whether she meant she hadn't been treated with such respect since then or she hadn't been treated as a gold brick since then, but knowing her views of Hemingway, it was most likely the latter.

Before her trip to California to conclude the movie deal, Pauline made an April jaunt to the Finca to meet the woman Patrick planned to marry. Henrietta Broyles of Baltimore expected to graduate from Radcliffe College in May and Patrick from Harvard University the same month. Pauline found "Henny" to be a charming girl and deeply devoted to Patrick. Even though Ernest tried to play hard to persuade, Henny won him over with her soulful eyes and assurances that she would be a good and faithful wife to Patrick. Mary suspected that Ernest acted reluctant for the fun of it, while Patrick thought it had to do with his lack of financial prospects.[23]

Ernest and Mary had recently returned from their second trip to Europe in less than a year, and the author remained in the throes of his infatuation with Adriana Ivancich. Sitting at the same Paris café where he had once gone with Pauline, Ernest had told Adriana that he loved her, causing a moment of panic for the young woman as she saw their friendship in jeopardy. Her consternation changed to relief, however, when he added, "I would ask you to marry me, if I didn't know that you would say no."[24]

With his muse in Italy and Ernest back in Havana, the author treated Mary like a servant, heaping verbal abuse on her in front of everyone.[25] Additionally distressing, Mary had just discovered she could never have children, making her unable to provide Ernest with the daughter he had longed for in all his marriages.[26] Patrick appreciated Mary's efforts to make everyone feel at home, and his father's lack of appreciation and brutish behavior toward her concerned him. He feared that Mary was not as tough as she attempted to appear.[27]

Patrick and Henny planned a June wedding in New York. When Pauline returned from her California movie trip, a letter from the mother of the bride awaited, providing details and asking Pauline and Ernest to forward lists of friends and relatives who should receive announcements. Pauline sent a copy of the letter on to Ernest, who responded to Pauline that he had no intention of going to the wedding. His justification for declining to attend included not receiving a thank you from his future daughter-in-law after her visit, Henny's mother's letter seemed too pushy, the Broyleses weren't his kind of people, and he never liked attending weddings, particularly church weddings.

Pauline responded, "I really don't know how you can behave so badly about the women your sons marry. They have had to take four of yours, and I think they have been damn cooperative and well mannered about it."[28] This wedding was not about him or whether he liked the girl or her family, she reminded him. This was about Patrick and the importance of being there to support him. As for his trumped-up excuses and concerns, it was not customary in this country to send a thank you for a midafternoon visit, she did not think the Broyleses pushy, and the wedding was to be in a magistrate's office and not a church. He could at least be civil and quit pampering himself. "Somebody has to tell you these things," she said, "and it is quite a bother to do it and having to read the letter you'll write back full of insults."[29]

Despite Pauline's entreaties, Ernest did not show up for the wedding, which took place with a few minor glitches. Told from the beginning that the wedding would take place on the seventeenth, Pauline learned on the fifteenth that the ceremony was the next day. As a result of the confusion, Gregory did not make it to the rehearsal dinner the night before. He also missed the wedding ceremony the next day because he slept through his clock alarm. He did make it to the wedding breakfast to feast on Crab Newburg and Champagne. Virginia arrived from the West Coast about the time all the festivities ended, but she met Henny and pronounced her intelligent, charming, and poised, with beautiful skin, "like a Renoir painting."[30] After a few days in Mantauk, the newlyweds departed for Europe. Pauline and Virginia remained in New York to spend time with Gregory.

Over the summer Gregory received a scholarship to work with the L. Ron Hubbard Foundation, where he became enamored with the concept of Dianetics as a spiritual healing technology developed by Hubbard.[31] Gregory decided to drop out of St. John's University and stay on with Hubbard after the summer. Virginia began looking into Dianetics as well, as a possible way of dealing with her many medical issues. Tired of Gregory contacting her only when he needed money, Pauline realized that she no longer had any influence over him. At one point during the visit Gregory told her that if she didn't quit correcting him about everything, he would just arrange never to see her.[32]

Ernest stoked the flames when he wrote to Gregory in August, complaining about Pauline and her family. "Mother won't answer even an
impeccably polite letter anymore," he told Gregory. And he certainly hoped
his son did not believe any of those stories about Ernest being "the little
poor boy who came into the wonderful rich family and stole the spoons."[33]
Ernest included his accounting of what Uncle Gus had contributed financially to the marriage, versus what he had spent throughout the marriage
and after the divorce. To top things off, Ernest griped to his son about
Pauline coming to the Finca that summer wanting more money. When Ernest
refused because of his tax situation and the need to pay back an advance on
his forthcoming book, he claimed that Pauline said, "Well, I suppose you
can't get blood out of a turnip."[34] Ernest's spiteful remarks about Pauline
may have had an opposite effect on Gregory, who turned around and contacted his mother. By the time Pauline left for another trip to Europe at the
end of August, she reported to Ernest that Gregory seemed back to his old
self and "sounded fine, relaxed and charming."[35]

Ernest's new book, *Across the River and Into the Trees,* was due out in
September, and Pauline told him "it is considered the big book excitement
of the year."[36] The book fared poorly with critics and friends, however.
Many found it boring, embarrassing, and trivial, more like a parody of
Hemingway's former style. Some critics believed that Hemingway had written the book because he thought he was dying. Thus, he wanted to finish
another book quickly, causing him to put a more ambitious novel aside.[37]
Ernest furthered the theory by developing an eye infection that spread to his
entire face on his first trip to Europe in 1949. Diagnosed with erysipelas, a
highly contagious disease, he landed in the hospital in Padua for penicillin
injections. He developed a similar infection on his return trip to Europe, followed by a major gash in his head requiring stitches while out on the *Pilar*
over the summer.

After reading a few installments of Ernest's book in *Cosmopolitan*
before the September release, Virginia Pfeiffer told her friend Elizabeth
Bishop that Ernest had become blind about his work and believed this book
the best thing he had ever done. "I can only think of one way by which it
could be thought that—as a true autobiography of the adult louse," Virginia
wrote.[38] She admitted to only being able to read the first and last installments, more than most of her friends had been able to do.

Martha Gellhorn weighed in as well, telling her friend Bill Walton that
she found the novel "revolting . . . he will never have to write his autobiography because he has been doing it, from the first novel, chapter by chapter,
each book keeping pace with his calendar years, building up his dream

vision of himself."[39] After hearing back from Walton, who agreed with her assessment, Gellhorn called it one of the most embarrassing things she had ever read, adding, "he has to write that pitiful monster woman of his dreams. . . . He will go on, from worthlessness to rot, always feeling misunderstood . . . always feeling everything is someone else's fault and I think . . . he will end in the nut house."[40]

Despite such criticism, Ernest insisted the book had merit. "But the readers didn't want a romantic novelist writing about getting old and dying and having a narcissistic affair with a young girl," he told Gregory, spending Christmas at the Finca.[41] During Gregory's visit, Adriana and her mother were houseguests as well, having come to see Adriana's brother Gianfranco, now working in Havana. Gregory could see that his father worshipped her.

Gregory also brought a woman to the Finca. Neither Pauline nor Ernest thought much of the girl, so both were glad when he left the L. Ron Hubbard Foundation after the holidays and moved to Los Angeles, where he got work as an airplane mechanic. A short time later, Gregory met Shirley Jane Rhodes, a former Powers model, and fell in love. Gregory, then nineteen, sent word to his mother that he wanted her to meet Jane, so Pauline scheduled a visit. Arriving on a Tuesday, she learned that Gregory and Jane wanted to marry on Saturday, since both had jobs and didn't want to lose time from work. Upon learning that Gregory had written Ernest for his blessing, Pauline cabled Ernest on Thursday, assuring him that she favored the wedding, all things considered.[42]

After Ernest failed to reach Gregory by telephone, he cabled both his son and Pauline saying he would give "absolutely no consent nor approval" without full details and an opportunity to check them out. As it stood, he didn't even know the name of the girl and instructed Gregory to call on Friday to discuss it with him.[43] On Saturday morning, Pauline cabled Ernest once again to say that Gregory had tried to call him the previous evening and that the wedding would take place that day, April 28.

Livid after receiving letters from Pauline and Gregory providing details of the wedding, Ernest fired off letters to each of them about their handling of the situation. He directed his anger toward Gregory, suggesting that his son start writing letters to family and friends when not in trouble or needing something. "That way they appreciate the ill-spelled, un-grammatical, introuble letters better," he said, suggesting that his son needed to learn how to write a grammatical and comparatively properly spelled letter regardless.[44]

Pauline responded to the curt letter she received from Ernest by asking him to get over being hurt and angry and write one of his "good" letters to Gregory. She agreed that he had every right to have his feelings hurt at not being included in the wedding plans, but the couple clearly had their minds made up to get married and seemed nervous about waiting any longer. Gregory was headstrong and had to learn things the hard way, she told Ernest, but if they stood by him and tried to understand him, perhaps he would realize they did not always try to thwart him. Ernest's anger at Pauline in the matter did not bother her, she told him, and she no longer needed his approval. "I have reached the age where I simply do what I think I must and that's that," she said. Not that she didn't value his opinions, but if by now she couldn't make decisions and take the consequences, she was "a poor thing indeed."[45]

Ernest claimed to be so sick and disgusted about the whole mess that he couldn't write if he tried.[46] All that spring and summer, he attempted to work on his novel about the sea, started in Bimini in 1936. Before getting too far, however, he received a cable on June 28 that his mother had died in Memphis. She had lived with Ernest's sister Sunny and entered a nursing home there when Sunny could no longer handle her. Though Ernest did not go to her funeral, he paid the funeral expenses. The news of Grace Hemingway's death surprised and saddened Pauline. She hastily wrote Ernest a note expressing her sympathies and quoting the line from Swinburne, "Life is not sweet in the end." She expressed hope that Grace's death "carries you back to when you were a happy little boy with her."[47] Still upset over confrontations with his family during his father's funeral more than twenty years earlier, Ernest wrote to Mary Hemingway, in Minnesota for a class reunion, that he had heard his sister Marcelline behaved shamefully at his mother's funeral and that her avarice made even Pauline look generous.[48]

By fall Pauline was in San Francisco preparing to head back East after visiting the McEvoys. She expected to meet Jay's mother and sister in New York for some Christmas shopping but planned first to stop by Los Angeles to see Virginia before leaving California. Virginia once again had health problems, and Pauline told Jay she hoped to talk Virginia into going back to the Mayo Clinic.

Pauline also experienced intermittent headaches and tired easily, so she scheduled a physical for a few weeks later at Mayo and thought Virginia should come with her. Despite her occasional problems, Pauline appeared to be in great shape during her trip to San Francisco. The day before she left for Los Angeles, Jay came to her room while she packed to give Pauline a new book on Paris as a going-away present. She struck him as looking particularly radiant and surprised him by saying, "Did I ever think of telling you what you've meant to me and what you've meant to my life ever since

I met you in New York?" Jay recalled responding rather sheepishly with "Oh, posh, or something like that," and Pauline gave him a big kiss. He never saw her again.[49]

Pauline had not yet left San Francisco when Gregory called his aunt Virginia's house looking for his mother. Upon receiving the call from Virginia, Pauline learned that Gregory had been arrested and needed her help. Pauline cabled Ernest to let him know that Gregory was in some kind of trouble and that she was en route to Los Angeles to check out the situation.

Though Gregory's offense was initially referred to as "taking a mind-stimulating drug before such things had become fashionable," the family understood that the real cause for Gregory's arrest related to his secret predilection for cross-dressing.[50] His issues with sexual identity became a lifelong problem for Gregory, who blamed his parents for never getting him the help he needed as he grew up, never wanting to admit their son had a problem, and later being more interested in hiding their embarrassment than in seeking help.[51]

In Gregory's mind, his troubles went all the way back to birth, when his parents wanted a girl. When his mother went off to Africa with Ernest for eight months, leaving him alone with Ada, the separation traumatized Gregory. Ada governed by fear, threatening to leave him just like his parents did if he misbehaved. For comfort, he retrieved his mother's silk stockings from her chest of drawers to feel close to her, beginning the habit of resorting to women's clothing whenever facing stressful situations.[52]

On this occasion, Pauline met with Gregory at the Los Angeles jail, retained a lawyer, and made arrangements to keep the incident out of the newspapers.[53] It appeared to Pauline that the problem could be straightened out without major consequences. Nevertheless, she felt Ernest should be notified of the full extent of the situation, particularly in light of his earlier concerns about not being brought in on everything going on with the family. When Gregory suggested that it might be simpler to leave his father out of it, Pauline responded with "Yes . . . a lot of things would be simpler if you had only one parent."[54]

Gregory thought his mother looked thin and haggard. By the time she got to Laura Archera and Virginia's house late that Sunday afternoon, she was in pain and put off calling. When Ernest called Pauline after not hearing anything, she pulled herself together enough to come to the phone and speak to him. The conversation apparently started out cordially enough but then elevated to major shouting and ended with Pauline sobbing. According to Ernest, Pauline bore the blame for all Gregory's problems; if she had been a better mother, and less permissive, none of this would have happened.

Pauline went to bed in tears. In the early morning hours, Virginia and Laura awakened to a "horrendous scream" from Pauline's bedroom. They rushed her to St. Vincent's Hospital, where doctors took her into surgery and began a search for the source of her pain. Due to Virginia's ill health, Laura took her back home after they got Pauline admitted. According to Laura, shortly after 4 A.M., a doctor called Virginia with the news: "We couldn't do anything."[55] Pauline's blood pressure had gone sky high, then dropped to nothing, causing her to die of shock on the operating table.

About five hours later, at 9 A.M. on Monday, October 1, Virginia notified Gregory, in his jail cell awaiting a hearing later that day, then cabled Ernest to let him know that Pauline had died of an apparent heart attack and that she would call later with more details. Ernest in turn cabled Patrick and Henny, now in Africa, letting them know he would send flowers for all of them after Virginia determined funeral arrangements. He extended his love and deepest sympathy.

All day Ernest waited in Cuba for more details, but Virginia never called. When he again called her house, Virginia coldly refused to tell him much. Grieving and blaming Ernest for contributing to Pauline's illness the night before, Virginia implied it no longer mattered what he knew. Ernest passed the next few days at the Finca silent and morose, while Virginia went about funeral arrangements. Mary, also shocked and grieved, later wrote, "I ran down to the rose garden to sit and try to find some sort of stability to contain this blow. Pauline, with her knowing eyes, was a high-spirited sharp-minded woman, an accidental friend to me, both generous and loving. I would miss her for a long time."[56]

Ernest's letter to his publisher that same day concluded with "The wave of remembering has finally risen so that it has broken over the jetty that I built to protect the open roadstead of my heart and I have the full sorrow of Pauline's death with all the harbour scum of what caused it. I loved her very much for many years and the hell with her faults."[57] His friend John Dos Passos wrote, "It's hard to think of Pauline gone, though she died suddenly and quickly, the way we would all like to die. I was very fond of her. Lord it seems longer than half a lifetime ago, when I first met the dark-haired Pfeiffer girls with you in Paris."[58] Ernest also received condolences from his sister Marcelline, who always attempted to be sympathetic to her brother in spite of his occasional digs at her. "She [Pauline] was such a darling," Marcelline wrote. "Tho' we had only known each other thru letters until 2 years ago, I was so very fond of her. . . . She meant a great deal to you, I know and she told me she had never ceased to love you."[59]

Rather than ship Pauline's body back to Key West, Virginia decided to bury her in Hollywood. She first checked on a burial plot in a Catholic cemetery but was upset to find out that Pauline's divorced status ruled out interment there. Instead, she purchased a plot in Hollywood Memorial Park Cemetery, off Santa Monica Boulevard, in the shadow of Paramount Studios. Her simple graveside service had only a few people in attendance, including Virginia, Gregory, Laura, Jay McEvoy, and Pauline's favorite cousin Garfield Merner. "My mother's face looked unbelievably white at the funeral, Gregory recalled, "and I remember thinking through sobs what a barbarous ritual Anglo-Saxon burial is."[60] The family placed no markers on her grave but buried her in a section of the cemetery with Cecil B. DeMille, Marion Davies, and Tyrone Power.

Pauline's will gave her business to the two partners and the building to Marjorie Stevens. Jack received ten thousand dollars, Virginia received five thousand dollars, and other bequests went to her longtime household employees. Monroe County Hospital in Key West received a gift to defray hospitalization expenses of charity patients. The remainder of her estate was divided equally between Patrick and Gregory. Pauline also instructed her executor that any personal correspondence or letters in her desk be burned. The equal bequest to both sons came as a surprise to Gregory, who had always assumed his mother loved Patrick more and would leave him more through her will. Although Ernest constantly carped about his rich ex-wife, Pauline's personal assets came to $188,122.11, not including the Whitehead Street property, which she owned 60–40 with Ernest. Pauline had not yet received the assets from her mother's estate.[61]

With Patrick in Africa, and Gregory still a minor, Ernest dispatched his lawyer to Key West to represent his sons, as well as himself, when the executor opened Pauline's safe and desk drawers. Ernest wrote a note to Pauline's executor letting him know "how much I appreciate the care with which you have looked after Pauline, Gregory and Patrick's interests. . . . I understand the difficulties of handling an estate of this kind. It is hard work and I appreciate the care you give it."[62]

CHAPTER 25

Afterward

Those who had been part of Pauline Hemingway's orbit began adjusting to life without her. Despite the fact that she and Ernest had divorced more than ten years before her death, their sons provided a common bond that kept them in each other's lives. For Pfeiffer family members, it was difficult to think about Pauline without thinking about Ernest. Their remembrances of how happy Pauline had been with Ernest alternated with their resentment of the great emotional pain and sorrow he had caused her.

Shortly after Pauline's death, Patrick and Henny returned from Africa and moved into the Key West guesthouse to sort out his mother's affairs and to decide, along with Patrick's father and brother, whether to sell or rent the Key West property. Ernest remained a 40 percent owner; Patrick and Gregory each had a 30 percent share. They decided for the time being to keep both the main house and guesthouse as rental property, with Patrick and Henny remaining in the small guesthouse and paying nominal rent to the other two owners. Patrick kept busy for a time looking after the property and tending to his mother's estate, particularly with his father in Cuba and his brother elsewhere. Decisions also needed to be made about investing the money arriving regularly from several sources in Piggott, including payments from Mary Pfeiffer's estate, distributions from Paul Pfeiffer's estate, and annual income from the Piggott Land Co.

Eventually, Patrick determined that he should move to Piggott, at least temporarily, to learn more about family operations and decide whether to join his uncle Karl and aunt Virginia in purchasing farm property in northeast Arkansas from the family land company. Patrick retained fond memories of his Pfeiffer grandparents and his time in Arkansas during childhood. "I loved my Grandfather Paul," Patrick recalled, remembering him as a banker and businessman, always in a suit and tie. "Every evening when I was there, he took me for a walk down the hill and all kinds of things would come out—especially toads." Patrick's time with his grandfather also included trips to Piggott State Bank, where Paul Pfeiffer served as president. "He would take me into the vault where all the money was. Give me change—dimes and quarters. I thought that was something—getting the change there in the vault where all the money was kept. It was a big deal to me at that age for a grandfather to pay attention and do things with you."[1]

Patrick and Henny arrived in Piggott during May 1952 and found life there much different without Patrick's grandfather. They moved into a tenant house in poor condition. To make matters worse, Patrick's uncle Karl and the townspeople seemed unreceptive to anyone with the last name Hemingway, even though he was Pauline's son. Few in town had read Hemingway's books, and many shared Karl's belief that Hemingway had taken advantage of Pfeiffer money. By mid-June, Patrick and Henny had had enough of rural Arkansas, and they made plans for a return to Africa. Their most pleasant experience while in Piggott was a quick visit from Jack, on the way to his Fort Bragg, North Carolina, duty station.

Notwithstanding Patrick's bad experience in Piggott—and Ernest's own chilly reception on occasion—Ernest still considered that Piggott had a lot of small-town charm. Several years after Patrick's departure, a film crew arrived in the town, thanks to Hemingway and his general factotum Toby Bruce. When Hemingway's friends Budd Schulberg and Elia Kazan were seeking a small-town setting for the now-classic 1957 movie *A Face in the Crowd,* Bruce had assured them they would not find a better place than Piggott, and Hemingway had concurred. After the picture premiered, Ernest called it "much better than most you ever see."[2]

The small-town charm of Piggott also held memories for Gregory, such as digging for worms in the Pfeiffer backyard with his grandfather, but his fondest memories were of Cuba, including fishing trips with his father and shooting competitions with the locals. Several months after his mother's funeral, Gregory made an effort to reconnect with his remaining parent by taking his wife and new baby Lorian to the Finca, financing the trip with an advance on his inheritance. The visit seemed to go well; Ernest liked his wife, and Gregory enjoyed introducing Jane to Cuba. Toward the end of the stay, however, a discussion with his father led to the subject of his arrest in California. When he told his father it wasn't really that bad, Ernest said, "No? Well, it killed Mother."[3] The remark devastated Gregory, and he never saw his father again, though he received his mother's estate payments from Ernest since Gregory did not turn twenty-one until November 1952. What bothered Gregory most was the possibility that his father might be right.

Accepting responsibility for his mother's death made Gregory feel guilty about his inheritance. He used some of it to finance a premed education at the University of California–Los Angeles but dropped out after two years and went to Africa, the vast continent that had captivated his father and brother. During his time in Africa, Gregory's marriage broke up, and his wife returned to the States with their daughter. After being drafted into the army, followed by another stint in Africa, Gregory finished premed and then entered medical school at the University of Miami. His acceptance into medical school prompted a letter from Ernest in Cuba. After extending congratulations, Ernest added, "But I doubt if you'll ever make much of a doctor—You can't even spell the word medicine correctly." Gregory said later he laughed at the response because he knew it meant his father "was proud of me in spite of the rough joking."[4]

Now understanding medical terminology, Gregory requested a copy of his mother's autopsy and learned that she had died of pheochromocytoma, a rare tumor of the adrenal gland. The tumor is unusual in that, rather than invading organs, it secretes large amounts of adrenaline, causing blood pressure to soar to the point where it can rupture arteries. He further learned that two types of such tumors exist—intermittent and constantly secreting. His mother's appeared to be the intermittent type, which could be set off by stress. The tumor had probably caused her many headaches, including the last one, which killed her.

Gregory provided this information in a letter to his father during the summer of 1960 to absolve himself of his mother's death. Instead, he suggested that Ernest's heated conversation with her earlier the evening of her death had upset Pauline to the point of causing her tumor to "fire off," sending adrenaline into her system and causing a blood vessel to rupture. When the tumor stopped discharging adrenaline, her blood pressure dropped to nothing, and she died of shock on the operating table. Gregory heard that after Ernest read his letter, "he raged at first and then walked around the house in silence for the rest of the day."[5]

At the time of Pauline's death, neither Gregory nor Patrick had received the Hemingway manuscripts being held by Uncle Gus. Though it had been his intent to give them to Pauline for her sons, she had not retrieved them before she died, and Gus's growing senility prevented him from altering his will to address their disposition. Thus, when Gustavus Pfeiffer died in New York on August 22, 1953, at age eighty-one—two years after Pauline's death—the status of the manuscripts was in legal limbo. Gus's estate included manuscripts of the novels *A Farewell to Arms* and *For Whom the Bell Tolls;* the short stories "Fifty Grand" (original manuscript of unpublished portion), "The Killers," and "The Undefeated" (first type-script); and the *Esquire* articles "Lion Hunting" and "Notes on Dangerous Game."

Immediately after Gus's death, executors retrieved the manuscripts from safekeeping at his Connecticut home, obtained an appraisal of twenty-five thousand dollars for the manuscripts, and turned them over to legal counsel for appropriate disposition.[6] Attorneys concluded after reviewing relevant correspondence, first, that Ernest had made an absolute gift of the manuscripts to Gus, free of trust; second, that Gus had not held the manuscripts in trust by virtue of any legal declaration of trust; and finally, that Gus remained absolute owner at the time of his death. In spite of the fact that they clearly belonged to the estate, executors had no doubt that Gus meant for the manuscripts to be preserved for Patrick and Gregory and that he intended for Pauline to take possession and place them in a safe-deposit box for the boys. Therefore, with approval of all residual beneficiaries, executors delivered the manuscripts to Patrick and Gregory.

The remainder of Gus's estate was valued at more than $15 million. The bulk of his holdings, more than $9 million, went into the Gustavus and Louise Pfeiffer Research Foundation established by Gus and his wife in 1942 to support research in medical and pharmaceutical fields. Gus's chess books and scrapbooks went to the New York Public Library, along with $25,000 for acquiring additional chess books. Prior to his death, he donated his collection of rare chess sets to the Metropolitan Museum of Art, and his will provided $200,000 in cash for additional acquisitions. Other cash gifts went to his personal secretary, household employees, and twelve charitable and educational organizations. In recognition of his strong family ties, the will dispersed $780,000 to thirty named nieces, nephews, and cousins. Pauline's $30,000 share passed to her sons, Patrick and Gregory.

Gus's death marked the end of many family ties, including the Aspetuck family compound. Since all the property, other than the Helen Keller home, belonged to Gus, it went on the market as part of his estate, along with his property in Fort Lauderdale and his New York apartment. As the only remaining tie to Aspetuck, Gus had specified that his body be cremated and his ashes scattered over a section of Aspetuck River known as Pfeiffer Pond in Connecticut. The eulogy delivered by his nephew Robert Pfeiffer remembered him as a man who took advantage of both ability and opportunity to achieve great personal and professional success. He was "daring without being reckless, firm without being stubborn, imaginative without being quixotic, practical without being an unrealistic theorist, idealistic without being inefficient."[7]

Gus's death also ended Pfeiffer involvement in pharmaceuticals. The original Pfeiffer Chemical Company established in St Louis by Gus and his brothers had become Warner-Hudnut. In the years after Gus's death, it merged to become Warner-Lambert and ultimately a part of Pfizer, the world's largest pharmaceutical company. The business principles that had guided Gus's success, along with his personal words of wisdom over the years, were preserved in a 1955 private publication, *Philosophical Writings and Aphorisms of Gustavus A. Pfeiffer.* The book included Gus's fundamental qualities for success in life (intelligence, personality, industry, and character), along with his guide for daily living, reflections on life's pleasures, and his personal objective "to give to all with whom I come in contact value-plus."[8]

With the death of Gus Pfeiffer, along with the earlier losses of Pauline Hemingway, Mary Pfeiffer, and Paul Pfeiffer, four of the key people who gave purpose to Virginia Pfeiffer's life were gone. She filled the empty space and attempted to give something of herself by adopting children. Virginia adopted eighteen-month-old Paula in 1951, followed by the infant Juanito in 1952, making her one of the first single parents allowed to adopt in California. Virginia's partner, Laura Archera, made a major life change as well. Shortly after their arrival in Hollywood, she and Virginia befriended Aldous Huxley, celebrated author of *A Brave New World,* and his wife, Maria. When Maria died of cancer in 1954, Laura increased her participation in his pioneering research on expansion of consciousness, which formed much of the basis for a human potential movement. Huxley experimented with several drugs, including mescaline (extracted from peyote cactus), psilocybin (extracted from mushrooms), and lysergic acid diethylamide (LSD—extracted from rye), long before they became controversial aspects of popular culture.

In 1956 Laura and Aldous married and moved to a house just five hundred yards up the hill from Virginia and her children. The five lived almost as one big family: Aldous, Laura, Virginia, Paula, and Juan. In May 1961, with Virginia and her children out of town for the weekend, a fire began in the canyon below their homes. While at Virginia's home attempting to feed the family pet, Edgarallencat, Laura looked out the window at flames nearing the house. Later she recalled in her book about life with Huxley that the flames mesmerized her. Although sufficient time probably remained to gather many of Virginia's things, she froze. "I looked around the charming kitchen and then went downstairs to the workroom, where, in the darkroom and in tin cans were the results of so many years of events in cinematography. In the typewriter was a letter, half finished. I thought of other writings that were there—a play Ginny had written. 'But Ginny doesn't care anyway,' I thought. Maybe I should take some clothes for her. I didn't. I saw her beautiful fur coat. 'Too hot for that now.' Fortunately, I took a box in which I knew she had some important papers—the only thing I did for her."[9]

Laura returned home and calmly told her husband, "Ginny's house is burning." They went back down the hill and found Virginia's house totally engulfed in flames and their own house the next target for the fast-moving fire. They lost almost everything in both homes—including Virginia's letters from Ernest, Pauline, and the rest of her family. In all, the canyon fire gutted twenty-four homes in the Hollywood hills. Virginia and her children returned two days later to find no home and no possessions. After several weeks of living in a hotel with Aldous and Laura, Virginia acquired another home near the burned-out area, and the five all moved in together. Until his death in 1963, on the same day as John F. Kennedy's assassination, Aldous Huxley replaced Ernest Hemingway as the most important writer in Virginia's life.[10]

Nevertheless, Virginia's memories of Hemingway—both good and bad —remained just below the surface: the handsome young man she met in Paris at Kitty Cannell's party, her sister's lonely lover whom she entertained during his one-hundred-day separation from Pauline, the brother-in-law she shared so many experiences with during his marriage to Pauline, and the selfish artist she fought with so heatedly when he mistreated her sister. Over the years that followed, until her death on February 24, 1973, Virginia refused to talk to the many reporters who wanted to know her views of Ernest Hemingway. She confided those thoughts only to friends and family. Virginia occasionally told people who inquired that she had never married because she did not want to end up like her sister, with a man who married her only for her money.

During the last years of Ernest's life, perhaps nothing galled him more than hearing such comments about his dependence on the Pfeiffers. "The popular theory that I was a bum who was picked up from poverty and supported on Pfeiffer money always seemed to me sort of strange," he told Patrick, citing his literary successes before and during his marriage to Pauline. In terms of Uncle Gus's support, every time he gave any kind of gift or financial contribution, "I gave him a manuscript which was at least double the value of the present. This was the value *at the time* they were given. Now they are much more valuable."[11]

Comments regarding Pauline's influence on his writing irritated him as well. Even though he "showed her" by creating *For Whom the Bell Tolls* without her editing assistance, his inability to produce anything of real merit for a time after that work weighed heavily on him. *Across the River and Into the Trees* became an abysmal literary failure, according to many critics, and his plan for a three-part masterpiece involving the land, the air, and the sea kept growing and changing without going anywhere. While working on the sea portion, he returned to an essay written for the April 1936 issue of *Esquire,* titled "On the Blue Water," and further developed aspects of that article. The result became *The Old Man and the Sea,* which told the story of an elderly Cuban fisherman in an epic struggle with a massive fish. Ultimately the old man defeats the giant marlin, only to have his prize destroyed by sharks as he attempts to get his catch back to land. For both the man and the fish, there is honor in the struggle, as well as the defeat. Published in 1952, the novella earned Hemingway the Pulitzer Prize that year and contributed to his being awarded the Nobel Prize for Literature in 1954, bringing the author the ultimate literary recognition that had eluded him in the past. Ironically it came from a piece out of the past, written while married to Pauline.

Though Hemingway tried to insist that the Nobel Prize meant little to him, he clearly thought he was more deserving than William Faulkner, who had captured the prize in 1949. Hemingway's views of Faulkner's writing were colored by being called a "coward" by Faulkner several years earlier, during a college lecture that made it into print.[12] Faulkner meant that, of all the leading American writers, Hemingway took the least risk in his writing. Faulkner apologized for the misinterpretation, but Hemingway was not one to forgive or forget easily. Thus, it was significant when Faulkner weighed in with high praise for *The Old Man and the Sea.* Reviewing the novella for a small magazine, he wrote, "Time may show it to be the best single piece of any of us, I mean his and my contemporaries. This time he discovered God, a Creator. . . . Praise God that whatever made and loves and pities Hemingway and me kept him from touching it any further."[13]

Hemingway did not accept his Nobel Prize in person, since he was recovering from several accidents during a trip to Africa with Mary. In January 1954, they walked away from a plane crash near Murchison Falls in Uganda with only minor injuries, even though initial reports indicated the crash left no apparent survivors. News of the Hemingways' presumed deaths circulated around the world. After they were located the next day, a would-be rescue plane burst into flames on takeoff, requiring Ernest to use his head as a battering ram to force his way through a jammed door. In addition to a concussion, he had crushed vertebrae; a ruptured kidney, liver, and spleen; temporary hearing and vision loss; first-degree burns, and an assortment of sprains, bruises, and other injuries. A month later, while helping put out a brush fire in Nairobi, he became disoriented from his concussion and toppled into the flames, adding second- and third-degree burns to his list of injuries.

Though accident-prone all his life, these latest assaults to Ernest's system may have inflicted more trauma than his body could bear, possibly escalating his descent into mental illnesses such as depression and paranoia. In 1960, Ernest made his first trip to the Mayo Clinic from Ketchum, Idaho, his home since Fidel Castro's takeover of Cuba. Along with other therapy there, he received electric shock treatments for his depression and paranoia. These treatments destroyed his memory and his ability to write, and that threw him into deeper depression, which required a second trip for treatment. He decided to end this depression permanently on July 2, 1961. Ernest rose that morning at his home, went quietly down the stairs to avoid waking Mary, retrieved a double-barreled shotgun from where Mary thought she had his guns safely locked away, put the barrels to his forehead, and pulled both triggers.

Ernest's funeral in Ketchum marked the first time his three sons had been together since the late 1940s, when they fished in Idaho. By 1961 Jack lived in San Francisco with Puck (pregnant with Mariel) and their daughters, Joan (Muffett), eleven, and Margot, six. Patrick returned for the funeral from Africa, where he enjoyed a successful career as head of a safari company. In March 1961, Ernest had written to thank Patrick for pictures of their newly adopted infant daughter, Edwina (Mina), and told Patrick he did not feel well, but there was no indication of the deepening depression. Gregory had last seen his father immediately after his mother's death, though they remained in contact. Told a few months earlier that his father had checked into the Mayo Clinic for treatment of a rare disease, Gregory reached a doctor by telephone who told him of Ernest's condition. Only then did Gregory become aware of the nature and severity of Ernest's situation. After his father's death, Gregory confessed in his memoirs that he "felt profound relief when they lowered my father's body into the ground and I realized that he was really dead, that I couldn't disappoint him, couldn't hurt him any more."[14]

While at the funeral, Gregory met his father's former secretary Valerie Danby-Smith, and a friendship developed. Though married at the time he met Valerie to his second wife, Alice Thomas, Gregory married Valerie in 1966, after his second marriage ended. He adopted Valerie's son, Brendan, and eventually gained custody of his children by his previous wife, including John, Maria, and Patrick. Gregory and Valerie added three children of their own—Sean, Edward, and Vanessa—bringing their brood to eight, counting his oldest daughter, Lorian, who lived with her mother. Gregory's marriage to Valerie ended in divorce as well, and in 1993 he married his fourth wife, Ida Galliher. Both of Gregory's brothers were widowed and remarried when they joined together on July 21, 1999, for Ernest Hemingway's one-hundredth-birthday celebration at his birthplace home in Oak Park, Illinois. Patrick and Carol came from their home in Bozeman, Montana; Jack and Angela traveled from Ketchum, Idaho; Gregory and Ida came from Miami, Florida. It became the last reunion of the three brothers to honor their father. In January 2001 Jack died of complications from heart surgery.

Gregory's death came later that same year, after an arrest related to his cross-dressing and five days in a Miami detention center. In the early morning hours of Monday, October 1, 2001, he died of heart disease in the jail cell where he was awaiting his hearing, scheduled later that day. Exactly fifty years earlier, in the early morning hours of Monday, October 1, 1951, Pauline Pfeiffer Hemingway had died as her son Gregory waited in a jail cell for a hearing scheduled later that day. Thus, death provided a connection between mother and son. Sadly, Gregory had sought this bond with his mother all of his life.

Though much has been written about Hemingway's storied literary career, little evidence remains of Pauline's connection to it. There are no editing notes on any of the manuscript drafts that he kept that might validate her role in honing his talents. Perhaps these went up in flames when the Piggott barn-studio caught fire and burned many of his papers. Regardless, the true extent of her contributions went with Ernest to his grave. Pauline's brother Karl always believed that his sister played a pivotal role in Hemingway's literary success and that he discarded her as soon as he could make it on his own. Further, according to Karl, Hemingway's personal insecurities prevented him from acknowledging that he owed any debt to the Pfeiffer family. Two years before Karl's death on December 11, 1981, he told a reporter, "[Ernest] was a pitiful character at times, but very talented. He wrote some great books and stories. But you know *For Whom the Bell Tolls*? I always used to say, 'It tolls for Ernest Hemingway.'"[15]

In the process of Hemingway becoming one of America's greatest writers of the twentieth century, Pauline's life—which started out with such promise—became subsumed into the Hemingway legend. Even the book that Hemingway might have written about her never became a reality. In a fragment from *A Moveable Feast,* not included in the first posthumous version but resurrected in the more recent edition, Hemingway noted his intent to leave out "the part with Pauline" and save it for another book. "It could be a good book," he wrote, "because it tells many things that no one knows or can ever know and it has love, remorse, contrition, and unbelievable happiness and final sorrow."[16]

NOTES

The following abbreviations are used in the notes for frequently cited sources:

Colby: Colby College Special Collections, Waterville, Me.
EH: Ernest Hemingway
Hadley: Hadley Richardson Hemingway Mowrer
HGW: Helen Guffey Weaver Estate, private collection
HMD: Honoria Murphy Donnelly Estate, private collection
HPMEC: Hemingway-Pfeiffer Museum and Educational Center, Piggott, Ark.
JFK: Ernest Hemingway Collection, John F. Kennedy Library, Boston
Lilly: Hemingway MSS III, Lilly Library, Indiana University, Bloomington, Ind.
Pauline: Pauline Pfeiffer Hemingway
PRF: Gustavus and Louise Pfeiffer Research Foundation Collection, Hemingway-Pfeiffer Museum and Educational Center, Piggott, Ark.
PSU: Ernest H. Mainland Collection, Special Collections Library, The Pennsylvania State University
PUL: Princeton University Library Special Collections, Princeton, N.J.
Texas: Hemingway Family Papers, Harry Ransom Humanities Research Center, University of Texas, Austin
UVA: University of Virginia Library, Charlottesville, Va.

Chapter 1: Introduction

1. Hemingway, *Moveable Feast,* title page.
2. Diliberto, *Hadley.* 36.
3. Cannell, "Scenes with a Hero," 146.
4. Cannell, "Scenes with a Hero," 146.
5. Cannell, "Scenes with a Hero," 146.
6. Kenneth Wells, interview with the author, Piggott, Ark., Mar. 20, 1997, based on conversations with Virginia Pfeiffer in 1950.
7. Cannell, "Scenes with a Hero," 146.
8. Wells, interview, Mar. 20, 1997.
9. Ayleene Spence, interview with the author, Piggott, Ark., Jan. 9, 1998.
10. Wells, interview, Mar. 20, 1997.

Chapter 2: The Pfeiffers

1. G. A. Pfeiffer to Family, Oct. 30, 1932, Jan. 9, 1937, PRF.

2. G. A. Pfeiffer to Family, Oct. 30, 1932, PRF.

3. G. A. Pfeiffer to Family, Jan. 17, 1937, PRF.

4. "540 Jahre Kluftinger in Kempten," *Allgäuer Zeitung/Allgäuer Tagblatt,* 1934, PRF

5. Alfredo Leonardi, "The Kluftinger, Pfeiffer and Leonardi Families: How Their Lives Were Affected by the City of Bologna, Italy," unpublished family history, 3, HPMEC.

6. Harris Franklin Rall, remarks at the dedication of the Henry Pfeiffer Chapel at Pfeiffer Junior College, Misenheimer, N.C., May 1–2, 1943, PRF.

7. George Pfeiffer, interview with the author, Los Angeles, Calif., Mar. 4, 1998.

8. G. A. Pfeiffer to Family, Dec. 31, 1941, PRF.

9. "Local Eyetems," *Parkersburg Eclipse,* Mar. 1, 1900.

10. "Local Eyetems," *Parkersburg Eclipse,* May 31, 1900.

11. "Local Eyetems," *Parkersburg Eclipse,* Nov. 14, 1901.

12. G. A. Pfeiffer, *Philosophical Writings.*

13. Lloyd Russell, interview with the author, Piggott, Ark., Oct. 8, 1997.

14. "Geo. M. Jackson, Socialist Leader of Clay Co., Stabbed Paul Pfeiffer of St. Francis Sunday," *Paragould Daily Press,* Oct. 14, 1912 (reprinted in *Corning Courier,* "G. M. Jackson in Bad in East End," Oct. 18, 1912).

Chapter 3: Pauline

1. "Visitation Academy," *Schools of the Catholic Archdiocese of St. Louis* (St. Louis: Archdiocese of St. Louis, 1995–96).

2. Faherty, *Deep Roots and Golden Wings,* 104.

3. Faherty, *Deep Roots and Golden Wings,* 112–13.

4. Witherspoon, *Remembering the St. Louis World's Fair,* 71.

5. Sheila Tybor, interview with the author, Piggott, Ark., July 19, 2005.

6. Pauline Pfeiffer, letter, Oct. 1925, *Alumnae Magazine,* Academy of the Visitation (St. Louis: 1926), 13.

7. Montgomery, *Leading Facts of French History.*

8. *Paragould Daily Press,* 1914.

9. Nancy Castrillon Militello, telephone interview with the author, Aug. 7, 1997.

10. *Savitar* (University of Missouri, Columbia: 1918), 35.

11. "Missouri Alumni in Journalism."

12. Paul Pfeiffer to Karl Pfeiffer, Nov. 5, 1918, Matilda and Karl Pfeiffer Foundation, Piggott, Ark.

13. Mary Pfeiffer to Karl Pfeiffer, Nov. 22, 1918, Matilda and Karl Pfeiffer Foundation.

14. Patty Johnson, "Colorful House That Cosmetics Preserved," *Iowan.* Feb.– Mar. 1961, 16.

15. Levin, *Wheels of Fashion,* 58.

16. Meade, *Dorothy Parker,* 43.

17. Frank J. Ryan, "To Whom it May Concern," Apr. 13, 1922, HPMEC.

18. Ursula Herold Harris, interview with the author, Walnut Creek, Calif., Feb. 11, 2000.

19. Harris, interview, Feb. 11, 2000.

Chapter 4: Ernest

1. Sanford, *At the Hemingways,* 54.

2. Sanford, *At the Hemingways,* 54.

3. Sanford, *At the Hemingways,* 81.

4. Ernest Hemingway, "Big Two-Hearted River: Part II." in Hemingway, *Short Stories,* 235.

5. Sanford, *At the Hemingways,* 67.

6. L. Hemingway, *My Brother,* 42.

7. Sanford, *At the Hemingways,* 12.

8. Baker, *Ernest Hemingway,* 31.

9. L. Hemingway, *My Brother,* 43.

10. Sanford, *At the Hemingways,* 41–42.

11. Baker, *Ernest Hemingway,* 5.

12. Sanford, *At the Hemingways,* 188.

13. Grace Hemingway to EH, July 24, 1920, Texas, in Reynolds, *Young Hemingway,* 138.

14. Sherwood Anderson to Lewis Galantière, Nov. 28, 1921, in Anderson, *Letters,* 82–83.

15. Sherwood Anderson to Gertrude Stein, Dec. 3, 1921, in Anderson, *Letters,* 85.

16. Ford, "Margaret Anderson," 257.

17. Ford, "Margaret Anderson," 257.

18. Diliberto, *Hadley,* 161.

19. Dos Passos, *Best Times,* 142.

20. Kuehl and Bryer, *Dear Scott/Dear Max,* 78 (ca. Oct. 10, 1924).

21. Sarason, *Hemingway and the Sun Set,* 118.

22. EH to Ernest Walsh, Jan. 29, 1925, JFK.

Chapter 5: Three's a Crowd (1925–1926)

1. "French Show Tonight," *New York Times,* Apr. 22, 1925; "Jusserand Opens French Exposition," *New York Times,* Apr. 23, 1925; "Four Towers to Remain from Paris Exposition," *New York Times,* Oct. 25, 1925.

2. Hotchner, *Papa Hemingway,* 52–53.

3. Dos Passos, *Best Times,* 143.

4. Pauline to Katy Smith, June 24, 1925, in Carr, *John Dos Passos,* 210.

5. Pauline to Harold Loeb, Aug. 1925, PUL, in Reynolds, *Paris Years,* 316.

6. Mellow, *Life without Consequences,* 295; Kert, *Hemingway Women,* 156.

7. Ernest Hemingway, "The Sea Change," in Hemingway, *Winner Take Nothing,* 42.

8. Ernest Hemingway, "Art of the Short Story," 88.

9. EH to Edmund Wilson, Nov. 8, 1952, Yale University Library, in Hemingway, *Selected Letters,* 793.

10. Fitzgerald to Boni & Liverright, before Dec. 30, 1925, PUL, in Fitzgerald, *Correspondence,* 183.

11. Diliberto, *Hadley,* 203.

12. EH to Harold Loeb, ca. Nov. 1925, JFK.

13. EH to William Smith, Dec. 3, 1925, Field Collection, Stanford University Library, in Reynolds, *Paris Years,* 332.

14. Pauline Pfeiffer, letter, Oct. 1925, *Alumnae Magazine,* Academy of the Visitation (St. Louis: Academy of the Visitation, 1926), 13.

15. Cannell, "Scenes with a Hero," 146.

16. Diliberto, *Hadley,* 142.

17. Reynolds, *Paris Years,* 318.

18. Hemingway, *Moveable Feast,* 209–10.

19. Reynolds, *American Homecoming,* 7–8; G. A. Pfeiffer to Pauline, n.d., JFK; G.A. Pfeiffer to Farmer's Loan and Trust Co., Jan. 16, 1926, JFK.

20. Pauline to EH and Hadley, Mar. 12, 1926, JFK. (Many of the Pfeiffer letters use an alternative spelling for "Bumby.")

21. Horace Liveright to EH, Dec. 30, 1925, UVA.

22. Pauline to EH and Hadley, Jan. 16, 1926, JFK.

23. Pauline to Hadley, Jan. 17, 1926, JFK.

24. Pauline to Hadley, Jan. 29, 1926, JFK.

25. Pauline to Hadley, Feb. 4, 1926, JFK.

26. Meade, *Dorothy Parker,* 167.

27. Pauline to Hadley, Mar. 16, 1926, JFK.

28. Pauline to EH, Mar. 8, 1926, JFK.

29. Pauline to EH and Hadley, Mar. 16, 1926, JFK.

30. Pauline to EH and Hadley, Mar. 16, 1926, JFK.

31. Boyle and McAlmon, *Being Geniuses Together,* 201.

32. Boyle and McAlmon, *Being Geniuses Together,* 204.

33. EH to Ernest Walsh, Apr. 7, 1926, JFK.

34. Manuscript fragment 648b, chap. 5, 43–44, JFK.

35. Manuscript fragment 648b, chap. 5, 44, JFK.

36. Diliberto, *Hadley,* 216.

37. Cannell, "Scenes with a Hero," 146.

38. EH to Clarence Hemingway, May 23, 1926, JFK, in Hemingway, *Selected Letters,* 207.

39. EH to Sherwood Anderson, May 21, 1926, Newberry Library, in Hemingway, *Selected Letters*, 205.

40. Sherwood Anderson to EH, June 14, 1926, in Anderson, *Selected Letters*, 80.

41. Griffin, *Less Than a Treason*, 141.

42. Diliberto, *Hadley*, 224.

43. Diliberto, *Hadley*, 224.

44. Diliberto, *Hadley*, 221.

45. Pauline to EH and Hadley, July 15, 1926, JFK.

46. Donnelly, *Sara and Gerald*, 25.

47. Gerald Murphy to EH, Sept. 6, 1926, JFK, in L. Miller, *Letters from the Lost Generation*, 21.

48. Gerald Murphy to EH, Sept. 6, 1926, 22.

49. EH to F. Scott Fitzgerald, Sept. 7, 1926, PUL, in Hemingway, *Selected Letters*, 217.

50. EH to Sherwood Anderson, Sept. 7, 1926, Newberry Library, in Hemingway, *Selected Letters*, 218.

Chapter 6: The One Hundred Days (1926)

1. Pauline to EH (multiple letters), Oct.–Nov. 1926, JFK.

2. Pauline to EH, Sept. 24, 1926, JFK.

3. Pauline to EH, Sept. 25, 1926, JFK. (This letter is probably misdated, as the boat departed Sept. 24, and she indicates they had been at sea for four days.)

4. Pauline to EH, Oct. 4, 1926, JFK.

5. Pauline to EH, Oct. 4, 1926, JFK.

6. Pauline to EH, Oct. 6, 1926, JFK.

7. Pauline to EH, Oct. 8, 1926, JFK.

8. Pauline to EH, Oct. 6, 1926, JFK.

9. Pauline to EH, Oct. 14, 1926, JFK.

10. Pauline to EH, Oct. 15, 1926, JFK.

11. Pauline to EH, Oct. 21, 1926, JFK.

12. Pauline to EH, Oct. 15, 1926, JFK.

13. Pauline to EH (multiple letters), Oct.–Nov. 1926, JFK.

14. Pauline to EH, Oct. 29, 1926, JFK.

15. Pauline to EH, Dec. 15, 1926, JFK.

16. Pauline to EH, Nov. 26, 1926, JFK.

17. Pauline to EH, Dec. 3, 1926, JFK.

18. Pauline to EH, Dec. 3, 1926, JFK.

19. Hemingway, "Art of Fiction XXI," 84.

20. Hadley to EH, Aug. 10, 1921, JFK.

21. Hemingway, *Sun Also Rises*, 146.

22. Hemingway, *Sun Also Rises*, 146.

23. Brian, *True Gen*, 58, 61.

24. Ayleene Spence, interview with the author, Piggott, Ark., Apr. 10, 1997.

25. Virginia Pfeiffer to EH, fall 1926, JFK.

26. Matilda Pfeiffer, interview with the author, Piggott, Ark., Mar. 28, 1997.

27. EH to Pauline, Nov. 12, 1926 (mistakenly dated Oct. 12), JFK, in Hemingway, *Selected Letters*, 220–22.

28. Pauline to EH, Oct. 30, 1926, JFK.

29. Pauline to EH, Nov. 2, 1926 (mistakenly dated Oct. 2), JFK.

30. Pauline to EH, Nov. 2, 1926, JFK.

31. Pauline to Hadley, Nov. 2, 1926, JFK.

32. EH to Pauline, Nov. 12, 1926 (mistakenly dated Oct. 12), JFK.

33. Hadley to EH, Nov. 16, 1926, JFK.

34. Pauline to EH, Nov. 22, 1926, JFK.

35. EH to Pauline, Dec. 2, 1926, JFK.

36. Pauline to Virginia Pfeiffer, Nov. 22, 1926, JFK.

37. Pauline to EH, Dec. 3, 1926, JFK.

38. EH to Pauline, Dec. 3, 1926, JFK, in Hemingway, *Selected Letters*, 234–35.

39. EH to Pauline, Nov. 12, 1926, JFK.

40. EH to Clarence Hemingway, May 23, 1926, JFK

41. Baker, *Ernest Hemingway*, 172.

42. EH to Perkins, Apr. 8, 1933, and EH to Perkins, Nov. 17, 1933, in Bruccoli, *Only Thing That Counts*, 188, 202 (listed in Hemingway, *Selected Letters*, as Nov. 16, 1933, PUL).

43. Ernest Hemingway, "Hills Like White Elephants," manuscript 473, JFK.

44. Hemingway, *To Have and Have Not*, 185–86.

45. EH to Pauline, Dec. 3, 1926, JFK.

46. Pauline to EH, Dec. 10, 1926, JFK.

47. F. Scott Fitzgerald to EH, Dec. 23, 1926, in Fitzgerald, *Letters*, 298.

48. Pauline to EH, Dec. 25, 1926, JFK.

Chapter 7: Wedding Plans (1927

1. Gerald Murphy to EH, Jan. 5, 1928, JFK, in L. Miller, *Letters from the Lost Generation*, 32.

2. Pauline to EH, Feb. 26, 1927, JFK.

3. J. Hemingway, *Misadventures of a Fly Fisherman*, 5–6.

4. Pauline to EH, Mar. 15, 1927, JFK.

5. Pauline to EH, Mar. 16, 17, 1927, JFK.

6. EH to Ernest Walsh, Jan. 2, 1926, JFK.

7. Pauline to EH, Mar. 16, 1937, JFK.

8. Pauline to EH, Mar. 21, 1927, JFK.

9. Pauline to EH, Mar. 23, 1927, JFK.

10. Hemingway, "Italy, 1927."

11. Baker, *Ernest Hemingway*, 183.

12. EH to F. Scott Fitzgerald, Mar. 31, 1927, JFK, in Hemingway, *Selected Letters*, 249.

13. G. A. Pfeiffer, *Philosophical Writings*.

14. Grace Hemingway to EH, Dec. 4, 1926, JFK, in Reynolds, *American Homecoming* 91.

15. Clarence Hemingway to EH, Dec. 13, 1926, JFK, in Reynolds, *American Homecoming*, 91.

16. Clarence Hemingway to EH, Jan. 27, 1927, JFK, in Diliberto, *Hadley*, 245.

17. Grace Hemingway to EH, Dec. 4, 1926, and Clarence Hemingway to EH, Dec. 13, 1926, both JFK, in Reynolds, *American Homecoming*, 92.

18. EH to Grace Hemingway, Feb. 5, 1927, JFK, in Hemingway, *Selected Letters*, 244.

19. EH to Madelaine Hemingway, Apr. 12, 1927, PSU.

20. EH to Madelaine Hemingway, Apr. 12, 1927, PSU.

21. EH to Madelaine Hemingway, May 6, 1927, PSU.

22. EH to Madelaine Hemingway, May 6, 1927, PSU.

23. M. Miller, *Ernie*, 107.

24. Madelaine Hemingway to EH, May 12, 1927, JFK, in Reynolds, *American Homecoming*, 130.

25. G. A. Pfeiffer to EH and Pauline, Apr. 28, 1927, PUL.

26. Leonhard Kluftinger to Pauline, May 8, 1927, PUL.

27. Henry Pfeiffer to EH and Pauline, May 19, 1927, PUL.

28. Annie Pfeiffer to Pauline, May 27, 1927, PUL.

29. Kate Downey Coffin to Pauline, May 17, 1927, PUL.

30. Emma Pfeiffer Merner to EH and Pauline, June 1, 1917, PUL.

31. Harriett Downey Younker to Pauline, May 24, 1927, PUL.

32. Paul and Mary Pfeiffer to Ernest and Pauline Hemingway, May 9, 1927, PUL.

33. Reynolds, *American Homecoming*, 124.

34. Donaldson, *Archibald MacLeish*, 164.

35. Brian, *True Gen*, 72.

36. Mary Pfeiffer to EH and Pauline, May 10, 1927, PUL.

Chapter 8: The Newlyweds (1927–1928)

1. Pauline to EH, Oct. 22, 1926, JFK.

2. Diliberto, *Hadley*, 79.

3. EH to Paul and Mary Pfeiffer, June 1927, PUL.

4. Pauline to EH, Dec. 15, 1926, JFK.

5. EH to Paul and Mary Pfeiffer, June 1927, PUL.

6. Mary Pfeiffer to EH, Sept. 7, 1927, JFK.

7. Mary Pfeiffer to EH, Sept. 7, 1927, JFK.

8. Mary Pfeiffer to EH, Sept. 7, 1927, JFK.

9. Mary Pfeiffer to EH, Sept. 7, 1927, JFK.

10. EH to Mary Pfeiffer, Oct. 1, 1927, PUL.

11. G. A. Pfeiffer to EH, Sept. 17, 1927, JFK.

12. G. A. Pfeiffer to EH, Sept. 17, 1927, JFK.

13. M. Miller, *Ernie*, 103.

14. Clarence Hemingway to EH, Aug. 8, 1927, JFK, in Reynolds, *American Homecoming* 137.

15. EH to Clarence Hemingway, Sept. 14, 1927, JFK, in Hemingway, *Selected Letters*, 258.

16. G. A. Pfeiffer to EH, Oct. 18, 1927, JFK.

17. G. A. Pfeiffer to EH, Oct. 18, 1927, JFK.

18. G. A. Pfeiffer to EH, Nov. 20, 1927, JFK.

19. Mary Pfeiffer to EH, Sept. 7, 1927, JFK.

20. EH to Mary Pfeiffer, Oct. 1, 1927, PUL.

21. G. A. Pfeiffer to EH, Jan. 22, 1928, JFK.

22. J. Hemingway, *Misadventures of a Fly Fisherman*, 6.

23. Virginia Pfeiffer to EH and Pauline, Mar. 1928, PUL.

24. Hadley to EH, Dec. 12, 1927, JFK, in Diliberto, *Hadley*, 252.

25. Pauline to EH, Feb. 3, 1928, JFK.

26. Hotchner, *Papa Hemingway*, 51.

27. Carr, *Dos Passos*, 231.

28. G. A. Pfeiffer to EH, Jan. 22, 1928, JFK.

29. EH to G. A. Pfeiffer, Mar. 16, 1928, JFK.

30. EH to Burton Emmett, Mar. 16, 1928, JFK.

31. Pauline to EH, ca. Mar. 21, 1928, JFK.

32. EH to Pauline, ca. Mar. 27, 1928, PUL.

Chapter 9: Homeward Bound (1928)

1. Wells, interview, Mar. 18, 1997; Spence, interview, Apr. 10, 1997.

2. Pauline to EH, May 20, 1928, JFK.

3. Matilda Pfeiffer, interview with the author, Piggott, Ark., Nov. 4, 2003; Dave Sanders, "Piggott Pandemonium: Hemingway Wasn't a Hit in This Town," *LGJ*, Spring–Summer 1975, 5 (Piggott Public Library).

4. Spence, interview, Apr. 10, 1997.

5. EH to Maxwell Perkins, May 31, PUL, in Hemingway, *Selected Letters*, 278.

6. EH to Grace Hemingway, June 1, 1928, PSU.

7. Sanders, "Piggott Pandemonium," 3.

8. McLendon, *Papa*, 49.

9. McLendon, *Papa*, 48; Charles Smart, interview with the author, Piggott,

Ark., Apr. 18, 1997; Russell, interview, Oct. 8, 1997; Kenneth Wells, interview with the author, Piggott, Ark., Mar. 18, 1997.

10. Lillie Jordan, interview with the author, Piggott, Ark., May 23, 1997.

11. Jordan, interview, May 23, 1997.

12. Lillie Jordan, interview with the author, Piggott, Ark., July 15, 1997.

13. Jordan, interview, May 23, 1997.

14. Hemingway, *Farewell to Arms,* 147.

15. EH to Waldo Peirce, June 17, 1928, Colby.

16. Mary Pfeiffer to EH, July 1, 1928, JFK.

17. EH to Mary Pfeiffer, July 2, 1928, PUL.

18. G. A. Pfeiffer to EH and Pauline, June 29, 1928, JFK.

19. G. A. Pfeiffer to EH, July 17, 1928, JFK.

20. EH to Waldo Peirce, July 5, 1928, Colby.

21. EH to Clarence and Grace Hemingway, July 4, 1928, JFK.

22. EH to Clarence and Grace Hemingway, July 4, 1928, JFK.

23. EH to Clarence and Grace Hemingway, July 15, 1928, JFK.

24. EH to Waldo Peirce, July 23, 1928, Colby.

25. Jordan, interview, May 23, 1997.

26. EH to Isabel Simmons Godolphin, Aug. 12, 1928, PUL, in Hemingway, *Selected Letters,* 283.

27. Pauline to Grace Hemingway, July 23, 1928, Lilly.

28. Pauline to EH, July 29, 1928 (misdated July 8, 1928), JFK.

29. Pauline to EH, July 31, 1928, JFK.

30. Pauline to EH, Aug. 9, 1928, JFK.

31. Jordan, interview, July 15, 1997.

32. Pauline to EH, Aug. 16, 1928, JFK.

33. Pauline to EH, Aug. 4 and 6, 1928, JFK.

34. Pauline to EH, Aug. 16, 1928, JFK.

Chapter 10: Family Matters (1928–1929)

1. Brian, *True Gen,* 79.

2. Brian, *True Gen,* 79.

3. Virginia Pfeiffer to EH and Pauline, Aug. 20, 1928, JFK.

4. Spence, interview, Apr. 10, 1997.

5. EH to Madelaine (Sunny) Hemingway, Oct. 1, 1928, PSU.

6. Ron Franscell, "Pfeiffer Barn Stores Only Memories," *Clay County Democrat,* May 30, 1979.

7. Dolph Moffatt, interview with the author, Campbell, Mo., Sept. 16, 1997.

8. EH to Madelaine (Sunny) Hemingway, Oct. 1, 1928, PSU.

9. G. A. Pfeiffer to EH, Oct. 16, 1928, JFK.

10. M. Miller, *Ernie,* 109–10.

11. M. Miller, *Ernie*, 110.

12. M. Miller, *Ernie*, 110.

13. M. Miller, *Ernie*, 112.

14. EH to Mary Pfeiffer, Dec. 13, 1928, PUL.

15. M. Miller, *Ernie*, 112.

16. Pauline to EH, Dec. 7, 1928, JFK.

17. M. Miller, *Ernie*, 115.

18. Mary Pfeiffer to EH, Dec. 12, 1928, JFK.

19. EH to Mary Pfeiffer, Dec. 13, 1928, PUL.

20. L. Hemingway, *My Brother*, 110–11.

21. Reynolds, *American Homecoming*, 211.

22. G. A. Pfeiffer to EH, Feb. 5, 1929, JFK.

23. EH to Paul and Mary Pfeiffer, Jan. 4, 1929, PUL.

24. EH to Mary Pfeiffer, March 4, 1929, PUL.

25. G. A. Pfeiffer to EH, Feb. 5, 1929, JFK.

26. EH to Perkins, July 31, 1929, in Bruccoli, *Only Thing That Counts*, 113.

27. EH to Perkins, July 31, 1929, in Bruccoli, *Only Thing That Counts*, 113.

28. G. A. Pfeiffer to EH, Feb. 28, 1929, JFK.

29. EH to Perkins, July 26, 1929, in Bruccoli, *Only Thing That Counts*, 110.

30. EH to Waldo Peirce, June 7, 1929, Colby.

31. G. A. Pfeiffer to EH, Feb. 28, 1929, JFK.

32. M. Miller, *Ernie*, 117.

33. "Ernest Hemingway, Author, Lands Sailfish during Trip at Key West: Noted Writer Featured in New York Paper," *Key West Citizen*, Mar. 11, 1929.

34. Paul Pfeiffer to EH and Pauline, Mar. 10, 1929, JFK.

35. EH to Paul and Mary Pfeiffer, Jan. 4, 1929, PUL.

36. Mary Pfeiffer to EH and Pauline, Mar. 30, 1929, PUL.

Chapter 11: Return to Paris (1929)

1. M. Miller, *Ernie*, 118–19.

2. Mary Pfeiffer to Pauline, June 5, 1929, PUL.

3. EH to Mary Pfeiffer, ca. May 11, 1929, JFK.

4. EH to Mary Pfeiffer, ca. May 11, 1929, JFK.

5. EH to Mary Pfeiffer, ca. May 11, 1929, JFK.

6. Hemingway, *Green Hills of Africa*, 141–42.

7. Guy Hickock to EH, July 23, 1929, JFK, in Reynolds, *1930s*, 16.

8. EH to Virginia Pfeiffer, Sept. 10, 1929, JFK.

9. Mary Pfeiffer to EH and Pauline, July 4, 1929, PUL.

10. Mary Pfeiffer to Pauline, July 15, 1929, PUL.

11. Mary Pfeiffer to EH and Pauline, Mar. 30, 1929, PUL.

12. Mary Pfeiffer to EH and Pauline, Mar. 30, 1929, PUL.

13. Paul Pfeiffer to EH and Pauline, Mar. 30, 1929, JFK.

14. Mary Pfeiffer to EH, May 4, 1929, JFK.

15. Mary Pfeiffer to EH, May 4, 1929, JFK.

16. Mary Pfeiffer to Pauline, July 15, 1929, PUL.

17. Mary Pfeiffer to EH and Pauline, Oct. 9, 1929. JFK.

18. Mary Pfeiffer to EH, May 4, 1929, JFK.

19. Paul Pfeiffer to EH, Oct. 14, 1929, JFK.

20. Archibald MacLeish to EH, June 24, 1929, JFK.

21. Sherwood Anderson to Ralph Church, Jan. 26, 1930, in Anderson, *Letters*, 205.

22. Callaghan, *That Summer in Paris*, 98–99.

23. Callaghan, *That Summer in Paris*, 161.

24. Maxwell Perkins to F. Scott Fitzgerald, Oct. 30, 1929, in Kuehl and Bryer, *Dear Scott/Dear Max*, 157.

25. Paul Pfeiffer to EH, Oct. 14, 1929, JFK.

26. G. A. Pfeiffer to Louise Pfeiffer, Dec. 21, 1929, PRF.

27. Mary Pfeiffer to Pauline, Aug. 17, 1929, PUL.

28. EH to Mary Pfeiffer, June 1927, PUL.

29. Gustavus A. Pfeiffer to Louise Pfeiffer, Dec. 21, 1929, PRF.

30. Virginia Pfeiffer to EH and Pauline, Sept. 29, 1929, JFK.

31. Sara Murphy to Pauline, Oct. 12, 1929, in L. Miller, *Letters from the Lost Generation*, 45.

32. Gerald Murphy to EH and Pauline, Oct. 12, 1929, in L. Miller, *Letters from the Lost Generation*, 44.

Chapter 12: A Place to Call Home (1930–1931)

1. G. A. Pfeiffer to EH and PH, Jan. 1930, JFK.

2. EH to Grace Hemingway, Jan. 27, 1930, PSU.

3. Donaldson, *Archibald MacLeish*, 199.

4. EH to Paul and Mary Pfeiffer, Apr. 23, 1930, PUL.

5. Mary Pfeiffer to EH and Pauline, Jan. 20, 1930, JFK.

6. EH to Guy Hickok, Dec. 5, 1930, PUL.

7. Paul Pfeiffer to EH and Pauline, Mar. 20, 1930, JFK.

8. G. A. Pfeiffer to Family, Feb. 20, 1943, PRF.

9. EH to G. A. Pfeiffer, Mar. 17, 1930, JFK.

10. G. A. Pfeiffer to A. Matas Teixidor, June 3, 1930, JFK.

11. Donaldson, *Archibald MacLeish*, 200.

12. EH to Waldo Peirce, June 1, 1930, Colby.

13. Virginia Pfeiffer to EH and Pauline, Mar. 1930, JFK.

14. G. A. Pfeiffer to EH, June 3, 1930, JFK.

15. J. Hemingway, *Misadventures of a Fly Fisherman*, 13.

16. EH to Archibald MacLeish, June 30, 1930, Manuscript Division, Library of Congress, in Hemingway, *Selected Letters*, 325.

17. J. Hemingway, *Misadventures of a Fly Fisherman*, 13–14.

18. EH to Archibald MacLeish, June 8, 1930, Manuscript Division, Library of Congress.

19. Mary Pfeiffer to Pauline, July 30, 1930, PUL.

20. J. Hemingway, *Misadventures of a Fly Fisherman*, 16–17.

21. Brian, *True Gen*, 82.

22. EH to Guy Hickok, Dec. 5, 1930, PUL, in Hemingway, *Selected Letters*, 333–34.

23. Donaldson, *Archibald MacLeish*, 207.

24. EH to Mary Pfeiffer, Jan. 28, 1931, PUL.

25. Mary Pfeiffer to EH, 1931, JFK.

26. EH to Karl Pfeiffer, Jan. 1, 1931, Stanford University Libraries.

27. EH to Karl Pfeiffer, Jan. 1, 1931, Stanford University Libraries.

28. Sanders, "Piggott Pandemonium," 5.

29. Pauline to Grace Hemingway, Sept. 10, 1930, Lilly.

30. Baker, *Ernest Hemingway*, 219.

31. Kert, *Hemingway Women*, 230.

32. "Mrs. Hemingway Is Newest Holder of Fish Record Here," *Key West Citizen*, Feb. 4, 1931.

33. "Visitor Nearly Drowned in the City Park Pool," *Key West Citizen*, Mar. 19, 1931.

34. G. A. Pfeiffer to Emma Merner, July 31, 1931, PRF.

35. G. A. Pfeiffer to Emma Merner, July 31, 1931, PRF.

36. McLendon, *Papa*, 74.

37. "To 'Love at First Sight' for Key West, Ernest Hemingway Attributes His Coming Here," *Key West Citizen*, Apr. 30, 1931.

38. McLendon, *Papa*, 76.

39. Pauline to Dr. Don Carlos Guffey, May 6, 1931, HGW.

40. Pauline to EH, May 21, 1931, JFK.

41. G. A. Pfeiffer to EH, July 16, 1931, JFK.

42. Diliberto, *Hadley*, 262.

43. Diliberto, *Hadley*, 263.

Chapter 13: Chaos Abounds (1931–1932)

1. Paul Pfeiffer to EH and Pauline, June 18, 1931, JFK.

2. Paul Pfeiffer to EH and Pauline, June 18, 1931, JFK.

3. EH to Paul and Mary Pfeiffer, Aug. 31, 1931, PUL.

4. Paul Pfeiffer to EH and Pauline, Sept. 18, 1931, PUL.

5. EH to Guy Hickock, Dec. 12, 1931, private collection, in Reynolds, *1930s*, 78.

6. Baker, *Ernest Hemingway*, 222.

7. G. A. Pfeiffer to Don Carlos Guffey, Oct. 21, 1931, JFK.

8. EH to Mary Pfeiffer, Nov. 12, 1931, PUL.

9. Reynolds, *1930s*, 77; G. Hemingway, *Papa*, 17.

10. EH to Mary Pfeiffer, Nov. 12, 1931, PUL.

11. Pauline to Grace Hemingway, Nov. 26, 1931, Lilly.

12. EH to Paul and Mary Pfeiffer, Nov. 16, 1931, PUL.

13. Pauline to EH, Nov. 30, 1931, JFK.

14. Sanders, "Piggott Pandemonium," 5.

15. Sanders, "Piggott Pandemonium," 3.

16. Sanders, "Piggott Pandemonium," 3.

17. Sanders, "Piggott Pandemonium," 4.

18. M. Pfeiffer, interview. May 8, 1997.

19. "To 'Love At First Sight' for Key West."

20. EH to Paul and Mary Pfeiffer, Jan. 5, 1932, PUL, in Hemingway, *Selected Letters*, 350.

21. EH to Paul and Mary Pfeiffer, Jan. 5, 1932, PUL.

22. Mary Pfeiffer to EH and Pauline, Mar. 12, 1932, JFK.

23. Mary Pfeiffer to EH and Pauline, June 7, 1932, JFK.

24. Pauline to EH, June 26, 1932, JFK.

25. EH to Guy Hickok, Oct. 14, 1932, PUL, in Hemingway, *Selected Letters*, 372.

26. EH to Dr. Don Carlos Guffey, July 26, 1932, HGW.

27. A mixture of ergot and apiol was used in the treatment of painful or missing menstrual periods or other menstrual cycle irregularities. In small quantities, it could also cause abortion in pregnant women.

28. Gerald Murphy to Archibald MacLeish, Sept. 8, 1932, Manuscript Division, Library of Congress.

29. Meyers, *Hemingway*, 160–80.

30. G. A. Pfeiffer to EH, Sept. 26, 1932, JFK.

31. Kert, *Hemingway Women*, 244.

32. Pauline to EH, Nov. 8, 1932, JFK.

33. Ernest to Grace Hemingway and Family, Dec. 19, 1932, PSU.

34. Debbie Miller, "Only Traces of Area Ties Linger," *Paragould Daily Press*, Jan. 8, 1989.

35. Sanders, "Piggott Pandemonium," 5.

36. Linda Houser, telephone interview with the author, Dec. 2004.

37. "Noted Writer Declines to Attend Piggott Premiere of Movie Version of Book," *Arkansas Democrat*, Dec. 5, 1932.

38. "Noted Writer Declines."

39. "Noted Writer Declines"; EH to Ralph Stitt, Nov. 1932, JFK.

40. "'A Farewell to Arms'" Has Sad Ending," Associated Press, Dec. 6, 1932.

41. EH to Ralph Stitt, November 1932, JFK.

42. G. A. Pfeiffer to EH, Dec. 8, 1932, JFK.

43. EH to G. A. Pfeiffer, Dec. 9, 1932, JFK.

44. G. A. Pfeiffer to EH, Dec. 10, 1932, JFK.

45. "'Farewell to Arms,' Hemingway Story, Triumph for Film Art," *New York American,* Dec. 9, 1932.

46. "'Farewell to Arms' Poignant Picture," *Daily News,* Dec. 9, 1932.

47. "'Farewell to Arms' Masterpiece," *Daily Mirror,* Dec. 9, 1932.

48. "Helen Hayes, Gary Cooper and Adolphe Menjou in a Film of Hemingway's 'Farewell to Arms,'" *New York Times,* Dec. 9, 1932.

49. L. Hemingway, *My Brother,* 123.

50. Wells, interview, Mar. 18, 1997.

51. "'A Farewell to Arms' Now Showing at New Franklin," *Piggott Banner,* Dec. 23, 1932.

52. "Over $100 Donated for Charity Work;" "Mrs. Virgil Smith Makes Record Sales," *Piggott Banner,* Dec. 23, 1932.

53. Hays, "Interview with Dr. John H. Jones," 36.

54. "Deepwater Resident Recalls 'Ernest,'" *Clinton Daily Democrat,* Clinton, Mo., Jan. 7, 1983.

55. Mary Pfeiffer to EH, Oct. 31, 1933, JFK.

Chapter 14: In Good Times and Bad (1933)

1. Bruccoli, *Only Thing That Counts,* 180–81.

2. G. A. Pfeiffer to Family, May 1, 1933, PRF.

3. Pauline to EH, Apr. 23, 1933, JFK.

4. EH to Mary Pfeiffer, Mar. 23, 1933, PUL.

5. Jack Hemingway, Hemingway Centennial Panel Discussion, Oak Park, Ill., July 21, 1999.

6. EH to Arnold Gingrich, Mar. 13, 1933, PUL, in Hemingway, *Selected Letters,* 511.

7. Baker, *Ernest Hemingway,* 240.

8. G. A. Pfeiffer to Family, May 1, 1933, PRF.

9. Karl Pfeiffer to EH, May 2, 1933, JFK.

10. G. A. Pfeiffer to Family, May 1, 1933, PRF.

11. Pauline to EH, Apr. 20, 1933, JFK.

12. Pauline to EH, May 15, 1933, JFK.

13. Pauline to EH, July 1933, JFK.

14. Pauline to EH, Apr. 28, 1933, JFK.

15. Pauline to EH, Apr. 28, 1933, JFK.

16. Kert, *Hemingway Women,* 249.

17. Kert, *Hemingway Women,* 250.

18. Virginia Pfeiffer to EH, Feb. 1999, JFK.

19. EH to Mary Pfeiffer, Mar. 23, 1933, PUL.

20. Mary Pfeiffer to EH, May 4, 1933, JFK.

21. Brian, *True Gen*, 90.

22. G. A. Pfeiffer to EH, June 1, 1933, JFK.

23. Mary Pfeiffer to Pauline and EH, July 1933, JFK.

24. Virginia Pfeiffer to Pauline, June 25, 1933, JFK.

25. M. Pfeiffer, interview, Mar. 28, 1997.

26. Mary Pfeiffer to EH, May 4, 1933, JFK.

27. Mary Pfeiffer to Pauline and EH, July 1933, JFK.

28. Paul Pfeiffer to EH and Pauline, July 17, 1933, JFK.

29. G. A. Pfeiffer to EH, July 20, 1933, JFK.

30. G. A. Pfeiffer to EH and Pauline, July 18, 1933, JFK.

31. Archibald MacLeish to EH, Apr. 7, 1932, in MacLeish, *Letters,* 247.

32. Brian, *True Gen*, 95.

33. EH to Mary Pfeiffer, Oct. 16, 1933, PUL, in Hemingway, *Selected Letters*, 397.

34. Pauline to EH, Oct. 19, 1933, JFK.

35. Pauline to EH, Oct. 18, 1933, JFK.

36. EH to Pauline, ca. Oct. 17, 1933, JFK.

37. EH to Pauline, Oct. 20, 1933, JFK.

38. Pauline to EH, Oct. 22, 1933, JFK.

39. Paul Pfeiffer to EH, Oct. 16, 1933, JFK.

40. Paul Pfeiffer to EH, Sept. 19, 1933, JFK.

41. Pauline to EH, Oct. 18, 1933, JFK.

42. EH to Mary Pfeiffer, Oct. 16, 1933, PUL.

43. Hemingway, "Paris Letter," 22.

44. Stein, *Autobiography of Alice B. Toklas,* 267–68.

45. Paul Pfeiffer to Pauline, Sept. 19, 1933, JFK.

46. EH to Mary Pfeiffer, Oct. 16, 1933, PUL.

47. Mary Pfeiffer to Pauline, Oct. 31, 1933, JFK.

48. Mary Pfeiffer to Pauline, Oct. 31, 1933, JFK.

Chapter 15: On Safari (1933–1934)

1. G. A. Pfeiffer to EH, Jan. 24, 1934, JFK.

2. Pauline Hemingway, "An African Safari 1933," diary entry, Dec. 23, 1933, Stanford University Library.

3. Virginia Pfeiffer to EH and Pauline, Jan. 1934, JFK.

4. EH to Mary Pfeiffer, Oct. 16, 1933, PUL.

5. Hemingway, *Green Hills of Africa,* 38.

6. P. Hemingway, diary entry, Dec. 29, 1933; Hemingway, *Green Hills of Africa,* 36–38.

7. Hemingway, *Green Hills of Africa,* 66.

8. P. Hemingway, diary entries, Feb. 6–16, 1934.

9. Hemingway, *Green Hills of Africa,* 205.

10. McLendon, *Papa,* 105.

11. G. A. Pfeiffer, data and comments on Ernest and Pauline Hemingway African Hunt, Apr. 19, 1934, JFK.

12. Invoice from Abelardo Linares, Madrid, Dec. 29, 1933, per order, Oct. 25, 1933, JFK.

13. Reynolds, *1930s,* 169.

14. G. A. Pfeiffer to EH, Apr. 30, 1934, JFK.

15. Samuelson, *With Hemingway,* 22–23.

16. EH to Arnold Gingrich, May 25, 1934, PUL, in Hemingway, *Selected Letters,* 404.

17. G. A. Pfeiffer to EH, June 5, 1934, JFK.

18. EH to Waldo Peirce, ca. May 26, 1934, in Hemingway, *Selected Letters,* 405–6.

19. Baker, *Ernest Hemingway,* 262.

20. Baker, *Ernest Hemingway,* 272–73.

21. Brian, *True Gen,* 92.

22. Brian, *True Gen,* 95–96.

23. EH to F. Scott Fitzgerald, May 28, 1934, PUL, in Hemingway, *Selected Letters,* 408.

24. EH to F. Scott Fitzgerald, May 28, 1934, PUL, in Hemingway, *Selected Letters,* 269.

25. Hemingway, *Green Hills of Africa,* 46.

26. Hemingway, *Green Hills of Africa,* 152.

27. Pauline to EH, May 31, 1934, JFK.

28. Pauline to EH, June 2, 1934, JFK.

29. Pauline to EH, June 10, 1934, JFK.

30. Pauline to EH, June 9, 1934, JFK.

31. Mary Pfeiffer to EH and Pauline, July 18, 1934, JFK.

32. Mary Pfeiffer to EH and Pauline, July 18, 1934, JFK.

33. G. A. Pfeiffer to EH, Aug. 10, 1934, JFK.

34. EH to Mary Pfeiffer (unsent), Aug. 14, 1934, JFK.

35. Samuelson, *With Hemingway,* 54.

36. G. A. Pfeiffer to EH, Apr. 30, 1934, JFK.

37. Pauline to EH, Sept. 15, 1934, JFK.

38. Pauline to EH, Sept. 18, 1934, JFK.

39. Pauline to EH, Sept. 20, 1934, JFK.

40. EH to Mary Pfeiffer, Aug. 14, 1934, JFK.

41. EH to Waldo Peirce, May 26, 1934, Colby, in Hemingway, *Selected Letters,* 406.

42. Pauline to EH, Oct. 7, 1934, JFK.

43. Pauline to EH, Oct. 7, 1934, JFK.

44. Pauline to EH, Oct. 7, 1934, JFK.

45. G. A. Pfeiffer to EH, June 5, 1934, JFK.

46. G. A. Pfeiffer to EH, June 5, 1935, JFK.

47. Mary Pfeiffer to EH, July 18, 1934, JFK.

48. EH to Mary Pfeiffer, ca. Aug. 14, 1934, JFK.

49. Paul Pfeiffer to Pauline and EH, Dec. 10, 1934, JFK.

50. G. A. Pfeiffer to C. Leonard Pfeiffer, Christmas 1934, PRF.

Chapter 16: More New Places (1935)

1. Hemingway, "Sights of Whitehead Street," 25.

2. McLendon, *Papa*, 135.

3. G. A. Pfeiffer to EH, Jan 26, 1935, JFK.

4. G. A. Pfeiffer to EH, Mar. 7, 1935, JFK.

5. Donnelly, *Sara and Gerald*, 93–94.

6. Pauline to Dawn Powell, Feb. 28, 1935, JFK.

7. Pauline to EH, Apr. 22, 1935, JFK.

8. Pauline to EH, May 12, 1935, JFK.

9. EH to Jane Mason, June 3, 1935, JFK.

10. G. A. Pfeiffer to EH, May 23, 1935, JFK.

11. G. A. Pfeiffer to EH, May 27, 1935, JFK.

12. Pauline to EH, June 14, 1935, JFK.

13. Pauline to EH, June 14, 1935, JFK.

14. Pauline to EH, Aug. 11, 1935, JFK.

15. Helen Keller to G. A. and Louise Pfeiffer, Nov. 9, 1939, American Foundation for the Blind.

16. *Bridgeport Post*, Bridgeport, Conn., July 31, 1938.

17. Louise Pfeiffer, interview with the author, Cambridge, Mass., Apr. 4, 2000.

18. M. Pfeiffer, interview, Mar. 28, 1997.

19. Jay McEvoy, interview with the author, San Francisco, Calif., Mar. 9, 1998.

20. EH to Perkins, Dec. 17, 1935, in Bruccoli, *Only Thing That Counts,* 229.

21. EH to F. Scott Fitzgerald, Dec. 16, 1935, PUL, in Hemingway, *Selected Letters,* 424.

22. EH to F. Scott Fitzgerald, Dec. 21, 1935, PUL, in Hemingway, *Selected Letters,* 428.

23. Karl Pfeiffer to EH, Nov. 28, 1935, JFK.

24. Oliver, *Ernest Hemingway A to Z,* 26.

25. EH to Mary Pfeiffer, Jan. 26, 1936, PUL.

Chapter 17: More New Faces (1936)

1. EH to Mary Pfeiffer, Jan. 26, 1936, PUL, in Hemingway, *Selected Letters*, 435–36.

2. EH to Sara Murphy, Feb. 11, 1936, in L. Miller, *Letters from the Lost Generation*, 156.

3. G. A. Pfeiffer to Family, Feb. 4, 1936, PRF.

4. G. A. Pfeiffer to EH, Mar. 1, 1936, JFK.

5. EH to Mary Pfeiffer, Jan. 26, 1936, PUL.

6. EH to Mary Pfeiffer, Jan. 26, 1936, PUL.

7. Pauline to EH, May 10, 1936, JFK.

8. Pauline to EH, May 9, 1936, JFK.

9. Brian, *True Gen*, 305.

10. EH to Mary Pfeiffer, Jan. 26, 1936, PUL.

11. EH to Mary Pfeiffer, Jan. 26, 1936, PUL.

12. EH to Maxwell Perkins, Feb. 7, 1936, PUL, in Hemingway, *Selected Letters*, 438.

13. F. Scott Fitzgerald to EH, Aug. 1936, in Fitzgerald, *Letters*, 311.

14. Ernest Hemingway, "The Snows of Kilimanjaro," in Hemingway, *Short Stories*, 59.

15. Hemingway, "Snows of Kilimanjaro," 58.

16. Hemingway, "Snows of Kilimanjaro," 60.

17. Hemingway, "Snows of Kilimanjaro," 54–55.

18. Hemingway, "Snows of Kilimanjaro," 60–61.

19. Hemingway, *To Have and Have Not*, 185.

20. Vaill, *Everybody Was So Young*, 273.

21. Vaill, *Everybody Was So Young*, 274.

22. Reynolds, *1930s*, 234.

23. EH to Jane Mason, Aug. 2, 1936, JFK.

24. EH to Jane Mason, Aug. 24, 1935, JFK.

25. Wilson, "Tenantry Comes Forward."

26. EH to Mary Pfeiffer, Aug. 11, 1936, PUL.

27. McLendon, *Papa*, 145.

28. Powell, *Diaries*, 127.

29. Powell, *Diaries*, 128.

30. Gingrich, "Scott, Ernest and Whoever," 374.

31. Gingrich, "Scott, Ernest and Whoever," 374.

32. Gingrich, "Scott, Ernest and Whoever," 374.

33. Arnold Gingrich to Jane Mason, Feb. 8, 1937, JFK.

34. Hemingway, *To Have and Have Not*, 245.

35. McLendon, *Papa*, 165.

36. Brian, *True Gen*, 101.

37. Brian, *True Gen*, 102.

Chapter 18: Trouble Ahead (1937)

1. Martha Gellhorn to Pauline, Jan. 14, 1937, in Moorehead, *Gellhorn,* 105.

2. Baker, *Ernest Hemingway,* 299.

3. Vaill, *Everybody Was So Young,* 280.

4. McEvoy, interview, Mar. 9, 1998.

5. Gerald Murphy to Pauline, Jan. 22, 1937, JFK, in L. Miller, *Letters from the Lost Generation,* 182.

6. Pauline to EH, Jan. 22, 1937, JFK.

7. Virginia Pfeiffer to EH, Feb. 9, 1937, JFK.

8. Gerald Murphy to Pauline, Jan. 22, 1937, JFK, in L. Miller, *Letters from the Lost Generation,* 182.

9. F. Scott Fitzgerald to Gerald and Sara Murphy, Jan. 31, 1937, HMD, in L. Miller, *Letters from the Lost Generation,* 184.

10. Pauline to Gerald and Sara Murphy, Feb. 8, 1937, HMD, in L. Miller, *Letters from the Lost Generation,* 187.

11. Franklin, *Bullfighter from Brooklyn,* 215.

12. Franklin, *Bullfighter from Brooklyn,* 214.

13. EH to Paul and Mary Pfeiffer, Feb. 9, 1937, PUL, in Hemingway, *Selected Letters,* 457–58.

14. EH to Paul and Mary Pfeiffer, Feb. 9, 1937, PUL.

15. EH to Paul and Mary Pfeiffer, Feb. 9, 1937, PUL.

16. McEvoy, interview, Mar. 9, 1998.

17. McEvoy, interview, Mar. 9, 1998.

18. Moorehead, *Gellhorn,* 106.

19. Reynolds, *1930s,* 260, 301.

20. Jack Latimer, interview with Bernice Kert, Apr. 5, 1979, in Kert, *Hemingway Women,* 293.

21. Pauline to EH, Mar. 15, 1937, JFK.

22. Pauline to EH, Apr. 20, 1937, JFK.

23. Pauline to EH, Apr. 27, 1937, JFK.

24. G. A. Pfeiffer to EH, May 31, 1937, JFK.

25. Pauline to EH, June 1937, JFK.

26. EH to Mary Pfeiffer, Aug. 2, 1937, PUL, in Hemingway, *Selected Letters,* 460–61.

27. EH to Mary Pfeiffer, Aug. 2, 1937, PUL, in Hemingway, *Selected Letters,* 460–61.

28. EH to Mary Pfeiffer, Aug. 2, 1937, PUL, in Hemingway, *Selected Letters,* 460–61.

29. Gerald Murphy to Sara Murphy, Sept. 4–7, 1937, HMD, in L. Miller, *Letters from the Lost Generation,* 199.

30. Baker, *Ernest Hemingway,* 322.

31. Reynolds, *1930s,* 281.

32. Sherwood Anderson to Henry Schumann, May 18, 1938, in Anderson, *Letters,* 397.

33. Paul Pfeiffer to EH, Nov. 15, 1937, JFK.

34. Katy Dos Passos to Sara Murphy, Nov. 12, 1937, UVA, in L. Miller, *Letters from the Lost Generation,* 203.

35. Jay Allen to Carlos Baker, March 6, 1963, in Kert, *Hemingway Women,* 312.

36. G. A. Pfeiffer to EH, Dec. 24, 1937, JFK.

Chapter 19: The Marriage Unravels (1938)

1. EH to Hadley, Jan. 31, 1938, PUL, in Hemingway, *Selected Letters,* 462.

2. EH to Maxwell Perkins, mid-Feb. 1938, in Bruccoli, *Only Thing That Counts,* 257.

3. G. A. Pfeiffer to EH, Apr. 25, 1938, JFK.

4. Pauline to EH, Apr. 29, 1938, JFK.

5. EH to Mike and Helen Lerner, May 25, 1938, JFK.

6. "Hemingway-Smart Accident Case Appears in Local Police Court," *Key West Citizen,* June 2, 1938.

7. Pauline and EH to Paul and Mary Pfeiffer, June 11–13, 1938, PUL.

8. Pauline and EH to Paul and Mary Pfeiffer, June 11–13, 1938, PUL.

9. EH to Maxwell Perkins, May 5, 1938, PUL, in Hemingway, *Selected Letters,* 467.

10. EH to Mary Pfeiffer, July 28, 1939, PUL, in Hemingway, *Selected Letters,* 494–95.

11. Donaldson, *Archibald MacLeish,* 276.

12. EH to Mary Pfeiffer, Aug. 18, 1938, PUL.

13. EH to Maxwell Perkins, July 12, 1938, PUL, in Hemingway, *Selected Letters,* 471.

14. Pauline to EH, Sept. 2, 1938, JFK.

15. Pauline to EH, Sept. 17, 1938, JFK.

16. EH to Arnold Gingrich, Oct. 22, 1938, PUL, in Hemingway, *Selected Letters,* 472.

17. Pauline to EH, Oct. 18, 1938, JFK.

18. EH to Maxwell Perkins, Oct. 28, 1938, PUL, in Hemingway, *Selected Letters,* 474.

19. "Hemingway's Spanish War Play, Four New Short Stories Out," *Key West Citizen,* Oct. 25, 1938 (reprint of Associated Press review by John Selby).

20. EH to Maxwell Perkins, Oct. 28, 1938, PUL, in Hemingway, *Selected Letters,* 474.

21. McEvoy, interview, Mar. 9, 1998.

22. EH to Pauline, Jan. 4, 1939, JFK.

23. EH to Mary Pfeiffer, Feb. 6, 1939, PUL, in Hemingway, *Selected Letters,* 475–78.

24. J. Hemingway, *Misadventures of a Fly Fisherman,* 30–31.

25. Patrick Hemingway, interview with Bernice Kert, Aug. 1978, in Kert, *Hemingway Women*, 323.

26. EH to Mary Pfeiffer, Feb. 6, 1939, PUL.

27. EH to Mary Pfeiffer, Feb. 6, 1939, PUL.

Chapter 20: The End of Something (1939)

1. EH to Thomas Shevlin, Apr. 4, 1939, PUL, in Hemingway, *Selected Letters*, 484.

2. EH to Maxwell Perkins, Mar. 25, 1939, PUL, in Hemingway, *Selected Letters*, 482.

3. Pauline to EH, Feb. 28, 1939, PUL.

4. Pauline to EH, Apr. 17, 1939, JFK.

5. Pauline to EH, May 28, 1939, JFK.

6. Pauline to EH, June 23, 1939, JFK.

7. Pauline to EH, June 23, 1939, JFK.

8. EH to Patrick Hemingway, June 30, 1939, Seymour Library, Knox College, Galesburg, Ill., in Hemingway, *Selected Letters*, 486.

9. Pauline to EH, July 6, 1939, JFK.

10. EH to Pauline, July 7, 1939, JFK.

11. Pauline to EH, July 8, 1939, JFK.

12. Pauline to EH, July 8, 1939, JFK.

13. Pauline to EH, July 8, 1939, JFK.

14. Pauline to EH, July 9, 1939, JFK.

15. Pauline to EH, July 12, 1939, JFK.

16. EH to Mary Pfeiffer, July 21, PUL, in Hemingway, *Selected Letters*, 491–92.

17. Pauline to EH, Aug. 5, 1939, JFK.

18. Pauline to EH, Aug. 10, 1939, JFK.

19. "Hemingway Will Go to Europe in Event of War," *Key West Citizen*, Aug. 24, 1939.

20. Diliberto, *Hadley*, 264.

21. J. Hemingway, *Misadventures of a Fly Fisherman*, 35.

22. EH to Hadley, Dec. 1, 1939, JFK.

23. EH to Mary Pfeiffer, Dec. 12, 1939, PUL, in Hemingway, *Selected Letters*, 499–500.

24. Mary Pfeiffer to EH, n.d., PUL.

Chapter 21: Acrimony and Alimony (1940–1941)

1. L. Hemingway, *My Brother*, 225–26.

2. M. Pfeiffer, interview, Mar. 28, 1997.

3. EH to Edna Gellhorn, Sept. 28, 1940, JFK.

4. EH to Maxwell Perkins, ca. Jan. 14, 1940, in Bruccoli, *Only Thing that Counts*, 277.

5. Baker, *Ernest Hemingway*, 349.

6. Kert, *Hemingway Women*, 421–22.

7. Kert, *Hemingway Women*, 422.

8. EH to Maxwell Perkins, May 18, 1943, in Bruccoli, *Only Thing That Counts*, 324.

9. McLendon, *Papa*, 201.

10. EH to Martha Gellhorn, late May 1940, JFK.

11. Baker, *Ernest Hemingway*, 349.

12. EH to Clara Spiegel, Aug. 23, 1940, PUL, in Hemingway, *Selected Letters*, 511.

13. EH to Maxwell Perkins, Aug. 26, 1940, PUL, in Hemingway, *Selected Letters*, 515–16.

14. EH to G. A. Pfeiffer, Aug. 28, 1940, JFK.

15. Note from EH with manuscript of *For Whom the Bell Tolls*, given to G. A. Pfeiffer, Oct. 1940, JFK.

16. G. A. Pfeiffer to EH, Dec. 3, 1940, JFK.

17. Diary entry, Oct. 24, 1940, in Powell, *Diaries*, 182.

18. G. Hemingway, *Papa*, 23.

19. G. Hemingway, *Papa*, 93.

20. McEvoy, interview, Mar. 9, 1998.

21. McLendon, *Papa*, 203.

22. "Divorce Granted Mrs. Hemingway: Key West Author Charged with Desertion; Suit Uncontested," *Key West Citizen*, Nov. 5, 1940.

23. McLendon, *Papa*, 202–3.

24. Kert, *Hemingway Women*, 345.

25. Dwight McDonald, review of *For Whom the Bell Tolls*, *Partisan Review*, Jan. 8, 1941, in Meyers, *Hemingway*, 326.

26. Dorothy Parker, review of *For Whom the Bell Tolls*, *PM*, Oct. 20, 1940, in Meyers, *Hemingway*, 315.

27. EH to Hadley, Dec. 1, 1939, PUL, in Diliberto, *Hadley*, 267.

28. Kert, *Hemingway Women*, 422.

29. Pauline to EH, Nov. 1940, in Fuentes, *Hemingway in Cuba*, 327–28.

30. Paul Pfeiffer to EH, Dec. 13, 1940, JFK.

31. Ruth Reynolds, "Love Collaborates with Hemingway," *New York Daily News*, Dec. 8, 1940.

32. EH to Hadley, Dec. 26, 1940, PUL, in Hemingway, *Selected Letters*, 521.

33. "Hemingway Here; Going to China," *Key West Citizen*, Dec. 21, 1940.

34. EH to Mary Welsh, Sept. 28, 1945, PUL, in Hemingway, *Selected Letters*, 602–3.

35. P. Hemingway, interview with Kert, Aug. 1978, in Kert, *Hemingway Women*, 269.

36. G. Hemingway, *Papa,* 17–18.

37. G. Hemingway, *Papa,* 18.

38. Gregory Hemingway, interview with the author, Piggott, Ark., July 4, 1999.

39. G. Hemingway, *Papa,* 19.

40. EH to Mary Welsh, Sept. 28, 1945, PUL, in Hemingway, *Selected Letters,* 602–3.

41. EH to Pauline, June 9, 1941, PUL, in Hemingway, *Selected Letters,* 524.

42. Pauline to EH, 1941, JFK.

43. EH to Pauline, June 9, 1941, PUL.

44. Baker, *Ernest Hemingway,* 366.

45. Reynolds, *Final Years,* 36.

46. Perkins to EH, Apr. 4, 1941, in Bruccoli, *Only Thing That Counts,* 307.

47. EH to Maxwell Perkins, Apr. 29, 1941, in Bruccoli, *Only Thing That Counts,* 309.

48. EH to Pauline, June 9, 1941, PUL, in Hemingway, *Selected Letters,* 524.

49. EH to Pauline, July 19, 1941, PUL, in Hemingway, *Selected Letters,* 525.

50. EH to Pauline, July 19, 1941, PUL, in Hemingway, *Selected Letters,* 525.

51. Perkins to EH, Aug. 29, 1941, in Bruccoli, *Only Thing That Counts,* 311.

Chapter 22: War on the Home Front (1942–1945)

1. L. Pfeiffer, interview, Apr. 4, 2000.

2. Diary entry, Nov. 5, 1942, in Powell, *Diaries,* 203.

3. G. A. Pfeiffer to Pauline, July 6, 1942, in "The Ownership and Distribution of the Ernest Hemingway Manuscripts," exhibit 3 of Estate of Gustavus A. Pfeiffer.

4. Pauline to G. A. Pfeiffer, July 26, 1942, in "Ownership and Distribution."

5. G. A. Pfeiffer Note to the File, Sept. 15, 1942, in "Ownership and Distribution."

6. Pauline to Patrick Hemingway, Oct. 1, 1943, PUL.

7. G. A. Pfeiffer to Family, Jan. 19, 1945, PRF.

8. Pauline to Patrick Hemingway, Nov. 21, 1942, PUL.

9. Pauline to Patrick Hemingway, Jan. 13, 1945, PUL.

10. Kert, *Hemingway Women,* 374.

11. Kert, *Hemingway Women,* 344.

12. Pauline to Patrick Hemingway, Jan. 13, 1945, PUL.

13. Pauline to Patrick Hemingway, Nov. 21, 1942, PUL.

14. Pauline to Patrick Hemingway, Jan. 13, 1945, PUL.

15. Pauline to Patrick Hemingway, Oct. 23, 1944, PUL.

16. Pauline to EH, Dec. 8, 1943, JFK.

17. Laura Archera Huxley, interview with the author, Los Angeles, Calif., Mar 5, 1998.

18. Huxley, *You Are Not the Target,* 150–53.

19. Huxley, interview, Mar. 5, 1998.

20. G. A. Pfeiffer to Family, Jan.19, 1945, PRF.

21. G. A. Pfeiffer to Family, Dec. 18, 1943, including Oct. 3, 1943, letter from Alfred Bachschmid, PRF.

22. G. A. Pfeiffer to Family, Dec. 18, 1943.

23. Kert, *Hemingway Women,* 373.

24. EH to Maxwell Perkins, Nov. 16, 1943, PUL, in Hemingway, *Selected Letters,* 554.

25. EH to Maxwell Perkins, Nov. 16, 1943, PUL, in Hemingway, *Selected Letters,* 553–54.

26. EH to Perkins, May 18, 1943, in Bruccoli, *Only Thing That Counts,* 324.

27. EH to Perkins, May 18, 1943.

28. Baker, *Ernest Hemingway,* 370; John J. McCusker, "Comparing the Purchasing Power of Money in the United States (or Colonies) from 1665 to 2003," Economic History Services, 2004, http://www.eh.net/hmit/ppowerusd/.

29. G. A. Pfeiffer to Family, Dec. 18, 1943, PRF.

30. Pauline to Patrick Hemingway, Jan. 27, 1944, PUL.

31. G. A. Pfeiffer to Family, Dec. 18, 1943.

32. Dolph Moffatt, interview, Sept. 16, 1997.

33. Jim Poole, interview with the author, Piggott, Ark., June 9, 1997.

34. Pauline to Henry (a friend), 1945, JFK.

35. Pauline to Patrick Hemingway, Oct. 5, 1944, PUL.

36. Pauline to Patrick Hemingway, Oct. 5, 1944, PUL.

37. J. Hemingway, *Misadventures of a Fly Fisherman,* 175.

38. Baker, *Ernest Hemingway,* 393.

39. Baker, *Ernest Hemingway,* 441.

40. Baker, *Ernest Hemingway,* 443.

41. M. Hemingway, *How It Was,* 133–34.

42. M. Hemingway, *How It Was,* 133–34.

43. Pauline to EH, Mar. 17, 1945, JFK.

44. Pauline to EH, Mar. 17, 1945, JFK.

45. Diliberto, *Hadley,* 271.

Chapter 23: New Beginnings (1946–1951)

1. Pauline to EH, May 16, 1945, JFK.

2. Virginia Pfeiffer to Mary Hemingway, Aug. 29, 1946, JFK.

3. Pauline to Patrick Hemingway, Jan. 16, 1946, PUL.

4. Pauline to Patrick Hemingway, Jan. 23, 1947, JFK.

5. Pauline to Patrick Hemingway, May 7, 1946, PUL.

6. Fountain and Brazeau, *Remembering Elizabeth Bishop,* 104.

7. EH to Patrick Hemingway, Apr. 13, 1946, in Kert, *Hemingway Women,* 425.

8. EH to Mary Hemingway, June 1946, JFK.

9. EH to Patrick Hemingway, June 21, 1946, JFK.

10. EH to Patrick Hemingway, June 30, 1946, JFK.

11. EH to Patrick and Gregory Hemingway, July 23, 1946, JFK.

12. Elizabeth Bishop to Margaret and Frani Muser, June 3, 1938, Vassar.

13. Pauline to Elizabeth Bishop, ca. Aug. 1946, Vassar.

14. Pauline to Mary Hemingway, Mar. 1948, JFK.

15. Fountain and Brazeau, *Remembering Elizabeth Bishop,* 365–66.

16. Later Pauline moved the store to the back, on the Ann Street side, and renamed it the Bahama Shop, with the apartment moving to the front.

17. M. Hemingway, *How It Was,* 199.

18. EH to Mary Hemingway, May 3, 1947, JFK.

19. Pauline to Buz (a friend), Apr. 1947, JFK.

20. Pauline to EH, May 1947, JFK.

21. M. Hemingway, *How It Was,* 203.

22. Pauline to EH and Mary, May 1947, JFK.

23. Pauline to EH, Jan. 15, 1948, JFK.

24. Reynolds, *Final Years,* 156–57.

25. EH to Mary Hemingway, July 8, 1947, JFK.

26. EH to Mary Hemingway, May 2, 1947, JFK.

27. EH to Mary Hemingway, May 3, 1947, JFK.

28. EH to Charles Scribner, June 28, 1947, PUL, in Hemingway, *Selected Letters,* 621–22.

29. M. Hemingway, *How It Was,* 207.

30. G. A. Pfeiffer to Pauline, Oct. 15, 1947, in "Ownership and Distribution."

31. Pauline to G. A. Pfeiffer, Oct. 26, 1947, in "Ownership and Distribution."

32. Pauline to G. A. Pfeiffer, Dec. 13, 1947, in "Ownership and Distribution."

33. Adele Brockoff to G. A. Pfeiffer, Jan. 11, 1948, in "Ownership and Distribution."

34. G. A. Pfeiffer to Adele Brockoff, Jan. 20, 1948, in "Ownership and Distribution."

35. Pfeiffer, interview, Mar. 4, 1998.

36. M. Hemingway, *How It Was,* 212.

37. M. Hemingway, *How It Was,* 215.

38. EH to Betty Bruce, July 5, 1949, JFK.

39. Pauline to EH, May 1948, JFK.

40. Kert, *Hemingway Women,* 430.

41. EH to Pauline, 1948, JFK.

42. Pauline to EH, Jan. 1949, JFK.

43. EH to Pauline, Jan. 26, 1948, JFK.

44. EH to Pauline, Jan. 26, 1948, JFK.

45. EH to Patrick Hemingway, June 11, 1952, JFK.

46. Pauline to EH, Feb. 3, 1949, JFK.

47. EH to Jack Hemingway, Feb. 22, 1949, JFK.

48. M. Hemingway, *How It Was,* 254.

Chapter 24: Last Rites (1949–1951)

1. Pauline to Mary Hemingway, May 1949, JFK.

2. Pauline to EH, Summer 1949, JFK.

3. Kert, *Hemingway Women,* 445.

4. Reynolds, *Final Years,* 208.

5. Reynolds, *Final Years,* 208.

6. J. Hemingway, *Misadventures of a Fly Fisherman,* 251.

7. G. Pfeiffer, interview, Mar. 4, 1998.

8. L. Pfeiffer, interview, Apr. 4, 2000.

9. EH to Adele Brockhoff, Aug. 1, 1949, JFK.

10. EH to Adele Brockhoff, Aug. 1, 1949, JFK.

11. EH to Adele Brockhoff, Aug. 1, 1949, JFK.

12. EH to Charles Scribner, Aug. 24, 1949, JFK.

13. Reynolds, *Final Years,* 175 (from Royalty Report, Aug. 30, 1948, JFK).

14. Huxley, interview, Mar. 5, 1998.

15. Wells, interview, Mar. 20, 1997.

16. Wells, interview, Mar. 20, 1997.

17. Wells, interview, Mar. 20, 1997.

18. Spence, interview, Apr. 10, 1997; Virginia Pfeiffer to Elizabeth Bishop, Feb. 5, 1950, Vassar.

19. *Piggott Banner,* Feb. 10, 1950; "He Returns $100,000 Find to Owner," Los Angeles newspaper clipping (unknown paper), ca. Feb. 1950.

20. Virginia Pfeiffer to Elizabeth Bishop, Feb. 5, 1950, Vassar.

21. McEvoy, interview, Mar. 8, 1998.

22. Virginia Pfeiffer to Elizabeth Bishop, June 28, 1950, Vassar.

23. M. Hemingway, *How It Was,* 261–62; Kert, *Hemingway Women,* 453.

24. Kert, *Hemingway Women,* 451.

25. Reynolds, *Final Years,* 221.

26. Kert, *Hemingway Women,* 452.

27. Kert, *Hemingway Women,* 453.

28. Pauline to EH, May 12, 1950, JFK.

29. Pauline to EH, May 12, 1950, JFK.

30. Virginia Pfeiffer to Elizabeth Bishop, June 28, 1950, Vassar.

31. Dianetics is defined by the Church of Scientology as "what the soul is doing to the body through the mind." Hubbard had just published the fundamentals of

Dianetics in 1950. Further research into the spiritual aspects of Dianetics led to Hubbard's founding of Scientology in 1954.

32. Pauline to EH, July 1950, JFK.

33. EH to Gregory Hemingway, Aug. 15, 1950, JFK.

34. EH to Gregory Hemingway, Aug. 15, 1950, JFK.

35. Pauline to EH, Aug. 26, 1950, JFK.

36. Pauline to EH, Aug. 16, 1950, JFK.

37. Alfred Kazin, review of *Across the River and Into the Trees, New Yorker,* Sept. 9, 1950, 101–3, in Meyers, *Hemingway,* 378.

38. Virginia Pfeiffer to Elizabeth Bishop, June 28, 1950, Vassar.

39. Martha Gellhorn to Bill Walton, Feb. 3, 1950, Boston University.

40. Martha Gellhorn to Bill Walton, Feb. 9, 1950, Boston University.

41. G. Hemingway, *Papa,* 111.

42. Pauline to EH, Apr. 26, 1951, JFK.

43. EH to Pauline, Apr. 26, 1951, JFK.

44. EH to Gregory Hemingway, May 2, 1951, JFK.

45. Pauline to EH, May 19, 1951, JFK.

46. EH to Gregory Hemingway, May 2, 1951, JFK.

47. Pauline to EH, June 30, 1951, JFK.

48. EH to Mary Hemingway, July 8, 1951, JFK.

49. McEvoy, interview, Mar. 8, 1998.

50. G. Hemingway, *Papa,* 6.

51. G. Hemingway, *Papa,* 252.

52. G. Hemingway, *Papa,* 236–37.

53. V. Hemingway, *Running with the Bulls,* 254.

54. G. Hemingway, *Papa,* 6.

55. Huxley, interview, Mar. 5, 1998.

56. M. Hemingway, *How It Was,* 290.

57. EH to Charles Scribner, Oct. 2, 1951, PUL, in Hemingway, *Selected Letters,* 737.

58. John Dos Passos to EH, Oct. 23, 1951, in Ludington, *Fourteenth Chronicle,* 597.

59. Sanford, *At the Hemingways,* 363.

60. G. Hemingway, *Papa,* 7.

61. Last Will and Testament of Pauline Pfeiffer Hemingway, Monroe County, Fla., June 25, 1949; Report of Appraisers, Estate of Pauline Hemingway, County Judge's Court, Monroe County, Fla.; Dec. 22, 1952.

62. EH to W. Curry Harris, Nov. 5, 1951, JFK.

Chapter 25: Afterward

1. Patrick Hemingway, telephone interview with the author, Feb. 10, 2000.

2. EH to Toby Bruce, Aug. 19, 1958, JFK.

3. G. Hemingway, *Papa*, 8.

4. G. Hemingway, *Papa*, 13.

5. G. Hemingway, *Papa*, 12.

6. "Ownership and Distribution."

7. Robert Pfeiffer, Gustavus A. Pfeiffer eulogy, Aspetuck, Conn., Aug. 25, 1953.

8. G. A. Pfeiffer, *Philosophical Writings*.

9. Huxley, *This Timeless Moment*, 71.

10. McEvoy, interview, Mar. 9, 1998; Roger Moss, interview with the author, Los Angeles, Calif., Mar. 6, 1998; Huxley, interview, Mar. 5–6, 1998.

11. EH to Patrick Hemingway, June 11, 1952, JFK.

12. Baker, Ernest *Hemingway*, 461.

13. William Faulkner, review of *The Old Man and the Sea*, *Shenandoah* (Autumn 1952): 55, in Meyers, *Hemingway*, 414–15.

14. G. Hemingway, *Papa*, 118.

15. Franscell, "Pfeiffer Barn Stores Only Memories."

16. Ernest Hemingway, *A Moveable Feast*—Starts and Incompletes, JFK.

BIBLIOGRAPHY

Special Collections and Archives

Carlos Baker Collection. Princeton University Libraries, Princeton, N.J.

Elizabeth Bishop Papers. Vassar College Library, Poughkeepsie, N.Y.

Honoria Murphy Donnelly Estate. Private collection.

Dos Passos Papers. Manuscripts Department, University of Virginia Library, Charlottesville.

Martha Gellhorn Papers. Special Collections, Boston University.

Hemingway MSS III. Lilly Library, Indiana University, Bloomington.

Ernest Hemingway Collection. John F. Kennedy Library, Boston.

Hemingway Family Papers. Harry Ransom Humanities Research Center, University of Texas, Austin.

Patrick Hemingway Papers. Princeton University Libraries, Princeton, N.J.

Hemingway-Pfeiffer Museum and Educational Center. Piggott, Ark.

Helen Keller Archival Collection. American Foundation for the Blind, New York.

Archibald MacLeish Papers. Manuscript Division, Library of Congress.

Ernest H. Mainland Collection. Special Collections Library, The Pennsylvania State University, State College.

Waldo Peirce Collection. Colby College Special Collections, Waterville, Me.

Gustavus and Louise Pfeiffer Research Foundation Collection. Hemingway-Pfeiffer Museum and Educational Center, Piggott, Ark.

Matilda and Karl Pfeiffer Foundation. Piggott, Ark.

Clara G. Spiegel–Ernest Hemingway Family Papers, 1939–1988. Newberry Library, Chicago.

Helen Guffey Weaver Estate, Private collection.

Books and Articles

Accetta, Kathleen J. "A Case Study on the Corporate Culture at Warner-Lambert: A Company Transition." Master's thesis, Fairleigh Dickinson University, 1994.

Anderson, Sherwood. *Letters of Sherwood Anderson.* Ed. Howard Mumford Jones. Boston: Little, Brown and Co., 1953.

Baker, Carlos. *Ernest Hemingway: A Life Story.* New York: Charles Scribner's Sons, 1969.

Bellavance-Johnson, Marsha. *Hemingway in Key West.* Ketchum, Idaho: Computer Lab, 1987.

Benson, Sally. *Meet Me in St. Louis.* New York: Bantam Books, 1958.

Boyle, Kay, and Robert McAlmon. *Being Geniuses Together: A Binocular View of Paris in the '20s.* New York: Doubleday & Co., 1968.

Brian, Denis. *The True Gen.* New York: Grove Press, 1988.

Bruccoli, Matthew J., ed. *The Only Thing That Counts: The Ernest Hemingway–Maxwell Perkins Correspondence.* New York: Scribner, 1996.

Burgess, Anthony. *Ernest Hemingway and His World*. New York: Charles Scribner's Sons, 1978.

Callaghan, Morley. *That Summer in Paris*. New York: Coward-McCann, 1963.

Cannell, Kathleen. "Scenes with a Hero." In *Hemingway and the Sun Set*, ed. Bertram D. Sarason. Washington, D.C.: NCR, Microcard Editions, 1972.

Carr, Virginia Spencer. *John Dos Passos: A Life*. New York: Doubleday & Co., 1984.

Conrad, Winston S. *Hemingway's France*. Emeryville, Calif.: Woodford Press, 2000.

Diliberto, Gioia. *Hadley*. New York: Ticknor & Fields, 1992.

Donaldson, Scott. *Archibald MacLeish: An American Life*. New York: Houghton Mifflin Co., 1992.

———. *By Force of Will: The Life and Art of Ernest Hemingway*. New York: Viking Press, 1977.

Donnelly, Honoria Murphy. *Sara and Gerald*. New York: Times Books, 1982.

Dos Passos, John. *The Best Times: An Informal Memoir*. New York: New American Library, 1966.

———. *The Fourteenth Chronicle: Letters and Diaries of John Dos Passos*. Ed. Townsend Ludington. Boston: Gambit, 1973.

Edwards, John Carver. *Airmen without Portfolio: U.S. Mercenaries in Civil War Spain*. Westport, Conn.: Praeger, 1997.

Eisenkramer, Henry. *The Boy Next Door: Memories of Kensington*. St. Louis: Maxamur, 1991.

Faherty, William Barnaby. *Deep Roots and Golden Wings: 150 Years with the Visitation Sisters in the Archdiocese of St. Louis 1833–1983*. St. Louis: River City Publishers, 1982.

Fitch, Noel Riley. *Walks in Hemingway's Paris*. New York: St. Martin's Press, 1989.

Fitzgerald, F. Scott. *Correspondence of F. Scott Fitzgerald*. Ed. Matthew J. Bruccoli and Margaret M. Duggan. New York: Random House, 1980.

———. "The Crack-Up," *Esquire*, February 1936, 41, 164.

———. *The Letters of F. Scott Fitzgerald*. Ed. Robert Turnbull. New York, Charles Scribner's Sons, 1963.

Ford, Hugh. "Margaret Anderson." In *Four Lives in Paris*. San Francisco: North Point Press, 1987.

Fountain, Gary, and Peter Brazeau. *Remembering Elizabeth Bishop*. Amherst: University of Massachusetts Press, 1994.

Franklin, Sidney. *Bullfighter from Brooklyn*. New York: Prentice-Hall, 1952.

Fuentes, Norberto. *Hemingway in Cuba*. Secaucus, N.J.: Lyle Stuart, 1984.

Gajdusek, Robert E. *Hemingway's Paris*. New York: Charles Scribner's Sons, 1978.

Gingrich, Arnold. "Scott, Ernest and Whoever." *Esquire*, October 1973, 151–54, 374, 380.

Giroux, Robert, ed. *One Art: Elizabeth Bishop Letters*. New York: Noonday Press, 1994.

Griffin, Peter. *Less Than a Treason*. New York: Oxford University Press, 1990.

Hall, Carolyn. *The Twenties in Vogue*. New York: Harmony Books, 1983.

Hansen, Arlen J. *Expatriate Paris: A Cultural and Literary Guide to Paris of the 1920s.* New York: Arcade Publishing, 1990.

Hays, Peter. "Interview with Dr. John H. Jones." *Hemingway Review* (Fall 1991): 36.

Hemingway, Ernest. "The Art of Fiction XXI." Interview. *Paris Review* (Spring 1958): 60–89.

———. "The Art of the Short Story." *Paris Review* (Spring 1981): 85–102.

———. *Ernest Hemingway: Selected Letters 1917–1961.* Ed. Carlos Baker. Paperback edition. New York: Charles Scribner's Sons, 1981.

———. *A Farewell to Arms.* New York: Charles Scribner's Sons, 1929.

———. *For Whom the Bell Tolls.* New York: Charles Scribner's Sons, 1940.

———. *Green Hills of Africa.* First Scribner Classics Edition. New York: Charles Scribner's Sons, 1998.

———. "Italy, 1927." *New Republic,* May 18, 1927, 350–53. Later published as "Che Ti Dice La Patria" in *Men Without Women.*

———. *Men Without Women.* New York: Charles Scribner's Sons, 1927.

———. *A Moveable Feast.* New York: Charles Scribner's Sons, 1964.

———. *A Moveable Feast: The Restored Edition.* New York: Scribner, 2009.

———. *The Old Man and the Sea.* New York: Charles Scribner's Sons, 1952.

———. "On Being Shot Again: A Gulf Stream Letter." *Esquire,* June 1935, 25, 156.

———. "On the Blue Water: A Gulf Stream Letter." *Esquire,* April 1936, 31, 184–85.

———. "A Paris Letter." *Esquire,* February 1934, 22, 156.

———. *The Short Stories of Ernest Hemingway.* New York: Charles Scribner's Sons, 1938.

———. "The Sights of Whitehead Street: A Key West Letter." *Esquire,* April 1935, 25, 156.

———. *The Sun Also Rises.* New York: Simon and Schuster, 1954.

———. *To Have and Have Not.* New York: Simon and Schuster, 1996.

———. *Winner Take Nothing.* New York: Scribner's Sons, 1970.

Hemingway, Gregory. *Papa: A Personal Memoir.* Boston: Houghton Mifflin Co., 1976.

Hemingway, Jack. *Misadventures of a Fly Fisherman.* Dallas: Taylor Publishing Co., 1986.

Hemingway, John. *Strange Tribe: A Family Memoir.* Guilford, Conn.: Lyons Press, 2007.

Hemingway, Leicester. *My Brother, Ernest Hemingway.* Cleveland: World Publishing Co., 1961.

Hemingway, Mary. *How It Was.* New York: Alfred A. Knopf, 1976.

Hemingway, Valerie. *Running with the Bulls: My Years with the Hemingways.* New York: Ballentine Books, 2004.

"Henry Pfeiffer." In *Prominent Men of New York: Individual Biographic Studies with Character Portraits.* Family ed. New York: Historical Records, 1941.

Hotchner, A. E. *Papa Hemingway.* New York: Random House, 1966.

Huxley, Laura Archera. *This Timeless Moment: A Personal View of Aldous Huxley.* San Francisco: Mercury House, 1968.

———. *You Are Not the Target.* New York: Farrar, Straus & Co., 1994.

Keats, John. *You Might as Well Live: The Life and Times of Dorothy Parker.* New York: Simon and Schuster, 1970.

Kert, Bernice. *The Hemingway Women: Those Who Loved Him—The Wives and Others.* New York: Norton Paperback, 1986.

Kuehl, John, and Jackson R. Bryer, eds. *Dear Scott/Dear Max: The Fitzgerald-Perkins Correspondence.* London: Cassell & Co., Ltd., 1971.

Lawrence, H. Lea. *A Hemingway Odyssey: Special Places in His Life.* Nashville: Cumberland House, 1999.

Leland, John. *A Guide to Hemingway's Paris.* Chapel Hill: Algonquin Books, 1989.

Levin, Phyllis Lee. *The Wheels of Fashion.* New York: Doubleday & Co., 1965.

Liddell, Donald M. With Gustavus A. Pfeiffer and J. Maunoury. *Chessmen.* New York: Harcourt, Brace & Co., 1937.

Loeb, Harold. *The Way It Was.* New York: Criterion Books, 1959.

MacLeish, Archibald. *Letters of Archibald MacLeish: 1907–1982.* Ed. R. H. Winnick. Boston: Houghton-Mifflin, 1983.

MacLeish, William H. *Uphill with Archie: A Son's Journey.* New York: Simon and Schuster, 2001.

McConathy, Dale. "Mainbocher." In *American Fashion,* ed. Sarah Tomerlin Lee for the Fashion Institute of Technology. New York: New York Times Book Co., 1975.

McIver, Stuart B. *Hemingway's Key West.* Sarasota: Pineapple Press, 1993.

McLendon, James. *Papa: Hemingway in Key West.* Key West: Langley Press, 1993.

Meade, Marion. *Dorothy Parker: What Fresh Hell Is This?* New York: Penguin, 1989.

Mellen, Joan. *Kay Boyle: Author of Herself.* New York: Farrar, Straus & Co., 1994.

Mellow, James R. *A Life without Consequences.* New York: Houghton Mifflin Co., 1992.

Metropolitan Museum of Art. *Chess: East and West, Past and Present. A Selection from the Gustavus A. Pfeiffer Collection.* New York: Metropolitan Museum of Art, 1968.

Meyers, Jeffrey, ed. *Hemingway: The Critical Heritage.* Boston: Routledge & Kegan Paul, 1983.

Miller, Linda Patterson, ed. *Letters from the Lost Generation.* New Brunswick: Rutgers University Press, 1991.

Miller, Madelaine Hemingway. *Ernie: Hemingway's Sister "Sunny" Remembers.* New York: Crown Publishers, 1975.

"Missouri Alumni in Journalism: Graduates and Former Students of the School of Journalism." *University of Missouri Bulletin.* Journalism Series, no. 27. Columbia, 1923.

Modlin, Charles E., ed. *Selected Letters: Sherwood Anderson.* Knoxville: University of Tennessee Press, 1984.

Montgomery, D. H. *The Leading Facts of French History.* Boston: Ginn & Co., 1903.

Moorehead, Caroline. *Gellhorn: A Twentieth-Century Life.* New York: Henry Holt and Co., 2003.

Nagel, James, ed. *Ernest Hemingway: The Oak Park Legacy.* Tuscaloosa: University of Alabama Press, 1996.

Oliver, Charles M., *Ernest Hemingway A to Z: The Essential Reference to the Life and Work.* New York: Checkmark Books, 1999.

Pfeiffer, G. A. *Philosophical Writings and Aphorisms of Gustavus A. Pfeiffer.* Foreword and ed. by Francis P. Farquhar. Privately printed. Grabhorn Press, 1955.

Pfeiffer, Matilde Valenti. "Memories That Haven't Faded." Unpublished memoirs. Cambridge, Mass, 1983.

Powell, Dawn. *The Diaries of Dawn Powell 1931–1965.* Ed. Tim Page. Vermont: Steerforth Press, 1995.

Reck, Michael. *Ezra Pound: A Close-Up.* New York: McGraw-Hill Paperbacks, 1973.

Reynolds, Michael. *Hemingway: The American Homecoming.* Cambridge, Mass.: Blackwell, 1992.

———. *Hemingway: The Final Years.* New York: W. W. Norton, 1999.

———. *Hemingway: The 1930s.* New York: Norton Paperback, 1997.

———. *Hemingway: The Paris Years.* New York: Norton Paperback, 1999.

———. *The Young Hemingway.* New York: Basil Blackwell, 1986.

Riley, Charles A. II. *The Jazz Age in France.* New York: Harry N. Abrams, 2004.

Samuelson, Arnold. *With Hemingway: A Year in Key West and Cuba.* New York: Random House, 1984.

Sanford, Marcelline Hemingway. *At the Hemingways.* Centennial ed. Moscow: University of Idaho Press, 1999.

Sarason, Bertram D., ed. *Hemingway and the Sun Set.* Washington, D.C.: NCR Microcard Editions, 1972.

Seebohm, Caroline. *The Man Who Was Vogue.* New York: Viking Press, 1982.

Sokoloff, Alice Hunt. *Hadley: The First Mrs. Hemingway.* New York: Dodd, Mead & Co., 1973.

Stein, Gertrude. *The Autobiography of Alice B. Toklas.* New York: Harcourt Brace, 1933.

Vaill, Amanda. *Everybody Was So Young.* Boston: Houghton Mifflin Co., 1998.

"Visitation Academy." *Schools of the Catholic Archdiocese of St. Louis.* St. Louis: Archdiocese of St. Louis, 1995–96.

Warner-Lambert Company. "A Company History." Morris Plains, N.J.: Warner-Lambert Company Corporate Library and Literature Services, 1966.

Wilson, Charles Morrow. "Tenantry Comes Forward." *Country Gentleman,* July 1936, 12–13, 42.

Witherspoon, Margaret Johanson. *Remembering the St. Louis World's Fair.* St. Louis: Comfort Printing Co., 1973.

Interviews and Remarks

Bruce, Otto (Toby). Interview with Marie Hillyer. Piggott, Ark., 1984.

Cole, Linnie. Interviews with the author. Piggott, Ark., June 17, July 15, 1997.

Jordan, Lillie. Interviews with the author. Piggott, Ark., May 23, July 15, 1997.

Harris, Ursula Herold. Interview with the author. Walnut Creek, Calif., February 11, 2000.

Hemingway, Gregory. Interview with the author. Piggott, Ark., July 4, 1999.

Hemingway, Gregory. Keynote remarks. Hemingway-Pfeiffer Museum and Educational Center Grand Opening, July 4, 1999.

Hemingway, Jack. Hemingway Centennial Panel Discussion, Oak Park, Ill., July 21, 1999.

Hemingway, Patrick. Telephone interview with the author. February 10, 2000.

Hemingway, Patrick. Hemingway Centennial Panel Discussion. Oak Park, Ill., July 21, 1999.

Houser, Linda. Telephone interview with the author. December 2004.

Huxley, Laura Archera. Interviews with the author. Los Angeles, Calif., March 5, 6, 1998.

McEvoy, Jay. Interview with the author. San Francisco, Calif., March 9, 1998.

Militello, Nancy Castrillon. Telephone interview with the author. August 7, 1997.

Moffatt, Dalton. Interview with the author. Campbell, Mo., March 22, 1997.

Moffatt, Dolph, Interview with the author. Campbell, Mo., Sept. 16, 1997.

Moss, Roger. Interview with the author. Los Angeles, Calif., March 6, 1998.

Pfeiffer, George. Interview with the author. Los Angeles, Calif., March 4, 1998.

Pfeiffer, Louise. Interview with the author. Cambridge, Mass., April 4, 2000.

Pfeiffer, Matilda. Interviews with the author. Piggott, Ark., March 28, May 8, 1997, November 4, 2003.

Poole, Jim. Interview with the author. Piggott, Ark., June 9, 1997.

Richardson, Jim. Interview with the author. Piggott, Ark. June 9, 1997.

Russell, Lloyd, Interview with the author. Piggott, Ark., October 8, 1997.

Smart, Charles. Interview with the author. Piggott, Ark. April 18, 1997.

Spence, Ayleene. Interviews with the author. Piggott, Ark., April 10, 1997, January 9, 1998.

Tybor, Sheila. Interview with the author. Piggott, Ark., July 19, 2005.

Wells, Kenneth. Interviews with the author. Piggott, Ark., March 18, 20, 1997.

Wilkins, Jody. Telephone interview with the author. October 1997.

INDEX

Ruth A. Hawkins has been an administrator at Arkansas State University in Jonesboro for more than thirty years and established its Arkansas Heritage Sites program, which includes the Hemingway-Pfeiffer Museum and Educational Center in Piggott. She has been recognized at the state, regional, and national level for her work in historic preservation and heritage tourism.